Musical Notations of the Orient

東洋音樂記譜法

BY WALTER KAUFMANN

INDIANA UNIVERSITY PRESS
BLOOMINGTON • LONDON 1967

Musical Notations of the Orient

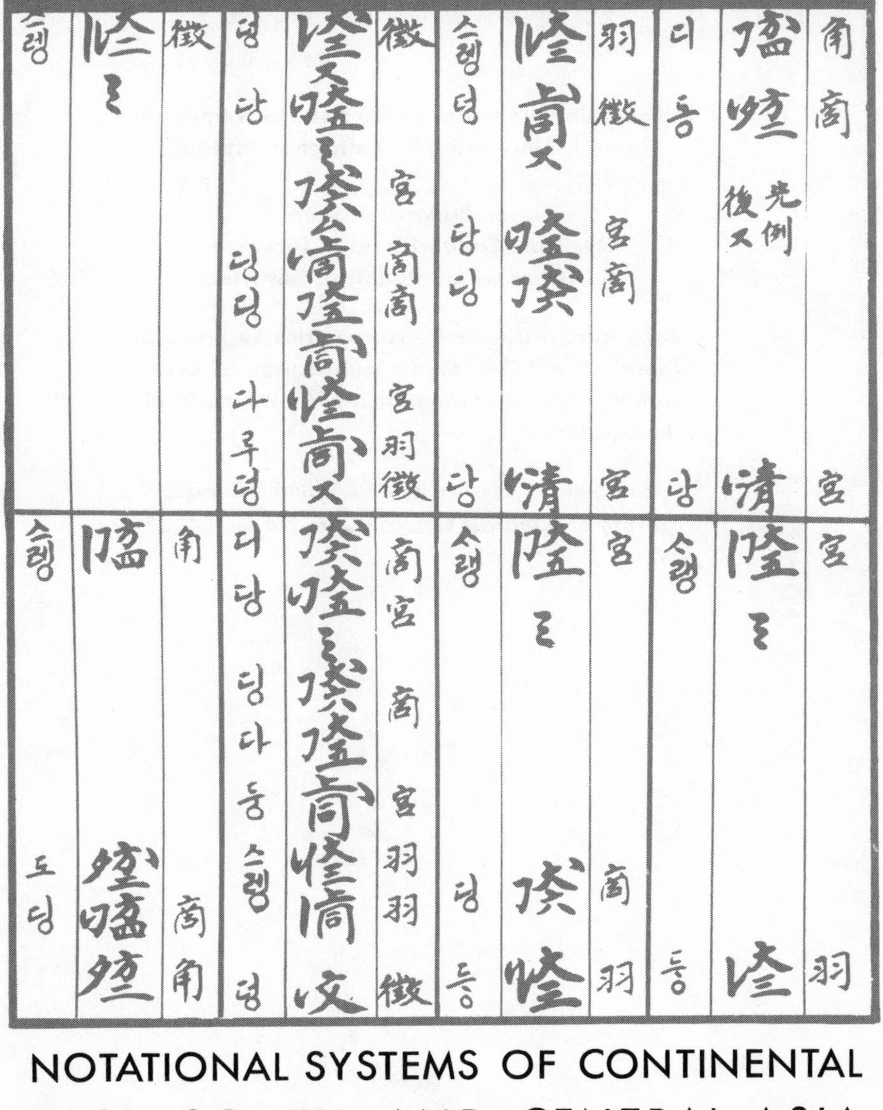

NOTATIONAL SYSTEMS OF CONTINENTAL EAST, SOUTH, AND CENTRAL ASIA

Indiana University Humanities Series Number 60
Indiana University, Bloomington, Indiana

***Editor:* Edward D. Seeber**
***Assistant Editor:* David H. Dickason**
***Assistant Editor:* Rudolf B. Gottfried**

The Indiana University Humanities Series was founded in 1939 for the publication of occasional papers and monographs by members of the faculty.

Library of Congress Catalog Card No. 66-64235

PREFACE

The impact of Western civilization upon Eastern cultures has caused so many changes that it is difficult to point out any Oriental community which does not reflect foreign influences in its diverse social and economic reforms, such as the creation of unions, the introduction of new strategies of expansion, far-reaching changes in industry and education, the effacing disappearance of the autocratic power of the family and of the divine rulers and living Buddhas, and many others. The indigenous arts, particularly music, by imitating and absorbing imported Western elements, often of remarkably mediocre quality, have frequently suffered a deterioration from which there is no recovery.

It is hardly necessary to repeat observations made by numerous authors about the "killing of indigenous music in the interest of poor and second-hand Western trash," about the "hopeless succumbing of native music to a technical age with military service and factory work, with rapid buses, planes, and cars, with phonographs, radios, and television sets" (Sachs).

Similar, perhaps less noticeable but equally severe and incessant changes have occurred in the notational systems of the East as a result of Western influence. Numerous indigenous Oriental notations were, and still are, so diverse, so ingeniously vague, so perfectly suited to denote the improvisational character of native music that, although we may not be able to decipher all of them, we feel profound regret about their being gradually and irresistably superseded by the rigid staff notation of the West or, in some instances, by an unimaginative, international system which employs Western (Arabic) numerals as notational symbols.

It is the aim of this book to collect and preserve these indigenous Oriental notational systems, which face a vulgarization similar to that felt by all other forms of native musical activity. The broad scope of this work necessarily entails shortcomings, probable errors, imbalance, and unusually lengthy explanations and notes, for all of which I beg clemency.

The difficulties in the preparation of this work arise from numerous facts: the sources are not as easily accessible and available as their counterparts in the West; authors, publishers, dates and places of publication are often obscure; copied notational examples are not always correct; the numerous languages and scripts may have subtleties and allusions which could have escaped me; and, finally, as most Oriental notations only serve mnemonic purposes, the symbols offer only vague instructions to the performer and transcriber and can lead to differing interpretations.

This book provides a description and preservation of Oriental notational systems, the study of which makes possible a deeper understanding of Eastern art music and demonstrates its character to the student more meaningfully than does the mere presentation of recordings and musical examples written in Western staff notation. The numerous problems arising from styles and techniques which are based upon improvisation and extramusical concepts are also considered.

The purposes of this study will have been fulfilled if it serves as a stimulus toward further research in this fascinating, but, alas, quickly vanishing field. The presentation of Eastern notations may also provide some aesthetic pleasure from the study of unusual and often complex systems and symbols.

Although I envisage two volumes, this one may be considered as a complete work in itself, as it deals mainly with musical notations used in continental East, South, and Central Asia. A second volume will describe the indigenous notations of Japan, the Ryukyu Islands, Indonesia, and the Islamic world.

In the chapters dealing with Chinese and Korean notations, Chinese characters and Korean letters are employed. The spelling of Chinese words is based upon Mathews' Chinese-English Dictionary (Cambridge, Mass., 1956). The terminology of the chapters dealing with the notations of India and Tibetan chant is presented in romanized letters because, unlike those chapters in which Chinese words are used, misunderstandings are far less likely to occur.

Acknowledgments and thanks are due principally to Professor Willi Apel, the distinguished authority in the field of musical notations and Gregorian chant; to the Graduate School of Indiana University; and to the Ford International Program (Indiana University). For permission to quote copyrighted material and to use notational examples in original and transcribed forms, I am very grateful to Dr. R. H. van Gulik (Tokyo), Dr. Lee, Hye-ku (Seoul), and Dr. Laurence Picken (Cambridge). These three scholars have been extremely kind and generous in various ways with their valuable advice.

I am also deeply indebted to Dr. Fritz Kuttner (New York) for his excellent help; to Mrs. Jeanette Snyder and the Lama Geshe Nornang (University of Washington) for translating and transcribing Tibetan texts; to my dear friend Dr. Arnold Bake (London University) for his permission to reprint two of his Tibetan manuscripts; to Professor Charles Kent for his most helpful advice in theoretical matters; and to Professor Pao-ch'en Lee (Monterey, California), who, despite his own heavy schedule, read through the Chinese and Korean chapters, made corrections, and offered excellent suggestions.

Finally, my very sincere thanks to Professors Wu-chi Liu (Indiana University), Tien-yi Li (Yale University), Arthur Corra (Indiana University), Mrs. Miranda Pao and, last but not least, to my untiring friend and assistant, Mr. Byongkon Kim, for his invaluable suggestions and for the help that he gave me with translations, copying, and miscellaneous checking.

Notwithstanding these acknowledgments of assistance, I must, of course, take responsibility for any errors that may occur in this book.

Walter Kaufmann

Indiana University
Bloomington, Indiana

CONTENTS

LIST OF ILLUSTRATIONS

To my Wife

INTRODUCTION

Notation, the craft of expressing music in written form, appears in a multitude of forms both in the Orient and Occident. The elements used in notational systems can be words, syllables, letters, numbers, curves, and other symbols or signs, many of which reflect the function and importance music has in the cultural lives of the various peoples.

Occidental notations, having developed from the use of letters and cheironomic signs to systems showing the increasing need to notate every minute detail of pitch, duration, speed, dynamics, and other features, eventually reached a point where in the staff notation of the present time notated music denotes everything the composer wishes to convey and, excepting the thorough-bass of the Baroque period, contemporary jazz, and some notational experiments of very recent time, allows no improvisational freedom by the performer.

Oriental notations, denoting in most instances monophonic music not bound by precise score-arrangements, often provide only sketchy outlines of the music, which receives its final form not from the composer but from improvising singers and players. The elements employed in Oriental notations occasionally indicate cosmological, metaphysical, or religious connotations. In contrast to Occidental systems which are accessible to all persons of adequate learning, Oriental notations are often guarded jealously by a few masters and may be kept vague purposely in order to avoid their use by uninitiated persons.

Before turning to the consideration of Oriental notational systems a brief description of Oriental art music in general will be of importance. We shall view this music from a time a few decenniums ago before Western music, not always of a high level, began to infiltrate into Oriental musical life, mainly through the mediums of radio, films, and, later, television. This Oriental art music is the music of civilized man in the following four cultural areas:

a) East Asia (China, Korea, and Japan)
b) Southeast Asia (Indonesia, the region of Indochina, Thailand, Malaya, and Burma)
c) South Asia (India)
d) West Asia and North Africa (Iran, Iraq, Arabia, Syria, Egypt, Libya, Algeria, and Morocco).

Music of these areas has two features in common: it is performed either by professional musicians or by members of special castes; and it is distinguished from primitive tribal music as well as from music of the Occident by its musical systems, theories, and notations. Although the various systems in Oriental art music differ considerably from one another, most are based upon or incorporated into wider philosophical, historical, or scientific concepts.

Many authors of the past – for example, Lü Pu-wei,[1] Ssŭ-ma Ch'ien,[2] Al-Fārābī,[3] and Al-Kindī,[4] in the Eastern world; and Plato,[5] Aristotle,[6] Euclid,[7] and Plutarch,[8] and many others in the West – did not deal with music separately but embedded their musical ideas in philosophical or scientific frameworks. This inclusion of music in a larger concept can also be observed in medieval European education where, in the Oriental manner, music was grouped together with the mathematical branches of arithmetic, geometry, and astronomy under the Quadrivium.[9]

Another feature common to all Oriental art music is that its practices, theories, systems, and notations, and even the shapes of musical instruments, have remained remarkably static, with very little, if any, development during the past, quite in contrast to the amazing changes which occurred in the same aspects of Western music. The reason for this unusual tenacity is the strong relationship of Oriental art music with the cosmos, magic, religion, philosophy, and other extramusical concepts.

It is important to note that to the Oriental mind, melodic patterns and scales, and even single notes and instruments, may have extramusical (e. g., magical) properties, and, only secondarily, esthetic ones. The Orient abounds in beliefs and legends that music can influence the cosmos, nature, and fate. For instance, in China the five basic notes are supposed to be closely related to the cardinal points, the elements, the seasons, the planets, colors, materials, numbers, parts of the human body, and to many other things. It is believed that several _rāgas_ of India possess magical properties and are tied in with certain periods of the day or night or, in some cases, the seasons of the year. Thus, the performance of _rāga Dipak_ is supposed to create fire and that of _rāga Kedar_ to melt stones and cure diseases. The _Mallār rāgas_ are reputed to have an influence on the rainy season; it is considered a grave mistake productive of disastrous consequences if morning _rāgas_ are performed in the evening, or vice versa. Similar convictions flourish throughout the Orient.

Except for some ritual and ceremonial pieces, music of the Oriental cultural areas makes extensive use of improvisation. No performer will play or sing a piece for the second time exactly as he did the first. There is unusual latitude in elaborating and embellishing a skeletal melody, and an Oriental performer places greater emphasis upon his virtuosity and his ability to improvise than upon giving an exact and literal reproduction of the musical notations. Significantly, the program of one of the first concerts of Western music in Japan omitted the names of composers but listed those of all performing musicians.[10]

As mentioned before, Western musical notations developed from letters and other signs which served as a mnemonic aid to the performers, who already knew the melodies, toward symbols which denote both pitches and rhythms in an increasingly precise manner. The East with only a few exceptions, used and retained in its notational systems the ancient symbols — syllables, letters, and neumatic signs — without ever aiming at greater precision and efficiency.

Besides its improvisational character, a reason for the remarkable tenacity of Oriental music is the typically Oriental manner of oral-aural teaching. The student seated in front of his master is even now required, as he has always been, to repeat over and over again what is shown to him, so that notational symbols rarely become more than a mnemonic help. Still another reason why the Oriental notational systems have remained static is that they were frequently kept secret. Among all those who performed music only a few of the most learned would master the symbols, and they would rarely impart their knowledge to all their students. Occasionally different schools would evolve their own notations, so that the same symbol might be given various interpretations by different masters.

Following a line of thought similar to that prevailing in the medieval West, where secular music was considered unworthy of being notated, the East employed notation mainly to preserve the melodies of ritual and ceremonial music. It was only gradually that there appeared tablatures and other notational systems for use in secular music as well. Even more than in the West, where manuscripts were rescued from oblivion by repeated copying, Oriental copyists often made mistakes in calligraphy, which were rarely corrected throughout the centuries, because sometimes the scribes could not read the notation.

Oriental notations can be grouped into systems according to whether or not they indicate rhythmic features, and, based on the notational elements employed, four categories can be distinguished:

a) phonetic systems which use words, syllables, or their abbreviations;
b) ideographic and diastematic systems which use notational curves, neumatic and ekphonetic signs;
c) tablatures;
d) systems which use Western devices such as meter signatures, Arabic numerals, bar lines, repeat signs, and others.

I

Chinese Lü and Related Notations

CHINESE NOTATIONS

An art catalogue of the Eastern Han period (25-220), written by the historian Pan Ku in A. D. 92,[1] is probably the earliest extant Chinese document to offer indirect information on notated music, although it contains no musical notations. This catalogue lists, in succession, four books: (a) Songs of the Chou period (1027-256) of Honan – seven poems; (b) "Tone-movements" of the Honan texts of the Chou period – seven items; (c) Texts of 75 folk songs of the Chou period – 75 items; (d) Tone-movements of 75 folk-song texts of the Chou period – 75 items. The term "tone-movements" seems to indicate some form of notation, and we can assume that items (b) and (d) were the notations of the texts contained in (a) and (c). These tone-movements could have been the p'ing-tsê (平仄),[2] signs which prescribe the tonal inflections of Chinese words. The earliest reference to these inflections is made in the Yüeh-chi (樂記) chapter on music, in the Li Chi (禮記), the "Book of Rites," one of the Chinese Classics.[3] The texts of the Li Chi seem to date back to a period from the late Chou to the early Han dynasties, and Pan Ku's tonal movements which were mentioned in A. D. 92 could have originated that early. The difficulty of combining these tone-movements with the p'ing-tsê is that the tonal inflections were not classified until the fifth century A. D., and that only since then, particularly during the T'ang and Sung periods (618-1279), did Chinese literati become fully aware of them and create an art of preset tonal patterns for poems and songs, about 500 years after Pan Ku wrote the catalogue.

The question as to whether notational systems existed in pre-Confucian periods cannot be answered with any certainty at the present time. Until the 23,000 (or more) bone, tortoise-shell, and bronze inscriptions have been examined in their entirety and definite assessments have been reached by sinologists and musicologists, we shall have to confine ourselves to assumptions and hypotheses.

Both "oracle bones," as the inscribed bones and shells are called, and some inscribed bronzes date back to early periods. The inscriptions are written in ideographic and pictographic ancient Chinese comprising a vocabulary of about 3,000 characters, of which roughly half have been deciphered.[4] These inscriptions show no literary efforts and are, in the main, brief statements dealing with divination; there are such questions as, how will the harvest be, when can rain be expected, when will winter come, what date will be auspicious for a sacrificial ceremony, what is the best time to go hunting, and so forth. Occasionally the inscriptions show also the date of the oracle consultation together with a brief statement indicating whether the oracle was fulfilled. "Among the thousands of these records, there is yet to be found a single poem, a single story, or anything that arouses our esthetic or emotional response. All entries are factual and brief."[5]

The inscriptions on Chou bronzes, however, are longer, and show literary efforts in the form of a refined style of language and some florid rhymes.[6] The written characters either agree with or resemble those incised in the oracle bones. We have to admit that it is possible that a few of these inscriptions may refer to music, musical instruments, or ritual. The question of whether any of the earliest inscriptions contain notational symbols remains hypothetical at the present time. A search in this direction was made by Fritz A. Kuttner several years ago. It met with no success. Yet (quoting from a letter by Dr. Kuttner sent to this author) we find that since the known early names of the twelve lü and the various scale degrees were represented by characters that simultaneously denote their names and functions in music, we may have had in early China a system of musical terms which begs overpoweringly for some sort of notation. Although the physical and documentary evidence is missing, it would be astonishing if such a system of pitches together with notational characters did not exist. "It seems probable that .... there must have been beautiful songs sung, touching prayers said .... [but] might these not have been committed in writing on some material more perishable than bones, shells, and bronzes and therefore irrevocably lost to posterity?"[7]

Probably the earliest extant musical notation can be observed in a manuscript[8] discovered by Sir Aurel Stein at the beginning of this century in the Caves of the Thousand Buddhas at Tun Huang, the westernmost Chinese city in Kansu. Several excavations brought to light valuable silks and other objects of the Han period (202 B. C. -A. D. 220) and numerous bundles and scrolls of Chinese and Tibetan writings. Among these scrolls were manuscripts containing ballads in various forms, passages of rhymed and plain prose, Buddhist stories, and song texts. The music is lost.[9] "Some manuscripts have musical indications above the verses; but these have not been satisfactorily explained. Only one piece of formal musical notation was found at Tun Huang (Pelliot 3808), and this gives the string accompaniment to lyric songs (ch'ü-tzu) and has no relevance to the ballad tunes. We also have two specimens of dance-script (Pelliot 3501 and Stein 5643, No.

5). The latter is wrongly called musical notation in the British Museum Catalogue."[10]

The music scroll (Pelliot 3808) is believed to date back to the T'ang period (618-907) or to a period several centuries earlier. A carbon 14 dating of this valuable manuscript would, once and for all, remove the doubts which are uttered occasionally concerning its age.

The Japanese scholar Hayashi Kenzo made an interesting attempt to decipher the notational symbols of this manuscript. He published a Study on the Explication of an Ancient Musical P'i-pa Score Discovered at Tun Huang, China in the Bulletin of Nara Gakugei University, Nara, Japan (V, No. 1, 1955). The author transcribed the notational symbols into Western notation without attempting any rhythmic interpretation. By comparing gaku biwa notation with that on a T'ang shō (Japanese mouth organ; the Chinese term is shêng) preserved in the Shōsōin, on which the pipes are marked with notational symbols that in some cases differ from the present shō notation, he is able to make plausible suggestions for all the signs. However, a final, undisputed assessment of the Tun Huang notation is still to be awaited.

We abstain from discussing this interesting manuscript any further at this time, because our concern is, first of all, to present the basic notational systems. It is planned to offer a detailed discussion of the Tun Huang notation and its ramifications in a later volume.

THE LÜ-LÜ (律呂)

The thought of omitting speculations about theoretical and cosmological matters has come to mind but, after careful consideration, has been discarded, because the sources abound with extramusical connotations and may offer the reader a clearer picture of the cultural background of early Chinese musical matters than would be possible otherwise. This necessitates some recapitulating of already often-related facts. Furthermore modern research (Kuttner) points to the view that some of these admittedly vague and mysterious connotations may possess factual, down-to-earth foundations, facts that still require careful investigation.

The fundamentals on which Chinese serious music of the past, i. e., the ritual music of the Confucian temple and the ceremonial music of the imperial court, is based are the pentatonic scale and the huang-chung (黄鐘). The pentatonic scale, although it has been frequently expanded into heptatonic and other scale-forms, appears constantly throughout the long history of Chinese music. The more remarkable feature, however, is the huang-chung ("Yellow Bell"), a more or less fixed pitch resembling the "Kammerton" of Western music. The widespread belief that musical sounds possess magical powers demanded a fixed pitch of this kind, from which all other pitches could be derived. In China it was believed that appropriate musical sounds could regulate the harmony between heaven and earth, darkness and brightness, peace and unrest, and that the balance created by the correct music was expressed in harmonious government, happiness of the people, and so forth. The first duty of every emperor upon his accession was to establish the correct pitch of the huang-chung. If the preceding government had been unsatisfactory in any manner, or if there had been epidemics, wars, earthquakes, floods, droughts, or other disasters, it was the duty of the new emperor and his yüeh-fu (樂府), the imperial music office (a section of the imperial office of weights and measures), to improve matters by revising the basic musical sounds in fixing the pitch of the huang-chung.

The book Lü-shih ch'un-ch'iu (呂氏春秋), "The Spring and Autumn of Lü Pu-wei,"[11] which was written in the third century B.C., relates how the huang-chung and the pitches derived from it were established. We read about twelve pitch-pipes, the lü-lü (律呂),[12] made of bamboo, whose origin is ascribed to the legendary emperor Huang Ti (c. 2700 B.C.); and we learn that in later periods the pipes were replaced by pitch bells. The first of this series of pitches, the huang-chung, possessed enormous importance not only in music but also in measures and weights. The size of the pipe determined the measure of one Chinese foot, and its volume had to be such that it would hold exactly 1,200 grains of wheat.

Various authors have attempted to reconstruct this Chinese "Kammerton." Van Aalst[13] places it at the pitch which corresponds to our note D. Courant[14] and Mahillon[15] place it at E; Amiot[16] at F, and others at Eb and F#, but the range of possibilities is even greater, for in China

> the foot measure itself was anything but constant; it varied between a minimum of twenty centimeters in the Chou period and a maximum of thirty-four centimeters under the Ming. The ratio of these extremes, 3:5, forcibly resulted in a musical variation within a minor sixth: if the pitch tone was C under the Chou, it was E below under the Ming![17]

Recent research has shown that the changes of the pitch of the huang-chung may have been much less than those indicated by Sachs.

The Princes-of-Han litophones at the Royal Ontario Museum of Archaeology in Toronto, excavated in Lo-Yang (Honan) have the precise standard pitches of 261 cps (C) and 440 cps (A) respectively, according to verbal information received from F.A. Kuttner.

Since it is impossible to reconstruct the exact pitch of the huang-chung, we shall arbitrarily represent it by the note C. Once the pitch of the huang-chung had been established, eleven other pitch-pipes were fashioned and their pitches derived from it. They were tuned in a succession of pure fifths, for Chinese theorists considered that the number 3 was the symbol of heaven and the number 2 the symbol of earth. Thus, the ratio 3:2 represented the harmony between heaven and earth.[18]

The excerpt, on page 16, from the Lü-shih ch'un-ch'iu (Book V) relates the story of how the huang-chung was created.

The characters denoting the huang-chung in the Lü-shih ch'un-ch'iu and in several other works are 鍾, not, as generally employed 鐘.

A rough translation of this excerpt reads as follows:

In olden times Huang-ti ("Yellow Emperor") ordered Ling Lun to establish the lü. Ling Lun travelled from the western to the shady northern side of Mount Yuan Yü. He selected bamboo grown in the Chieh Ch'i valley. He chose only a piece which was hollow and of even thickness. He cut off its knots and used the hollow section between the two joints, the length of which was 3.9 ts'un (inches). And he blew the pipe and produced the sound kung (the basic tone) of huang-chung. He then brought twelve other pipes of different lengths down from the mountain and he listened to the sounds of the male and female Phoenix birds. He grouped their sounds into the twelve lü. There were six sounds of the male bird, and another six of the female. He related them to the kung of the huang-chung and found that the huang-chung was the foundation of the lü-lü.

This story has been repeated over and over again in numerous works

昔黃帝令伶倫作爲律伶倫自大夏之西乃之阮隃
之陰取竹於嶰谿之谷以生空竅厚鈞者斷兩節間
其長三寸九分而吹之以爲黃鍾之宮吹曰含少次
制十二筒以之阮隃之下聽鳳皇之鳴以別十二律
其雄鳴爲六雌鳴亦六以比黃鍾之宮適合黃鍾之
宮皆可以生之故曰黃鍾之宮律呂之本

on Chinese music. It is a typical example how Chinese writers of later periods invented pretty little stories which made the readers search for deeper meanings. We have to admit that it is difficult to free oneself from the assumption that there is more to these stories than what the text offers.

Ssŭ-ma Ch'ien (163-85), who completed the Shih Chi, "Records of the Historian," begun by his father Ssŭ-ma T'an (who died in 110 B.C.), offers a frequently quoted explanation of how the pipes were to be tuned by stating the well-known formula san-fen-sun-i-fa (三分損益法): "Subtract and add one third." The lengths of the bamboo pipes, all of the same diameter, were calculated in such a manner that the second pipe was one third shorter than the first, the third pipe one third longer than the second, and so forth. The ratio of the length of the second pipe to that of the first was 3:2, making the pitch of the second tone a perfect fifth above that of the first, while the ratio of the length of the third pipe to that of the second, being 4:3, made the third tone a perfect fourth below that of the second. By continuing this process (san-fen-sun-i-fa) of ascending fifths and descending fourths in an alternating manner, the following system resulted:

	G		A		B		C#		D#		E#	
C		D		E		F#		G#		A#		B#

The notes of the upper progression were called lü (律), "rules"; the notes of the lower progression were originally called t'ung (同), "companions." Gradually, however, all twelve tones came to be called lü.

A system such as the one above, which can be thought of as formed by a succession of pure fifths and octave transpositions, is not a circle of fifths but a spiral, for it can never close. The b#, twelve fifths above C, is not quite the same as the c seven octaves above C. There are two methods of "overcoming" the spiral. One is to continue the succession of pure fifths until a point is reached when all tones of the spiral can be projected into the range of one octave by octave-transposition so that a more or less satisfactory group of sounds can be found among them. The second method is to alter deliberately the natural pitches and create a tempered system which will form a closed circle.

Although it has no direct bearing upon notation, we shall continue the consideration of the lü in order to offer a comprehensive view of the complex problem. Both methods mentioned above were explored by Chinese music theorists. The first was used by several scholars, among them Chiao Yen-shou (c. 70 B. C.), who extended the spiral to 60 fifths, and Ching Fang (43 B. C.), whose system included 60 fifths, but perhaps also 53. The latter system, which actually divided the octave into 53 commas, proved more satisfactory than the former, for it permitted transposition of the pentatonic scale onto each of the 53 tones. Ching Fang called the 53 tones the "Inner Circle" and the basic twelve lü the "Outer Circle." Among other experiments of his was a spiral of 60 fifths, which resulted in a system of great complexity,[19] and another system of 84 seven-tone scales formed by transposing the seven basic scales onto each of the twelve lü. This latter system was further developed by several theorists, one of whom was Wang Fo, who died A. D. 959.

The theorist Ch'ien Lo-chih (425-453) in a treatise called Lü-lü sin-p'u (律呂新譜), "New Treatise on the Lü"), extended the spiral to 360 tones; and, during the Sung period (960-1279), another, Ts'ai Yüan-ting, explored the possibility of adding six additional tones to the twelve basic lü, thus creating a system of eighteen lü. However, no extension of the spiral of pure fifths could ever lead to a true closing of the spiral, for no power of 3 ever equals a power of 2.

Possibilities of creating tempered systems were also explored. Van Aalst[20] assumes the existence of a tempered system before the disastrous Great Burning of Books (ordered by Ch'in Shih-huang-ti, the "First Exalted Emperor of the Ch'in," in 213 B. C.); but, since none of the stone or metal chimes of this period reveal any form of tempered tuning, the matter remains entirely hypothetical; it is true, however, that a scholar by the name of Ho Ch'eng-t'ien (370-447) was accused of "having done violence to figures."[21]

The pure fifth (3:2) contains 702 (actually 701.955) cents. The interval formed by adding twelve fifths (702 x 12) contains, therefore, 8424 cents, and seven octaves cover a span of 8,400 cents (1,200 x 7). The difference between these intervals (i. e., between B# and c) is approximately 24 cents, the Pythagorean comma.

Kurt Reinhard,[22] whose report we quote below, includes a statement about an author named Huai-nan-dsi that requires a few remarks: Huai-Nan-Tzu (淮南子) is actually the title of a work consisting of twenty-one parts written by Liu An (劉安), the Prince of Huai-Nan, who died in 122 B. C. Reinhard's statement is not incorrect because Liu An was also known as Huai-Nan-Tzu. Liu An calculated the twelve lü in a manner which makes us think of the remarkable mixture of number mysticism with scholarly observation of ancient Greek music theory:

Note	Number relationship		Cents
B	43	43, 000	1, 096
A#	45	45, 000	1, 017
A	48	48, 000	906
G#	51	51, 000	801
G	54	54, 000	702
F#	57	57, 000	602
E#	60	60, 000	519
E	64	32, 000	408
D#	68	34, 000	303
D	72	36, 000	204
C#	76	38, 000	110
C	81	40, 500	0

The lower five numbers (we read the list from bottom to top) in the first "Number relationship" column are to be multiplied by 500, the upper seven by 1, 000. The starting point (C) is 81. Thus:

81 x 500 = 40, 500.

Another number, 749, is now used to divide the result:

40, 500/749 = 54 plus a remainder of 54.

54 now becomes the numerical representation of the G, a perfect fifth above the original C. Since this is one of the upper seven tones, 1, 000 is the multiplying factor:

54 x 1, 000/749 = 72 plus a remainder of 72.

This represents the D below the G.

72 x 500/749 = 48 plus a remainder of 48.

This represents A above the D, and so forth.

The number representing E# is 60. The number for B# is computed thus:

60 x 1, 000/749 = 80 plus a remainder of 80.

The ratio of the interval C-B# is, therefore, 81:80, the syntonic comma (the comma of Didymos).

The ingenious, though devious, arithmetic employed to produce this system results in eight pure fifths and four tempered fifths. Thus it is in no sense an equal-tempered system. The four tempered fifths are of unequal sizes; their decimal ratios are shown below:

E - B	1.4883721
B - F#	1.3255813
C# - G#	1.4901960
D# - A#	1.5111111

Why 81 has been used as numerical starting point has been a puzzle to numerous authors. One can assume that 81, being 3 x 3 x 3, shows already a certain refinement in the calculation of pitches and may represent the first cautious step in the direction toward a tempered system. It may be of importance to point out that the numbers 81 (for C), 54 (for G), 72 (for D), 48 (for A) and 64 (for E) appear in the <u>Shih Chi</u> (c. 90 B. C.), where the lengths of the standard pipes are described. The actual Chinese text appears on page 22 and is a quotation translated in the legend below the text.

Two further endeavours to reach a satisfactory temperament were made by Prince Chu Tsai-yü (朱載堉) in 1584 and 1596. He calculated numbers to the ninth decimal point in order to define more exactly the tempered pitches. It is interesting to note that in his work, <u>Lü-lü ching-i</u> (律呂精義, "The Exact Meaning of the Lü"), Chu Tsai-yü established a usable temperament 100 years before Andreas Werckmeister. This system was not put into practice in the lifetime of Chu Tsai-yü.

First column (right side): 9 x 9, 81 as *kung*
Second column: Of three parts, adding one, as *shang*
Third column: Of three parts, adding one, as *chiao*
Fourth column: Of three parts, taking off one, as *chih*
Fifth column: Of three parts, taking off one, as *yü*.

(The names *kung*, *shang*, *chiao*, *chih*, *yü* will be discussed on page 53.)

In 1664, the beginning of the Ch'ing period (1644-1911), the trend toward equal-temperament was forcibly halted by the imperial music office, and the ancient spiral of the twelve *lü* was again adopted – at least in theory. Practice, however, was by now subject to increasing influences from Europe and inclined more and more toward tempered tunings based upon those of the West.

It is important to note that the twelve *lü* were never thought of as forming a chromatic scale. True scales were derived only from melodies and never from "rows," such as those formed by the twelve pitch-pipes. The *lü* were, however, grouped into basic and auxiliary and into *yang* (male) and *yin* (female) tones.

Before we present the characters which serve as notational symbols representing the *lü*, we have to point out that their written forms have changed since the early sources were first written. At the Great Burning of Books in 213 B.C. most of the primary sources were destroyed with the exception of the *Shih Ching*, the Book of Odes, and some works on divination, medicine, and agriculture. We can assume that these early works contained chapters on music together with notational symbols written in the "old script."[23] The characters shown below represent the "modern script," a manner of writing which came into use during the Han period – that is, several centuries after the original works had been written.

The Five Basic *Lü*

Names:			Pitches (assuming C as the first *lü*):
Huang-chung	黄鐘,	"Yellow Bell"	C
Lin-chung	林鐘,	"Forest Bell"	G
T'ai-ts'u	太簇,	"Great Frame"	D
Nan-lü	南呂,	"Southern Tube"	A
Ku-hsi	姑洗,	"Old, purified"	E

The Seven Auxiliary *Lü*

Ying-chung	應鐘,	"Answering Bell"	B
Jui-pin	蕤賓,	"Luxuriant Vegetation"	F#
Ta-lü	大呂,	"Greatest Tube"	C#
I-tsê	夷則,	"Equalizing Rule"	G#

The Seven Auxiliary Lü (cont.)

Names:			Pitches (assuming C as the first lü):
Chia-chung	夾鐘,	"Pressed Bell"	D#
Wu-i	無射,	"Not Determined"	A#
Chung-lü	仲呂,	"Mean Tube"	E#

Besides the division into basic and auxiliary tones, the lü were also grouped into yang and yin. In addition, the lü were linked to the months of the year. With every month the key of the hymns performed in the Confucian temple was changed so that one lü after the other served as the basic note.

Yang ("The light side of the mountain"), the male, the positive, and the moist principle:

A# appropriate for September
G# appropriate for July
F# appropriate for May
E appropriate for March
D appropriate for January
C appropriate for November

Yin ("The dark side of the mountain"), the female, the negative, and the dry principle:

B appropriate for October
A appropriate for August
G appropriate for June
E# appropriate for April

D# appropriate for February

C# appropriate for December

The two rows of yang and yin, the only whole-tone "scales" outside of Europe, had little practical value in Chinese music and were based upon philosophical speculation.[24] The only practiced exception occurred in the grouping of stone and metal chimes.

The names of the twelve pitch-pipes have been used, in an abbreviated form, as a unique system for denoting absolute pitches. It was mainly employed in ritual music where absolute pitches had important extramusical connotations. The age of this unusual notation cannot be stated clearly, but we know that the names of the pitch-pipes had already appeared in the Chou Li,[25] which was written about the first century B.C. If used as a notation, only the first words of each of the twelve lü names are used. Instead of huang-chung only huang, or instead of lin-chung only lin is employed, and so forth.

The twelve abbreviated lü names, if used as notational symbols, are (in modern script):

Huang 黄, C

Ta 大, C#

T'ai 太, D

Chia 夾, D#; alternative symbols: 圜 or 員

Ku 姑, E

Chung 仲, E# (F); alternative symbols: 中(呂) or 小(呂)

Jui 蕤, F#

Twelve Abbreviated *Lü* Names (*cont.*)

Lin 林, G; alternative symbol: 函

I 夷, G#

Nan 南, A

Wu 無, A#; alternative symbol: 亾

Ying 應, B

Chinese music theory is similar to that of India, which groups all musical sounds into a lower octave (*mandra saptaka*), a middle octave (*madhya saptaka*), and an upper octave (*tar saptaka*). The Chinese theorists do the same: the *lü* are grouped into *pei-lü* (倍呂, "double pitch-pipes"), the lowest; the *chêng-lü* (正呂, "principal pipes"), the middle; and the *pan lü* (半呂, "half pipes"), the upper octave. These three octaves are also called *cho shêng* (濁聲, "muddy sound") for the lowest; *chung shêng* (中聲, "middle sound") for the middle; and *ch'ing shêng* (清聲, "clear sound") for the upper octave.

Of the lowest octave only the following four notes below the 黃 are used:

Huang 黃, C

Pei-ying 倍應, B

Pei-wu 倍無, Bb (A#)

Pei-nan 倍南, A

Pei-i 倍夷, Ab (G#)

These four symbols have been in use only since the Manchu period (1644-1911). They represent sounds which are derived from the spiral of perfect fifths. This implies that there will be a difference in pitch when the octave has been reached or passed. Hence pei-wu, for instance, is not a pure octave duplication of wu. The same concerns the upper octave, which is indicated by the affix ch'ing (清, "clear"), placed either to the left or the right of the lü character. Thus, a sound an octave higher than 黄 (of the middle octave) would be notated 清黄 or 黄清.

This notational system made up of the first characters of the twelve lü names served to notate important melodies of the Confucian temple and the imperial palace and, occasionally, to notate "lute"-songs, such as the songs by Chiang K'uei.[26] Although this notation lacked all rhythmic indications, it was an important tool in the hands of the learned musicians because it enabled them to prescribe absolute pitches.

Lü symbols can also be found in pieces notated in systems not denoting absolute pitches. In such cases, at the beginning of a piece, a complete lü symbol indicates the required pitch of the basic or initial note of the melody. For instance, at the beginning of the hsiao[27] part of the "Spring Hymn to Confucius," which is notated in kung-ch'ê,[28] we find the following annotation:

chia	夾	The lü chia-chung, which stands for D#
chung	鐘	
wei	爲	acts [here as]

kung 宫 kung, the basic note — expressed by means of solmization syllables of the Chinese five-tone notation. Kung has the same significance as the Western (movable) "do."[29]

The abbreviated lü characters (e.g., chia) are employed only in notating entire melodies. Whenever a single absolute pitch is prescribed, as in the present case, the complete lü name is used.

The following example, Figure 1, represents a score written much later, and shows the first eleven measures of the first ode of the Shih Ching.[30] In order to offer as full an explanation as possible we shall transcribe every character and symbol, irrespective of whether or not they are lü, although this may cause some deviation from our consideration of the lü notation. We begin reading from the top right-hand corner of page 29:

The first four characters are:

樂 yüeh (music)

正 chêng (principal, chief)

倡 ch'ang (to lead, to direct)

賛 tsan (to assist, to help).

The next characters, written in a frame below, are:

合 ho (joined, together)

樂 yüeh (music)

關 kuan ("kuan," onomatopoetical, the sound of ...)

雎 chü (the osprey, a kind of fish-hawk).

Figure 1

樂正倡贊
合樂關雎
播鞉第一通止
播鞉第二通止
播鞉第三通止
關
非禮勿視非禮勿聽非禮勿言非禮勿動
關
非禮勿視非禮勿聽非禮勿言非禮勿動

Figure 1 (cont.)

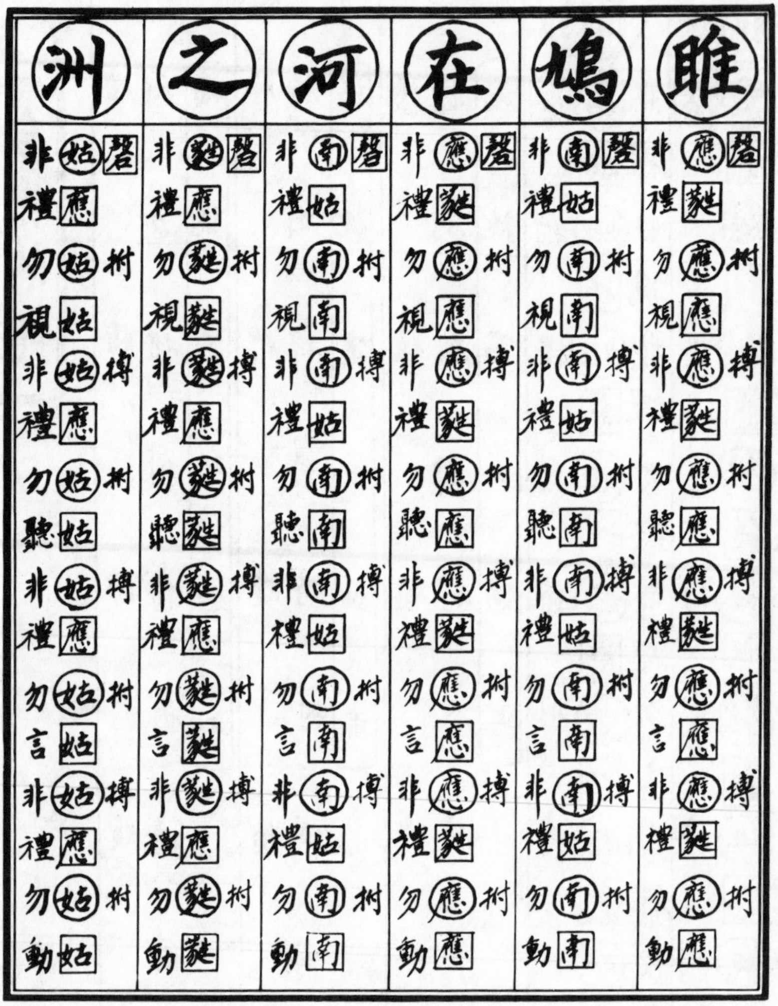

The whole title column thus reads in full: "The music director leads and assists... (in frame): the accompaniment ('together music') of the Kuan-chü Ode."

The subsequent columns, each of which represents a "measure," are to be read from top to bottom and from right to left. The music begins with the second column; here we observe symbols outside and inside an oblong frame. The ones outside, immediately to the right of the frame, are:

搏 po (lit., "to strike," "to beat with the fist")

and, below it,

拊 fu (lit., "to slap," "to tap")

The two characters indicate "loud and soft," respectively. When 搏 and 拊 are combined, they are the name of a small drum (called po-fu) which is used in the Confucian temple.[31] To the right of po we find only the second of the two characters ch'ung tu (舂 牘), "pounding tablet," which, in this instance, stands for "wooden clapper."

The characters po-fu and tu appear throughout columns two, three, and four. The characters placed in the oblong frame offer the following instructions (read from top to bottom):

播 po ("beat," "strike")

鞉 t'ao (abbreviation of t'ao ku[32])

第一。第二。第三。 "first," "second," "third," in columns two, three, and four, respectively.

通 "stanza"

止 "stop"

These six characters are not to be considered as notational symbols but merely as instructions concerning the use of percussion instruments in the first three stanzas ("measures"). In short, we are dealing here with a brief "instrumental prelude" to the ensuing ode.

The transcription of columns two, three, and four is as follows:

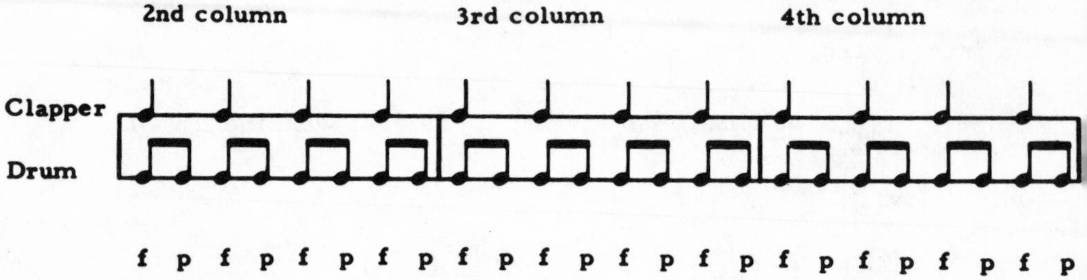

The fifth column begins the melody and its accompaniment. At the top of Figure 1 (pp. 29-30) the large characters in circles represent the text.[33] Each column is headed by one text word which is sung to one note and is held for the whole measure. Below the text, in small circles and squares in the center of each column, are the *lü* symbols indicating a quick-moving accompaniment performed by the *pien-ch'ing*.[34] The music for this instrument is always notated with *lü* symbols. At the top of the fifth column, to the right, immediately below the textual character, we observe in a square the character 磬 which means *ch'ing* (abbreviation of *t'ê ch'ing*[35]). The small signs below *ch'ing* indicate drum beats, soft and loud, as has already been explained. Of considerable interest are the characters to the left of the *lü* symbols. They read: *fei li wu shih*; *fei li wu t'ing*; *fei li wu yen*; *fei li wu tung*. This sixteen-syllable sequence appears unaltered in each subsequent column. A rough translation of one column reads as follows: "Do not see anything improper; do not hear anything improper; do not speak anything improper; do not do anything improper." These words are not sung but are used merely as a mnemonic formula for the accompanists. The words "fei" and "wu," notated with the same *lü* symbol, represent the melody note. The word "li" represents the interval of a fourth or fifth above the melody note; and "shih," "t'ing," "yen," and "tung" correspond again with the respective melody note or its higher octave, as shown in Figure 2 on page 34.

The *lü* notation does not show any duration of the sounds; the symbols indicate only pitches and nothing else. Yet, Chinese musicians were able to convey in this notation a certain pulse by placing the evenly flowing words *fei li wu shih*, etc., side by side with the *pien-ch'ing* notes and, furthermore, by placing the *lü* symbols in small circles and squares. The regular succession of circle-square-circle-square conveys the idea of a uniform, regular pulse:

Figure 2, following (pp. 34-36), is a transcription of columns two to eight.

Occasionally the *yang-yin* principle can be observed in some *lü* notations of Confucian hymns. Figure 3, following (p. 37), is the *pien-ch'ing* part of the first strophe of the Hymn to Confucius.[36]

Figure 2

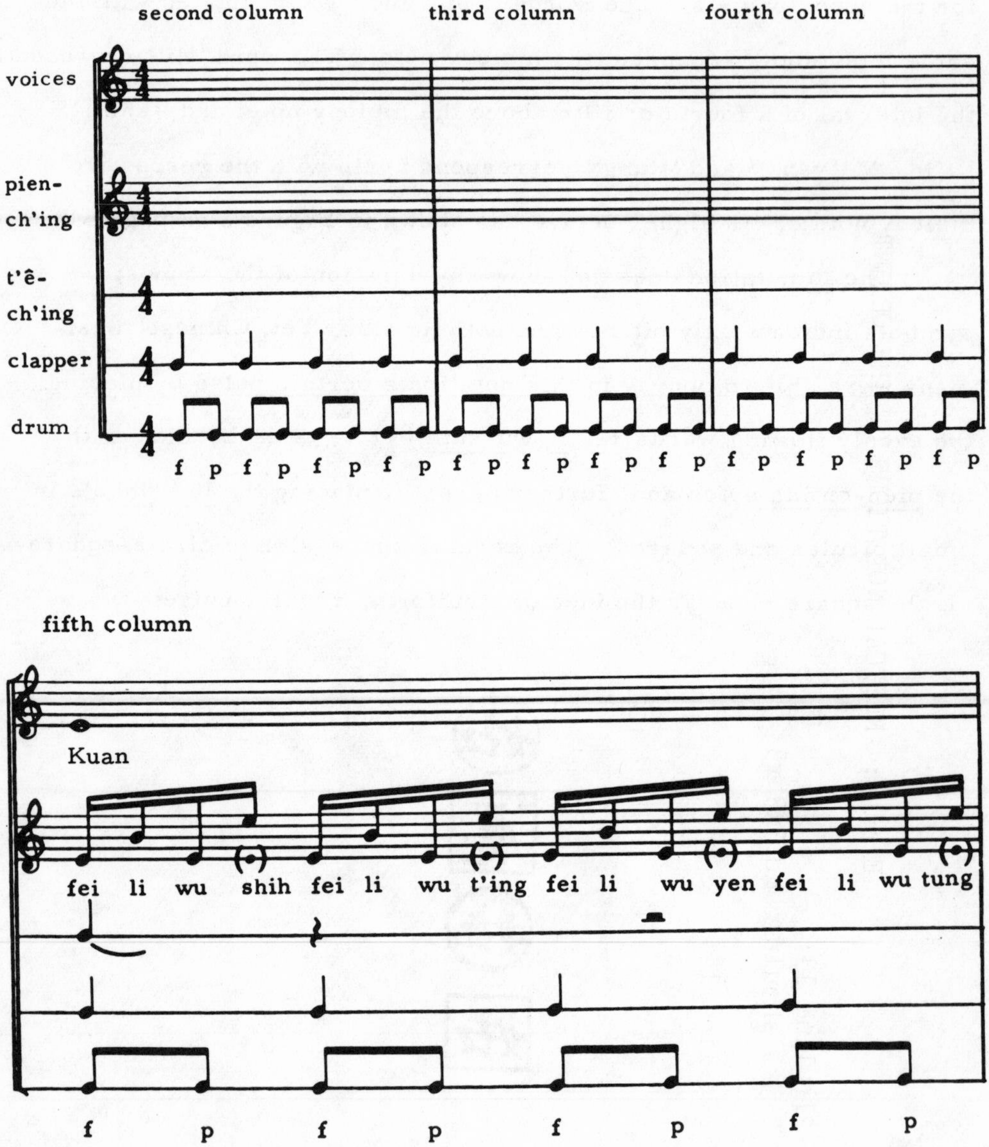
second column
third column
fourth column
voices
pien-
ch'ing
t'ê-
ch'ing
clapper
drum
f p f p f p f p f p f p f p f p f p f p f p f p
fifth column
Kuan
fei li wu shih fei li wu t'ing fei li wu yen fei li wu tung
f p f p f p f p

Errata: MUSICAL NOTATIONS OF THE ORIENT

Page 21, line 13:
$3x3x3$ should read $3x3^2x3$

Page 40, line 18:
"pantomines" should read "pantomimes"

Page 44, line 6:
"became effective" should read "began"

Page 97:

In the musical example, both alternatives placed below the triplet, representing the first quarter of the bar GAG, EDCD, E, D, should read GAG and not GGG.

Page 170, line 11:
"Nan ryu" should read "Nam-ryu"

Page 232, Figure 55:
TE should read ṬE

Figure 2 (cont.)

sixth column

seventh column

Figure 2 (cont.)

eighth column

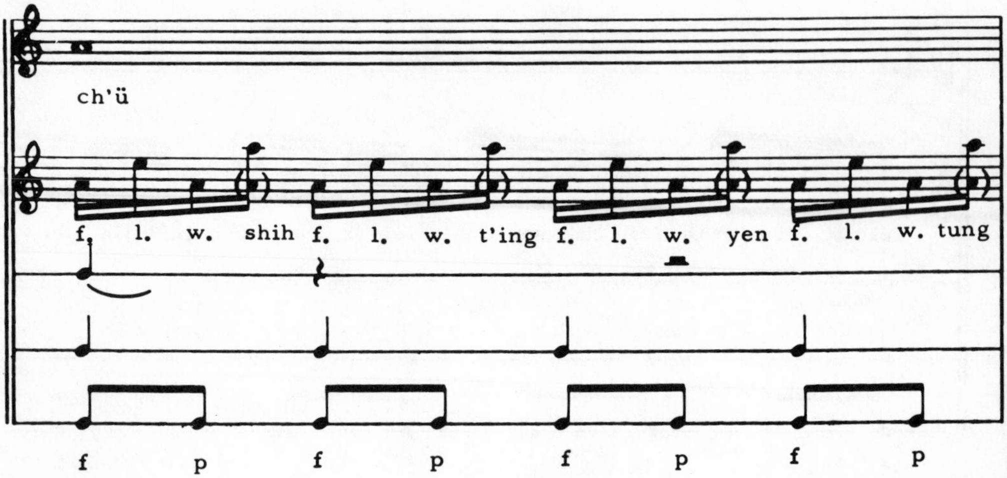

In the excerpt on page 37 (Fig. 3), all notational symbols indicate the sounds of the yang row. It is obvious that by using only one of the two rows of slabs of the pien-ch'ing an anhemitonic pentatonic scale cannot be performed. If, however, custom ruled that only yang notes were to be used on the pien-ch'ing in this hymn, the missing sounds of the pentatonic scale had to be replaced by others that approximated the intended sounds and yet were degrees of the yang row.

Let us assume that the melody would have to begin with the low note A. As A belonged to the yin,[37] the female row, the nearest tone in the yang row, the pei-i (Ab), had to be substituted. As the slabs of the pien-ch'ing were tuned to the spiral of pure fifths, Ab (or G#) being the ninth fifth, the sounds were somewhat "out of tune." This, however, was of no consequence, for the aim was to use yang notes exclusively. A literal transcription of the hymn would read as follows, (Fig. 4, p. 37):

倍夷黃太姑倍夷夷姑

太黃太夷姑倍夷夷姑

姑姑夷黃太黃夷倍夷

夷黃太倍夷姑黃太黃

倍夷

Figure 3

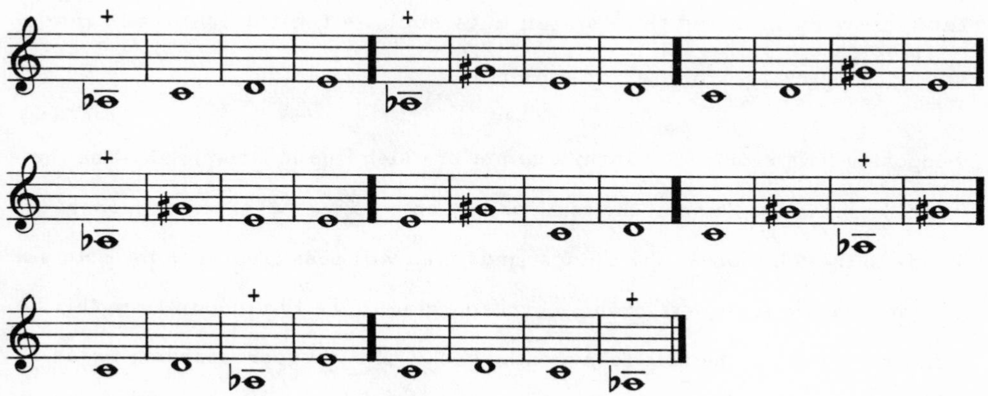

Figure 4

The *Aufführungspraxis* of these particular hymns was such that the *pien-ch'ing* part used only the *yang lü* while the vocal part was performed in its proper pentatonic shape, beginning with the note D, a pure fourth above the intended initial note A.[38] In other words, the vocal part did not consist exclusively of *yin* notes but employed the entire gamut of tones in an anhemitonic pentatonic melody. It is most probable that other accompanying instruments, in addition to the *pien-ch'ing*, also did not use *yang* notes exclusively and, as with the vocal line, played the melody in its proper shape.[39] There must have been severe dissonant clashes during such a performance, which is remarkable considering the acute hearing of the Chinese. This strange custom can also be observed in Korea. Andreas Eckardt[40] has observed that when two slabs of a set of chimes were hung in the wrong order, the leading musician refused to have this obvious mistake corrected. The argument was that the slabs had always hung in this way and that no change could be made on such a revered instrument. This, it is assumed, shows how strongly extramusical considerations influenced musical practice. One cannot help but severely doubt this view although every now and then statements such as the following are made which support the former assumption:

> Supposing it is required to form a gamut of which [the *lü*] *jui-pin* shall be the base: knowing the name of the tonic or key note (蕤 賓 , which corresponds to the 5th moon), the Chinese musician will pass from it to the note six moons forward (thus, 黃 *huang*, corresponding to the 11th moon); from this he will retrograde to the note four months back (夷 *i*, corresponding to the 7th moon); then he will go to the sound six moons forward (太 *t'ai*, corresponding to the 1st moon); then four moons back again (無 *wu*, 9th moon). He will thus create a scale of five sounds to which he will give the names *kung*,

shang, chiao, etc.[41] If we put this pentatonic gamut in apposition to the corresponding western notes, we shall have

and it will be readily perceived that the C and D are nearly half a tone too flat; but to the Chinese this is no objection, their aim being to prove the irrefutable connection of their music with astronomy and nature . . . .[42]

Although the Chinese musical past deals mainly with two scale-forms, the anhemitonic pentatonic and the heptatonic, at various times China may have used more complex scales, compelling scholars to enlarge the number of their notational symbols. Symbols for microtonal alterations can be found in the notations of Chiang K'uei (1155-1229),[43] in which appear a slightly sharpened E and B, both notated with the same symbol: 折字 . This symbol always occurs either between two 姑 (E) or between two 應 (B). If written in Western notation it would appear in the following manner:

The Chinese term for microtonal alterations is chê-tzŭ (折字),

"bent letters (notes)." These two sharpened notes seem to function merely as ornaments of E and B respectively.

Following is an example (Fig. 5) containing such microtonal alterations and their notational symbols. This example, a composition of the above-mentioned Sung composer, Chiang K'uei, is followed (Fig. 6) by a transcription in Western notation[44] in which the note

 indicates the microtonal sharpening of the notes E and B.

In Figure 5 the *lü* notation appears to the right side of the textual columns. We find that Chiang K'uei's melody uses the material D E ($\overset{+}{\text{E}}$) F# G A B ($\overset{+}{\text{B}}$) d. We observe that there is a resemblance between this scale and that of the North Indian rāga *Khamaj* *(Khammaja)*.[45]

It may be of interest to deviate here from the discussion of the *chê-tzŭ* in *lü* notation in order to trace briefly some influences from India and Central Asia on the music of China, especially during the Sung period, the time when Chiang K'uei composed his pieces. For many centuries there had been a strong link between China, Central Asia, and India. Pantomines, a rich variety of dances, and other theatrical shows gained such popularity in China that this imported foreign music (*Hu-yüeh*, 胡樂)[46] threatened to obliterate the indigenous ritual and ceremonial music. The imperial music offices of the various emperors had to create special music departments in order to deal with these imported musical styles. There were seven "departments" (with their own orchestras) during the brief Sui dynasty (590-618), and ten during the T'ang period (618-907); and later, especially during the Sung period (960-1279), the introduction of impressive theatrical performances of Islamic origin could be observed. These had come to China via Central Asia. The Confucian philosopher Chu Hsi (朱熹) 1130-

應南應清太太姑應林蕤姑字折姑應字折應林南應
鞭臥龍躍鏡浦靈之來噎如雨 環玉廂翠繽紛
蕤林蕤姑太姑 南應字折應南應南林蕤姑蕤林
靈之逝扉出雲 我行其野有穧有秭入其闉闍
太蕤太姑 南應字折應林南林應字折應南林太蕤
載歌載儛 祓我家室旱予父母高田萊蕪下田
太姑 南應字折應蕤林南應林清太太姑字折姑
烏乎 爾澤毋三爾煦毋五葢嚴祀其終古

Figure 5

Transcription of the melody notated in Figure 5:

Figure 6

1200) composed twelve melodies to texts of the Book of Odes. To illustrate this, here is the first of these melodies:[47]

Figure 7

If we replace A# with Bb and D# with Eb we get the scale F G A Bb C D Eb f (or, transposed, C D E F G A Bb c), which also corresponds to the North Indian rāga Khamaj. Although Khamaj is a rāga of Hindu origin, it is not too fantastic to assume that with the Muslim invasion of Northern India, which became effective during the Ghaznavid (Yamin) dynasty in the tenth century, Mohammedan singers imported Khamaj and other popular rāgas as far as China. It is to be expected that the original Indian scales underwent some modifications before that time or when they were used in China. Further evidence in support of this assumption can be found in another song by Chiang K'uei, "The Spirit of the Billows,"[48] as shown in Figure 8 below.

Figure 8

Figure 8 (cont.)

If we read Bb instead of A#, Eb for D#, and Ab for G#, we get the scale F G Ab Bb C D Eb f corresponding to the ancient and popular North Indian rāga Kafi, which even today is a favorite of Muslim musicians in North India.

YUL-CHA-PO (律字譜)

YUL-CHA-PO, which means "principal letter notation," is the Korean name of the Chinese lü notation. Yul-cha-po can be found in the famous Ak-hak-koe-pŭm (樂學軌範, Music Study Guide Model), a handbook on music in nine volumes. This important work was written by order of the King, Sung-chong, in 1493.[49] In collaboration with other scholars of the Hong-mun-kwan College, the author, Sŭng Hyŭn (成俔, 1439-1504), describes general musical matters, the history of Chinese music,[50] dance and popular music, accessories used in dancing, and the prescribed costumes to be worn by musicians and dancers. Sŭng Hyŭn emphasizes in his work the most important features of ancient serious Korean music, the Ah-ak (雅樂, "pure music").

Before we continue, a brief description of Ah-ak, which denotes the ancient (pure) music of temple and palace, may be of interest. The term appears first in a Chinese work, the Confucian Analects

(論語), where we read that "the bad music of the territory of Chêng spoils the pure music."[51] Gradually the term Ah-ak was applied to all music performed at festive gatherings of the nobility.

The beliefs in the divine origin of music, in its divine message to all, and in its divine powers of influencing fate, guiding education, and maintaining prosperity are still noticeable in Ah-ak. From the remote past, China had supposedly been under the guidance of the twelve heavenly and human legendary emperors, more or less symbolical figures of great ancestral importance, to whom were ascribed the invention of music, the arts, sciences, and crafts. Each of these legendary emperors had his own music which was called by a special name. Although today these ancient types of music have disappeared, Korean Ah-ak still reverently retains some of the old names. Korean court musicians of the recent past distinguished six kinds of Ah-ak, each differing from the others in the use of specific instruments and in its functions at the various ceremonies:

a) Un-mun-ak (雲門樂, lit. "cloud-gate music"), music in honor of the spirits of heaven. Un-mun-ak represents the music and dances of the legendary Chinese emperor Huang Ti (黄帝).
b) Ham-chi-ak (咸池樂, lit. "entire influence of King's virtue music"), music in honor of the spirits of the earth. Ham-chi-ak represents the music of the legendary emperor Yao (堯) of China.
c) Tae-kwŭn-ak (大卷樂, lit. "big turn music"), dance music appeasing and honoring the spirits of the four directions (cardinal points); the "four directions" (sa mang, 四望) can also be interpreted with the "four views" — sun, moon, stars, and ocean.

d) Tae-ha-ak (大夏樂 , lit. "big summer music"), music in honor of the mountain and river spirits. Tae-ha-ak represents the music of the Chinese legendary emperor Yu (禹); the character 夏 (in Korean: ha) stands for the Chinese Hsia dynasty, which was founded by Yu.

e) Tae-ho-ak (大護樂 , lit. "great protection music"), music in honor of the (female) ancestors. Tae-ho-ak represents the music of the Chinese legendary emperor Shêng T'ang (成湯), the founder of the Shang (商) dynasty (1523-1027).

f) Tae-mu-ak (大武樂 , lit. "great Mu [military] music"), music in honor of the rulers Mun and Mu. The character 文王 represents the Chinese ruler Wên (Korean: Mun), the ancestor of the Chinese emperor Wu (武 , Korean: Mu), the founder of the Chou dynasty (1027-256).

A seventh kind, not included in the official six types, was Tae-so-ak (大韶樂, lit. "great beauty music"), music in remembrance of the virtues of emperor Shun (舜), also described as music for the "four views" and "five mountains." This music was highly praised by Confucius: "When Confucius heard the Tae-so of the Chê country he lost his appetite for three months – he was so deeply impressed by it."[52] According to Shimonaka Yasaburo (下中彌三郎),[53] the six kinds of Ah-ak in China were listed in a slightly different manner: Un-mun-ak and Tae-kwŭn-ak were grouped together, and Tae-so-ak was listed as the third of the six kinds of Ah-ak.

Today Korean Ah-ak can be heard in the ceremony in honor of Confucius (Mun-myo, 文廟), where it is called Che-chŭn-ak 祭典樂 , lit. "ceremony-law music"). This ceremony is performed twice a year, in spring and in fall. Ah-ak of recent and present times includes not only ritual and ceremonial melodies of T'ang and Sung China, but has added to its repertoire some popular Chinese melodies and a few original Korean tunes and melodies of Buddhist origin; the latter music is called Hyang-ak (鄉 樂 , "indigenous Korean music"). It appears that Hyang-ak melodies are based upon six-tone scales, contrary to the strictly pentatonic character of real Ah-ak.

Continuing now our consideration of yul-cha-po, we observe that this notation can be found in the Sae-chong shillok (世 宗 實 錄) a famous historical document dealing with the events which occurre during the reign of King Sae-chong (fifteenth century A.D.). This work contains thirteen pieces of court music compiled by the Korean imperial music office.[54] During the second half of the fifteenth century, yul-cha-po was less frequently used. Occasionally, some learned court musicians of later periods would revert to this notational system, as for instance in the book Sok-ak won-po (俗 樂 源 譜), "Original Source of Popular Music."[55] This collection of songs, probably compiled during the eighteenth century by the imperial music office, contains only one piece still notated in yul-cha-po. Lee reports[56] that court musicians were not always able to read the yul-cha-po symbols correctly and that manuscripts copied by them showed numerous mistakes. Gradually yul-cha-po disappeared and became replaced by the simpler O-ŭm-yak-po (五 音 略 譜), "Abbreviated Notation of the Five Sounds."[57] This new notational system, which appeared sporadically during the reign of King Sae-cho, quickly gained in popularity during the following centuries.

The symbols of *yul*-*cha*-*po* are identical to those of the abbreviated Chinese *lü* names but, of course, are pronounced in Korean:

Hwang	黃	(e.g.,) C
Tae	大	C#
Thae	太	D
Hyŭp	夾	D#
Ko	姑	E
Chung	仲	F
Yu	蕤	F#
Im	林	G
I	夷	G#
Nam	南	A
Mu	無	A#
Ŭng	應	B

The following is an example[58] of *yul*-*cha*-*po* as quoted from the *Ak*-*hak koe*-*pŭm*, Vol II ("*Shi*-*yong*-*a*-*bu*-*jae*-*ak*," 時用雅部祭樂):

南 應 太 黃
林 南 姑 南
黃 蕤 南 林
太 姑 林 姑

If we transcribe this example into Western notation, we see that the resulting melody probably represents a part of the Chinese "Hymn to Confucius."[59]

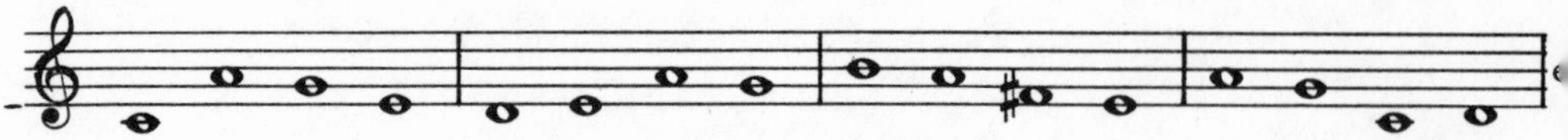

This Korean version of the famous hymn now employs heptatonic tone-material: C D E F# G A B.

Japanese imperial court music (gagaku), too, established a system of absolute pitches. Unlike the Korean usage of Chinese lü characters, Japanese musical practice employed different characters and names for the twelve pitches, maintaining only one of the Chinese lü, the huang-(chung). This tone, which is called ōshiki in Japan, does not represent the first note of the twelve sounds as it did in China and Korea. The basic tone of the Japanese system of twelve semitones corresponds to the Western note D. Its name is ichikotsu (壹越 or 一越). The tone ōshiki (黄鐘), the Chinese huang-chung, is here represented by the Western note A. The following are the Japanese names of the twelve sounds within the octave and their Western equivalents:

Character and	name	Western equivalent	popular designation by numbers	
盤渉,	Banshiki	B	三	(3)
鸞鏡,	Rankei	A#	二	(2)
黄鐘 (黄鐘),	Ōshiki	A	一	(1)
鳥鐘 (鳥鐘),	Husho	G#	十二	(12)

Character and	name	Western equivalent	popular designation by numbers	
双調,	Sōjō	G	十一	(11)
下無,	Shimomu	F#	十	(10)
勝絶,	Shōsetsu	F	九	(9)
平調,	Hyōjō	E	八	(8)
斷金,	Tangin	D#	七	(7)
壹越,	Ichikotsu	D	六	(6)
上無,	Kamimu	C#	五	(5)
神仙,	Shinsen	C	四	(4)

Besides the three notational systems of more or less absolute pitches thus far discussed, we must mention the Japanese shakuhachi tablature[60] and some endeavors to utilize — partially or wholly — Western staff notation.[61]

In order to complete our review of absolute-pitch notations, we digress here from our consideration of the lü and symbols derived from the lü and describe two unusual attempts made by Indian musicians to establish absolute pitches. Indian music theory of the past derived the pitches of its seven-tone scale from the cries of various animals. The argument was that animal cries remain unchanged and thus could serve, to some degree, to establish pitches. The lowest pitch was derived from the cry of the peacock, the next higher from that of the chataka, the fever-bird of the rainy season, the third from the bleat of the goat, the fourth from the call of the crane, the fifth from the sound of the koil bird, the sixth from the croak of the frog, and the seventh from the trumpeting of the elephant. It is obvious that this method could not have led to satisfactory results. During the nineteenth century missionaries from Europe had taken into India a small portable harmonium which quickly gained great popularity and which, up to the middle of the present century, could be found in the homes of many music-loving Indians. The keys of this harmonium served to determine absolute pitches: "white one" (safed ek), the first white key, indicated the note C; "white two" (safed do), indicated D; "black one" (kali ek), stood for Db or C#; and so forth. These pitch definitions were never used in Indian notations. At the beginning of a concert, however, the Tanbura[62] player and the drummer and any other accompanists would consult the soloist concerning his basic note. This basic note, the Indian SA (the Chinese kung) would then be defined by reference to the keys of the European harmonium.

THE OLD CHINESE FIVE-TONE NOTATION

This notation uses five characters which represent the five degrees of a pentatonic scale. The five-tone scale was, and still is, the main feature of Chinese music. Although many other scales appeared in the course of China's long history, eventually there was always a return to the basic pentatonic anhemitonic scale. This five-tone notation is the favorite medium of Chinese, Korean, and, to a certain degree, Japanese[63] music theorists who employ the five characters not only in their descriptions of scales and modes, but add them to other, more complex notational systems as a technique of clarification.

The earliest source that mentions the names of the degrees of the ancient five-tone scale of China is the *Tso Chuan* (左傳), a commentary to the *Ch'un-ch'iu* (春秋 – *Annals of Spring and Autumn*), one of the Confucian classics.[64] The *Tso Chuan* was written in the fourth century B. C. by Tso Shih Ch'iu-ming (左 史 丘 明), the so-called "father of Chinese prose." In this and numerous other works the five degrees of the scale are:

Kung 宮

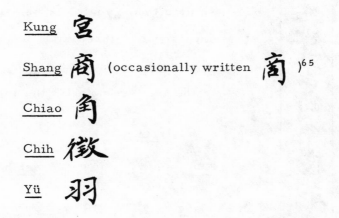

Shang 商 (occasionally written 啇)[65]

Chiao 角

Chih 徵

Yü 羽

These names are comparable to the solmization syllables of the West. *Kung* can represent any of the twelve *lü* and, in the same manner as the European "movable do," denotes the first degree of any pentatonic (or heptatonic) scale.

The excerpt on page 54 (Fig. 9) is taken from a copy of the *Chou Li* (Book 21), where the notational symbols are recorded in modern script.

Roughly translated the passage reads: ... these are represented by the following five tones: *kung*, *shang*, *chiao*, *chih*, and *yü*. All these tones can be produced by the "eight sounds" [the eight materials from which musical instruments are constructed]: metal, stone, earth (clay), skin, silk, wood, gourd, and bamboo.

Of interest is the writing of *chih* in the following passage: the

皆文之以五聲宮商角徵羽皆播之以八音金石土
革絲木匏竹

Figure 9

tenth character of the first column is written 徵 while in all other instances we fin[d] 徵.

Although these five degrees do not signify absolute pitches, they were considered to be part of the yang and yin "rows," similar to the male and female lü, and wer[e] arranged into three male and two female degrees. Assuming that kung corresponds to the Western note C, the grouping is:

	Yang			Yin	
kung	宮	(C)	chih	徵	(G)
shang	商	(D)	yü	羽	(A)
chiao	角	(E)			

Kung has been described as the man who takes a wife, chih; their son, shang, marries yü; but their offspring, chiao, can not marry, for the next fifth (B), would lie a semitone from C and would thus mar the peaceful effect of the pentatonic (family) group.[66] These five notes are included in the Chinese philosophical concept of the "Five Agents." Within this concept numerous connotations are ascribed to the five degrees of the scale on page 55.[67]

Kung	Chih	Shang	Yü	Chiao
Earth	Fire	Metal	Water	Wood
"5"	"7"	"9"	"6"	"8"
Saturn	Mars	Venus	Mercury	Jupiter
Center	South	West	North	East
	Summer	Autumn	Winter	Spring
Wind	Heat	Cold	Rain	Sunshine
Ox	Chicken	Dog	Pig	Sheep
Naked	Feathered	Hairy	Shell-covered	Scaly
Millet	Beans	Hemp	Chinese sugar-cane	Wheat
Emperor	Works	Official	Things	People
Fragrant	Burnt	Rancid	Rotten	Goat-smell
Sweet	Bitter	Sharp	Salty	Sour
Yellow	Red	White	Black	Green
Desire	Cheerfulness	Anger	Grief	Joy

The excerpt on page 56 (Fig. 10), taken from a copy of the *Shih Chi*, XXIV (*Yüeh-shu*, 2), illustrates this concept.

Roughly translated the excerpt reads:

Kung symbolizes the emperor, *shang* the government officials, *chiao* the people, *chih* the national affairs (actions), and *yü* the harvest (material things).

If the five (tones) are not disturbed then there is no disorder. If *kung* is wrongly intoned, suffering follows, because the emperor is arrogant and proud. If *shang* is wrongly intoned, depravity follows, because the officials are idle and corrupt. If *chiao* is wrongly intoned, sadness arises, because the people are disturbed and harbour resentment. If *chih* is wrongly intoned, pain follows, because the affairs (actions) will be wearisome. If *yü* is wrongly intoned, danger arises, because the wealth is exhausted. If all five tones are wrongly intoned, everything deteriorates, and the country will face destruction in the near future.

宮為君商為臣角為民徵為事羽為物五者不亂則
無怗懘之音矣宮亂則荒其君驕商亂則趍其臣壞
角亂則憂其民怨徵亂則哀其事勤羽亂則危其財
匱五者皆亂迭相陵謂之慢如此則國之滅亡無日
矣

Figure 10

This passage from the *Shih Chi* is nearly identical with one in the *Li Chi* (*Yüeh-chi,* V). In the *Shih Chi* excerpt the seventeenth and nineteenth characters of the second column are 搥 ("throw," "beat") and 臣 ("subject"), while in the corresponding places in the *Li Chi* the characters 陂 ("uneven") and 官 ("official") are used.

The foregoing passage is another of the frequently quoted ones. It cannot be dismissed as easily as the phoenix-and-pitch-pipes story because it aims at a description of the relationship of the five basic notes and grades them according to their importance. The second part of the passage which threatens the performer with various punishments if the tones are incorrectly presented deserves to be considered because we observe similar phenomena in the music of medieval India. There are numerous authors who threaten the performer and listener with poverty and a reduced span of life if the *rāgas* are not correctly sung or played (e. g., Nārada, *Saṅgīta-Makaranda,* written some time between the seventh and eleventh centuries).

As already mentioned, these five characters appear in Chinese, Korean, and Japanese works; their forms remain unaltered, but, of course, the pronunciations vary in the three countries:

China	Korea	Japan
Kung	Kung	Kyū
Shang	Sang	Shō
Chiao	Kak	Kaku
Chih	Chih	Cho (Chi)
Yü	U	U

The notes represented by the third and fifth characters (*chiao* and *yü*) vary in their relationship to *kung*, as can be seen in the following chart:

	宮	商	角	徵	羽
China:					
Early five-tone scale:	C	D	E	G	A
Ming scale:	C	D	F	G	A
Korea:					
Kung scale:	C	D	E	G	A
Chih scale:	C	D	F	G	A
Sang scale:	C	D	F	G	Bb
Japan:					
Ryo mode:	C	D	E	G	A
Ritsu mode:	C	D	F	G	A

An example in which the five characters are used to clarify other notational systems can be seen in Figure 11. This example, taken from the *Ak-hak koe-pŭm*,[68] is notated in Korean *yul-cha-po* with the additional Chinese five-tone symbols.

太商　黃宮
姑角　南羽
南羽　林徵
林徵　姑角

Figure 11

THE OLD CHINESE SEVEN-TONE NOTATION

This notational system adds two symbols to the Five-Tone Notation and is, therefore, only an enlarged form of it. Neither indicates any absolute pitches, and the notational symbols signify only the relative positions of the tones within the octave.

The Tso Chuan[69] states that the seven-tone scale had been adopted in ritual music as early as the Chou period (1027-256). At this time two auxiliary tones were added to the basic five degrees of the scale: the pien-kung and the pien-chih (B and F# respectively, provided kung is transcribed as C). These two tones were not considered as basic scale-degrees and were of lesser importance than the other five sounds. The word pien (變), meaning "to change," "to alter," or "to lead up to," indicates the dependence of these two tones upon the basic notes of kung and chih. Thus, the ancient heptatonic scale was C D E (F#) G A (B) c.

During the Chou period the two pien tones were also called ho (和, "harmony") for pien-kung (B); and miu (繆 , "misleading") for pien-chih (F#).[70] During the T'ang dynasty (618-906) the same two pien tones were called chun (準 , "regulating," "equalizing") and pien. In the late sixteenth century Prince Chu Tsai-yü refers to pien-kung (B) again as ho, and pien-chih (F#) as chung (中 , "middle").[71] During the Yüan dynasty (1260-1368) the Mongols introduced an eight-tone scale: C D E F F# G A B c. Unlike the earlier scale, the Mongolian scale made no distinction between basic and auxiliary tones; all were considered equally important.[72] The endeavors during the Ming period (1368-1644) to revive national consciousness and to remove all foreign influences from music are reflected in the official Ming scale. All semitones were deleted, and, although the resulting pentatonic scale did not duplicate its predecessor, it definitely helped to restore the dignity and simplicity of Ming music. Thi new scale was: C D F G A c.

Toward the end of the Ming period and during the Ch'ing dynasty (1644-1911) a new heptatonic scale consisting of the Ming scale and two additional tones was established. This scale, similar to but not identical with the corresponding tempered major scale of the West, w approximately C D E F G A B c. Eventually the official Ch'ing scale consisted of fourteen degrees within the octave, and its notes did not coincide with the spiral of pure fifths.[73] The degrees of this impracti and purely theoretical scale were not notated with the symbols of the ancient Seven-Tone Notation, but with the symbols of the simple and flexible kung-ch'ê-p'u system,[74] which had become increasingly popular with musicians and theorists since the Yüan and Ming dynasties.

During more recent times, Western influence became so strong that both the pentatonic and the heptatonic forms of the Chinese scale moved toward equal temperament.[75]

Assuming that kung represents the Western note C, the ancient heptatonic scale was notated as follows:

宮	kung	C
商	shang	D
角	chiao	E
變徵	pien-chih	F#
徵	chih	G
羽	yü	A
變宮	pien-kung	B

Instead of the complicated pien symbol (變), abbreviations in the form of ○ or 亠 were used. Thus, pien-chih could be notated by 徵 or (徵); pien-kung by 宮 or (宮).[76]

The higher octave was indicated by adding the character 少 (shao, "little") to the notational symbol. Thus if 宮 denotes C, 宮 少 (the "little kung") would be c.

The use of the Old Five and Seven-Tone Notations diminished considerably during the late Sung (Southern Sung) and Yüan dynasties (1127-1368) because another notational system, the kung-ch'ê-p'u[77] was rapidly gaining in popularity.

In the Ming period (1368-1644), which followed the Yüan dynasty, the ancient symbols again came into use, although kung-chê-p'u continued to be the most frequently employed notation. The Ming scale, as mentioned before, differed from the ancient pentatonic form in the interpretation of the chiao (角):

Old Scale:					Ming Scale:				
C	D	E	G	A	C	D	F	G	A
宮	商	角	徵	羽	宮	商	角	徵	羽

During the Ch'ing period (1644-1911), which followed the Ming, Chinese musicians and theorists – undoubtedly influenced by Western musical practice – employed the seven-tone symbols together with some affixes to notate all twelve degrees of the chromatic scale. We remind the reader that none of these symbols represent absolute pitches but are merely "solmization characters." Assuming that kung represents the Western note C, the chromatic scale was notated as follows:

宮	kung	C
⿰氵宮	ch'ing-kung[78]	C#
商	shang	D
⿰氵商	ch'ing-shang	D#
角	chiao	E
涌	ch'ing-chiao	E# (F)
變徵	pien-chih	F# (Gb)
徵	chih	G
瀓	ch'ing-chih	G#
羽	yü	A
⿰氵羽	ch'ing-yü	A# (Bb)
變宮	pien-kung	B (Cb)

The symbols of the Old Chinese Five and Seven-Tone Notations occasionally appeared also in Japan. There they were used in some notations of the imperial court music (gagaku), in the music books of the Buddhist chant (shōmyō),[79] and in theoretical works.

While the symbols for the various scale-degrees were the same as in China, in Japan one additional symbol was employed: it denoted the raising of certain notes, particularly the notes 商 and 羽, by a semitone; this symbol, called ei, is 嬰, or in its abbreviated form, 妥.

(Ryo scale)

宮	商	角	變徵	徵	羽	變宮
Kyū	Shō	Kaku	Hen-chi[80]	Chi	U	Hen-kyu

(Ritsu scale)

宮	商	嬰商	角	徵	羽	嬰羽
Kyū	Shō	Ei-shō	Kaku	Chi	U	Ei-u

In the foregoing scale-forms[81] the symbols of hen-chi and hen-kyu should be transcribed with Ab and db, respectively, and those of ei-shō and ei-u with E# and B#, because hen indicates an alteration by a lower semitone and ei an alteration by a higher semitone. We use the enharmonic alternatives of G#, c#, and F, c, respectively, because they are more plausible in Western notation and because neither Chinese nor Japanese performing musicians make any distinction between enharmonic degrees.

The piece shown in Figure 12[82] on page 64 is a short excerpt from a Japanese saibara (催馬樂), a song accompanied by a small instrumental ensemble, usually without drums and patterned after folk music, which had become fashionable in gagaku during the Heian period (794-1185). The saibara imitated or utilized the materials of horsemen's songs, Tibetan love songs, devotional songs, and others. The melodies of saibara were written in the two official modes

Figure 12

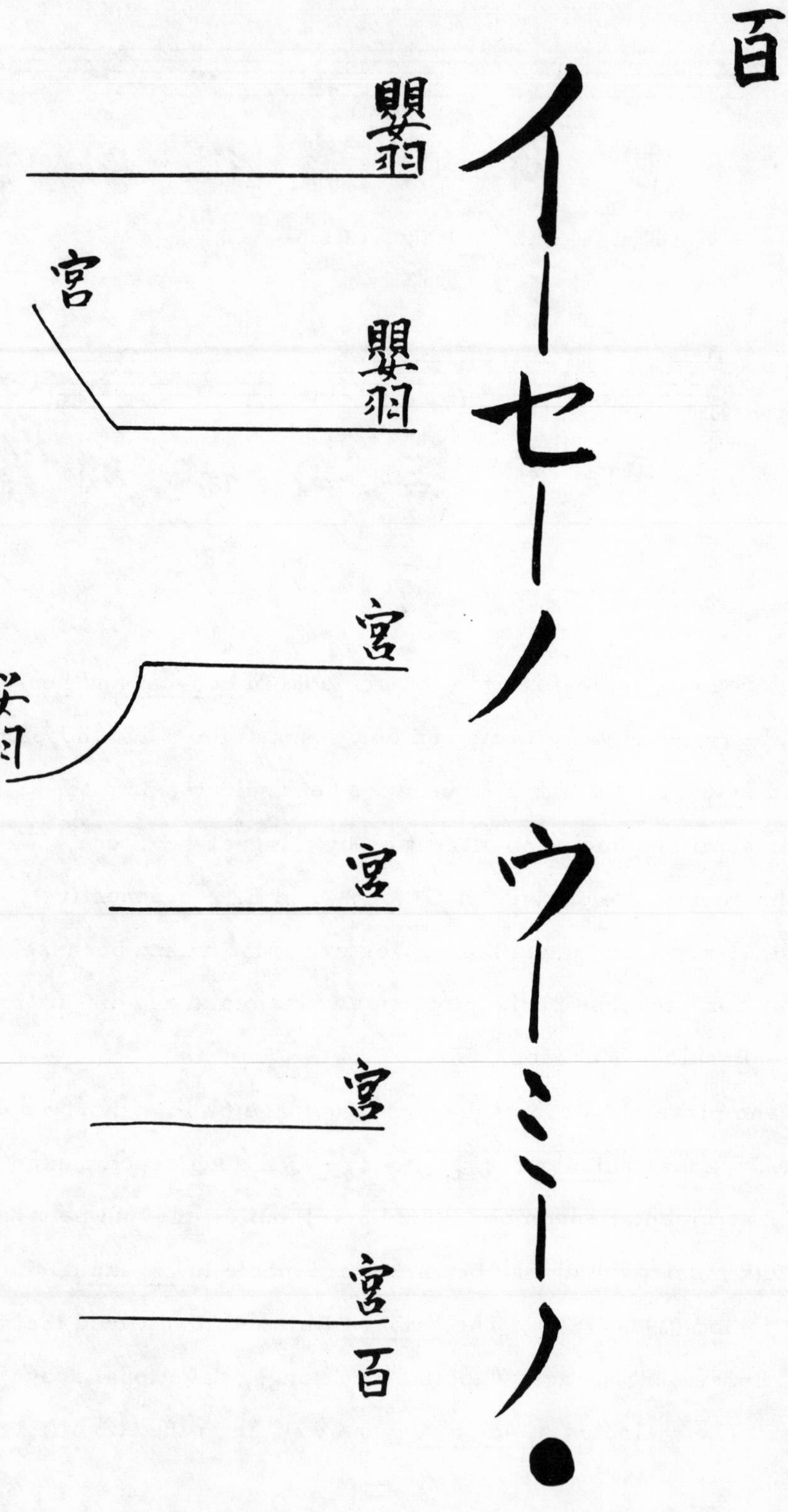

of imperial court music: ryo and ritsu.[83] The adaptation of these melodies into the prescribed musical limitations of gagaku made them acceptable to the imperial household.[84]

The horizontal lines and curves of Figure 12 are read from right to left and top to bottom. They show the movement of the melody. The second curve rises from ei-u to kyū (c to d), the third descends from ei-u to kyū (d to c); here ei-u is notated in its abbreviated form. The straight lines represent held notes: : the first ei-u, the fourth, fifth, and sixth kyū. The large letters on the right side represent the text: Ise no umi no. . . , "Ise of the sea of. . . ."[85] The symbols 百 (hyaku, lit. "hundred") indicate percussive features.[86] Transcribed into Western notation the excerpt would read:

In works dealing with music theory, scales can be described by placing the symbols of the old Five-Tone Notation in a system of twelve horizontal staves which represent the twelve semitones in the octave. In such cases it becomes unnecessary for the writer to elaborate the description of the notes by adding ei or hen, because any alterations of the basic degrees (kyū, shō, kaku, etc.) are demonstrated by their positions in the twelve staves as shown in Figure 13, page 66. In Figure 13 a rising and descending scale is notated in which shō (商) represents Eb (D#) in ascent and Db (C#) in descent. U (羽) stands here for Bb (A#) in ascent and descent.

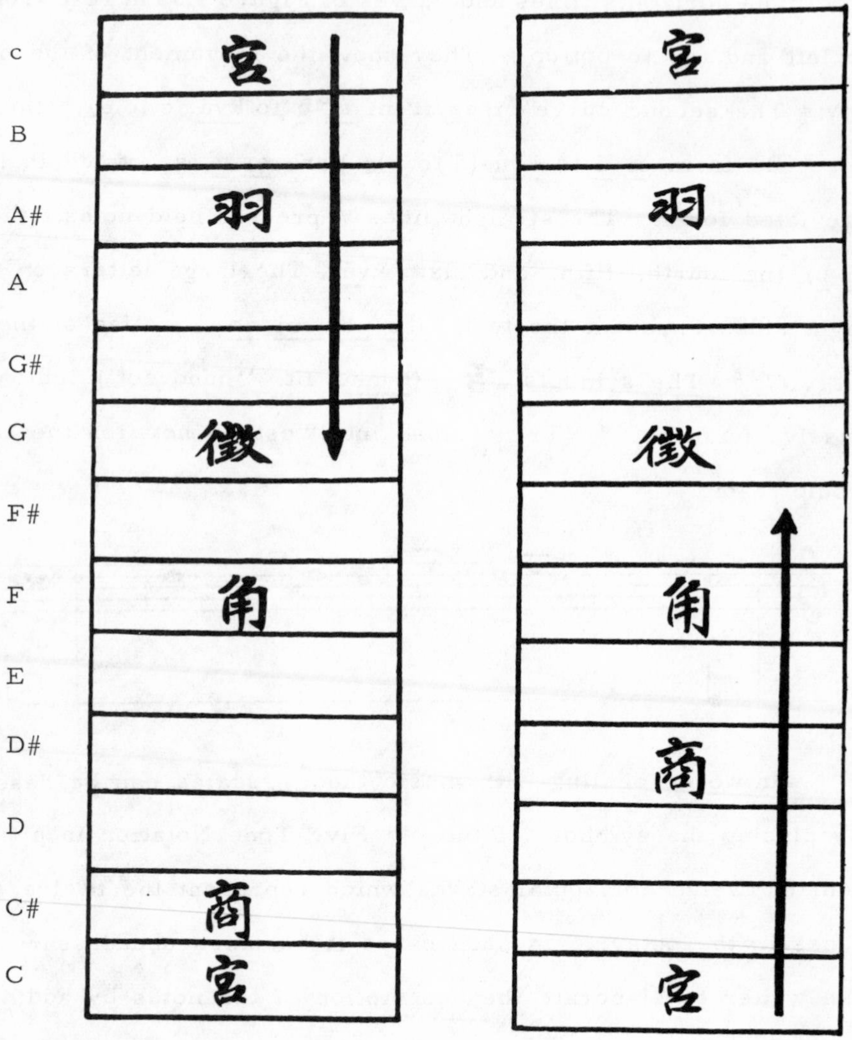

Figure 13

II

The Chinese Kung-Ch'e-P'u and Related Notations; Indian Notations and North Indian Drumming

KUNG-CH'Ê-P'U (工尺譜)[1]

The kung-ch'ê-p'u is often described as the notational system of the Yüan (元) dynasty (1260-1368), the period of Mongol rule over China. Although it is true that kung-ch'ê-p'u became widely popular during this period, it originated earlier – probably in the Sung (宋) dynasty (960-1279), or perhaps in the restless times of the Five Dynasties (五代 , 906-959), or even, as Courant assumes,[2] in the late T'ang (唐) dynasty (618-906).

The most likely period of origin was the Sung dynasty. Although as a rule less glorious than the T'ang, the Sung dynasty was a time of political relaxation which tolerated flourishing antimilitary theories and esteemed literati, philosophers, and dilettanti. It was then that books were first printed with movable type, so that for the first time a large portion of the population had access to the Confucian Classics; and it was a period when growing political stability fostered increased artistic activities. Thus, one can imagine that a simpler, more flexible system of notation might have come into use – one that was no longer the exclusive property of learned scholars but available to everyone interested in music.

Political stability was short-lived for, after the death of Genghis Khan in 1227, the savage and pitiless Mongols turned against China, and the Sung empire began to disintegrate; but the comparatively simple kung-ch'ê-p'u endured and was used by both invaders and invaded. It was adequate for notating the newly imported Mongol scale[3] as well as the established scales of the Sung and T'ang dynasties and those of earlier periods. Indeed, it became the most popular notational system and has held its ground down to the present time. Chinese operatic music was notated almost exclusively with kung-ch'ê symbols, and the operas, produced not only in large cities but taken by traveling companies to the most remote villages, helped to spread the use of this system of notation. Moreover, the provincial audiences who watched these dramas became informed about Chinese legends and heroes, history, literature, and music. One can assume that both city-dwellers and villagers who were interested in music adopted this notation because it was available and comparatively easy to learn.

The earliest source containing a description of the kung-ch'ê-p'u symbols is a work called Mêng-ch'i-pi-t'an (夢 溪 筆 談), "Brush Talks from the Dream Book," written A. D. 1093 by the North Sung author Shên Kua (沈 括).[4] The work consists of twenty-six volumes and two appendices (later a twenty-seventh volume was added) and deals with history, fine arts, tools, medicine, dialectics, divination, government, miracles, and, in the fifth and sixth volumes, music In volume six the author explains the notational symbols of the kung-ch'ê system by comparing them with the symbols of the older Chinese notations. Of particular interest is his comparison with the lü. In the page cited in Figure 14 (which bears no number in the Chinese text) Shên Kua writes that the gamut of the twelve lü (十二律) spread over sixteen semitones from C (宮) beyond its octave (清 宮) to the note e, a range which he describes as that of ancient music. According to Shên Kua, this range has changed to fifteen semitones

十二律并清宮當有十六聲今之燕樂止有十
五聲蓋今樂高於古樂二律以下故無正
黄鐘聲只以合字當大呂猶差高當在大
呂太簇之間下四字近太簇之高四字近
夾鐘下一字近姑洗高一字近中呂上字近
蕤賓勾字近林鐘尺字近夷則工字近南
呂高工字近無射六字近應鐘下凡字爲
黄鐘清高凡字爲大呂清下五字爲太簇
清高五字爲夾鐘清法雖如此然諸調殺
聲不能盡歸本律故有偏殺側殺寄殺元
殺之類雖與古法不同推之亦皆有理知
聲者皆能言之此不備載也

Figure 14

(C - d#), the range of the Yen-yüeh (燕 樂, "banquet music").[5] He also states that the absolute pitch of the huang-chung (黃 鐘) has "ceased to exist" (無正黃鐘聲), which implies that now the huang-chung represents an arbitrary pitch. In his comparison of kung-ch'ê-p'u with the ancient lü notation Shên Kua states that ho (合), the first kung-ch'ê symbol, only approximates ta-lü (大呂), that hsia-ssŭ (下四), the next kung-ch'ê symbol indicating a note a semitone higher than the former, only approximates t'ai-ts'u (太簇), and so forth. The reason why these tones are only approximate is that he does not relate them to any absolute pitches but uses the lü only to demonstrate the equidistant semitone intervals between the notes indicated by the kung-ch'ê symbols. The following list represents an extract of Shên Kua's explanation.

Kung-ch'ê-p'u:			Lü:	
合	(ho)	approximates	大	(ta)
下四	(hsia-ssŭ, "low ssŭ")	approximates	太	(t'ai)
四	(ssŭ)	approximates	夾	(chia)
下一	(hsia-yi, "low yi")	approximates	姑	(ku)
高一	(kao-yi, "high yi")	approximates	仲	(chung)
上	(shang)	approximates	蕤	(jui)
勾	(kou)	approximates	林	(ling)
尺	(ch'ê)	approximates	夷	(i)
工	(kung)	approximates	南	(nan)

Kung-ch'ê-pu:			Lü:	
高工	(kao-kung, "high kung")	approximates	無	(wu)
六	(liu) [sic]	approximates	應	(yin)
下凡	(hsia-fan, "low fan")	approximates	黄清	(huang, ch'ing)
高凡	(kao-fan, "high fan")	approximates	大清	(ta, ch'ing)
下五	(hsia-wu, "low wu")	approximates	太清	(t'ai, ch'ing)
高五	(kao-wu, "high wu")	approximates	夾清	(chia, ch'ing)

The order of Shên Kua's kung-ch'ê symbols differs from that of all subsequent kung-ch'ê systems. In Shên Kua's explanation kao-kung is followed by liu, while in all later forms kao-kung, or its equivalent, is followed by hsia-fan and kao-fan, which in turn are followed by liu, hsia-wu and kao-wu.[6]

The symbols of kung-ch'ê-p'u represent solmization syllables written in simple, sometimes abbreviated, Chinese characters. In the South it had become habitual to transcribe ho (合), the first symbol, as the western note C, while the North seemed to incline toward transcribing ho as the note D. We shall transcribe ho as C, in the same manner as we transcribe the huang-chung and the kung of the older notations.

The kung-ch'ê symbols after Shên Kua's time are devoid of all kao signs. Chromatic alterations, with the exception of kou (勾 , F#), are only indicated by the affix hsia (下乙 , "flat"); C#, D#, G#, and A# become Db, Eb, Ab, and Bb (hsia-ssŭ, hsia-yi, hsia-kung, and hsia-fan), respectively. The accepted and correct[7] sequence of the kung-ch'ê symbols (and some of their variants) used in North China, where this system was first adopted, is as follows:

Name:	Symbol:	Variants:	Western equivalent:
Ho	合		C (e. g.)
Hsia-ssŭ	下四	四	Db
Ssŭ	四	(宮四)	D
Hsia-yi	下乙	一	Eb
Yi	乙	一 (宮一)	E
Shang	上		F
Kou	勾		F#
Ch'ê	尺		G
Hsia-kung	下工	丅	Ab
Kung	工	(宮工)	A
Hsia-fan	下凡	儿	Bb
Fan	凡	凡 (宮凡)	B
Liu	六		c
Hsia-wu	下五	万	db
Wu	五		d
Hsia-yi	亻一		eb

Name	Symbol:	Variants:	Western equivalent:
Yi	亿		e
Shang	仩		f
Kou	佝		f#
Ch'ê	伬		g

The variants representing hsia-ssŭ, hsia-yi, hsia-kung, and hsia-fan are incomplete in that one horizontal stroke is omitted in each symbol.

In theory the kung-ch'ê symbols cover a gamut of three octaves;[8] in practice, however, the entire range is never used. The three octaves are called:

cho-shêng (濁聲), "muddy," lowest notes,

chung-shêng (中聲), middle notes,

ch'ing-shêng (清聲), "clear," highest notes.

The symbols denoting tones of the upper octave beyond 五 are usually notated with the affix 亻:

五 亿 仩 伬 仜

Symbols denoting tones below 合 are marked with a small comma:

合 凡 工 尺 上 乙

Occasionally we notice some inconsistency in the use of affixes indicating notes of the highest and lowest octaves. In some instances the affix 亻 denotes the lowest, and 彳 the highest notes of the gamut. Thus, while 亿 may read e (a tenth above middle C) in one manuscript, it may denote E (a sixth below middle C) in another. The latter version is easily discernible because its notes above 五 have the affix 彳.

In South China (Canton) only nine *kung*-*chê* symbols are used, eight of which are the same as those of the North. The one which differs is *shih* (士), another reading of the northern *ssŭ* (四):

Ho	合	C (e. g.)
Shih	士	D
Yi	乙	E
Shang	上	F
Ch'ê	尺	G
Kung	工	A
Fan	凡	B
Liu	六	c
Wu	五	d

The system which prevails in the South uses neither *kao* nor *hsia* signs for sharpening and flattening notes. Chromatic alterations are made by transposition. If Bb is required, 合 is considered to be F, whereupon 上, being a fourth higher than 合, can become Bb. The shifting of *ho* (合), comparable to the "movable *do*" of the West, led to the creation of a number of scales, some with a pure fourth, others with an augmented fourth, which facilitated transpositions and changes of mode. This method was employed in various ways in the diverse musical categories of China,[9] especially in the operatic styles, where stringed instruments such as the *êrh-hsien* (二 絃 , lit., "two strings")[10] or the *hu-ch'in* (胡 琴 , "foreign *ch'in*")[11] play an important role. As a detailed discussion of these systems would lead far beyond the scope of this book,[12] we shall confine ourselves to one example: the two strings of the *êrh-hsien* are tuned to 合 and 尺 (C and G, the *mu-hsien* 母 絃 , "mother string," and *tzŭ-hsien* 子 絃 ,"son string," respectively). An *êrh-hsien* player, who as a rule knows little about *kao* and *hsia* notes, is able to master the various modes required in operatic music by memorizing a few transposing scales without even altering the tuning of his two strings. If the two strings are called by different tone names, a number of scales (comparable to the western *do*-mode, *re*-mode, etc.) are created in the following manner:[13]

Lower (*mu*) string:			Upper (*tzŭ*) string:	
C (*ho*)	D E F	⟶	G (*ch'ê*)	A B c
D (*shih*)	E F G	⟶	A (*kung*)	B c d
E (*yi*)	F G A	⟶	B (*fan*)	c d e
F (*shang*)	G A B	⟶	c (*liu*)	d e f
G (*ch'ê*	A B c	⟶	d (*wu*)	e f g

and others.

The player would thus name the various scales according to the tone names given to his two strings: *ho-chê-t'iao* (合尺 調 , *ho-chê* scale), *shih-kung-t'iao* (士工調 , *shih-kung* scale), *yi-fan-t'iao* (乙凡調, *yi-fan* scale), and so forth.[14] As the tuning of the two strings remains unaltered (C and G), all scales have to begin with C:

	Mu:				Tzŭ:			
Ho-ch'ê-t'iao	C	D	E	F	G	A	B	c
Shih-kung-t'iao	C	D	Eb	F	G	Ab	Bb	c
Yi-fan-t'iao	C	Db	Eb	F	G	Ab	Bb	c
Shang-liu-t'iao	C	D	E	F#	G	A	B	c
Ch'ê-wu-t'iao	C	D	E	F	G	A	Bb	c

and others.[15]

In addition to the scales mentioned above, there are others which can be compared to the "fixed *do*" system.[16] Among them are scales used in the operatic styles of *êrh-huang* (二 黄)[17] and *pang-tzŭ* (梆 子).[18] For instance, the basic *êrh-huang* scale is

尺	工	凡	六	五	一	生	伬
G	A	Bb	c	d	e	f#[19]	g.

In this scale 凡 invariably stands a minor third above 尺 . Such practices in this and other scales may have been the reason for the eventual appearance of additional symbols in the *kung-ch'ê-p'u* of the South. We observe occasionally two symbols for *fan*, two for *shang*, and two for *yi*. While in the *kung-ch'ê-p'u* of the North similar pairs of symbols were in common use and each symbol had its specific significance, in the South (Canton) they were employed indiscriminately; each member of a pair could be used for notating either the basic tone or its alteration.

However, the fact that the notation of the South possessed two symbols for the degrees mentioned – even if the symbols were used carelessly – seems to indicate that originally each symbol may have had a specific significance. One could assume that originally 凡 may have denoted Bb; 反, another symbol for fan may have denoted B; 乙 may have stood for Eb; 一 for E; 上 for F; and 生 (shêng) for F#. The last symbol (shêng) in particular was and is often used to represent a tone a pure fourth above ho as well.

A similar method of transposition is applied in the notations of music for the hsiao [20] and the ti. [21] While in ti notation ho is transcribed with the note c, [22] in hsiao notation ho represents a tone a fourth lower: G. [23]

Ti		Hsiao	
合	c	合	G
四	d	四	A
乙	e	乙	B

Occasionally the tones of the ti and the hsiao are notated as they sound:

Ti:	六	五	乙	上	尺	工	凡	𠆾	伍	亿	仩	伬
	c	d	e	f	g	a	b	c'	d'	e'	f'	g'

Hsiao:	尺	工	凡	六	五	乙	上	伬	仜	𠆩	𠆾	伍
	G	A	B	c	d	e	f	g	a	b	c'	d'

Similarly the tones produced on the yüeh-ch'in (月琴) [24] and san-hsien (三絃) [25] are notated as follows:

Yüeh-ch'in		San-hsien		
Inner string:	Outer string:	Low string:	Middle string:	High string:
上	六	四	尺	五
尺 工 凡 六 五 乙 仩 伬 仜	伍乙 仩 伬 仜 仉 亻六 伍 亿 仩 伬 仜	乙 上 尺 工 凡 六 五 乙 仩 伬 仜 仉	工 凡 六 五 乙 仩 伬 仜 仉 亻六 伍 亿	乙 仩 伬 仜 仉 亻六 伍 亿

The foregoing ti, hsiao, yüeh-ch'in, and san-hsien scales illustrate the use of the affix 亻. If a scale begins with high notes, such as 六 and 五, the affix 亻 is frequently omitted in the notation of either the next higher note 乙 (六 五 乙 仩, etc.), or of all subsequent notes up to 亻六.

In recent times Chinese musicians, with the exception of those who use Western staff notation or the highly popular chien-p'u (簡譜), an abridged notation employing Arabic numerals,[26] have, mainly in the North (Peiping), ceased using signs for flat and sharp notes in kung-ch'ê-p'u. North China confines itself to the use of three scales, similar to the transposing scales of the South: a "major," a "minor," and the hsi-p'i (西皮)[27] scale, which is a "Dorian mode." In all these instances simple kung-ch'ê symbols are used without any kao or hsia indications.

Kung-ch'ê-p'u was used to notate both ritual and secular music; the many styles of secular music led to a number of methods of notating rhythmic features. The prevailing syllabic style of ritual music required few, if any, rhythmic signs because the monosyllabic words of Chinese sacred texts were set mainly to chains of long notes of equal length. These uniform beats were organized into groups (measures) of four or eight, and the end of each group was often indicated by the sound of a percussion instrument. Accompanying instruments could be used to sub-divide each beat into halves or quarters,[28] but the meter, the strict succession of four or eight uniform beats, remained unchanged.

The following represents the Hymn in Honor of Confucius performed

according to a decree issued in the eighth year of Ch'ien Lung (A. D. 1743). The same words and the same music are always used, the only difference being the change of lü or key-note. The hymn is always sung in the lü corresponding to the moon during which the ceremony takes place; for instance, during the second moon chia-chung is assumed as lü, and during the eighth moon the keynote is nan-lü. The hymn is divided into six stanzas:

1. Ying shên, receiving the approaching spirit.
2. Ch'u hsien, first presentation of offerings.
3. Ya hsien, second presentation.
4. Chung hsien, third and last presentation.
5. Ch'ê chuan, removal of the viands.
6. Sung shên, escorting the spirit back.[29]

The notational symbols are placed to the left of the textual characters of the six strophes of the hymn shown on pages 82 and 83. Each strophe is read from top to bottom and from right to left.

Figure 15

工大 合哉 四孔 乙子
工先 尺覺 乙先 四知
合與 四天 尺地 乙參
工萬 尺世 乙之 乙師
乙祥 尺徵 合麟 四紱
合韻 尺答 四金 尺絲
合日 四月 工既 乙揭
合乾 四坤 合清 工怡

工予 合懷 四明 乙德
尺玉 合振 工金 尺聲
四生 合民 尺未 乙有
合展 四也 乙大 四成
乙俎 合豆 工千 乙古
四春 四秋 尺上 四丁
工清 尺酒 合既 工載
合其 四香 合始 工升

工式 合禮 四莫 乙愆
尺升 乙堂 合再 乙獻
尺響 乙協 合鼗 四鏞
乙誠 尺孚 乙罍 工獻
乙肅 乙肅 四雍 四雍
合譽 工髦 尺斯 工彥
尺禮 乙陶 合樂 四淑
乙相 四觀 合而 工善

Figure 15 (cont.)

終獻

工自 合古 四在 乙昔
尺先 乙民 合有 四作
乙皮 乙弁 合祭 工菜
尺於 乙論 四思 合樂
乙惟 尺天 工膺 乙民
合惟 尺聖 合時 四若
乙彝 乙倫 尺攸 工敘
尺至 乙今 合木 工鐸

徹饌

工先 合師 四有 乙言
仜祭 尺則 仜受 乙福
合四 仜海 乙黌 尺宮
合疇 四敢 合不 仜肅
乙禮 尺成 仜告 乙徹
乙毋 四疏 合毋 仜瀆
乙樂 尺所 合自 仜生
乙中 四原 合有 工菽

送神

工鳧 合繹 四峨 乙峨
尺洙 仜泗 合洋 四洋
尺景 乙行 乙行 尺止
合流 四澤 乙無 四彊
乙聿 尺昭 合祀 仜事
仜祀 尺事 合孔 四明
仜化 乙我 仜烝 尺民
合育 四我 合膠 工庠

We have already observed that occasionally writers take libertie with the use of the affix 亻. In the fifth and sixth strophes of Figure 15 we notice 仜 appearing several times in conjunction with notes of the middle octave. Let us consider the last sixteen notes of the sixth stanza:

乙 尺 合 仜 仜 尺 合 四 仜 乙 仜 尺 合 四 合 工

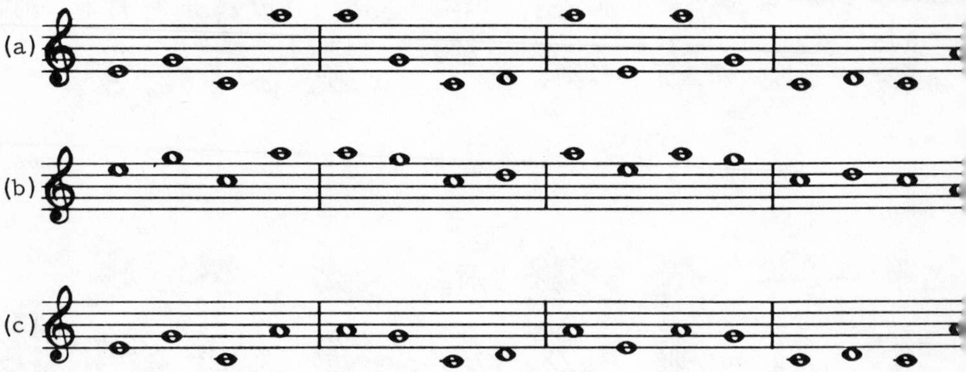

Of the three transcriptions shown above, (a) represents a literal reading with unusually large intervals, (b) shows transpositions of notes belonging to the middle octave into the high range of 仜 (for the purpose of avoiding these improbable intervals), and (c) shows a reading in which the affix 亻 is ignored, suggesting that the write: may have employed it for other than musical purposes. The third version seems to be more acceptable than the other two because 仜 is not used throughout the hymn; in the first four stanzas the writer uses 工 exclusively; only in the last two stanzas does he use the affix, and even then not constantly.

Another interpretation of 仜, less plausible than the previous one, could be that occasionally the sign 亻 was used for denoting the high-alteration of a note by a semitone.[30] In such instances 仜 could be transcribed as A#. This reading is highly improbable here because the melody has a purely anhemitonic pentatonic character in its first four stanzas, and the sporadic use of 仜 in the last two stanzas cannot possibly mean a sudden change from A to A#, which would thus destroy the pentatonic character, particularly in ritual music.

Figure 16 (pp. 86-87) is the score of the Confucian heptatonic hymn Ssŭ-wên (思 文), "Contemplation of refined writing":[31]

The score has to be read horizontally from right to left across pages 86 and 87. The characters at the top of both pages read:

Chin	tzŭ	ching	êrh - shih - ssŭ	pai
(Golden	words	classic (books)	twenty-four	strikes
ku	pan	chieh	tsou	p'u
drum	wooden block		rhythm	score).

Below the heading we find three annotations in oval frames on page 86 and three others on page 87. Further down on both pages we find another three horizontal rows of such annotations. These inform us about "measure one," "measure two," and so forth, up to "measure twenty-four" (). Each annotation, placed at the first beat of each measure, is marked with a black dot representing a percussive beat. In all there are twenty-four strokes (measures), a fact which is also indicated in the heading. Below these annotations we observe the melody notated in kung-ch'ê symbols, each of which is placed in a small circle.

The meter of the hymn is clearly indicated by the fact that there

Figure 16

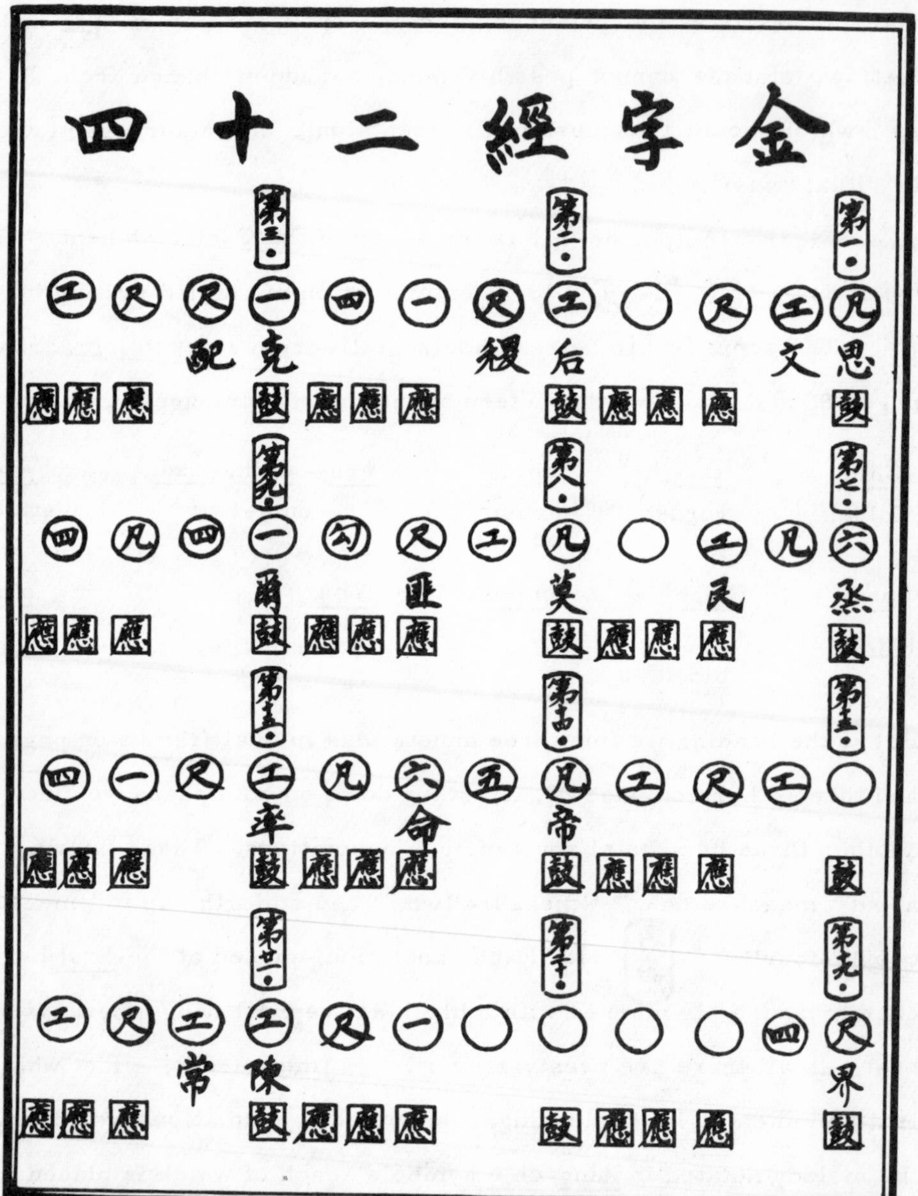

Figure 16 (cont.)

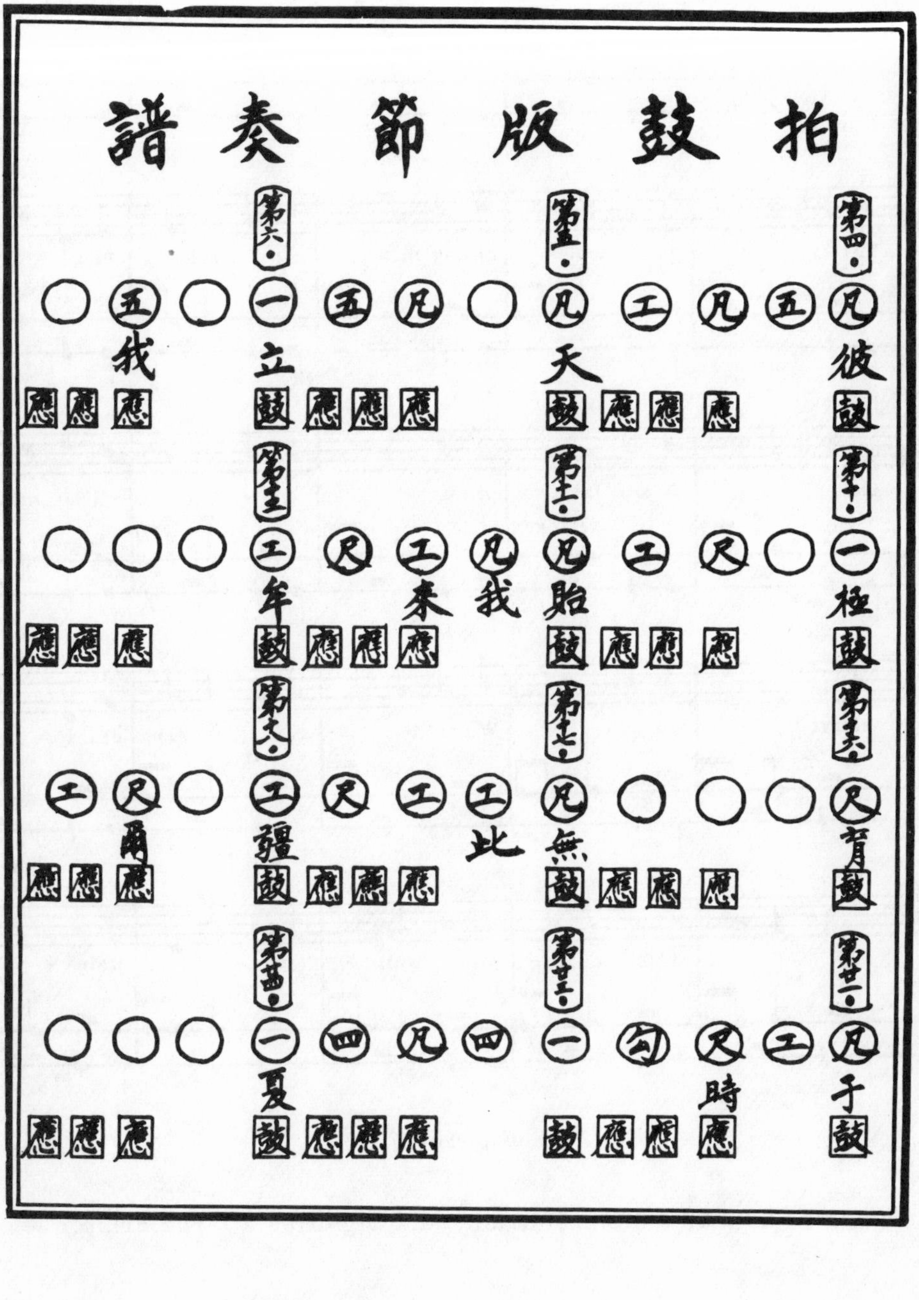

Figure 17

1. Signifies a small drum; 2. Signifies a large drum.

are four circles in each measure. Whenever a rest (or held note) occurs, an empty circle is used. The text[32] appears below the circles in small characters. In this hymn the rigid syllabic style of ritual music is not strictly observed because some of the words are held over more than one note (and beat). Below the text we find characters placed in square frames which denote the percussion part; these characters are:

鼓 Ku, the general term for drum,

應 Ying (ying-ku), "corresponding drum."[33]

A transcription of the hymn is shown on page 88.

In various instrumental parts of ritual, and in many notations of secular music where there are neither textual characters nor such clearly organized scores as that of the hymn Ssŭ-wên to guide the reader, several methods of notating rhythmical features are employed.

The simplest was to write notes of long duration in large characters and notes of shorter duration in small ones. Writing music by means of large and small notational symbols occurred only sporadically and did not become a popular method because it was indistinct and showed no marked endeavor to notate rhythm clearly. Another device used to indicate notes of long duration was to leave one or more spaces open immediately after (below) the note to be prolonged. An example of an instrumental part of the Tao-yin (導引), "The Imperial Guiding March,"[34] on page 90 will illustrate this. The march is to be performed by two mouth organs (shêng, 笙),[35] two ti,[36] two hsiao,[37] two gong chimes (yün-lo, 雲鑼),[38] two drums, and wooden clappers.[39]

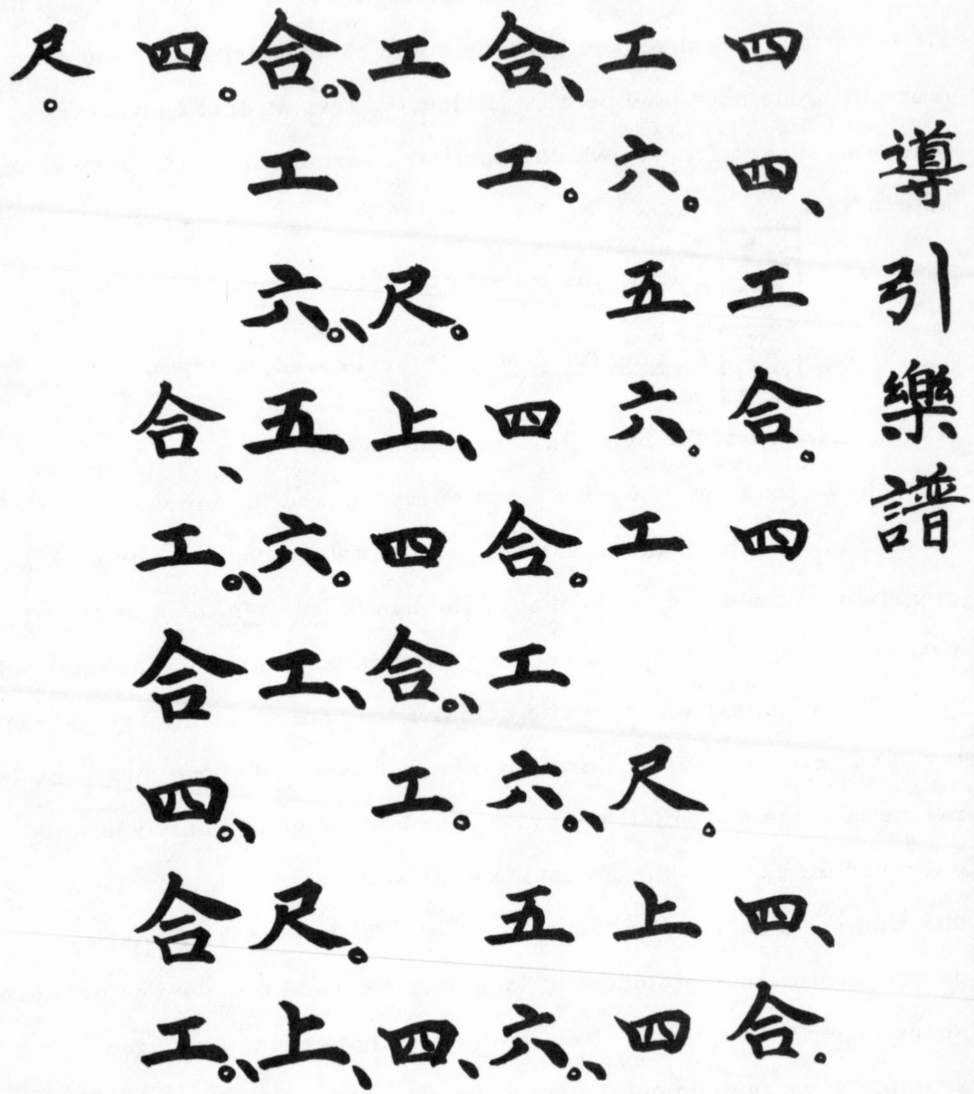
導引樂譜
尺 四 合 工 合 工 四
工 工 六 四
六 尺 五 工
合 五 上 四 六 合
工 六 四 合 工 四
合 工 合 工
四 工 六 尺
合 尺 五 上 四
工 上 四 六 四 合

Figure 18

As already stated, the gaps after (below) the symbols indicate prolongations of the preceding notes. Each gap corresponding to the size of one notational symbol represents one beat — in the transcriptions shown below, a quarter note. Thus, if a wide gap the size of two or more notational symbols appears, it signifies a correspondingly longer duration of the preceding note.

Occasionally, however, the gaps are not clearly spaced — they may be too large or too small and thus cause some ambiguity in transcription.

The first column of Figure 18 shows a gap large enough to contain two notational symbols. We therefore assume that the note preceding the gap has to be held for three beats, one beat being represented by the notational symbol (ssŭ) itself, the other two by the gap. A similar gap appears in the sixth column. The other gaps, being smaller, denote the prolongation of the preceding notes by one beat only.

The drumbeats are notated by small circles and the beats to be performed by the wooden clapper by commas. In ritual and ceremonial music it was customary to place a drumbeat at the end of a measure, a habit not strictly observed, as can be seen in the notation of the "Imperial Guiding March." If we adjust our transcription to the exact sizes of the gaps, we get:

This version, if continued, may cause some doubts as to whether a "literal" transcription is the proper solution and whether the gaps are correctly spaced. If, according to custom, we expect the drumbeat to appear at the end of every four-beat measure, we find that the large gap of the first column has to be reduced to a one-beat duration. In this case the note ssŭ will be held only for two beats:

Continuing the transcription, it becomes obvious that in this particular piece a drumbeat cannot be placed at the end of every measure.

From the preceding discussion we conclude that this method of notating rhythmic features may have served mainly as a mnemonic aid to the performer who already knew the rhythmic shape of the melody and did not require detailed rhythmic information. However, for persons not acquainted with the rhythm of this melody, it can be expected that different transcribers will achieve different results. To show the ambiguity of interpreting the gaps we give two transcriptions (p. 93) of the Tao-yin, one written by Kurt Reinhard,[40] the other by J. A. van Aalst.[41] A comparison of these two transcriptions shows not only rhythmic differences but a number of octave transpositions as well. As stated before in the discussion of flute notations,[42] symbols denoting sounds of the middle octave occasionally were used for sounds of the upper octave, and, in some cases, vice versa.[43] Van Aalst's transcription places the majority of low notes in the higher octave in

(Reinhard)

(Van Aalst)

Figure 19

A. Signifies clapper; B. Signifies drum.

order to achieve a less angular form of the melody than the one by Reinhard, which adheres to the notated symbols.

Another method of notating rhythmic features is shown in Figure 20, a song called "The Fresh Beautiful Flower" (鮮 花).[44]

Figure 20

In this method, which is similar to the one just described, the prolongations of notes are indicated by dots placed at the right side of the notational symbols, with each dot prolonging the note by one beat. In addition to the dots, small circles are used (with a few exceptions) to denote the final beats of eight-beat measures. These circles may occur as well on the fifth, sixth, or seventh beats, in which case they indicate a prolongation of the respective note to the end of the measure. Although this method has an advantage over the one that uses gaps, errors can still occur. Thus, an ambiguity can be observed if we consider the last symbol of the fifth and the first four symbols of the sixth columns. The passage allows two different transcriptions which can be seen in the first half of the last line of Figure 21. Conceivably copyists commit errors and, just as in the case of the widening and narrowing of gaps, add or omit dots. The upper stave of the first half of the last system of Figure 21 shows the literal, the lower one a probable and, perhaps, more plausible interpretation of the doubtful passage; that is to say, we assume that the notes concerned may have been 士. 上. 尺. 工 士 。 and not, as written, 士.. 上.. 尺. 工 士。. Following is the transcription of "The Fresh Beautiful Flower":

"The Fresh Beautiful Flower," (cont.)

Figure 21

Still another method[45] of notating rhythmical features which aims at greater accuracy uses a considerable number of metrical signs plac as usual, to the right side of the notational symbols. There are two se of signs: those which indicate notes which occur on any of the four beat of a measure, and those which denote syncopated or held notes.

The first group consists of the following signs:

First beat ▼
Second beat •
Third beat ○
Fourth beat •

In practice the signs are used in the following manner:

合 ▼
四 •
一 ○
尺 •
工 ▼
六 •
工 ○
尺 •

Occasionally the black triangle which represents the first beat can be replaced with ∖ or ✕. Especially in pieces in 2/4 meter[46] the main beat (opening beat) is usually denoted by the sign ∖ , called chêng-pan, (正板), "main beat," or t'ou-pan (頭板), "head beat," or hung-pan (紅板), "red beat."

In pieces with four-beat measures the first beat can also be notated with ✕ , called tsêng-pan (贈板), "conferring, bestowing beat," or hêh-pan (黑板), "black beat."

The sign o , called chêng-yen (正眼), "main eye," indicates the third beat of a measure. The second and fourth beats of this group, if notated, are each marked by a single dot. If two or more notes are to be performed within any of the four beats, they are notated as follows:

A second set of metrical signs is used if notes are held from one into the next beat or beats. Each of the following signs represents not the starting point of a note (), but that part of a note which is held over into the next beat ():

First beat L or 乂 or 一
Second beat L
Third beat △
Fourth beat L

The sign L is called t'ou-chih-pan (頭制板), "head restrained beat," and 乂 , hêh-chih-pan (黑制板), "black restrained beat." These two signs denote the metrical main beat applied to notes which are held over from the preceding beat; and, as stated before, they never occur when a note begins with the main beat. The sign L , ch'ê-yen (折眼), "cut-off eye," denotes the second or fourth beats, notes which are held over from the preceding beats. These signs are used in the following manner:

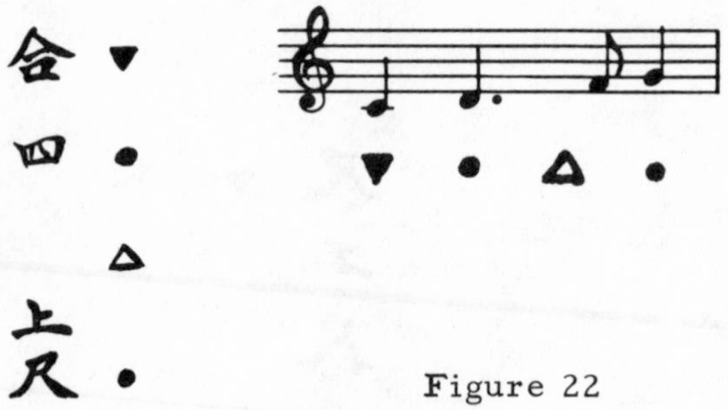

Figure 22

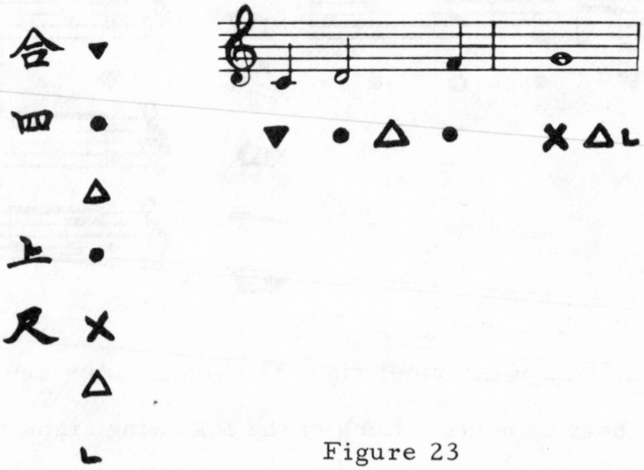

Figure 23

In the foregoing example (Fig. 23) we note that the sequence × △ ∟ stands for 1 (2) 3 4. It is unnecessary to insert a sign for the second beat because × △ ∟ suffice to indicate that the note is to be held from the first to the third and beyond it, to the subsequent fourth beat.

The metrical sign notated with 一, which must not be confused with the abbreviated <u>yi</u> symbol (一) of <u>kung-ch'ê-p'u</u> is used in the following manner:

or:

If notational symbols are placed in the column of metrical signs, they represent grace notes (short appoggiaturas) which approach the succeeding note from below:

Grace notes which are higher than their succeeding notes — that is, ornamental notes which approach the main notes from above — are not indicated by specific notational symbols but by the general sign ◡ . This sign usually denotes a grace note which is one tone higher than the preceding note and, of course, higher than the succeeding note:

An exception is made if the grace note occurs, for example, between two main notes the second of which is a tone higher than the first. In such instances the grace note has to be two tones higher than the preceding main note:

Repeated notes are indicated by dots placed below the notational symbols:

We notice that the down beat of a measure in a succession of repeated notes is notated not only with the customary dot but also by the metrical sign IX , an abbreviated <u>hêh</u>-<u>chih</u>-<u>pan</u> ([illegible]). Trills and glissandi are shown by an oblique line in the notational column:

The end of a phrase is indicated by a 乚 framing the last notational symbol in the following manner:

All Chinese dramas use music, most of which is written and arranged by professional musicians of a much lower social level than the distinguished literati. Many operas use the same standard melodies, "song labels" (ch'ü-p'ai, 曲牌), "leitmotifs" (ya-ti, 雅笛), and "leit-rhythms" which are the common property of the Chinese operatic repertoire.[47] They refer to certain situations, and when performed are immediately recognized by Chinese audiences.

Before considering Chinese operatic melodies, it is important to discuss briefly some of these features, particularly the rhythms characteristic of certain operatic styles. A typical êrh-huang[48] rhythm is:

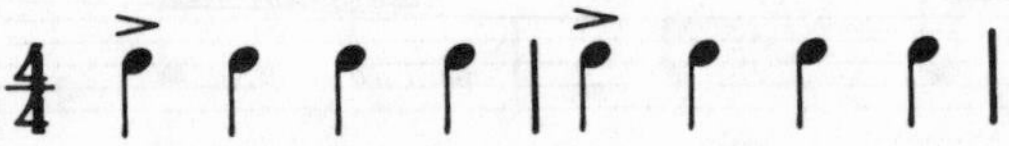 etc.,

called i-pan san-yen (一板三眼), one accented, three light beats ("eyes"); another êrh-huang rhythm is:

 etc.,

called i-pan i-yen (一板一眼), one accented, one light beat. In hsi-p'i (西皮)[49] style the characteristic rhythms are also i-pan san-yen and i-pan i-yen, but both have to begin with up-beats:

 etc.,

and

 etc.

Occasionally these and other rhythms are mentioned in operatic manuscripts; hence it may be of some interest to list here the important ones: Chêng-pan (正板), "principal beat," refers to a succession of main beats:

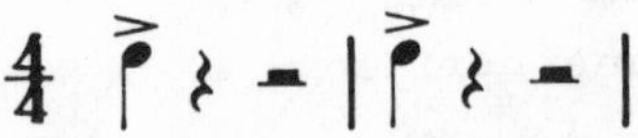

or

San-pan (散板), "scattered beat," or Yao-pan (搖板), "rocking beat," refer to free rhythms; K'uai-pan (快板), "fast beat," consists of a series of quick, accented (drum) beats without any yen; Man-pan (慢板), "slow beat," is, as the term implies, a succession of slow beats, usually performed in a free manner; Yüan-pan (原板), "original beat," consists of the sequence i-pan i-yen and refers to a return to the original rhythm after an arioso, recitative, or spoken dialogue.

The next two terms, although they use the word pan, have no relation to rhythmical features. They are: Fan-pan (反板), "turned back pan," which refers to the reversed tuning of the strings of the hu-ch'in in hsi-p'i operas; and Tao-pan (倒板), "falling back pan," which denotes a brief introductory melody sung by the actor behind the curtain before his appearance on the stage.

In order to round out the list, it is necessary to mention the tzŭ-pai (自白), "self-introduction," performed by the actor, either in the form of a recitative or as a spoken monologue.

We now turn to an operatic example which shows to what extent the foregoing symbols, signs, and annotations are used. Figure 24 represents a brief excerpt from Lao-yüan (老圓), "The Old Buddhist Priest," a drama by Yü Yüeh (俞樾), who lived during the late Ch'ing (清) period. Yü Yüeh, a former admiral, who in later years turned to the study of ancient Chinese literature, wrote approximately 500 volumes dealing with various literary subjects.[50] As the author of this drama, which deals with the story of an old Buddhist priest, a general, and a prostitute, Yü-Yüeh probably had little to do with the music, for as stated before, operatic music was provided by professional musicians who drew their material from the common pool of motives, melodies, and rhythms and adjusted it to the text.

Following (Fig. 24, p. 105) is the excerpt from the drama *Lao-yüan*. This figure shows two broad vertical columns both containing at their left sides the text[51] and, to the right of each textual character, *kung-ch'ê* symbols written in slanting rows. The reading of the two broad columns is from top right to bottom right, then from top left to bottom left. The slanting rows of *kung-ch'ê* symbols, each headed by a textual character, are to be read from *left to right* because it was impossible for the copyist to place them vertically. The fact that each slanting row of the left column appears to be joined to one in the broad column at the right is of no consequence.

Some of the notational symbols are variants created by the copyist: the symbol *ho* (合) becomes 仝 , and *ssŭ* (四) becomes の . This alternative writing of *ssŭ* is derived from the common (commercial) writing (碼 字 , *ma-tzŭ*) of the number 四 (four): 乂 .[52] If written carelessly 乂 becomes の. It is of interest to note that the same 乂 was also an ancient form of the number 五 (five).[53] In *su-tzŭ-p'u*, symbols such as の and め can represent both 四 (D) and 五 (d), the higher octave and their alterations. We also find that the main beats are not only indicated by 乂 and 以 , but also by 丶 , the sign of the main beat in 2/4 meter.

Following (Fig. 25, p. 106) is a transcription of the *Lao-yüan* excerpt. It does not claim to be the only possible one because, as we have noticed before, there are still certain ambiguities in the notation, and furthermore, we must take into account traditional motives and rhythms which, although not indicated in the manuscript, were known to performers and listeners of the late Ch'ing dynasty.

Figure 24

Figure 25

P'ING-TSÊ (平仄)

The notations of art songs frequently contain the p'ing-tsê ("level-oblique"), symbols which we must examine before discussing the song notations themselves. A most remarkable feature of the Chinese language is the use of level (even), falling, and rising tones in the pronunciation of its monosyllabic words. The basic Chinese vocabulary consists of only about 400 separate syllables, but each syllable may have numerous meanings; some, more than 150. For instance, the word fu when uttered with a high even tone means "a sage"

(夫), with a lower even tone, "a raft" (桴), a rising tone alters its meaning to "dried meat" (脯), and a falling tone changes it to "pot" (釜), and so forth. In writing, however, every meaning of a word is expressed by a different character.

In dictionaries these tones are indicated by the numbers 1-4. According to the introduction of Mathews' Chinese English Dictionary,[54] they are listed in the following manner:

1 (陰平(聲)) yin-p'ing Upper Even (Tone) – High level

2 (陽平(聲)) yang-p'ing Lower Even (Tone) – High rising

3 (上(聲)) shang Rising (Tone) – Low rising

4 (去(聲)) ch'ü Falling or Going (Tone) – High falling

An excellent description of these tones is offered by Professor Teng Ssu-yü:[55]

First tone –	Slight surprise –	oh?
Second tone –	question –	oh?
Third tone –	doubt –	o-oh?
Fourth tone –	emphasis –	oh!

If we notate the four tones above and below one stave, we get:

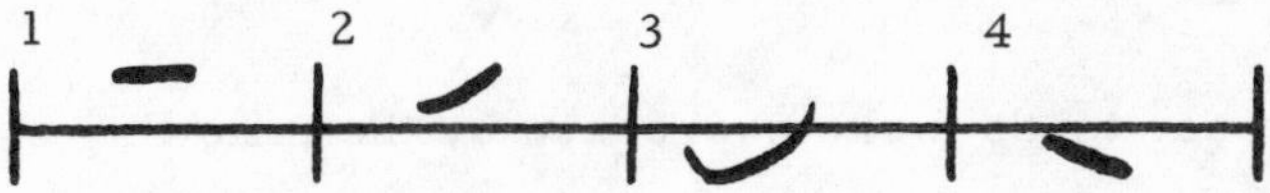

In their relationship to music the four tones[56] are generally called:

Upper even (shang p'ing, 上平)

Lower even (hsia p'ing, 下平)

Rising (shang, 上)

Falling (ch'ü, 去)

During the T'ang and Sung periods (618-1279) the linguistic tones of poetic song texts were correlated with the tonal movements of the vocal lines and thus had considerable influence upon the shape of the melody.

These tones, called sheng (聲), probably reach back into the early history of the Chinese language. There is vague reference to them in the Yüeh-chi, the music chapter of the Li Chi, the "Book of Rites."[57] In the fifth century A.D., Shên Yüeh [Shên Yo] (沈約 441-513, classified these tones,[58] and roughly a hundred years later, T'ang poets began creating poetry (lü-shih, 律詩, "regulated poetry") by making conscious use of them. A new style of poetry called hsin-t'i (新體) was devised in which preset tonal patterns provided strict rules for the writing of poems.

A Chinese poem is at best a hard nut to crack, expressed as it usually is in lines of five or seven monosyllabic root-ideas, without inflection, agglutination, or grammatical indication of any kind, the connection between which has to be inferred by the reader from the logic, from the context, and least perhaps of all from the syntactical arrangement of the words. Then, again, the poet is hampered not only by rhyme but also by tone.... the natural order of words is often entirely sacrificed to the exigencies of tone, thus making it more difficult than ever for the reader to grasp the sense....[59]

In writing, these tones were expressed by the following symbols:

1. 平 p'ing, "even tone" — 陰平 yin p'ing (high level)
2. 平 p'ing, "even tone" — 陽平 yang p'ing (high rising)
3. 上 shang, "rising tone," (low rising)
4. 去 ch'u, "falling tone," (high falling)

A fifth symbol, often employed in the writing of the dialects of the South, does not denote a type of inflection but represents the shortening of a syllable:

入 ju.

This latter symbol, frequently described as "entering tone," has been abolished in the Mandarin dialect (national language) and combined with the other tones.

A comparison of the shêng with the medieval neumes of the West shows that p'ing corresponds to the punctum and virga, shang to the podatus or pes, and ch'ü to the clivis. The neumes, like the shêng,

indicated not so much accentuation in the modern sense of the word, but rather an inflection of the voice, the acutus (a), a raising, the gravis (b), a lowering of the pitch. The former became the virga (which, as a rule, is used for a higher note), the latter, the punctum (which usually indicates a lower tone).[60]

Linguistic tones were related to the yang and yin principle in the same manner as musical tones. High tones (high and low could be applied to even, rising, and falling inflections) would be ascribed to the yin and low tones to the yang principle. Another classification placed both high and low even tones into the yin, and all oblique forms, rising, falling, and "entering," into the opposite, yang. This remarkable technique of creating poems (and, subsequently song melodies) to preset tonal patterns reached its greatest refinement during the Sung period (960-1279). We refer particularly to the tz'ŭ (詞), an important form of poetry of the late T'ang and Sung dynasties in which this art can be studied.[61] Numerous Chinese authors discuss the relationship between the shêng and the tonal movement of melodies.

In the history of the Southern Sung period (A. D. 420-478)[62] there is a biography of a certain Lu Chüeh (陸厥) (A. D. 472-499), author of a History of the Four Neumes. The following passages from this biography, quoted by Ku Yen-wu (顧炎武) are significant: "At the end of Yün Ming (A.D. 483-493) various scholars, including Shên Yüeh, wrote poems and compositions using kung shang [the tones of the scale – J.H.L.] with p'ing, shang, ch'ü and ju... using these as the basis for arranging the rhymes and rules according to the eight rules of Shên Yüeh." ... and Chiang K'uei (姜夔) in the music section of the official history of the Sung dynasty (宋史樂志) only repeats...: "It is inherent in their very nature, that the seven musical tones [of the scale – J.H.L.] should be matched in harmony with the four linguistic neumes" (七音之協四聲各有自然之理).[63]

After the Sung dynasty this art of writing poetry and music to pre-set tonal patterns[64] became neglected, and it happened not infrequently that a linguistic even tone would be linked to an oblique musical tonal movement, or vice versa.

We now turn to the consideration of the kung-ch'ê notation of an untitled song (p. 111).[65] The large characters in the middle of each of the four columns are the text. To their right we notice the kung-ch'ê symbols and to their left the p'ing-tsê annotations. Although the notation shows no rhythmic signs, the placing of one or more notational symbols against each textual character shows how many notes are to be performed with each word (and beat).

The basic movement form, which includes the distribution of themes and metres, is by an unknown composer, but preceded the writing of the words of the poem.

The words were by Ts'ao Kuan (曹冠) during the Sung dynasty.

The tonal superstructure [the melody] was composed in 1848 by Hsieh Yüan-huai (謝元淮) in the Ch'ing dynasty, and follows the musical character of the words of Ts'ao Kuan and the preconceived movement,

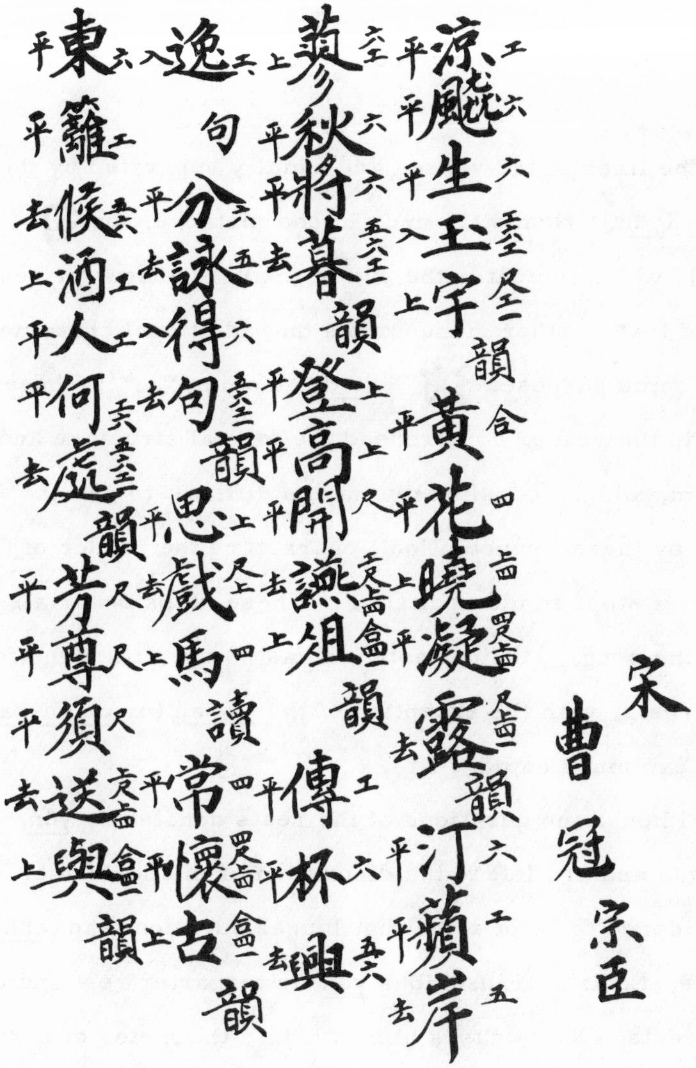
宋
曹冠 宗臣
涼颷生玉宇韻黃花曉凝露韻汀蘋岸
蓼秋將暮韻登高開讌俎韻傳杯興
逸句分詠得句韻思戲馬讀常懷古韻
東籬候酒人何處韻芳尊須送與韻

Figure 26

thematic and metric form of the unknown original composer. This music-poem is taken from the *Sui Chin Tz'u P'u* (碎金詞譜), Vol. 5, p. 2.[66]

At the outer right of Figure 26 we read the name of the Sung poet Ts'a-Kuan.

The lines of the verses are usually separated by the character 韻 (*yün*, "rhyme"), and, in one instance, by 句 (*chü*, "sentence"), which indicates the end of textual phrases or sentences. We may add that in other manuscripts one additional character can be use for the same purpose, 讀 (*tou*, "comma").[67] These three charac-ters help the reader comprehend the formal structure and meaning of the poem, which occasionally may be difficult to grasp. At spots indicated by these "punctuation" characters the reader of the poem allows brief stops in his recitation. These stops occur also in the vocal line of the song. Musical notation has no specific signs for the indication of rests, with the exception of the *ti-pan* (or *chieh-pan*), which will be explained on page 114.

Although the durations of the rests denoted by *yün*, *chü*, and *tou* are vague and are left to the discretion of the performer, *yün* usually is considered to be of somewhat longer duration than *chü* and *tou*. Fo instance, Levis[68] transcribes *yün* as a quarter rest and *chü* and *tou* a eighth rests. This causes him to notate the meter of certain phrases as $\frac{4\,^1/_2}{4}$, $\frac{7\,^1/_2}{4}$, etc.:

(9th measure of Figure 26, page 111)

(11th and 12th measures of Figure 26, page 111)

The indefinite durations of the rests allow us to simplify the matter by interpreting the various rests so that they always complete a measure:

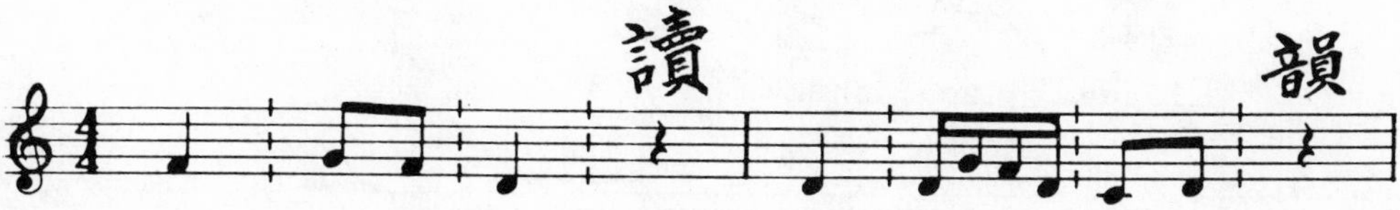

Each textual character will be transcribed with one beat of the duration of a quarter note. For instance, if three notational symbols are placed against one textual character, they will be transcribed as triplets. The three notes could also be considered as one eighth and two sixteenths, or two sixteenths and one eighth; such rhythmic subtleties are not notated in <u>kung-ch'ê-p'u</u> and are left to the discretion of the performer.

The <u>kung-ch'ê</u> symbols next to the fifth textual character of the first column (right-hand side) are:  The third symbol, a short horizontal line, can easily be confused with the abbreviated <u>yi</u> symbol (一). The reasons why it cannot be <u>yi</u> are: (1) the melody is purely anhemitonic pentatonic; and (2) immediately below this short line appears <u>yün</u> (韻), the indication of a rest. This short horizontal line in the notational column indicates the end of a phrase, a short rest. It is called *ti-pan* (底板), "end beat" or *chie* *pan* (截板), "cut-off beat." Other *ti-pan* can be noticed next to the tenth, seventeenth, twenty-second, thirtieth, thirty-sixth, forty-third, and forty-eighth characters of Figure 26.

The following transcription of Figure 26 is provided with (a) the original text written in Chinese characters, (b) transliteration and translation (literal),[69] (c) a general translation, and (d) the original *shêng* (and the modern tones of each word), in order to enable the reac er to compare linguistic with musical tonal movements.

Figure 27

韻

涼 颷 生 玉 宇

Liang piao sheng yü yü

Cool wind arises jade vault

Cool wind blows in the firmament

平 平 平 入 上

2 1 1 4 3

韻

黄 花 曉 凝 露

Huang hua hsiao ning lu

Yellow flowers morning congealed dew

In the morning the yellow chrysanthemum is heavy with dew

平 平 上 平 去

2 1 3 2. 4 4

Figure 27 (cont.)

韻

汀 蘋 岸 蓼 秋 將 暮

Ting p'ing an liao ch'iu chiang mu

Beach duck-weeds bank smart-weeds autumn toward late

Duckweeds and smartweeds on the beaches and banks herald the approach of late autumn

平 平 去 上 平 平 去

1 2 4 3 1 1 4

韻

登 高 開 讌 俎

Teng kao k'ai yen tsu

Ascending heights open feast dishes

Ascending the heights we give a banquet

平 平 平 去 上

1 1 1 4 3

句

傳 杯 興 逸

Ch'uan pei hsing i

Pass cups spirit wanders

A round of drinks — and our spirits wander joyfully

平 平 去 入

2 1 1 4.5

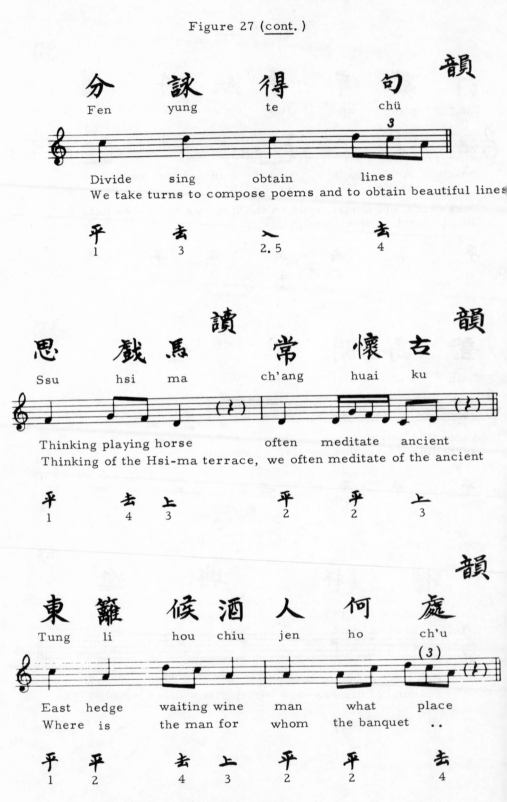

Figure 27 (cont.)

韻

分 詠 得 句

Fen yung te chü

Divide sing obtain lines

We take turns to compose poems and to obtain beautiful lines

平 去 ㇏ 去

1 3 2.5 4

讀 韻

思 戲 馬 常 懷 古

Ssu hsi ma ch'ang huai ku

Thinking playing horse often meditate ancient

Thinking of the Hsi-ma terrace, we often meditate of the ancient

平 去 上 平 平 上

1 4 3 2 2 3

韻

東 籬 候 酒 人 何 處

Tung li hou chiu jen ho ch'u

East hedge waiting wine man what place

Where is the man for whom the banquet ..

平 平 去 上 平 平 去

1 2 4 3 2 2 4

Figure 27 (cont.)

韻

芳 尊 須 送 與

Fang tsun hsü sung yü

Fragrant goblet await give with
is served at the East hedge

平 平 平 去 上
1 1 1 4 3

If we compare the shêng with the tonal movement of the melody (Figure 27), we find that in several instances the melody does not follow the prescribed rise and fall of linguistic tones. Next to the eighth character of the first column in Figure 26 we find: 上曉上四 . Shang (上) indicates a rising linguistic tone, whereas the melody actually descends from 上 to 四 . A similar instance can be observed next to the first character of the second column.

In the year 1713 the Imperial Music Office of the Ch'ing dynasty (1655-1911) established a new official (theoretical) scale with fourteen degrees in the octave.[70] The first twelve of these fourteen degrees were named after the twelve lü (huang, ta, t'ai, etc.), and the last two (the thirteenth and fourteenth degrees) were again called huang and ta; thus, the next higher octave would not begin with huang, but with t'ai:

(C)	1	huang	6	chung	11	wu	
	2	ta	7	jui	12	ying	
	3	t'ai	8	lin	13	huang	
	4	chia	9	i	14	ta	
	5	ku	10	nan	1	t'ai	(c)

	Lü name	Ti	Hsiao	Courant's definition
11	I(-tsê)	凡	上	ut# 3
12	Nan	仉	仩	re
13	Wu	合	尺	re
14	Ying	六合	伬	re#
1	Huang	四	工	mi
2	Ta	五	仜	fa
3	T'ai	乙	凡	fa#
4	Chia	亿	仉	sol
5	Ku	上	合五	sol#
6	Chung	仩	六五	la
7	Jui	尺	四五	la
8	Lin	伬	五合	la#
9	I	工	乙	si
10	Nan	仜	亿	ut
11	Wu	凡	上	ut#
12	Ying	仉	仩	re
13	Huang	六	尺	re
14	Ta	亻六	伬	re#
1	T'ai	五	工	mi

This nomenclature shows that the ancient significance of the lü as absolute pitches had disappeared; only the names of the lü were still in use. In notating this scale by means of kung-ch'ê-p'u, additional symbols had to be employed. The chart on page 118 shows the lü names in the left-hand column, the kung-ch'ê symbols as used in ti music in the center, and the kung-ch'ê symbols as used in hsiao music in the right-hand column. A simple calculation shows that the interval between any two of the fourteen degrees consists of $\frac{1200}{14} = 85.714$ cents. The notation of the fourteen equidistant notes utilizes the affix 亻. This symbol, which formerly indicated the higher octave, now means that the notes are altered. Moreover, we observe a number of combinations of symbols such as  the significance of which has been shown in the foregoing chart.

KONG-CHŬK-PO

Kong-chŭk-po is the Korean pronunciation of 工 尺 譜 (the Chinese kung-ch'ê-p'u), the popular notational system of China which appeared in Korea in the fifteenth century. Unlike China, where kung-ch'ê-p'u was used mainly to notate operatic and other secular music, Korea confined its use to the notation of ritual and ceremonial melodies. Korean musicians had a profound respect for Chinese musical culture and valued melodies, instruments, and notations imported from China as highly as they did the ritual and music of their own temple and imperial palace. This was perhaps one reason why kong-chŭk-po never gained popularity in Korea;

another was the invention of an indigenous Korean notational system, the o-ŭm-yak-po (五音略譜), which will be discussed on pages 124-27.

Kong-chŭk-po is first mentioned and used in the Sae-cho shillok (世祖實錄), a historical document dealing with the events and achievements of the reign of King Sae-cho (1456-1469).[71] The musical pieces in this work are grouped in the following manner:

a) Chong-myo-ak (宗廟樂), "Imperial Temple Music";

b) Hwan-ku-ak (圜丘樂), lit., "Around the Hill Music," a royal ceremony, performed at the winter solstice upon and around a circular platform, the "hill," which represents heaven;

c) Ch'ang-su-chi-kok (創守之曲), "Song of Creation and Protection";

d) Kyong-kŭn-chi-kok (敬勤之曲), "Song of Respect and Diligence."

Another fifteenth-century work which contains kong-chŭk notatio is the seventh volume of the Ak-hak-koe-pŭm.[72]

Contrary to Chinese kung-ch'ê-p'u, the symbols of kong-chŭk po are devoid of all affixes; and 四, 一, 工, 凡, and 五 can denote both D and Db, E and Eb, A and Ab, B and Bb, and d, db, and d# respectively. The Korean names of the symbols are:

Hap	合	C
Sa	四	Db and D
Il	一	Eb and E
Sang	上	F
Ku	勾	F#
Chŭk	尺	G
Kong	工	Ab and A
Pŭm	几	Bb and B
Yuk	六	c
O	五	db, d, and d#.

Following is an example from the Sae-cho shillok, a hymn of Chong-myo-ak (宗廟樂).[73] It is notated in kong-chŭk-po and yul-cha-po:

Figure 28

一	夾	惟
六	潢	皇
几	無	昊
尺	林	天

Figure 28 (cont.)

臨下有赫
仲林潢南
上尺六工

敢用菲儀
林夾潢無
尺一六几

以御來格
汰潢仲夾
五六上一

The text of the hymn, written in Chinese characters but pronounced in Korean, reads as follows: "Yu hwang ho chŭn; im ha yu hyŭk; kam yong bi ui; ui u re kyuk." Its meaning is: "Only you, my heavenly, imperial emperor, to us, your subjects, you appear in divine majesty how should I dare to offer you my trifling presents and approach [invoke] you?"

The eighth and thirteenth symbols of the center and left-hand columns of Figure 28 are somewhat surprising. Although it is possible that in addition to Eb, F, G, Bb, c, the hymn uses the "pien" notes A (南) and d (汰), one should expect at first hearing to find anhemitonic pentatonic tone material and assume that the copyist made some mistakes. The symbol 五, as we know, could be interpreted as d# (eb), but its transcription into 汰 clearly shows that the note d was intended. The symbol 工, too, allows no other interpretation, as it is transcribed with 南.[74] Such doubtful instances, probably caused by the widespread illiteracy among court musicians who were expected to read and write the notational systems, necessitated the adoption in the fifteenth century of a simple system which employed mainly numbers and the signs 上 (up) and 下 (down), a notation called o-ŭm-yak-po,[75] which caused increasing neglect of the older notational systems.

As in Korea, kong-chŭk-po did not gain widespread popularity in Japan. There are only two instances of this system's coming into use: in the notations of imported Ming and, later, Ch'ing compositions from China. Since 1877 Ming and Ch'ing music have usually been mentioned together in Japan as Minshin-gaku (明 清 樂). Chinese Ming music became known in Japan in 1629 in the form of vocal pieces with instrumental accompaniment.[76] Although imported Ming music contains some heptatonic and hexatonic melodies, the majority are anhemitonic pentatonic. About 200 pieces are extant, and these are notated in kong-chŭk-po. Music of the Ch'ing period appeared in Japan in 1804.[77] This too consists of vocal pieces with instrumental accompaniment, also notated in kong-chŭk-po. However, when denoting the next higher octave, their symbols are provided with the affix 亻 (伵, 亿, 仩, etc.), and the octave above that with 彳

(伵, 亿, 仩, etc.). In Japan the notational symbols in Minshin-gaku are called:

symbol	Japanese name
乙	i (イ)
上	shang (シャン)
尺	chieh (チェ)
工	kong (コン)
凡	hang (ハン)
六	liu (リウ)
[合	hō (ホー)]
五	u (ウ)
四	sui (スイ)

In the Japanese language the characters 乙, 上, 尺, 工, and so forth, are pronounced quite differently from the manner in which they are pronounced in musical notation. In the latter the symbols are spoken in imitation of their Chinese (or Korean) names.

O-ŬM-YAK-PO (五音略譜)

During the reign of King Sae-cho (1456-1469) yul-cha-po becam obsolete, and a much simpler system, the o-ŭm-yak-po, "Five-Soun Abbreviated Notation," became established in Korea. The earliest mention of this system is made in the Sae-cho shillok. Extensive us of o-ŭm-yak-po is made in the important Tae-ak-hu-po (大樂

後譜, lit., "Great Music Later Notation"),[78] a collection of twenty-seven pieces dating from the period of King Sae-cho and compiled in 1759 under the auspices of King Yong-cho. The music contained in the Tae-ak-hu-po is cho-ak (朝樂, imperial court music), notated in several systems: yul-cha-po, o-ŭm-yak-po, and chŭng-kan-po.[79] Items 3 to 7 in the Tae-ak-hu-po represent several versions of an important piece of ah-ak, called Chung-tae-yŭp (中大葉), that has been notated in different modes.[80] Another source is Shi-yong-hyang-ak-po (時用鄉樂譜), a collection of twenty-six pieces. The date of its origin is unknown; it was reprinted in 1945 by the Institute of Oriental Literature, Yŭn-sae (延世) College (Christian College), at Seoul.

O-ŭm-yak-po, like kong-chŭk-po, does not indicate any absolute pitches. With the exception of the first (basic) note of the scale, which is represented by kung (宮), o-ŭm-yak-po uses the numbers 1 to 5 (一, il; 二, i; 三, sam; 四, sa; and 五, o) instead of solmization syllables. The system encompasses a gamut of two octaves the center of which is kung, which we shall transcribe as the note C, although any other tone could be used as well. Notes above kung use the affix 上 (sang, "upper"), below kung, 下 (ha, "lower").

O-ŭm-yak-po, which denotes the anhemitonic pentatonic scale, was (and still is) the popular Korean counterpart of the Old Chinese Five-tone Notation (宮, 商, 角, 徵, 羽); its notational symbols are:

上五	or	上五 (or 宮)	sang o	c'
上四	or	上四	sang sa	a
上三	or	上三	sang sam	g

Five-tone Notation (cont.)

上二	or	上二	sang i	e
上一	or	上一	sang il	d
宮			kung	c
下一	or	下一	ha il	A
下二	or	下二	ha i	G
下三	or	下三	ha sam	E
下四	or	下四	ha sa	D
下五	or	下五 (or 宮)	ha o	C

These symbols were applied to the four modes of Korean music,[81] particularly to pyong-cho (平調) and u-cho (羽調), and less frequently to their respective kae-myon-cho (界面調) forms:[82]

Symbol	Old Chinese notes	Pyong-cho	Pyong-cho kae-myon-cho	U-cho	U-cho kae-myon-cho
上五	c	c	c	f	f
上四	A	A	Bb	d	eb
上三	G	G	G	c	c
上二	E	F	F	Bb	Bb
上一	D	D	Eb	G	Ab
宮	C	C	C	F	F
下一	A	A	Bb	D	Eb
下二	G	G	G	C	C
下三	E	F	F	Bb	Bb
下四	D	D	Eb	G	Ab
下五	C	C	C	F	F

As in Chinese custom, Korean musicians would define the required pitch of kung by stating a yul-cha-po symbol at the head of the notated piece. For instance, we find formulas such as: kung is hwang-chong: 宮 is 黄 = C; or: kung is hyŭp chong (the Chinese chia-chung): 宮 is 夾 = Eb, and so forth.

Although o-ŭm-yak-po denotes only the degrees of a pentatonic scale, some efforts were made to indicate the pyŭn (變 ; Chinese: pien) tones in two pieces of the Sae-cho shillok.[83] In these two instances in which o-ŭm-yak-po is used to notate "T'ang music"[84] we find the symbols 一 (il) and 凡 (pŭm). Both are borrowed from kong-chŭk-po and are used without the affixes sang or ha in order to avoid confusion. The symbol 一 corresponds to the Chinese pien chih (F#), and 凡, of course, to the Chinese pien kung (B).

As o-ŭm-yak-po appears frequently in conjunction with another system, the chŭng-kan-po (井 間 譜), we shall delay presenting notational specimens until that system has been discussed.

CHŬNG-KAN-PO (井 間 譜)

Chŭng-kan-po (井 間 譜)[85] is one of the earliest systems which permits notating the duration of notes. According to the Sae-cho shillok, its invention was ascribed to King Sae-cho (1456-1469). However, chŭng-kan-po is already mentioned and used in the Sae-chong shillok (世宗實錄),[86] the historical document of King Sae-chong (1450-1452), who ruled before Sae-cho.

From the time of its appearance[87] chŭng-kan-po was combined with most Korean musical notations with the exception of some tablatures and the neumatic system of yŭn-ŭm-pyo (連 音 標).[88] Chŭng-kan-po is notated in the form of a chart in which each of the smallest rectangles represents one metrical unit (chŭng-kan). These chŭng-kan (which we shall notate with quarter notes) are usually organized into six groups (kang, 綱) of 3, 2, 3, 3, 2, 3 chŭng-kan, respectively, amounting to a total of sixteen metrical units. These sixteen chŭng-kan – or six kang – constitute one haeng (行). Thus, a composition consists of several haeng, each haeng contains six kang, and each kang consists of two or three chŭng-kan:

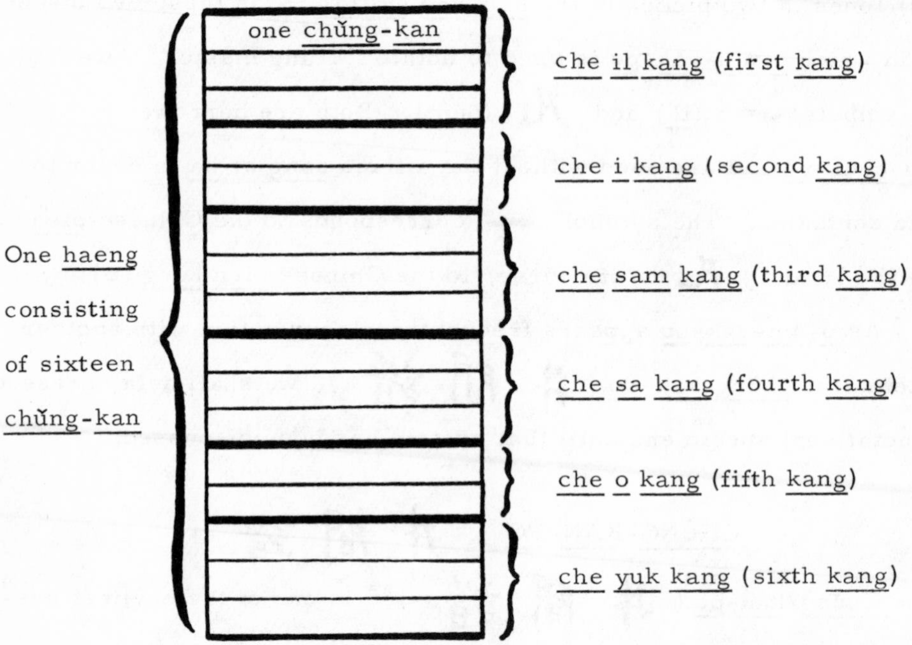

The six kang are often called yuk tae kang (六 大 綱 , "six great principles"). As stated before, there are generally sixteen chŭng-kan in one haeng, but in some rare instances twenty chŭng-kan may be used.[89] In the Yang-kŭm shin-po,[90] a famous zither book of 1610, only two large kang are indicated in each haeng, and the subdivision into chŭng-kan is omitted.

Not every piece begins with the first chŭng-kan; some begin with the second or third, in a way similar to upbeats in Western music.[91] The following excerpt (Fig. 29) illustrates the combination of chŭng-

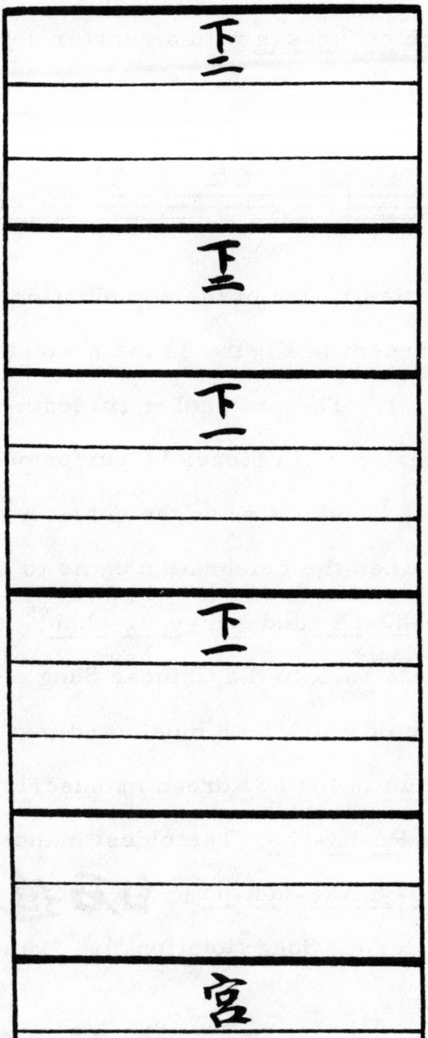

Figure 29

kan-po with o-ŭm-yak-po; the piece is called Himun-ak-po (熙文樂譜 ,"Bright Literary Music"), as recorded in the Sae-cho shillok. If we represent each chŭng-kan with a quarter note, the transcription of Figure 29 would read:

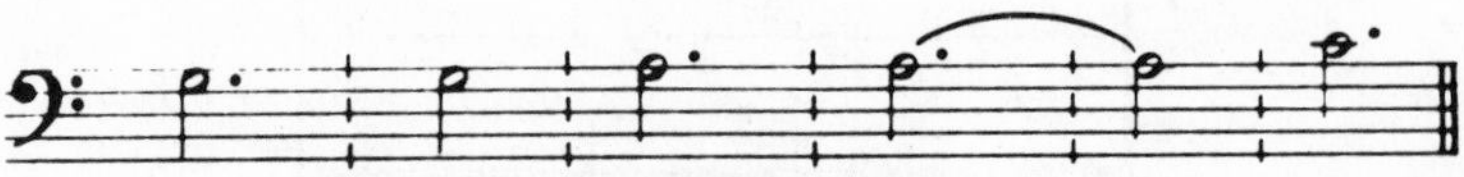

As a further illustration of the combination of o-ŭm-yak-po with chŭng-kan-po we present in Figure 30 the ancient song Po-hŭ-cha (步虛子). The protocol of fifteenth-century Korean court music prescribed that certain pieces be performed when the king entered the throne hall,[92] others when the subjects paid their homage,[93] and one Po-hŭ-cha when the celebration came to an end and the king left the hall.[94] Po-hŭ-cha and Nak-yang-chun[95] are the only two melodies extant which date back to the Chinese Sung period,[96] and Po-hŭ-cha is the only piece of which both music and text are preserved; the text of Nak-yang-chun is lost. Korean manuscripts of varying ages contain notations of Po-hŭ-cha. The oldest manuscript, pronounced in Korean Paek-sŭk-to-yin-ka-kok-po (白石道人歌曲譜 , lit., "White Stone Hermit Song Notation"),[97] shows Po-hŭ-cha notated without any ornaments.

The An-sang-kŭm-po (安瑺琴譜), a zither book of 1572,[98] and later works such as the Tae-ak-hu-po (大樂後譜 of 1759, the Sok-ak-won-po (俗樂源譜),[99] written before 1776 and the Yu-yae-ji (遊藝誌),[100] written after 1776, notate the same melody with an increasing amount of ornamentation.[101]

Po-hŭ-cha differs in a few details from other, similar compositions, and it is these differences which make it difficult to determine whether the melody is of Chinese or Korean origin. In order to explain these points a brief digression on the formal structure of Po-hŭ-cha is necessary:

	1st line	2nd line	3rd line	4th line
First verse:	7 words	5 words	10 words	6 words
	Different melody in first and second verses	Same melody in first and second verses		
Second verse:	7 words	6 words	10 words	6 words

Or, briefly expressed:

First verse:	A	B	C	D
Second verse:	E	B	C	D.

This rare song form is characterized by the two opening phrases (A and E), called hwan-tu (換頭 , "exchanged heads") and the longer recurrent sections in both verses (B, C, D), are called to-tŭ-ri 도 드 리 , "coming again"). The to-tŭ-ri sections usually show a quickening of tempo and a characteristic 6/8 meter that is not common to related Chinese forms.

Po-hŭ-cha is performed vocally with instrumental accompaniment, but unlike other important pieces such as Man-tae-yŭp (慢大葉),[102] Chung-tae-yŭp (中大葉), and Sak-tae-yŭp (數大葉), which have instrumental interludes and postludes, Po-hŭ-cha has none.[103]

In the Tae-ak-hu-po version every fourth word of the text is marked by a percussive beat – a style called sa-kyun-pak (四均拍 , "Four Even Beats") – whereas in Chinese ritual music percussive beats would occasionally appear with every word.

Po-hŭ-cha differs from related Chinese pieces in form and Aufführungspraxis. We have to repeat that it is impossible to determine whether these differences were added to a piece imported from China or whether the song was created in this manner in Korea.

Figure 30 (pp. 132-40) is the Tae-ak-hu-po version of this ancient melody.[104]

Figure 30

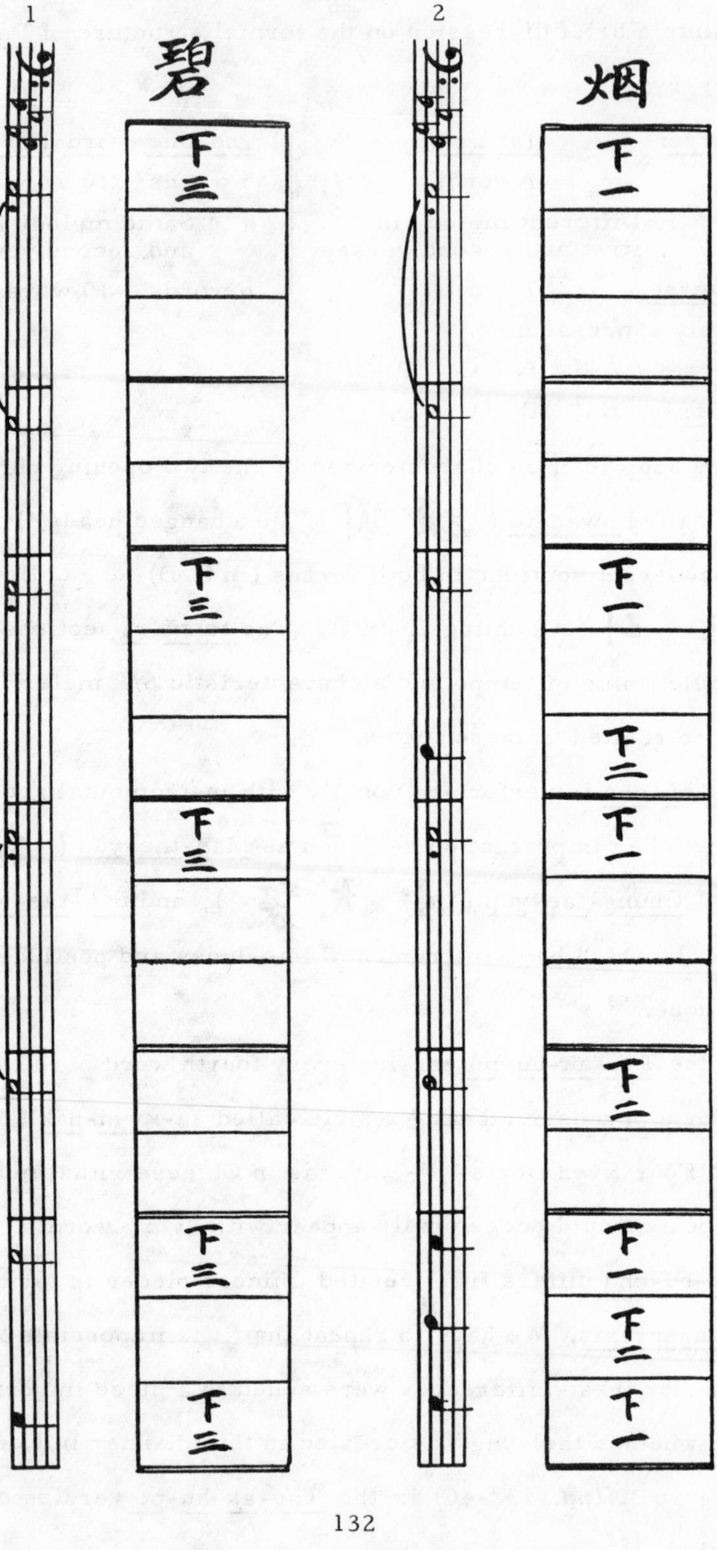

Figure 30 (cont.)

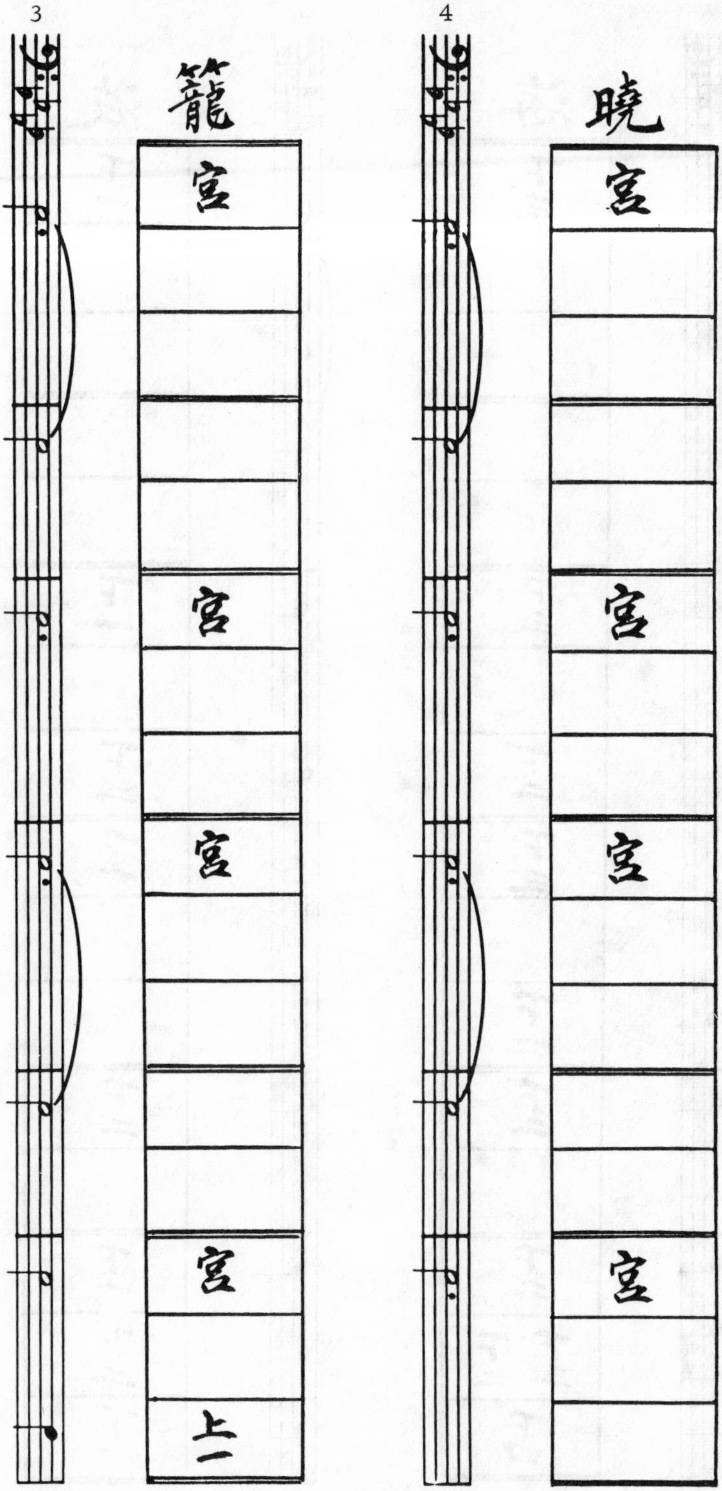

Figure 30 (cont.)

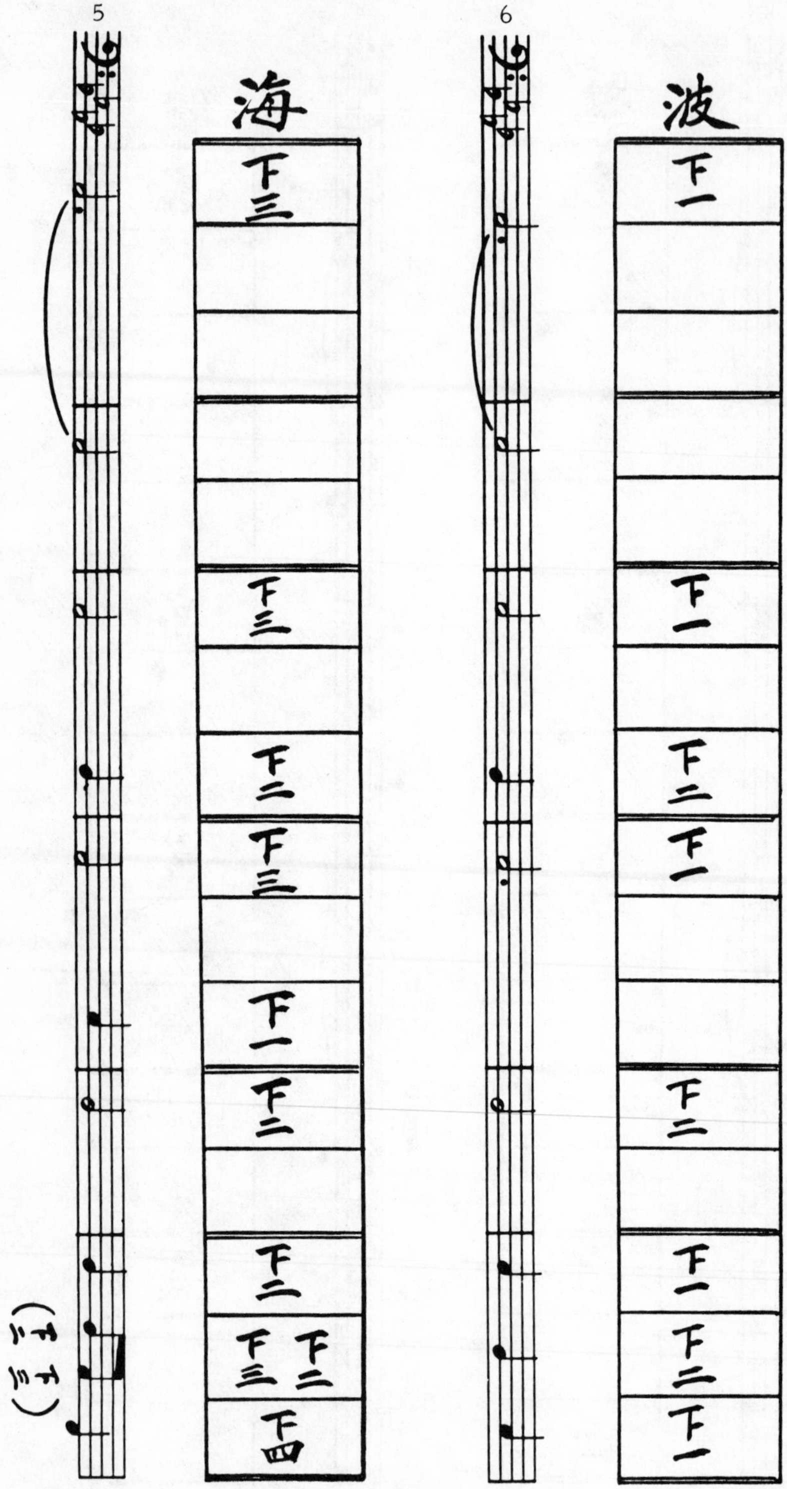

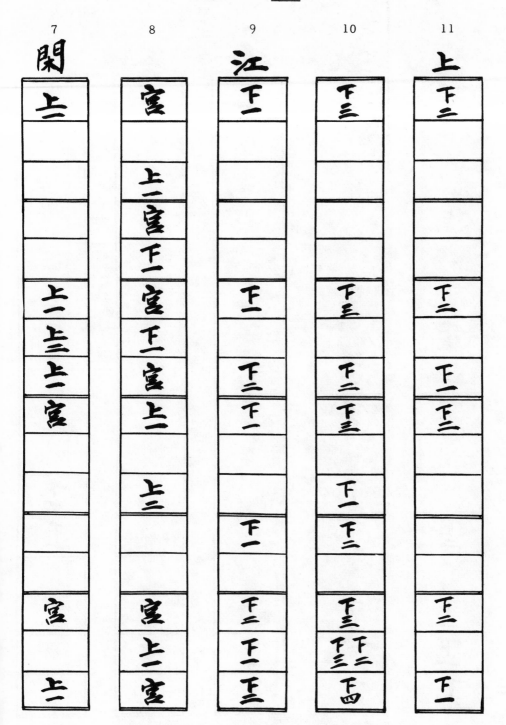

Figure 30 (cont.)

7	8	9	10	11
閑		江		上
上二	宫	下一	下三	下二
	上一			
	宫			
	下一			
上一	宫	下一	下三	下二
上三	下一			
上一	宫	下二	下二	下一
宫	上一	下一	下三	下三
	上三		下一	
		下一	下二	
宫	宫	下二	下三	下二
	上一	下一	下三 下二	
上二	宫	下三	下四	下一

Figure 30 (cont.)

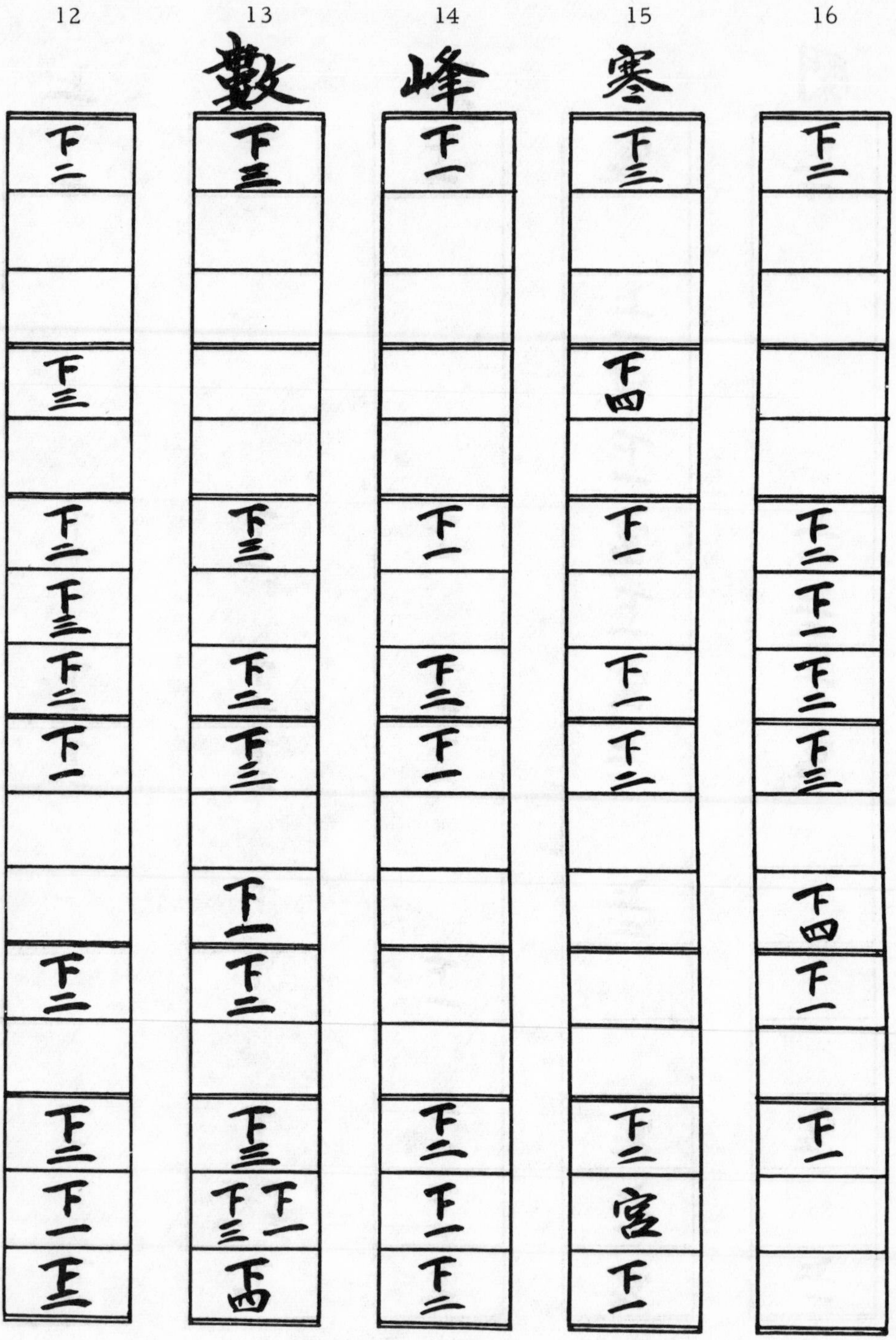

Figure 30 (cont.)

Figure 30 (cont.)

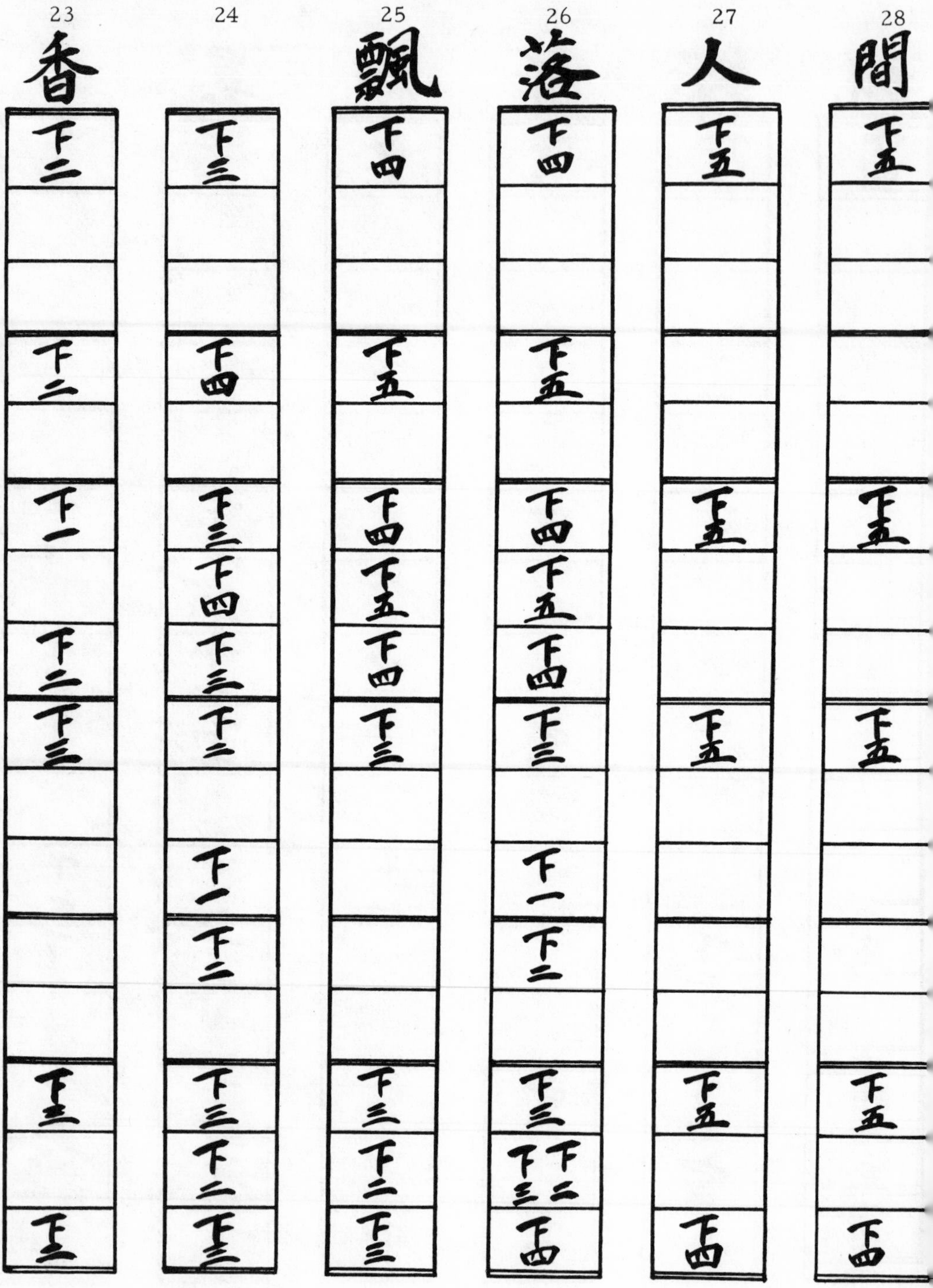

Figure 30 (cont.)

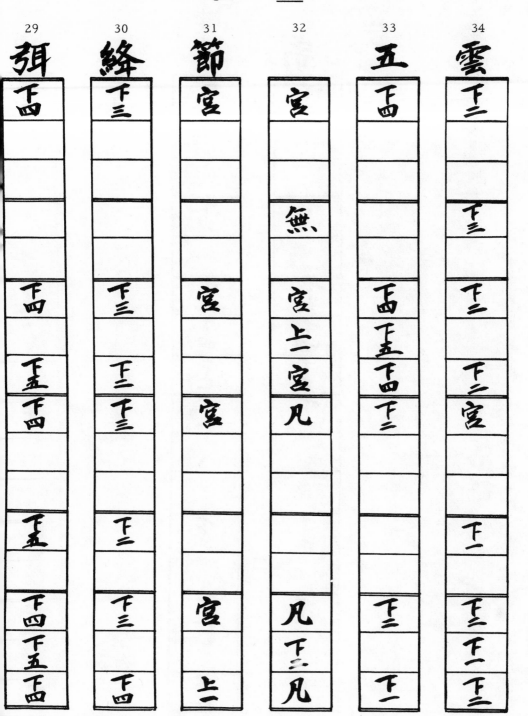

29	30	31	32	33	34
弭	絳	節		五	雲
下四	下三	宮	宮	下四	下二
			無		下三
下四	下三	宮	宮	下四	下二
			上一	下五	
下五	下二		宮	下四	下二
下四	下三	宮	凡	下二	宮
下五	下二				下一
下四	下三	宮	凡	下二	下二
下五			下二		下一
下四	下四	上一	凡	下一	下三

Figure 30 (cont.)

35 36

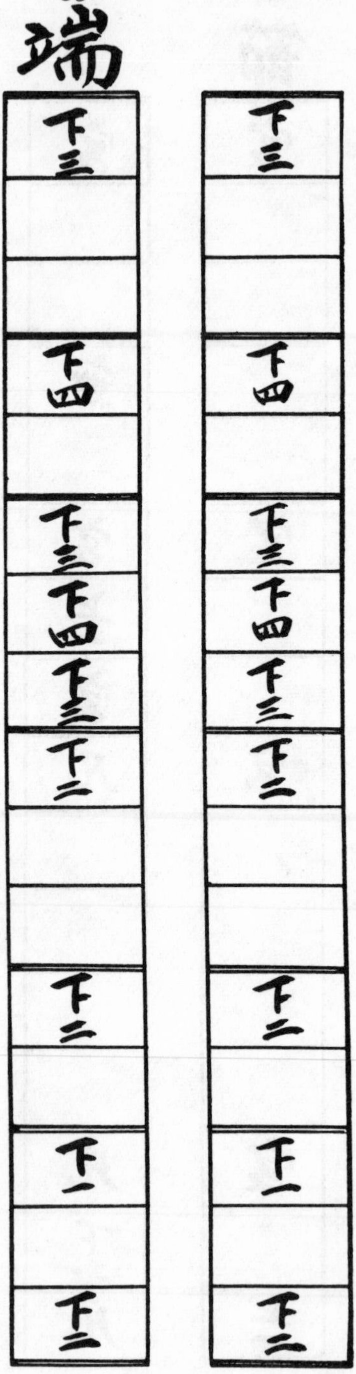

The text of Po-hŭ-cha, written in Chinese, pronounced in Korean, follows below, together with a general translation:

碧	Pyŭk	The blue mist covers the sea in the haziness of dawn;
烟	In	
籠	Nong	
曉	Hyo	
海	Hae	
波	Pa	The moving waves encircle the numerous hills which protrude out of the water, as a cool, ornamental bracelet of precious stones clings around one's wrist.
閑	Han	
江	Kang	
上	Sang	
數	Su	
峰	Pong	
寒	Han	
珮	Pae	
環	Hwan	
聲	Sŭng	The rare beauty of music flutters in the wind;
裡	Ri	
異	I	
香	Hyang	

Text of Po-hu-cha (cont.)

飄	Pyo	
落	Rak	As it reaches the earth it merely rests above the clouds – for such heavenly music is not understood by men.
人	In	
間	Kan	
弭	Mi	
絳	Kang	
節	Chŭl	
五	O	
雲	Un	
端	Sŭ	

With the exception of eight haeng (8, 12, 16, 22, 24, 32, 36, 44), all other haeng show at their heads textual characters. Each word has to be held throughout the duration of its haeng, or, if there is no text at the head of the following haeng, the preceding text has to be held over.[105] We have transcribed only the first six haeng of the song, but the reader will have little difficulty in completing the transcription. Two unusual features may be observed in haeng 32; first, the use of 無 (mu, Chinese: wu), a symbol borrowed from yul-cha-po. Originally mu represented the "absolute" pitch of Bb (A#), a tone which is untenable in o-ŭm-yak-po because its kung is variable and, with it, all degrees above and below. Mu, being a minor seventh above the hwang-chong (Chinese: huang chung), therefore, has to be treated as a relative pitch, representing a note which stands a minor seventh above kung of o-ŭm-yak-po. Since kung is Eb in the present instance, mu will be Db. The use of the symbol mu is justified because there is no specific symbol in o-ŭm-yak-po for notating the minor seventh above kung.

Second, similar considerations apply to the use of 凡 (pŭm), borrowed from kong-chŭk-po. Since kung is Eb, pŭm must be transcribed as D.

Figure 31 on page 144 represents Nak-yang-chun (the second extant melody of the Chinese Sung period), as notated in the Sok-ak-won-po.[106] In this instance chŭng-kan-po and yul-cha-po are combined. The reader will have no difficulty in transcribing this famous piece.

In Figure 32 (p. 148) we present another important melody of Korean court music, called Yŭ-min-ak (與 民 樂 , lit., "Grant People Music").[107] Originally it was vocal music accompanied by a chang-ko,[108] but it gradually became an instrumental piece. According to the Ak-hak-koe-pŭm[109] it was used as opening and closing music for court celebrations in the fifteenth century.[110]

The text of Yŭ-min-ak was derived from 龍飛御天歌 (Korean: Yong-pi-ŭ-chŭn-ka, lit., "Dragon Flying Royal Heaven Song"), a sequence of poems in 125 strophes, selected by Chŭng-in-ch'i (鄭 麟 趾) by order of King Sae-chong in 1446. The words were written in Chinese characters and in the newly created Korean script.[111] The Chinese poem, together with the melody to which it was sung, is called Yŭ-min-ak. The text consists of two versions, one of five verses, the other of ten. The first five (Chinese) characters of the text are to be found at the top of p. 145.

Figure 31

洛陽春

	林	太	林	無	潢	黃
太	仲	潢	仲	林	潢	
仲						黃
太	仲	汰	南	林	南	
黃		汰	潢			太
	太	潢	南	林	潢	
還		南	林	林	潢	太
入	黃	潢	仲	仲	南	太
	太	潢	仲	汰	林	
南	太					黃
潢		汰	太	潢	林	
潢	仲	潢	仲	潢	林	太
	姑	南	太	南	仲	太
	太		太	林		黃
		林			南	
	黃	南	仲	林	南	南

	pronounced in Korean:		
海	Hae	Sea	(meaning: Korea)
東	Tong	East	
六	Yuk	Six	
龍	Yong	Dragons[112]	
飛	Pi	Flying	

There were four types of Yŭ-min-ak:

1) Yŭ-min-ak-man (與民樂慢),

2) Yŭ-min-ak-yŭng (與民樂令),

which were ascribed to T'ang-ak,[113]

3) Yŭ-min-ak-man, and

4) Yŭ-min-ak-yŭng,

the latter two ascribed to Hyang-ak.[114]

Yŭ-min-ak-man of T'ang-ak is notated in the Sae-chong shillok (ten verses), in the Sok-ak-won-po (five verses), and is also preserved in the archives of the former Royal Band of Seoul (originally five verses; later, verses 6-10 of the Sae-chong shillok were added to it). Yŭ-min-ak-yŭng of T'ang-ak is preserved in the Sok-ak-won-po, and in two versions, pon-ryŭng (本令) and hae-ryŭng (解令), in the archives of the former Royal Band. Yŭ-min-ak of Hyang-ak is notated in the An-sang-kŭm-po; and Yŭ-min-ak-yŭng of Hyang-ak in the Sok-ak-won-po (hyŭn-po, "string-notation"), in the Shin-sŭng-kŭm-po (申晟琴譜), and preserved by the former Royal Band. The T'ang-ak forms of Yŭ-min-ak preserved by the former Royal Band are often simply called man-po (man-notation), and the Hyang-ak forms preserved by the Royal Band are called yŭ-min-ak without the additional words man and yŭng.

The term man (慢) means "slow" and denotes the original form performed at a slow speed. Yŭng (令), "special," denotes a variation of man — the variation is made by adding rhythmic embellishments to the melody and performing it in a lively tempo.

Lee contradicts this by stating that one verse of yŭng was performed in seven minutes, while ten (all) verses of man were performed in twenty minutes.[115] The explanations concerning man and yŭng forms[116] are so contradictory that it seems impossible to arrive at an intelligible definition. The Ak-hak-koe-pŭm states that if Yŭ-min-ak-man of T'ang-ak (as notated in the Sae-chong shillok) is used as dance music, it is called Yŭ-min-ak-yŭng. The Sae-chong shillok, however, describes the same piece (used with or without dancing) as Yŭ-min-ak-man.

The only distinct difference between the various types can be noted in the instrumentation of the T'ang and hyang forms of Yŭ-min-a the T'ang forms, both man and yŭng, are performed by the T'ang-p'iri (唐觱篥), a type of oboe with seven holes, played by the leader of the ensemble; the pang-hyang (方響), metal chimes (which consisted of two rows of eight iron slabs each and which appeared in Korea in A. D. 1115); the T'ang-chŭk (唐笛), the Chinese ti, a cross flute with seven holes; the t'ong-so (洞簫), the Japanese shakuhachi, a vertical flute with five holes and one side hole (one hole near the mouthpiece is covered with paper); the T'ang-p'i-pa (唐琵琶), the Chinese p'i-pa, a lute with four strings; and the a-jêng 牙箏), a bowed zither with seven strings. The basic note of all these instruments has to be the hwang-chong (Chinese: huan-chung).

The hyang-ak forms of Yŭ-min-ak are performed by the hyang-p'iri (鄉觱篥), the hyang-oboe, a little larger than the T'ang-p'iri, played by the leader of the ensemble; the tae-kŭm (大笒), a flute with six holes; the hae-kŭm (奚琴), related to the Chinese hu-ch'in, a fiddle with two silken strings; the kaya-kŭm (伽倻琴), a zither with twelve strings;[117] and the chang-ko. The basic note of all these hyang-ak instruments has to be hyŭp (the Chinese chia-[chung]).

All types of Yŭ-min-ak were required material in the national examinations for court musicians.

Following (p. 148) is the beginning of Yŭ-min-ak-man as notated in the Sae-chong shillok (Vol. CXL).

The score specimen (Fig. 32) shows thirty-two chŭng-kan in each of the three vertical columns. Although the chŭng-kan are not grouped into kang, they can be read without difficulty. Each of the three columns contains: at the right-hand side, the yul-cha-po (Chinese: lü) symbols; in the middle, annotations for the chang-ko player; and, at the left, textual characters.

The chang-ko words are:

鼓 ko, "drum-side" (left side)

鞭 pyŭn, "whip-side" (right side)

搖 yo, "roll"

雙 ssang, a beat performed by both hands on both sides simultaneously.

The text is already known to us[118] except for the fourth character, 拍. This character pak, literally meaning "to clap," signifies

Figure 32

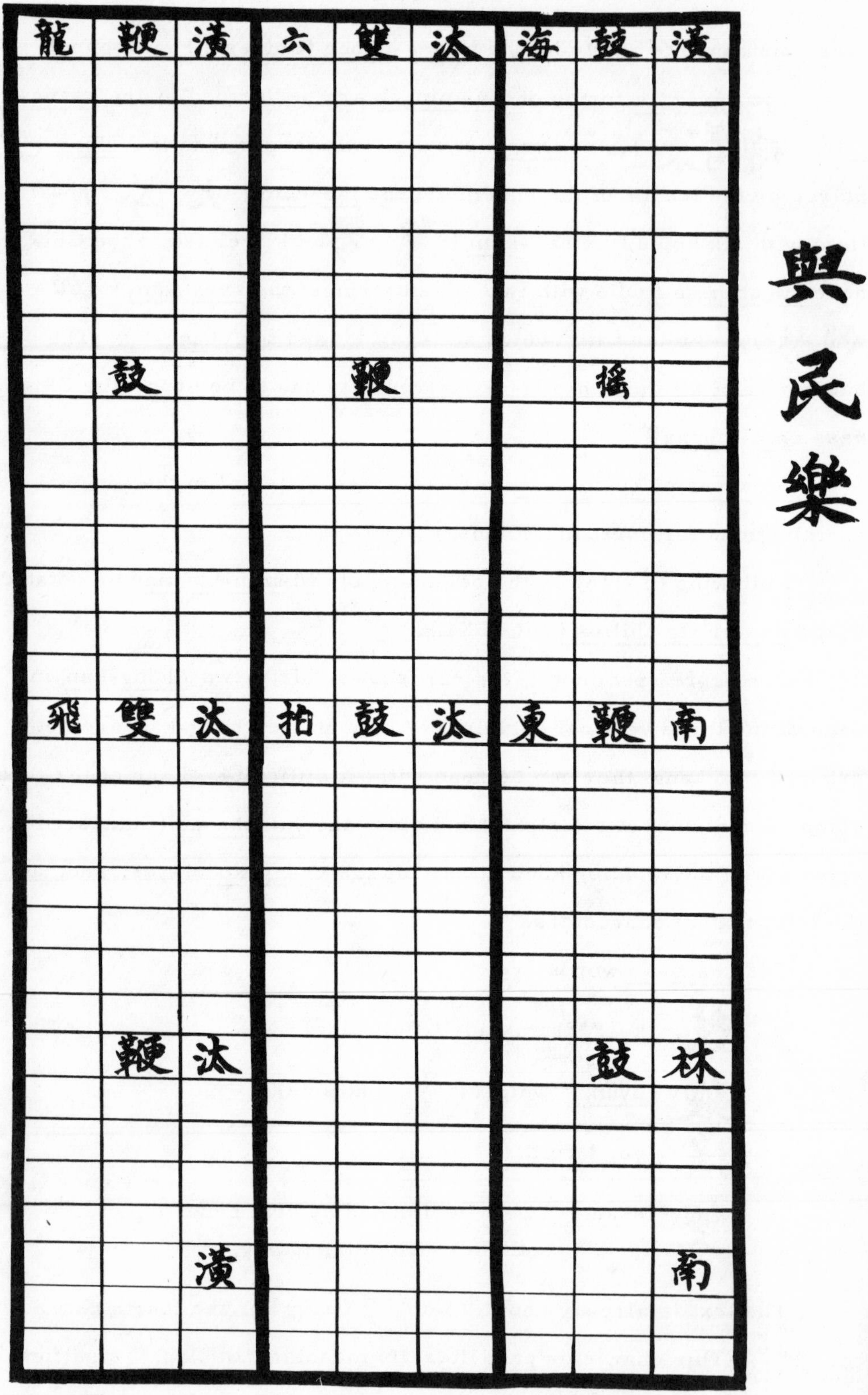

to the performer that the word yuk (六) is to be held over into the second half of the thirty-two chŭng-kan of the second column.

As we are dealing with thirty-two chŭng-kan in each column, we reduce the metrical unit from a quarter note to an eighth note. Transcribed, the excerpt will read:[119]

Figure 33 (p. 150) represents Yŭ-min-ak-yŭng as notated in the Sok-ak-won-po.[120]

The title of Figure 33 informs us that we are dealing with hyŭn-po (絃譜), "string notation." There is some doubt as to whether this piece was performed solely by string instruments, as the notational symbols show no differences from those of other scores cited previously.

The man version of Yŭ-min-ak as notated in the Sok-ak-won-po begins as follows (Fig. 34, p. 151).[121]

Figure 33

與民樂

絃譜

六	雙	汰	東	鞭	南	海	鼓	潢
					南			
		汰			林			潢
	搖	潢		鞭	南			潢
					汰			
		汰			潢			南
		潢		搖	南			汰
	鞭	汰		掬	林		搖	潢
					仲			南
	鞭	汰		鼓	林			潢
	搖	淋		搖	潢		搖	沖
		湳			南			
		淋			林			汰
		沖			仲			潢

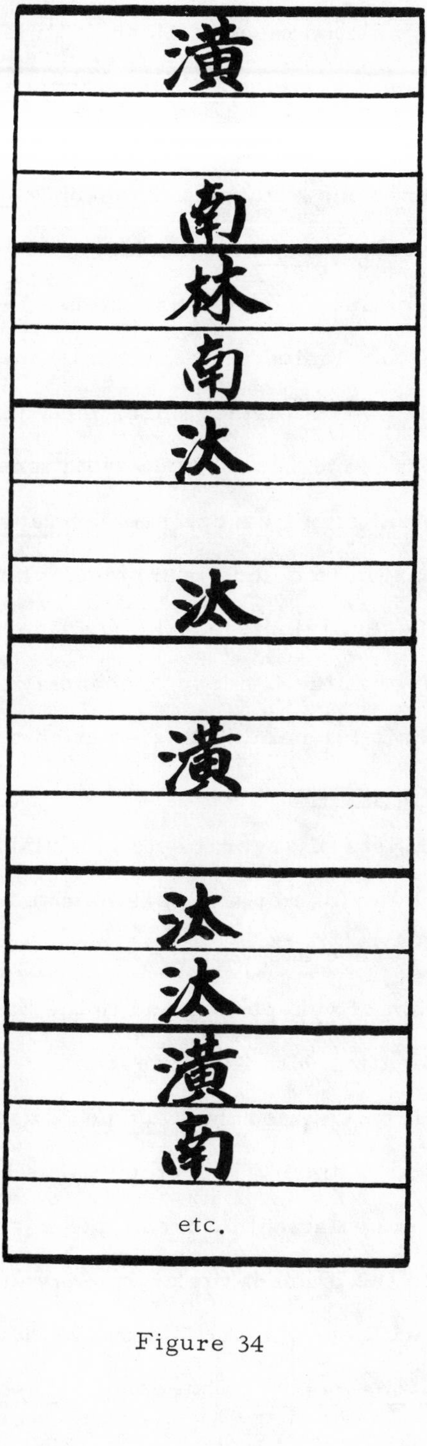

Figure 34

YUK-PO (肉譜)

Yuk literally translated means "flesh," "meat," or "body"; thus, yuk-po, a notational system of Korea, suggests a manner of notating the "mere flesh" of a melody. In comparison to yul-cha-po, the old Five and Seven-Tone Notations, kong-chŭk-po, o-ŭm-yak-po, and the zither tablatures, yuk-po is considered to be an inferior system because it does not use Chinese characters, the medium of writing of learned people, but indicates the notes by means of Korean syllables written in hangŭl.[122] Furthermore, the characters used in yul cha-po and the old Five and Seven-Tone Notations have connotations far beyond their musical significance, such as yang and yin characteristics and the relationship to colors, numbers, planets, and so forth.[1] Yuk-po has none of these attributes. Although there is no proof, one is tempted to surmise that the Chinese pronunciation of 肉, rou, ma have served as the basis for naming this notation because it often employs the syllables rŭ, ru, ro, etc.

The system consists of several sets of syllables which serve as a mnemonic aid to the performer and resemble to some extent the solmization systems of Europe and Japan.

The first mention of yuk-po is made in the Sae-cho shillok, the historical document dealing with King Sae-cho's reign in the fifteenth century. In this work it is stated that yuk-po is used only in notations of instrumental music. Although it seemed vague to the uninformed, yuk-po became highly popular with Korean musicians and amateurs an has remained so up to the present time. In Korean music books it is frequently combined with other more "learned" notational systems, particularly with hap-cha-po.[124] Extensive yuk-po notations can be found in the An-sang-kŭm-po (1572),[125] the Yang-kŭm shin-po (1610), the Hong-kee-hu-po (洪基厚譜 , n. d.),[127] and the Cho-sŭng kŭm-po (趙晟琴譜 , after 1759),[128] as well as in other works of lesser importance.

The yuk-po syllables vary with every instrument. In notations of the hyŭn-kŭm (玄琴)[129] and occasionally, in kaya-kŭm (伽倻琴)[130] music, the following five syllables are used:

Tŭng 덩
Tung 둥
Tang 당
Tong 동
Ting 딩

When used in notating music of the p'il-lyul (觱篥),[131] a variant of the p'iri (篥), a type of oboe, the yuk-po syllables are changed to:

Rŭ 러
Ru 루
Ra 라
Ro 로
Ri 리

which, for the sake of easier pronunciation, are usually read: Nŭ, Nu, Na, No, Ni. In tae-kŭm (大笒)[132] music the syllables begin with a strong T, e.g., Tta (따). As already stated, in kaya-kŭm music the yuk-po syllables can begin either with the letter T, or, in some instances, with K. When representing high notes the syllables begin with J, JJ, or CH. When two successive sounds are slurred, combinations of two syllables occur; for instance: Tang and Tong become Tarong (다롱); Tang and Jing become Taring (다링). Similarly, we find combinations such as Sareng (스랭), Sŭreng (스렝), and occasionally others.

In the famous Korean hyŭn-kŭm book — the Yang-kŭm shin-po — the yuk-po syllables begin, of course, with the letter T. In this work where symbols of hap-cha-po are placed side by side with yuk-po syllables, we find that the note Bb, performed on the fifth fret of the "big string" (大絃),[133] and the note Eb, a fourth higher, performed on the fourth fret of the "play string" (方絃), are both notated with the syllable Tang. The same syllable is also applied to the note F performed on the fifth fret of the "play string," and to Ab, performed on the seventh fret of the same string, if the fourth finger is used to stop the string in all four instances. The syllable Tong is used if the index finger stops the "play string," or if the middle finger stops the "big string." Jing is used if the thumb stops the "play string." Tung occurs when the index finger or the thumb stops the "big string."

Although these features do not occur invariably, they appear frequently enough to create the impression that the playing technique rather than the representation of notes is being referred to.

If we investigate the yuk-po (notation) of a whole piece and count the frequently occurring yuk-po syllables, we find, for instance that in Chung-tae-yŭp (中大葉),[134] the note produced by th index finger on the sixth fret of the "play string" is notated ten times with Tong and twenty times with Ting. In the same piece, the note pro- duced by the index finger on the seventh fret of the "big string" is notated nine times with Tung and twice with Ting.

Before trying to reach a conclusion regarding the significance of yuk-po syllables, let us consider a prescript concerning the tuning of two Korean zithers in terms of yuk-po and afterwards investigate the use of these syllables in p'iri notations.

According to Lee,[135] the tuning procedure of the kaya-kŭm is as follows: the fourth string is to be tuned to Tang, the fifth to Tong; the third string is to be tuned to Tung, and the second to Hŭng. The intervals between Tang and Tong, Tung and Hŭng have to be "little weak" seconds,[136] while the interval between Tŭng and Tang has to be a pure fourth. If the tuning is correct, the interval between Tang (also called An-tang, (안 당) and Pat-tang (밧 당), that is, the interval between the open fourth and seventh strings, has to produce a perfect fifth, and the interval between Tŭng and Pat-tang, that is, between the open third and seventh strings, an octave. The remaining twelve strings[137] are to be tuned in octaves to the strings already tuned. The only exception to the octave-tuning method is the eighth string, which has to be tuned to Ji (지), a note usually a major second or, in some instances, a minor third higher than Pat-tang. Thus, the following strings would be tuned in octaves: 2 and 6, 3 and 7, 4 and 9, 5 and 10, 6 and 11, and 7 and 12. The tuning of the first string is not yet known to us, but, we may suppose that as far as the tuning of the octave-pairs is concerned, the change from four strings (2-6, 3-7) to five (4-9, 5-10, etc.) is caused by the tuning of the eighth string (Ji), which does not fit into the octave pattern. At present all of this is still doubtful on account of the indefinite instructions, which offer no help as to definite pitches. Nevertheless, we may risk drawing a tentative chart containing the few points we have elucidated:

strings:	1	2	3	4	5	6	7	8	9	10	11	1
yuk-po:		Hŭng	Tung	Tang (or An-tang)	Tong		Pat-tang	Ji				

intervals:

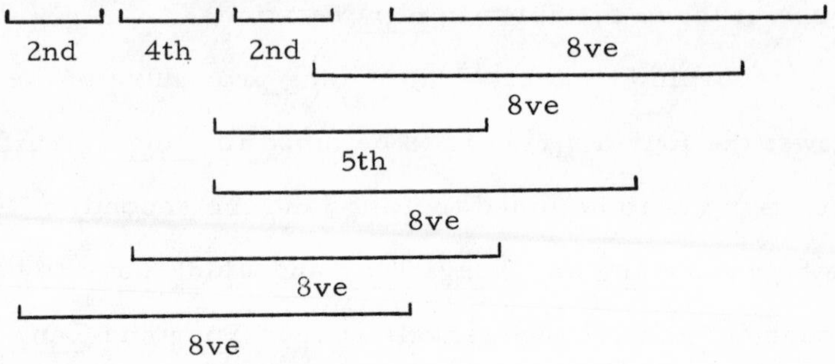

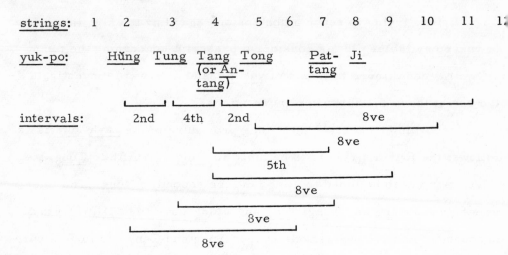

Eckardt relates[138] that in early ages there were two tunings, but he offers no definite information as to how they were arrived at. The sole intelligible tuning given, which dates back to only 1927, is:

D E G A* d e g a c* d' e' g'.

At A* and c* the bridges can be moved in order to achieve an occasional alteration by a semitone, e. g., Bb and b respectively. A comparison of the notes we have established with the modern tuning stated by Eckardt shows that the two coincide if we shift the modern tuning one step to the left:

(Lee)	1	2	3	4	5	6	7	8	9	10	11	12
		Hŭng	Tung	Tang	Tong		Pat-tang	Ji				

(Eckardt) (D E G A d e g a c d' e')
D E G A d e g a c' d' e' g' ?

In the Han-kuk-ŭm-ak-yon-gu (after p. 82) Lee presents the following tuning of the kaya-ko (kŭm):

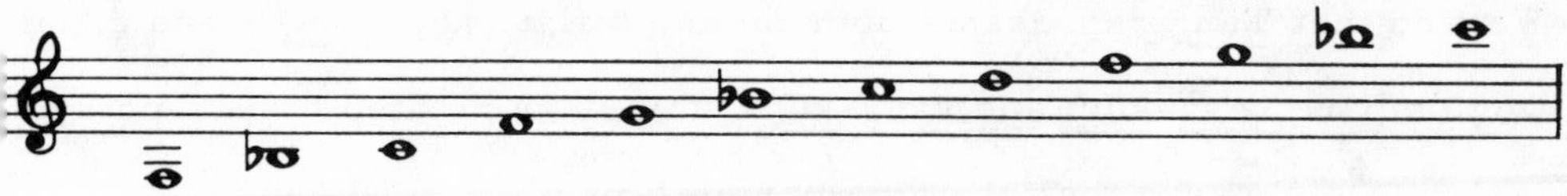

청 흥 둥 당 동 징 땅 지 찡 칭 종 찡

Chŭng Tung Tong Ttang Jjing Ching Jong Jjing
Hŭng Tang Jing Ji

The strings most frequently used are F, G, and Bb (Tang, Tong, and Jing). The eighth string, tuned to d (Ji), is called the ''lonely widower's string'' because it is not used in an octave pair.

We notice that again the intervals Hŭng and Tung, Tang and Tong, Ttang (or Pat-tang) and Ji, are seconds, that the interval Tung and Tang is a fourth, that Tung and Ttang (Pat-tang) form an octave, and that strings 1-4, 2-6, 3-7, 4-9, 5-10, 6-11, and 7-12, are tuned in octaves.

The yuk-po syllables in notations of yang-kŭm (洋琴)[139] music are applied to the thirteen (or fourteen) strings of the instrument. In this instance we are able to lay them out at once in scale form without any preliminary investigation:

홍 둥 등 당 동 지 징 당 동 디 딩 팅 쫑
(밧당)(밧동)

Ab	Bb	C	Eb	F	Gb	ab	bb	c	db	eb	f	ab'
Hŭng	Tung	Tŭng	Tang	Tong	Ji	Jing	Tang or Pat-tang	Tong or Pat-tong	Ti	Ting	T'ing	Jjong

We find that Tang represents both Eb and b flat, and Tong F and c. If we compare kaya-kŭm and yang-kŭm tunings as notated by yuk-po syllables, we observe the following parallels:

Intervals:

	second	fourth	octave
Kaya-kŭm	Hŭng-Tung Tang-Tong	Tung-Tang	Tung-Pat-tang
Yang-kŭm	Hŭng-Tang Tung-Tŭng Tang-Tong, etc.	Tung-Tang etc.	Tung-Pat-tang, etc.

Continuing our investigation, we now consider the first page of a piece called Man-tae-yŭp (慢大葉)[140] as it is notated in the Yang-kŭm-shin-po of 1610.[141] In this work three notational systems are used side by side: the old Chinese Five Tone Notation, hap-cha-po,[142] and yuk-po. Hap-cha-po and the old Five Tone Notation enable us to interpret the yuk-po syllables with comparative certainty. For t present, we can disregard the hap-cha-po symbols and confine ourselv to the other two notations.[143] They read as follows:

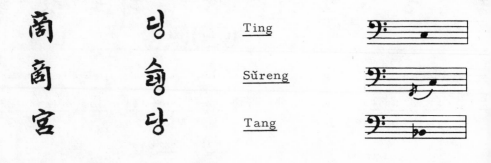

商	딩	Ting	
商	스렝	Sŭreng	
宮	당	Tang	

宮	스랭	Sareng	
商	딩	Ting	
宮	다	Ta . . (calligraphic mistake for 당, Tang).	
羽	등	Tŭng	
徵	덩	Tŭng	

徵	스렝	Sŭreng	
宮	청	Chŭng	
角	딩	Ting	
商	동	Tong	
宮	스랭	Sareng	
徵	딩	Ting	
角	스랭	Sareng	

角	딩	Ting	
商	동	Tong	

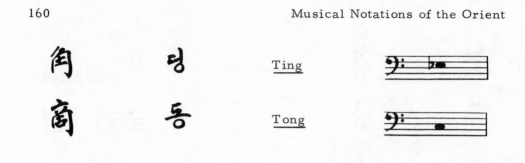

In somewhat the same way as do the yuk-po syllables of kaya-kŭm and yang-kŭm music, hyŭn-kŭm syllables denote the following intervals:

Second:	Fourth:	Octave:
Tŭng – Tung	Tŭng – Tang	Tŭng – Ting
Tang – Tong		

The combinations Sŭreng and Sareng do not indicate specific notes but only imitate the sounds of appoggiaturas. The syllable Chŭng is employed to represent a slow arpeggio across the three "chong" strings:

[144]

If we arrange these syllables (excepting the combinations) in an ascending order we get:

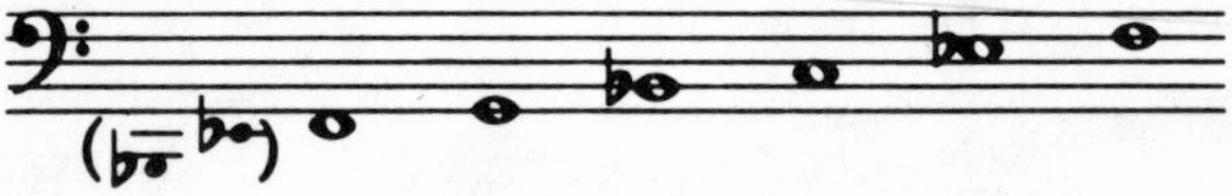

Tŭng Tung Tang Ting Ting Ting
Ta. . Tong

The following four examples (Fig. 35)[145] show the use of yuk-po syllables in p'iri[146] and chang-ko[147] notations:

(a)
念 佛
피리
♩= 50
느니루로 누나히레나 레 노 니레 나시루 루나 시루니로
etc.
장고
떵 떵 기덕 덩더러러 쿵 기덕 쿵 더러러 덕
(b)
打 令
피리
♪= 69
루로 느 나네 네 레 레 네네레라레노 느 네네레라레노 느 루로느나
장고
(c)
도 드 리
피리
♩= 66
렌 띠 시렌 띠 시레 니레나 레 노 느 로 나
장고
(d)
굿 거 리
피리
♩.= 60
노 나 니레나 난 시로니 노 내라 (南道굿거리장단)
장고
덩 기덕 쿵 덩 더러 덩 기덕 쿵 덩 더러 덩 기덕기덩 드로로

Figure 35

Item (a) of Figure 35 is called *Yŭm-pul*, "Buddhist Meditation." The *yuk-po* syllables of the *p'iri* part (upper line) read:

First measure:		Second measure:	
느	*Nŭ*	노	*No*
니	*Ni*	니	*Ni* (♪)
루	*Ru* (♪)	레	*Re*
로	*Ro*	나	*Na*
느	*Nŭ*	시	*Shi* (♪)
나	*Na*	루	*Ru*
히	*Hi* (♪)	루	*Ru* (♪)
레	*Re*	나	*Na*
나	*Na*	시	*Shi*
레	*Re*	루	*Ru*
		니	*Ni*
		로	*Ro*

The *yuk-po* syllables denoting the *chang-ko* rhythm (lower lin are:

First measure:		Second measure:	
떵	*Ttŭng*	쿵	*K'ung*
떵	*Ttŭng*	기	*Ki* (♪)
기	*Ki* (♪)	덕	*Tŭk*

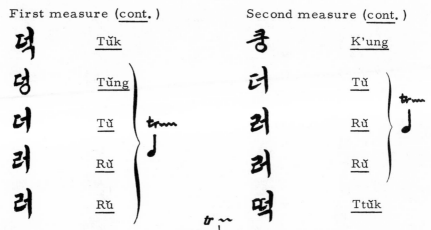

First measure (cont.)			Second measure (cont.)		
덕	Tŭk		쿵	K'ung	
덩	Tŭng		더	Tŭ	
더	Tŭ		러	Rŭ	
러	Rŭ		러	Rŭ	
러	Rŭ		떡	Ttŭk	

Lee transcribes both drum rolls with ,[148] although the yuk-po syllables indicate a difference between the roll of the first and that of the second measure: the first roll is denoted by Tŭng-Tŭ-Rŭ-Rŭ, showing that the beginning of the roll is an "appoggiatura" (Tŭng) to the subsequent roll (Tŭ-Rŭ-Rŭ). The second roll (Tŭ-Rŭ-Rŭ), however, is performed without the initial Tŭng.

The second item (b) of Figure 35 is a version of Tha-ryŭng (lit., "Hit the Bell"), a popular court dance melody which is supposed to have had its origin in the music imported from T'ang China.[149] Its meter is 12/8 or 6/8.[150] According to Mr. Won Kyung Cho, of Seoul, the dancer has to wear a green costume with rainbow-colored sleeves and a crown when performing Tha-ryŭng. The yuk-po syllables of the p'iri part are:

First measure:

루	Ru	
로	Ro	
느	Nŭ	
나	Na	
네	Ne	

Second measure:

네	Ne
레	Re
레	Re
네	Ne
니	Ni
레	Re
라	Ra
레	Re
노	No
느	Nŭ

Third measure:

네	Ne
니	Ni
레	Re
라	Ra
레	Re
노	No
느	Nŭ
루	Ru
로	Ro
느	Nŭ
나	Na

The chang-ko part is not provided with yuk-po syllables.

The third item (c) of Figure 35 is a section of a piece called to-tŭ-ri.[151] The yuk-po syllables of the p'iri part[152] are:

First measure:

렌	Ren
띠	Tti
시	Shi ([illegible])
렌	Ren
띠	Tti

Second measure:

시	Shi ([illegible])
레	Re
니	Ni
레	Re
나	Na
레	Re
노	No

Second measure (cont.)

느	Nŭ
로	Ro
나	Na

The fourth item (d) of Figure 35 is called kut-kŭ-ri ("Ritual Things"). The yuk-po syllables of the p'iri part[153] are:

First measure:

노	No
나	Na
니	Ni
레	Re
나	Na

Second measure:

난	Nan
시	Shi
로	Ro
니	Ni
노	No
네	Ne
라	Ra

The yuk-po syllables of the chang-ko part are:

First measure:

덩	Tŭng	
기	Ki	
덕	Tŭk	
쿵	K'ung	
덩	Tŭng	
더	Tŭ	
러	Rŭ	

Second measure:

덩	Tŭng	
기	Ki	
덕	Tŭk	
쿵	K'ung	
덩	Tŭng	
더	Tŭ	
러	Rŭ	

Third measure (<u>Kut</u>-<u>kŭ</u>-<u>ri</u>,
rhythm of the South):

덩	<u>Tŭng</u>		덩	<u>Tŭng</u>
기	<u>Ki</u>	(♪)	드	<u>Tŭ</u>
덕	<u>Tŭk</u>		르	<u>Rŭ</u>
기	<u>Ki</u>	(♪)	르	<u>Rŭ</u>

The frequently occurring <u>yuk</u>-<u>po</u> syllables of the four <u>p'iri</u> pieces represent the following long and short notes:

Piece:
↓

(a)	long note			Ro, No Ru	Nŭ	Na			
	short note	Ru		Nŭ, Ru	Re, Shi Ni	Ni, Na	Re	Hi, Ni	
(b)	long note			Ro, No	Nŭ		Ne, Re		
	short note	Ru		Ro	Re	Ra	Na, Re Ne	Ni	
(c)	long note			No	Re	Na	Ren		Tti
	short note			Ro	Re, Nŭ		Shi, Re	Ni	
(d)	long note			No		Na			
	short note	Ra	Ne	No, Ro	Na, Shi Ni	Nan	Re	Ni	

Although Lee maintains that yuk-po cannot be considered as a solmization system because the syllables are used without order and purpose,[154] we notice that the foregoing chart does show a certain deliberate intent: syllables with dark vowels, such as u or o, represent lower sounds, with brighter vowels, a, e, or i, representing higher sounds; and, although there are a few exceptions, the general method of correlating vowel and pitch cannot be disregarded. This method is applicable to both p'iri and zither music. The highest sounds are denoted by syllables with the vowel i and by an intensified opening consonant as, for instance, in Jjing (찡), Tti (띠), and so forth.

The syllable Ttŭl (뚤 or 쑬) indicates the repetition of a note, for instance, in:

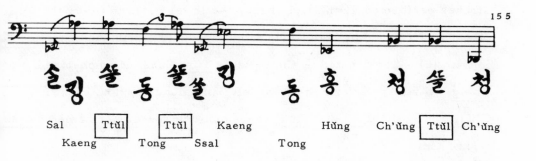

As already mentioned, in zither music appoggiaturas are denoted by combinations of syllables such as Sureng, Sareng, Sal Kaeng (Ssal Kaeng), and other similar ones. In p'iri music appoggiaturas are indicated by syllables such as Ru Ro, Hi Re, Ni Re, Shi Ru, Shi Ren, and so forth. With the exception of Shi Ru (), we find that the syllables containing bright vowels such as Hi, Ni, and occasionally Shi represent grace notes which are higher in pitch than the succeeding main notes, while syllables with dark vowels (Ru, Ro, etc.) denote grace notes lower in pitch than the succeeding main notes.

The yuk-po syllables of the chang-ko parts imitate the sounds produced on the drum and use the vowel ŭ. Only when the drummer performs a brief, dry-sounding appoggiatura-like initial stroke (succeeded by a stroke of longer duration) is the syllable Ki employed. If, after the stroke, the skin is allowed to reverberate, the syllable Tŭng is used; if the sound is stopped abruptly, Tŭk is applied. The quality of drum sounds is discernible by the syllables used: Tŭng, Ttŭng, K'ŭng, for dark, reverberating beats; Tŭ, Rŭ, for strokes which constitute drum rolls; Tŭk, Ttŭk, for dry-sounding beats.

Items (a) and (d) of Figure 35 show how the right and left hands strike the drum: the upper notes of the chang-ko line indicate the strokes performed by the right hand, the lower notes those by the left. Strokes performed by both hands simultaneously — with one exception in item (d) — are denoted by the syllable Tŭng, and, if emphasized, by Ttŭng. Strokes performed by the left hand alone are notated with K'ŭng. Tŭk (Ki-Tŭk) and Ttŭk represent dry sounds performed by the right hand.

Features related to yuk-po can be found in Japan in Shakuhachi and, to some degree, in Samisen notations.[156] Another similar system can be noticed in Bali in the notations of Kidung[157] songs. The symbols are:

Ding	Dong gedé	Dang gedé	Deng	Dung	Dang tjenik	Dong tjenik
E	F	G	A	B	c	d

Dong and Dang can be either gedé ("big," "loud") or tjenik ("small," "high"). As can be noted, neither Dong gedé and Dong tjenik, nor Dang gedé and Dang tjenik have octave relationships. This notation is more vague than the Korean yuk-po, and the date of its origin is unknown. It served as a mnemonic aid in vocal music, although occasionally the symbols were employed also in instrumental music, as, for instance, in the music of the ritual Wayang Kulit (Shadow Plays), which is performed by the Gendér Wayang orchestra, a gamelan consisting of four gendér.[158] The tones of the Gendér Wayang are called Ding, Dong, Déng, Dung, and Dang, roughly corresponding to E, F#, G#, B, and c#. These notations were scratched into palm leaves.[159] Schlager reports[160] that the vowel of each text syllable was the key for the note to be used with it. For instance, the syllables madu, containing the vowels a and u, were set to music to the tones Dang and Dung. This "literal" setting to music of the text receives little attention today.

KU-ŬM (口音, lit., "Mouth Sound")

This unusual Korean notational system uses the full lü names[161] written in Korean letters and employs these words merely for mnemonic purposes. The original significance of the lü, the indicating of absolute pitches, is completely ignored.

The origin of ku-ŭm is unknown. One can assume that the habit of using lü names freely dates back to the fifteenth century, when yul-cha-po became neglected and less cumbersome notational systems were adopted. Figure 36, following, represents a part of a Confucian hymn, Mun-myo-ak (文廟樂) notated by Cho-sŭng,[162] as preserved by the National Institute of Music at Seoul:[163]

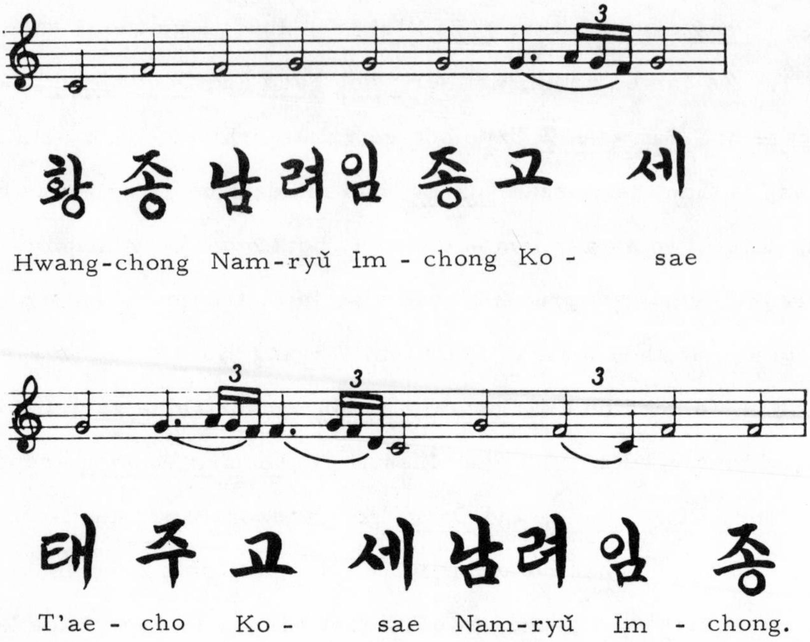

Figure 36

It will be noticed that the lü names and the notes of the melody do not tally. The actual pitches of the lü stated above should be:

Hwang-chong	C
Nan-ryŭ	A
Im-chong	G
Ko-sae	E
T'ae-cho	D

This habit of using pitch names in an indiscriminate manner shows how even musicians of the imperial court and the Confucian temple had become ignorant of the ancient significance of the lü. In addition to having a mnemonic function, these words sounded impressive to the listeners and gave a certain nimbus of learnedness to the performers.

YŬN-ŬM-PYO (連 音 標 , "Continued Sound Symbols")

Yŭn-ŭm-pyo is the only real ekphonetic notation of Korea. Its symbols do not indicate specific pitches but the rising and falling of two or more sounds in succession.

The history of yŭn-ŭm-pyo is unknown, and the available material is exceedingly scarce. The symbols of this system appear to be related to the Japanese Heike-biwa notation.[164] The symbols of yŭn-ŭm-pyo are:

\ , called nu-rŭ-nŭn-pyo (누르는표 , lit., "press down symbol"), indicating a falling of two or more notes.

/ , called tŭ-nŭn-pyo (드 는 표 , lit., "lift up symbol"), indicating a rising.

✓ , called nul-lŭ-se-nŭn-pyo (눌러세는표 , lit., "press down and rise symbol"), indicating a progression of notes from a lower to a higher level.

·✓ , called tŭn-hŭl-lim-pyo (든 흘림표 , lit., "float, shake symbol"), indicating a progression from high to low and a return to high, performed legato.

口 , called mak-nae-nŭn-pyo (막 내는표 , lit., "random produce symbol"), denoting even, level sounds.

乙 , is called chŭp-ŭ-tŭ-nŭn-pyo (접 어드는표 , lit., "fold, lift sound symbol"). The interpretation of this symbol is somewhat vague; the common reading is a slight descent followed by an ascent, generally at the end of a phrase.

) , called yŭn-ŭm-pyo (연음표 , lit., "continued sound symbol"), from which the name of this notational system is derived. It denotes the slurring of two or more successive notes.

⋮ , called pan-kak-pyo (반각표 , lit., "add another eight-beats symbol"). This symbol appears only once – in the fifth verse of the song pyŭk-sa-ch'ang (碧紗窓 , lit., "sapphire-blue lace window").[165]

The yŭn-ŭm-pyo symbols are placed at the right-hand side of the text and are used only by singers who are already acquainted with the melody. They cannot be deciphered by uninformed persons.

Figure 37, following (p. 173), represents the song Pyŭk-sa-ch'ang.[166]

The Korean text of Pyŭk-sa-ch'ang reads as follows:

Pyŭk-sa-ch'ang-i ŭ-run kŭ-nŭl nim-man-yŭk-yŭ. Pŭl-ttŭk ttwi-ŭ ttuk na-sŭ po-ni nim-ŭn a-ni o-ko. Myŭng-wŭl-i man-chŭng hŭn-tui pyŭk-o-tong chŭ-chŭn-nip-hoe pong-huang-i wa-sŭ kin-mok-ŭl hwi-ŭ-ta-ka chit-ta ta-tŭm-ŭn. Kŭ-rim chae-ro-ta. Mat-ch'o-a pam-il saet-mang-chŭng haeng-yŭ nat-i rŭn-tŭl nam u-hil pŭn-ha-yŭ-ra.

Roughly translated, the words mean:

As the sapphire-blue lace curtain at her
window trembles

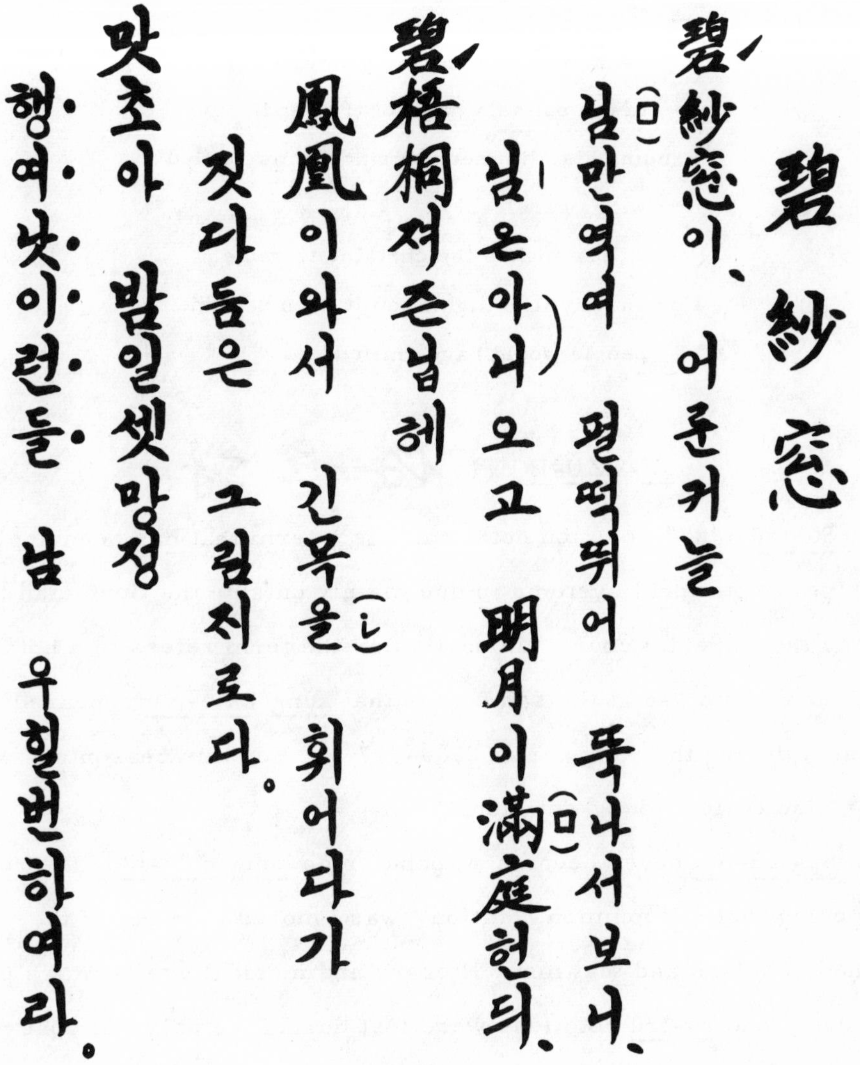
碧紗窓
碧紗窓이、어룬커늘
(口) 님만역여 펄떡뛰어 뚝나서보니、
님은아니오고 明月이 (口) 滿庭헌듸、
碧梧桐져즌닙헤
鳳凰이와서 긴목을 (ㄴ) 휘어다가
짓다듬은 그림지로다。
맛초아 밤일셋망정
행여낫이련들 남 우힐번하여라。

Figure 37

She rises quickly and leaves the room to see
whether the beloved has arrived.
But only the silver of the full moon floods
the garden.
A phoenix settles upon the glistening leaves
of the sultan's parasol tree and
Bending his slim neck to smooth his ruffled
wings carelessly
His shadow makes the curtains tremble.
Fortunately it is night; had it been daytime
people would have smiled.

SU-TZŬ-P'U (俗字譜)

Su-tzŭ-p'u, "common notation," is a term that has been applied to Chinese notational systems in use mainly outside the Confucian temple and the imperial court. In particular the term refers to a notation which came into use at the same time that kung-ch'ê-p'u appeared — probably during the Sung period (960-1279). For this reason su-tzŭ-p'u is also called "Sung-notation."

Su-tzŭ-p'u never became as popular as kung-ch'ê-p'u, the reasons being that a "common notation" was ignored by many of the learned scholars and that many literary and musical works which probably contained su-tzŭ notations were lost during the political upheavals which occurred with the change from the Sung to the Mongol-dominated Yüan period.

Courant[167] believes that the Sung-notation was employed by the Ch'itan (契丹),[168] originally a nomadic Tungus tribe which had settled in northeastern China (Liao, 遼) between 907 and 1125. The bellicose Ch'itan gradually acquired civilization, adopted Chinese customs, and became devoted students of Chinese literature. In the year 1124 the Ch'itan were driven into western Turkestan, where they were called Kara Kitan or Kitay, and, by European writers, Cathayans. These people, who had become completely assimilated by the Chinese, preserved Chinese literary works and, probably, also possessed and used one or the other form of su-tzŭ-p'u.

The symbols of su-tzŭ-p'u were subject to more variations in writing than those of any other of the Chinese notational systems. Courant assumes that the symbols were abbreviations of the lü characters; but since the graphic resemblance between the two notations is very vague, no definite conclusion as to the origin of su-tzŭ symbols can be made.

The first information concerning su-tzŭ-p'u appears in the works of the Sung philosopher Chu Hsi (朱熹, 1130-1200),[169] who compares su-tzŭ symbols with those of the (abbreviated) lü and kung-ch'ê notations.

We extend in the following table (p. 176) Chu Hsi's comparison by presenting the symbols of several su-tzŭ systems together with those of the lü and kung-ch'ê notations.

Columns 1 and 2 represent the lü and kung-ch'ê symbols respectively. Columns 3 and 8 contain su-tzŭ symbols as used by Chu-Hsi: column 3 shows the symbols as quoted by Courant,[170] column 8 shows them according to the Ch'in-lü-shuo (琴律說).[171] Columns 4 and 7 represent su-tzŭ symbols as used in the second volume of the Tz'ŭ-yüan (詞源, "Source of Poetry"), a work written in 1248 by Chang Yen (張炎).[172] Column 5 contains su-tzŭ symbols as used in the eighth volume (p. 10) of T'ien-wên-ko-ch'in-p'u-chi-ch'êng (天聞閣琴譜集成),

a collection of zither pieces in sixteen volumes, by T'ang I-ming (唐彝銘), published in 1876.[173] Column 6 shows the *su-tzŭ* symbols of Chiang K'uei (姜夔), a famous author and composer of the South Sung period (1127-1279); the symbols appear as they were in the third volume of his *Pê (pai)-shih-tao-jên-ko-ch'ü* (白石道人歌曲).[174] Along with other song cycles this work contains the *Yüeh-chiu-ko* (越九歌), (Nine) Songs of Yüeh,[175] which are notated in *lü* notation. Another group of songs in the same work (Vol. IV), called *Tzŭ-tu-ch'ü* (自度曲),[176] "Personally thought-out Songs," however, are notated in *su-tzŭ-p'u*, a system which no one has been able to satisfactorily decipher since the Yüan and Ming dynasties (Hsia Ch'êng-ch'ou).[177]

Column 9 represents *su-tzŭ* symbols of the Sung encyclopedia *Shih-lin-kuang-chi* (事林廣記), by Ch'ên Yüan Ching (陳元靚).[178] Column 10 shows the *su-tzŭ* symbols as stated by Levis.[179]

It may be of interest to quote here in free translation, together with our comments, some of the remarks of Hsia Ch'êng-ch'ou[180] concerning the origin, interpretation, and ambiguities of some of the *su-tzŭ* symbols:

厶, △, 厶⃝, (黄): according to Chang Wên Hu (張文虎),[181] this symbol is derived from the upper half of 合.

一, ㊀, 二, 丶⃝, (夾): according to the collected works of Chu Wên Kung (朱文公),[182] of the Ming period, 二 and 下一 are the same as 夷. However, 二 and 二 are mistaken for each other, as are 夷 and 夾.

絲, 厶, マ, ㊀, (仲): Chiang K'uei notates this tone with ㄣ; the same symbol is used in the Tz'ŭ-yüan. It is possible that this symbol was derived from 乚, the common script form of 上. In a commentary on 律呂 (lü-lü) it is stated that 丄 and 姑 represent the same tone. Hsia Ch'êng-ch'ou adds: "I really do not know which of these is the correct one."[183]

厶, ㄥ, ㊁, (蕤): there are various symbols to denote this tone. The music theorist Hsü Hao[184] writes that the kung-ch'ê symbol 勺 is the combination of the Sung notation symbols ㄣ and ㄥ. In the notations of Chiang K'uei 勺 is used in only two songs;[185] in other instances the symbols ㄥ, ㄣ, ㄱ, and マ, are employed.

人, ㊇, (林): Chu Hsi states that this tone was notated with 厶; according to Hsia Ch'êng-ch'ou, this is erroneous.

夊, 么, 六, ㊅, (潢): Chang Wên Hu, a music theorist of the nineteenth century and an authority on Chiang K'uei's songs, believes that this note was notated with 久, which is the script form of 六.

ゆ, ㊂, 丌, (大清): in a commentary to the Tz'ŭ-yüan this tone is notated with 可; T'ang Lan[186] believes that it has the same meaning as 尖五, which, according to Hsia Ch'êng-ch'ou, is erroneous.

ゆ, 可, 丌, ㊂, (太清): in a commentary to the Tz'ŭ-yüan this tone is notated with ㊉.

万, 万, 万, (夾清): in the Tz'ŭ-yüan this tone is notated with 高五 (d#). In music books of the Sung period[187] this note is called "tight d" (緊五), a term derived from p'i-pa playing.[188] The Ch'in-lü-shuo does not use this symbol. Occasionally the symbol ㄱ is used, but no supporting reference can be found. T'ang Lan states that with the exception of the symbols used by Chiang K'uei, all others are unreliable or incorrect.

一ㄣ , ㄅ少 , (尖一 , being the higher octave of 姑): T'ang Lan argues that this tone is incorrectly notated in the Tz'ŭ-yüan with ㄅ少 ; it should be 一少 ; Chiang K'uei uses 一ㄣ . Nevertheless, both ㄣ and 少 (radicals) are in use. Occasionally ㄣ has been considered as a rhythmic sign, which is incorrect. Only in the Pê-shih-tao-jên-ko-ch'ü of Chiang K'uei,[189] is the symbol 一ㄣ interpreted as 一 , together with 折 (chê), "possibly a rhythmic sign" (Hsia Ch'êng-ch'ou).[190] Hsia Ch'êng-ch'ou writes: "I thought that ㄣ and 少 were equivalent. Looking them up in several music books I find that 尖一, 尖上 , 尖凡, 尖尺 , 尖工 , and 尖凡 are identical with the notations in the 'Kuang Book'."[191] The question whether ㄣ may have had some rhythmic significance in notations other than the one mentioned above remains unanswered.

幺ㄣ , 幼 , 紗 , (尖上 , being the higher octave of 仲): T'ang Lan believes that the notation of this tone, 幼 , as used in the Tz'ŭ-yüan, is erroneous; it should be 紗 . T'ang states that Chen Wên Chüeh[192] corrected this symbol to 妙 .

◎ , 〈少 , (尖勾 , being the higher octave of 蕤): this is wrongly notated with 尖八 in the "Kuang Book"[193] –

it should be 尖勾.

𠆢ㄅ , 𠆢ゆ , (尖尺, being the higher octave of 林): in the Kuang Book this tone is notated with 尖∧ because ∧ is the common script form of 尺. Chang Yen in his Tz'ŭ-yüan wrongly notates this tone with 𠆢ㄢ or 𠆢ゆ.

忕 , (大凡, being the higher octave of 應): in the Tz'ŭ-yüan this tone is notated with 大住.[194] (反): this symbol occurs in neither the Tz'ŭ-yüan nor the Kuang Book. It seems that 反 is used only when the rhythm is agitated. It is possible that ㇇ is an abbreviation of 反.

And so forth. We have noticed some of the numerous discrepancies and doubtful features which first have to be clarified before this remarkable notational system can be fully deciphered. Figure 38 (p. 181), is a song by Chiang K'uei.[195] It contains a number of unknown and several composite symbols, many of which cannot be transcribed.

Although su-tzŭ-p'u never gained popularity, it had survived during the six centuries since the Sung period and occasionally still comes into use. The symbols of nineteenth-century su-tzŭ-p'u are:[196]

ㄥ	Ho	(e.g.)	C
ⓥ	Hsia Ssŭ		Db
>	Ssŭ		D
㊀	Hsia Yi		Eb
一	Yi		E
𢆶 or ㄣ	Shang		F

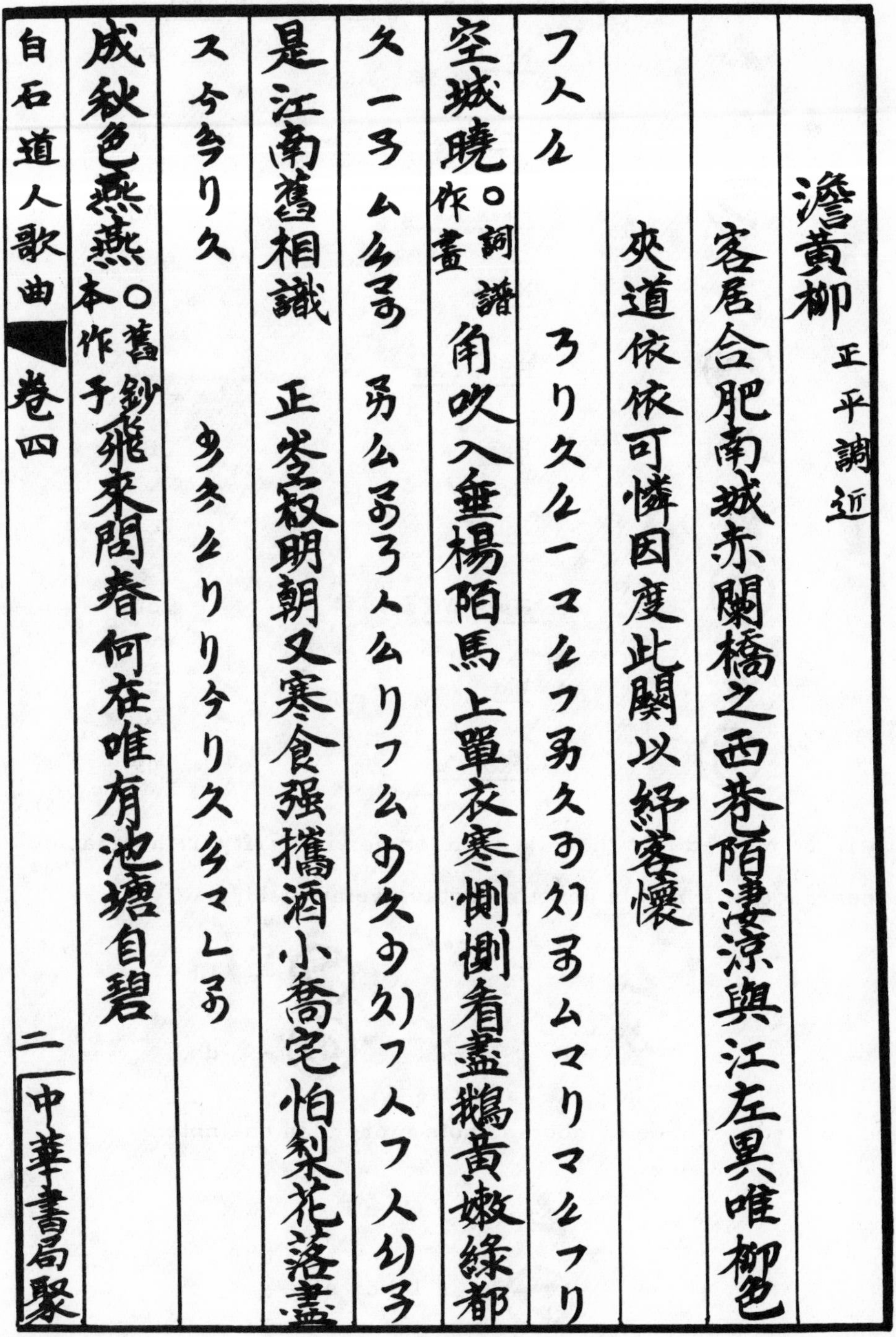

淡黃柳 正平調近

客居合肥南城赤闌橋之西巷陌淒涼與江左異唯柳色夾道依依可憐因度此闋以紓客懷

空城曉○詞譜作畫 角吹入垂楊陌馬上單衣寒惻惻看盡鵝黃嫩綠都是江南舊相識 正岑寂明朝又寒食強攜酒小喬宅怕梨花落盡成秋色燕燕○舊鈔本作子 飛來問春何在唯有池塘自碧

白石道人歌曲 卷四 二 中華書局聚

Figure 38

Symbols of nineteenth-century *su-tzŭ-p'u* (*cont.*)

	*Kou*	F#
	*Ch'ih*	G
	*Hsia Kung*	Ab
	*Kung*	A
	*Hsia Fan*	Bb
	*Fan*	B
	*Liu*	c
	*Hsia Wu*	db
	*Wu*	d
	*Kao Wu*	d#

It will be noticed that there is little or no similarity in the graphic appearance of symbols denoting octave relationships:

	– C		– Db
	– c		– db,

and so forth. Three symbols denote more than one note:

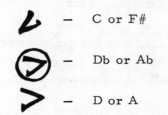

 – C or F#

 – Db or Ab

 – D or A

THE NOTATIONS OF INDIA

In India, as in many other Oriental countries, music teaching is done by rote. The teacher presents a musical phrase and the student repeats it until, after it is mastered, another phrase can be proffered. This method of instruction has its advantages because the Indian musician, before performing a rāga, has to be acquainted not only with the tone material, but with the characteristic intonations, ornaments, "strong and weak" notes and other, often minute, but highly essential details, most of which cannot be notated and have to be learned by frequent listening and imitating.

As Indian music is basically an art of improvisation, it is of little importance to the musician whether the first and the subsequent performances of a piece are literally the same. What matters is his observing all the rules and regulations of the rāga, a tightly knit framework of more or less important notes and phrases, within which the performer is expected to demonstrate his artistry by skillful improvisation. Notation which "freezes" a melody into a rigid form would not assist but hinder a performance based upon the spontaneity of improvisation.

With the exception of tone words or tone syllables used in theoretical treatises, musical notation in India did not come into widespread use until the late nineteenth century, and even then it was employed mainly for didactic, analytical, and referential purposes. At the end of the nineteenth, and particularly in the first third of the twentieth century, when the eminent Pandit V. N. Bhatkhande of Bombay successfully endeavored to unify different interpretations of rāgas into more or less standardized forms and created a satisfactory classification of the northern rāgas, the use of tone syllables developed into a notational system, a valuable tool in the hands of numerous Indian authors. As a result, the tone syllables have been more recently employed to notate not only scales and characteristic phrases, but extended pieces as well.

Like the West at the present time, India possesses only one notation, which, with a number of modifications, is used by musicians of both North and South. In the North the tone syllables are written in the Nagari script, in the South either in Nagari or in Tamil script. Muslims occasionally write the syllables in Urdu script, but the pronunciation of these syllables is basically the same throughout India.

Although Indian art music occasionally employs microtonal alterations,[197] musical notation has created no specific symbols for them. While the contemporary northern notation clearly indicates the chromatic alterations of the seven basic degrees within the octave, southern notation, as a rule, does not; it confines itself to the notation of the seven basic notes.[198] The performer who consults a notated melody before his recital already knows the tone material, the chromatic alterations, ornaments, and all the other essential details of the rāgam.[199] In order to read South Indian notation, irrespective of the fact that it may be written in Nagari or Tamil script, the knowledge of the elaborate system of the 72 Melakartas[200] of Karnatic music is essential[201]

The aim of Indian music theorists of the past was to establish workable basic scales and derive from them definitions and classifications of the multitude of other subordinate scales. At the present time North Indian musicians use as their basic scale the notes of rāga Bilaval, which is very similar to the Western major scale. South

India's basic scale, rāgam Kanakangi, expressed in Western terms, is C Db Ebb F G Ab Bbb c. The degrees of this scale are the shuddha svaras, the pure (i. e., "natural") notes.

In the past India used various basic scales, the notes of which served to define the degrees of other scales with chromatic alterations. Since theorists often were vague in defining both basic and derivative scales, misunderstandings arose. For instance, a most famous theoretical work in Indian music, the Saṅgītaratnākara by Śārṅgadeva, written in the second half of the thirteenth century, offers no clear definition of the basic scale; therefore, every scale description derived from this basic scale is vague.[202] If we consider that almost every Indian author after Śārṅgadeva used to quote from the Saṅgītaratnākara and that the Indian musician Kallinātha (fifteenth century) wrote a frequently quoted commentary (the Saṅgītaratnākaratīka) on it and – furthermore – that hundreds of authors referred to different basic scales, the confusion in theoretical matters becomes apparent.[203]

While the South Indian system of the 72 Melakarta rāgams is comparatively distinct, North Indian music, subject to numerous foreign influences, particularly the Islamic invasions, suffered considerably from this confusion until a solution was introduced first by Mohammed Rezza in 1813 (Naqmat-e-Asaphi) and finally perfected by Pandit V. N. Bhatkhande, whose works Lakshya Saṅgītam (in Sanskrit) and Hindusthani Saṅgīt Paddhati[204] employed the notes of rāga Bilaval as a basic scale and presented an efficient classification of North Indian rāgas.

NORTH INDIA: TONE SYLLABLES

If we transcribe the first note of the scale with the Western note

C, the notes of Bilaval are indicated as follows:

Tone syllable	Tone name	Western equivalent
SA (सा)	Ṣaḍja (Shadja)	C
RI (or RE) (री or रे)	Ṛṣabha (Rishabha)	D
GA (ग)	Gāndhāra	E
MA (म)	Madhyama	F
PA (प)	Pañcama (Panchama)	G
DHA (ध)	Dhaivata	A
NI (नि)	Niṣāda (Nishāda)	B

These tone syllables do not represent absolute pitches; they constitute a solmization system with a "movable do."

The notes SA and PA are never sharped or flatted. The notes RI, GA, DHA, and NI can be flatted only by a semitone and cannot be sharped as is done to their corresponding degrees in the West. The flat is indicated by a horizontal line below the syllable:

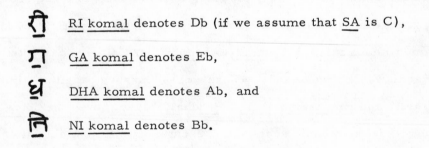

री̱ RI komal denotes Db (if we assume that SA is C),

ग̱ GA komal denotes Eb,

ध̱ DHA komal denotes Ab, and

नि̱ NI komal denotes Bb.

The only note which can be sharped by a semitone (but not flatte[d]) is MA. The high alteration is indicated by a short vertical line above the syllable: म॑ , MA tīvra (F#).

The practice of placing a line below the syllable to indicate a low alteration and a vertical line above it to indicate a high alteration exists in the notations of the vedic chant. For instance, the hymns of the oldest veda, the Rig Veda, were recited on three tones within the gamut of a third. The middle tone was called udātta (raised tone), the one below, anudātta (not a raised tone), and the upper one svarita (a resounding tone). These three tones were applied according to the meaning of the words and thus represent the ancient melody of spoken Sanskrit based upon three accents of high, medium, and low, similar to the accents of classical languages of European antiquity. The melodies were not of an independent character; each of these three tones depended upon the correct recitation of the sacred text.

Anudātta and svarita were denoted by a short horizontal line below the textual syllable and by a vertical dash above it, respectively. The udātta used for the pracaya, the "multitude" of unaccented syllables, was not marked.

In some treatises we can find terms such as MA komal, or GA tīvra, which mean nothing but MA shuddha ("pure," natural MA) and GA shuddha, the notes F and E respectively, in contrast to any altered forms that may have occurred before. Indian music theory uses terms such as atikomal, "very flat," and tīvratar, "very sharp," but musical notation has no symbols for these terms. The gamut of notes is divided into three octaves:[205] mandra saptaka, the lowest, madhya saptaka, the middle, and tāra saptaka, the highest octave.[206] Recent authors,[207] particularly in South India, have enlarged the range to five octaves, adding a very low and a very high one which are called anu mandra sthāyī and ati tāra sthāyī, respectively. The adoption of a range of five octaves seems to be the result of influences from the West. As Indian music is basically vocal, a gamut of three octaves is fully adequate. Notes of the lower octave are marked with a dot below the syllable, those of the upper octave with a dot above the syllable.

If we again transcribe SA as the note C, the Western chromatic scale can be notated as follows:

THE RHYTHMIC MODES OF NORTH AND SOUTH INDIAN MUSIC

Before discussing the notation of durational values, we must survey briefly the rhythmic modes (tālas). The modes and melody patterns of Indian rāgas find their counterparts in the rhythmic modes which, although more complex, resemble somewhat the rhythmic mod of thirteenth-century music in Europe.

Although there are numerous rhythmic modes, a perusal of notated Indian songs of the North and the South shows that only a comparatively small number of them is in frequent use. The simplicity of North Indian notation permits transcriptions into Western notation without an intimate knowledge of the rhythmic modes because the *vibhāgas* ("divisions," "bars") are clearly indicated by short vertical lines which correspond to the Western bar lines. South Indian notations do not always use dividing marks between the *vibhāgas*. Occasionally commas are used which can be interpreted as bar lines, but since commas are also used to indicate prolongations of notes, this method can create misunderstandings. However, the use of specific signs indicating the durations of shortened and extended notes facilitates the reading even if there are no bar lines; moreover, South Indian notations always state at the head of a piece the name of the rhythmic mode (*tālam*), a practice which serves the reader and transcriber as a reliable guide.

Indian *tāla* proceeds in groups of bars (*āvartas*) in which each bar may contain a different number of beats. For instance, the *āvarta* of the North Indian *Dhamār Tāl* has the following structure:

The *āvarta* of northern *Jhaptāl* is:

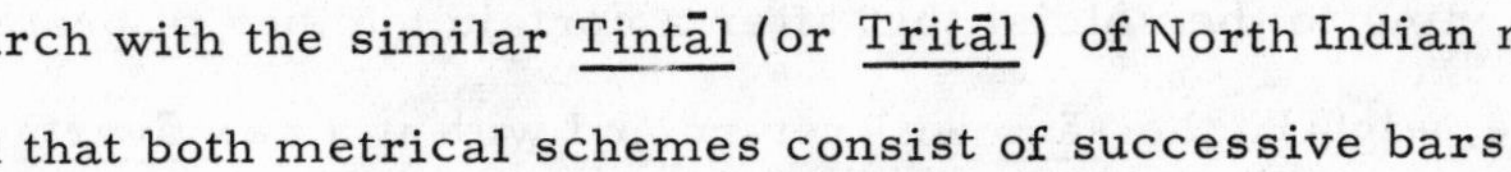

It is important to note that each *vibhāga* (bar) in an *āvarta* has a distinct significance. If we compare the simple 4/4 meter of a Western march with the similar *Tintāl* (or *Tritāl*) of North Indian music, we find that both metrical schemes consist of successive bars each containing four beats. In *Tintāl*, however, the four *vibhāgas* within an *āvarta* differ from each other in character and require specific drum beats. North Indian notation marks the beginning of each vibhāga in the following manner:

x 2 o 3

One vibhāga – in our example it is the first of the āvarta – has as its first beat the sam (lit., "complete," "total"), the musical accent of the āvarta, which is marked with an x placed below the first tone syllable. The sam shows no dynamic stress; it is the point at which soloist and accompanying drummer are expected to meet, where melody ar rhythm of singer and drummer coincide. The soloist, when reaching the sam will usually perform either the basic note (SA), or the highly important vādī (aṃśa), the predominant note of the rāga.[208] The drummer, when reaching the sam, has to perform a special beat, usually executed on both heads of the tabla pair[209] or the mridanga.[210]

If the performers, particularly after intricate elaborations both melodically and rhythmically, achieve a precise and musically satisfactory coincidence, it is acknowledged by nods and smiles from performers and audience.

The vibhāga marked with the number 2 has no particular significance; in it and in the fourth vibhāga, marked 3, the performers are free in their improvisations. The first beat of the third vibhāga is generally marked with an o. This beat is called khāli, the "empty" beat. It too is produced by a special sound on the drums and serves as a warning to the soloist that after a certain number of beats (in our example, eight), the sām will return and with it a new āvarta will begin. The khāli is most useful, particularly in complicated tānas (fiorituras and melodic variations), in which the soloist is apt to stray from the metric pattern. In short, the vibhāgas of an āvarta are frequently marked with X 2 o 3 (for instance in the northern *Tintāl* or *Tritāl*), or, if there are more than four *vibhāgas* in the *āvarta*, with X o 2 o 3 4 (for instance in the northern *Ektāl* and *Chautāl*), or with X 2 o 3 o 4 o (in northern *Ādachautāl*), or with X o 2 3 o (in the northern *Sultāl*), and so forth. Occasionally it may happen that the drummer becomes so enthusiastic in his performance of complex syncopations that the *khāli* is produced in an indistinct manner. This can mislead the soloist and the *sām* may not come off as clearly as intended with the result that angry arguments between soloist and drummer may ensue when the performance is over.

For the purpose of transcribing Indian melodies into Western notation a knowledge of the general structure of the *āvarta* will be helpful because, in order to present a clear picture of both melody and rhythm, the transcriber should write each *āvarta* on a separate line.

The following table shows the frequently used *tālas* of North Indian music:

Ādachautāl:

1	2	3	4	5	6	7	8	9	10	11	12	13	14
X		2		o		3		o		4		o	

Brāhmtāl:

1	2	3	4	5	6	7	8	9	10	11	12	13	14
X		o		2		3		o		4		5	

15	16	17	18	19	20	21	22	23	24	25	26
6		o		7		8		9		10	

27	28
o	

Chautāl:

1	2	3	4	5	6	7	8	9	10	11	12
X		o		2		o		3		4	

Dādra:

1	2	3	4	5	6
X			o		

Dhamārtāl:

1 2 3 4 5	6 7	8 9 10	11 12 13 14
X	2	o	3

Dipchandi:

1 2 3	4 5 6 7	8 9 10	11 12 13 14
X	2	o	3

Ektāl:

1 2	3 4	5 6	7 8	9 10	11 12
X	o	2	o	3	4

Jhampa:

1 2	3 4 5	6 7	8 9 10
X	2	o	3

Jhaptāl:

1 2	3 4 5	6 7	8 9 10
X	2	o	3

Jhumra:

1 2 3	4 5 6 7	8 9 10	11 12 13 14
X	2	o	3

Panjabi: (same as Tritāl)

Rūpak:

1 2 3	4 5	6 7
X	2	3

Shikar:

1 2 3 4 5 6	7 8 9 10 11 12	13 14	15 16 17
X	o	3	4

(The second vibhāga is usually not indicated by a number)

Sultāl:

1 2	3 4	5 6	7 8	9 10
X	o	2	3	o

Tilvada:

1 2 3 4	5 6 7 8	9 10 11 12	13 14 15
X	2	o	3

Tivra:

1 2 3	4 5	6 7
X	2	3

Tritāl (Tintāl):

1 2 3 4	5 6 7 8	9 10 11 12	13 14 15
X	2	o	3

The tālas Chautāl and Ektāl, Dipchandi and Jhumra, Tilvada, Tritāl, and Panjabi, and others, are structurally the same. They differ, how ever, in the types of drum beats used. For instance the basic drum beats, expressed by specific drum words, of Tilvada and Tritāl are:

	1	2	3	4	5	6	7	8
	X				2			
Tilvada:	DHA	TUKA	DHAN	DHAN	DHA	DHA	TI	TI
Tritāl:	TA	DHAN	DHAN	DHA	TA	DHAN	DHAN	DHA
	9	10	11	12	13	14	15	16
	0				3			
Tilvada:	TA	TUKA	DHAN	DHAN	DHA	DHA	DHAN	DHAN
Tritāl:	DHA	TIN	TIN	TA	TA	DHAN	DHAN	DHA

South Indian music, too, possesses a considerable wealth of rhythmical modes, many of which resemble those of the North. In contrast to the northern modes, Karnatic tālas are organized into five groups (jātis). This tendency to group rhythms and scales is characteristic of the Indian South, where the absence of foreign influences allowed the systems of rāgas and tālas to become astonishingly orderly.

Karnatic notation does not, as a rule, indicate the sam and khāli features. The performers are expected to know the various significances of the vibhāgas within the āvarta. The following chart shows the grouping of rhythmic units into jātis and tālas:

Tāla	Jāti				
	Trisra	Chatusra	Khaṇḍa	Miśra	Saṅkīrṇa
Eka	3	4	5	7	9
Rūpaka	2 + 3	2 + 4	2 + 5	2 + 7	2 + 9
Jhampa	3 + 1 + 2	4 + 1 + 2	5 + 1 + 2	7 + 1 + 2	9 + 1 + 2
Triputa	3 + 2 + 2	4 + 2 + 2	5 + 2 + 2	7 + 2 + 2	9 + 2 + 2
Matya	3 + 2 + 3	4 + 2 + 4	5 + 2 + 5	7 + 2 + 7	9 + 2 + 9
Dhruva	3+ 2+ 3+ 3	4 + 2+ 4+ 4	5+ 2+ 5+ 5	7+ 2+ 2+ 7	9+ 9+ 2+ 2
Āṭa	3+ 3+ 2+ 2	4 + 4+ 2+ 2	5+ 5+ 2+ 2	7+ 7+ 2+ 2	9+ 9+ 2+ 2

The indications trisra, chatusra, etc., refer to the number of metrical units contained in the first vibhāga: trisra, three; chatusra, four; khaṇḍa, five; miśra, seven; and saṅkīrna, nine.

The āvarta of Eka tāla possesses only one anga ("member") or vibhāga; Rūpaka tāla consists of two angas; Jhampa, Tripuṭa and Maṭya tālas consist of three angas; and Dhruva and Āṭa tālas of four.

In notated songs we observe that in certain instances the jāti of the tāla is not indicated. This method refers to specific jātis: Triputa tāla, without any jāti indication, signifies only its Trisra jāti form. Eka, Rūpaka, Maṭya, and Dhruva tālas, without jāti indications, refer always to their Chatusra jāti forms. Āṭa tāla, without jāti indication, refers only to its Khaṇḍa jāti form; and Jhampa tāla, without jāti indication, denotes only its Miśra jāti form.

One of the most popular Karnatic rhythmic modes is Ādi tāla, which is nothing else but Tripuṭa tāla in its Chatusra jāti form (4 + 2 + 2). In addition, there exist several irregular tālas, such as Chapu tāla ("Trisra jāti," 1 + 2), Chapu tāla ("Miśra jāti," 1 + 2 + 2 + 2), both frequently employed in folk and popular music. One rather complex tāla is Siṁhanandana tāla, which contains seventeen angas with a total of 100 rhythmic units in the following order: 8 + 8 + 4 + 8 + 4 + 8 + 2 + 2 + 8 + 8 + 4 + 8 + 4 + 8 + 8 + 4 + 4.

Nomenclature of Durational Values

The durations of notes are measured by fractions or multiples of the mātrā ("unit," "instant") in the North and of the laghu ("short") in the South. If we represent the mātrā (or laghu) with a quarter note the other note values are:

North	South
Anumātrā ("under-mātrā")	*Anudrutam* ("under-quick")
Ardhamātrā ("half-mātrā")	*Drutam* (*Durut*) ("quick")
Mātrā (or *Hrasva*, "short")	*Laghu* ("short")
Adhyardha (1 1/2 mātrā)	*Laghu druta(m)*
Dirgha ("long")	*Guru* ("heavy")
Ardhatisra (2 1/2 mātrās)	*Guru druta(m)*
Pluta (or *Vṛddha*, "augmented")	*Pluta(m)*
	Kākapāda(m) ("crow's foot")

Occasionally the following symbols are employed to denote the various note values of South Indian music:

∪	*Anudruta(m)*
o	*Drutam*
|	*Laghu*
8	*Guru*
|8	*Plutam*
+	*Kākapādam*

According to Sambamoorthy,[211] the signs + and — are used together with fractions (written in Arabic numerals): — $\frac{3}{4}$, for instance, indicates that the melody begins after $\frac{3}{4}$ of an *anudrutam* has passed once an *āvarta* ( in our interpretation) has begun. Similarly + shows that the melody starts with an upbeat of half of an *anudrutam* before the first beat of the *āvarta* ( in our interpretation).

These signs appear only in a few contemporary treatises and cannot be considered to be part of the generally accepted notational system of the South.

As already stated both northern and southern notations can use short vertical "bar" lines after each vibhāga. The older South Indian manuscripts, particularly those notated in Nagari script, omit bar lines altogether.

The Northern Notation of Durational Values

Each tone syllable, if not otherwise indicated, has the duration of one rhythmic unit, a mātrā. A short horizontal line placed at the right side of the syllable prolongs the note by one mātrā; two horizontal lines, one after the other, by two mātrās; and so forth:

सा 

सा- 

सा-- 

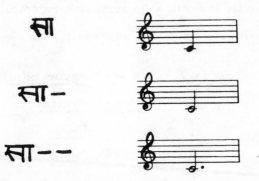

Subdivisions of a mātrā are notated by slurs placed below the tone syllables:

| ग॒ ग॒ म रे ग॒ म प म ग॒ रे सा | रे - - - |

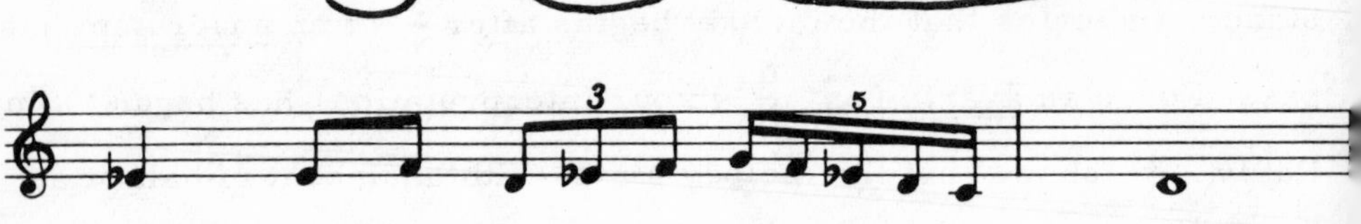

Dotted and syncopated notes are denoted by means of a comma, usual[ly] in combination with the lower slur which brackets together all notes that comprise one mātrā. For instance, | मप , प | can read  or . With the exception of rests at the beginning or end of an āvarta, North Indian notation makes no distinction between dotted notes and rests which would occur instead of the extension of the note. Occasionally the writer makes sure that the note is to be held by using a very short and thinly written horizontal line:

सा,-रे 

सा, रे, however, can also be transcribed as 

or  . म॑ग,म॑म॑ can be transcribed in four different ways:

The second version could be notated as म॑ग,-म॑म॑. रें̱

सांनि̱सां नि̱ध̱प can be only 

while रें̱ सां,नि̱सां नि̱ध̱प can read either

 or 

Appoggiaturas are indicated by placing the ornamenting note (written as a small letter) above and slightly to the left of the main note. For instance, प सां will read: 

A mīnd (glide) is notated by a slur placed above the notes involved: प नि̱ प is  ; साध़सा– is  . If a tone syllable is placed in parentheses, it means that a particular ornament is to be performed on it. For instance, (सा) will read:  or (प) ,

. If the tone material of the rāga contains Ab and F# instead of A and F, the ornament will read

.

The text is placed below the notes. If a textual syllable is to be held for two or more notes, the sign ऽ is used in the textual line in the following manner:

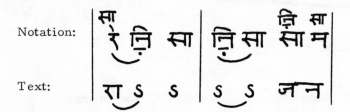

Notation:	सा रे ऩि सा	ऩि सा ऩि सा सा म
Text:	रा ऽ ऽ	ऽ ऽ जन

which reads:

Text: Ra – – – – ja – n

The sign ऽ (avagraha, lit., "separation," the mark of an interval) occasionally appears also at the beginning of an āvarta when the melody does not start with the first beat or beats. While in the notational line there is no indication of rests at the beginning of a section (sections such as sthāyī [asthayi], antara, and others),[212] the textual line shows the

Notation:	मप पगं गं
Text:	ऽ मेऽ हीऽ क

or:	रे – रे
	ऽ ज ऽ ने

If the melody begins late in the *āvarta*, for instance with the last *vibhāga*, or with only one or two beats at the end of the *āvarta*, the space preceding the actual start is left blank both in the notational and textual lines, and the bar line indicating the beginning of the last *vibhāga* is omitted. For instance:

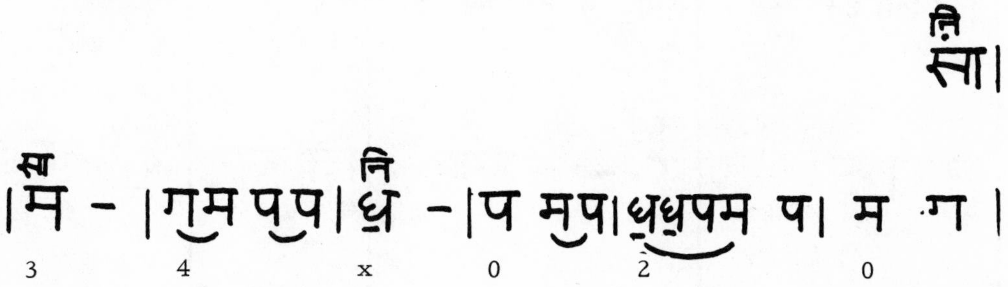

Figure 39, following (p. 200), is the first section (*sthāyī*)[213] of a song in *rāga* *Bhairav* (*Dhamārtāl*). The notes of *Bhairav* are C Db E F G Ab B c, both ascending and descending. The *vādī* is Ab, the less important *saṃvādī*, Db. On both notes heavy vibratos have to be performed.

The melody begins with the *khāli* bar which appears at the end of the line. The sequence of bars is not X 2 o 3, but 3 X 2 o, which is permissible.

The *sam* in this particular song coincides first with the first note of the scale, C, and, at its second occurrence, with Db, the *saṃvādī*. As the *vādī* is Ab, belonging to the upper half of the scale, it will appear in the second section of the song, the *antara* (which is not shown here), in which the notes of the upper half of the scale predominate.[214]

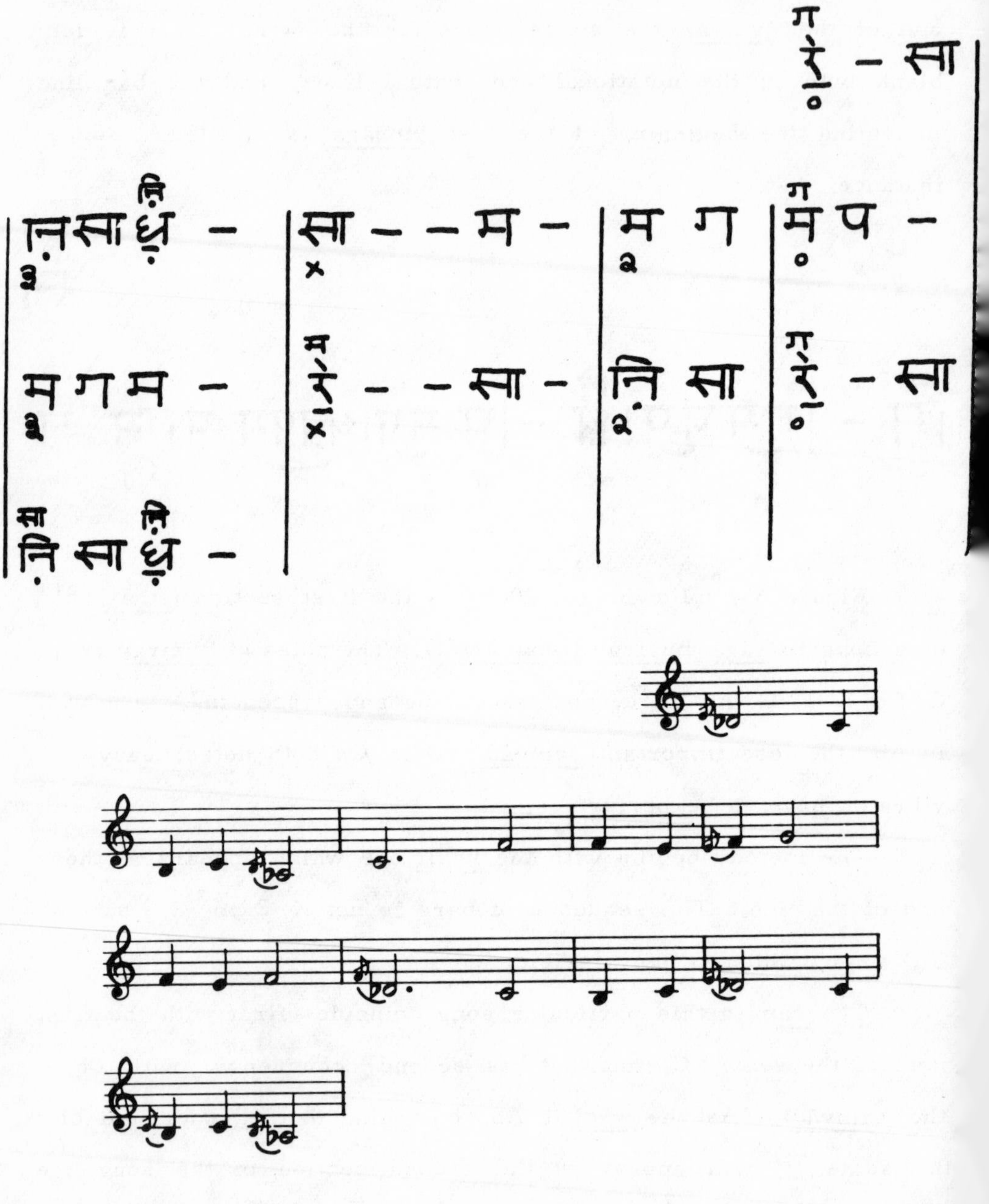

Figure 39

SOUTH INDIA: MELAS AND NOTATIONS

Although related to the northern notational system, the southern notation differs from the former in avoiding signs denoting chromatic alterations of the seven basic (shuddha) notes within the octave, by almost never indicating sam and khālī features, by frequently omitting "bar lines," and by notating durational values in a different manner.

We shall turn first to a brief consideration of the southern system of the 72 melakarta rāgams,[215] because as already stated, without this information it is impossible to read South Indian notations.

In contrast to the music of the northern half of the peninsula which, in the past, was frequently exposed to foreign influences, the system of South Indian scales has remained comparatively undisturbed and shows considerable orderliness. The word melakarta, meaning "group maker," represents a primary scale, the notes of which are the same as, or related to, the notes of a number of subordinate and derivatory scales (janya rāgams). The melakartas (melas) represent 72 straight (in contrast to certain vakra, "zig-zag" types), heptatonic (sampurna) scales which are grouped into twelve chakras ("wheels") of six melas each. The first and fifth notes (SA and PA) remain unaltered in all 72 scales. The first 36 use the pure fourth, shudda MA (F), the other 36 the augmented fourth, prati MA (F#). The first three notes, identical in the six scales of each chakra, change from the first to the sixth chakra in the following manner: C Db Ebb, C Db Eb, C Db E, C D Eb, C D E, to C D# E, respectively. The seventh to the twelfth chakras use the same notes as the first six chakras but, as stated before, change the note F to F#.

The upper three notes of the six scales of each of the twelve chakras change from Ab Bbb c, via Ab Bb c, Ab B c, A Bb c,

A B c, to A# B c, respectively. We simplify this information in the form of two charts, the first showing the notes of the lower tetrachord, the second those of the upper:

Chart I

Chakra	1:	C	Db	Ebb	F
Chakra	2:	C	Db	Eb	F
Chakra	3:	C	Db	E	F
Chakra	4:	C	D	Eb	F
Chakra	5:	C	D	E	F
Chakra	6:	C	D#	E	F
Chakra	7:	C	Db	Ebb	F#
Chakra	8:	C	Db	Eb	F#
Chakra	9:	C	Db	E	F#
Chakra	10:	C	D	Eb	F#
Chakra	11:	C	D	E	F#
Chakra	12:	C	D#	E	F#

Chart II

Chakra:															
1	2	3	4	5	6	7	8	9	10	11	12				
Rāgam															
1	7	13	19	25	31	37	43	49	55	61	67	G	Ab	Bbb	c
2	8	14	20	26	32	38	44	50	56	62	68	G	Ab	Bb	c
3	9	15	21	27	33	39	45	51	57	63	69	G	Ab	B	c
4	10	16	22	28	34	40	46	52	58	64	70	G	A	Bb	c
5	11	17	23	29	35	41	47	53	59	65	71	G	A	B	c
6	12	18	24	30	36	42	48	54	60	66	72	G	A#	B	c

If we wish to determine the notes of a certain mela we have to consult the two charts in the following way: suppose we wish to ascertain the notes of mela 48; Chart II informs us that it belongs to chakra 8. Chart I shows that the lower notes of chakra 8 are C Db Eb F#; the note G remains unaltered, and the upper four notes can be found in Chart II to the right of number 48; they are G A# B c. Thus melakarta 48 consists of the notes C Db Eb F# G A# B c.

Following is the list containing the names of the 72 melakartas and showing their organization into twelve chakras:

I. Indu Chakra
1. Kanakāngi
2. Ratnāngi
3. Gānamūrti
4. Vanaspati
5. Mānavati
6. Tanarupi

II. Netra Chakra
7. Senāvati
8. Hanumattodi
9. Dhenuka
10. Nātakapriya
11. Kokilapriya
12. Rūpavati

III. Agni Chakra
13. Gāyakapriya
14. Vakulābharanam
15. Māyāmālavagaula
16. Chakravākam
17. Suryakāntam
18. Hātakāmbari

IV. Veda Chakra
19. Jhankāradhvani
20. Natabhairavi
21. Kiravāni
22. Kharaharapriya
23. Gaurimanohari
24. Varunapriya

V. Bhana Chakra
25. Nāraranjani
26. Chārukeshi
27. Sarasāngi
28. Harikāmbhoji
29. Dhirashankarābharanam
30. Nāganāndi

VI. Rutu Chakra
31. Yāgapriya
32. Rāgavardhani
33. Gāngeyabhushani
34. Vāgadhishvari
35. Śūlini
36. Chalanāta

VII. Rishi Chakra
37. Sālagam
38. Jalārnavam
39. Jhālavarāli
40. Navanitam
41. Pāvani
42. Raghupriya

VIII. Vasu Chakra
43. Gavāmbhodi
44. Bhavapriya
45. Śubhapantuvarāli
46. Shadvidhamārgini
47. Suvarnāngi
48. Divyamani

IX. *Brahma Chakra*
49. Dhavalāmbari
50. Nāmanārāyni
51. Kāmavardhani
52. Rāmapriya
53. Gamanashrama
54. Viśvambari

X. *Disi Chakra*
55. Śyāmalāngi
56. Shanmukhapriya
57. Simhendramadhyam
58. Hemavati
59. Dharmavati
60. Nitimati

XI. *Rudra Chakra*
61. Kāntāmani
62. Rishabhapriya
63. Latāngi
64. Vāchaspati
65. Mechakalyani
66. Chitrāmbari

XII. *Aditya Chakra*
67. Sucharitra
68. Jyotisvarūpini
69. Dhātuvardhani
70. Nāsikabhūshani
71. Kosalam
72. Rasikapriya

South Indian musicians can state almost at once the number of any particular *mela* (abbr. for *melakarta*) if they are given its name or state the name if they are given the number. This surprising feat of memorizing 72 names and their numbers is based upon a comparatively simple method which can be learned by anyone acquainted with the Sanskrit alphabet (practically all Indian languages use its sequence of letters). Its consonants are grouped into the *kāṭapayādi* system — four categories, the first consisting of letters related to *ka* (the *kādinav* category), the second referring to *ṭa* (*ṭādinava*), the third to *pa* (*padinava*), and the fourth to *ya* (*yādyashṭa*):

I. *Kādinava:*	K	Kh	G	Gh	Ng	Ch	Chh	J	Jh	Jn
	1	2	3	4	5	6	7	8	9	0
II. *Ṭādinava:*	Ṭ	Ṭh	Ḍ	Ḍh	Ṇ	T	Th	D	Dh	N
	1	2	3	4	5	6	7	8	9	0
III. *Pādipancha:*	P	Ph	B	Bh	M					
	1	2	3	4	5					
IV. *Yādyashṭa:*	Y	R	L	V	Ś	Sh	S	H		
	1	2	3	4	5	6	7	8		

Most people in the South who can read and write know these four groups of letters. Even a child who has learned in school the correct sequence of the letters can find out their numbers within each group by counting the letters on his fingers. We notice that there are ten in the kādinava and ṭādinava groups, five in the pādipancha, and eight in the yādyashṭa. In the first two groups, Jn and N — the tenth letters — are not numbered with 10 but with 0.

Knowing these four groups of letters and their numbers, we are fully equipped to determine the numbers of the 72 melas. Suppose we wish to find out the number of mela Rūpavati; we take the first two consonants of the name, R and P, and note their numbers: R is 2 of the yādyashṭa, P is 1 of the pādipancha groups. This gives us two digits, 2 and 1; if we reverse the two numbers to 1 and 2, we have the correct number of Rūpavati (12).

It is of no consequence which of the four groups of letters is referred to when the number of a mela is being determined. A few more examples will illustrate this:

Melakarta rāgam:					
Kosala(m)	K	is	1	of I	1 7, reversed: 71,
	S	is	7	of IV	
Dhenuka	Dh	is	9	of II	9 0, reversed: 09,
	N	is	0	of II	
Simhendramadhyama	S	is	7	of IV	7 5, reversed: 57,
	M	is	5	of III	
Śūlini	Ś	is	5	of IV	5 3, reversed: 35.
	L	is	3	of IV	

In several instances care has to be taken about the correct spelling of a name such as Śūlini where the first letter is a Ś.

Some other difficulties arise when conjunct consonants are employed. For instance, in *Ratnāngi* the letters *R* (2 of IV) and *N* (0 of II) have to be considered. The rule is that when two conjunct consonants occur, the second letter which precedes the second vowel has to be used for counting. However, in *Chakravāka*, *Divyamani*, *Viśvambhari*, *Simhendramadhyama*, and *Chitrāmbari*, not the second but the first of the conjunct consonants has to be used.

To describe the origin of this remarkable system of *melas*, names, numbers, and letters, would require a lengthy chapter dealing with the history of South Indian music, a history which has not yet been written in its entirety.

Briefly and incompletely stated, we can assume that by the middle of the seventeenth century South Indian music had evolved most of its characteristics. We know that then the center of musical activity was Tanjore and that a musician-author of great fame, Veṅkaṭamakhin, wrote under the auspices of the court, his *Caturdaṇḍīprakāśikā* (1637 or 1660), a treatise in which a system of 72 *melakartas* is mentioned.[21]

The views about Veṅkaṭamakhin's merit of having introduced the system of the 72 *melakartas* differ considerably. T. R. Śrinivāsa Ayyaṅgār, in his introduction to the *Saṃgraha-Cūḍā-Maṇi*[217] by Govinda (eighteenth century), states that Veṅkaṭamakhin's names for the 72 *melas* were based upon the *kaṭapayādi* system, that is, upon the system which derives *melạ* numbers from the first two consonants of the name

P. Sambamoorthy in his *South Indian Music*[218] is of the opinion that Veṅkaṭamakhin's *melas* are not related to the *kaṭapayādi sankhyā*. We fully agree because numerous *mela* and *janya* names of Veṅkaṭamakhin differ from those of Govinda and from those of later systems.

During the last two centuries two systems evolved: the Kanakambari-Phenadyuti, partly different from, partly related to the list of Veṅkaṭamakhin, and another, employing mostly new mela names established by Govinda in his Saṃgraha-Cūḍā-Maṇi, the Kanakangi-Ratnangi system. The latter represents, excepting a few minor modifications, the modern system. It contains 72 krama sampurna (straight heptatonic) scales, the names of which conform with the kaṭapayādi sankhyā (kaṭapayādi numeration).

Numerous musicians and theorists have endeavored to adjust the names in order to make them conform to the numbers, an effort that has been in progress throughout the last two centuries. Today the system is well established if we take into consideration the exceptions mentioned before. The various conferences, particularly those of the Madras Music Academy, the All India Music Congresses, and the activities of the Music Department of the University of Madras have contributed considerably toward a final clarification of the complex system.

As we have mentioned before, South Indian music can be notated either in Nagari or in Tamil scripts. The Nagari script does not contain any rhythmic indications. Occasionally commas are employed at the ends of groups consisting of five to seven tone syllables which can be sung within one breath. The rhythm of the melody is indicated by an annotation at the head of the piece which states the tālam. The relationship between tone syllables and beats is regulated by the text.

The following is the beginning of a song in the first mela Kanakāngi and, according to the title annotation, should be performed in Triputa rhythm (3 + 2 + 2):

Melody: सा, निधनिसारिगारि, मगारिगारिसस, . . .

Text: चा णू र म ल्ल मु ह . . .

We notice that a long SA is written सा, a short one स, that a long RI is written री, a short one रि, and so forth. The tone syllables are not provided with dots which indicate the use of mandra and tara saptakas. As we already know, the tone material of Kanakangi is C Db Ebb F G Ab Bbb c. The melody fragment stated above can be transcribed as follows:

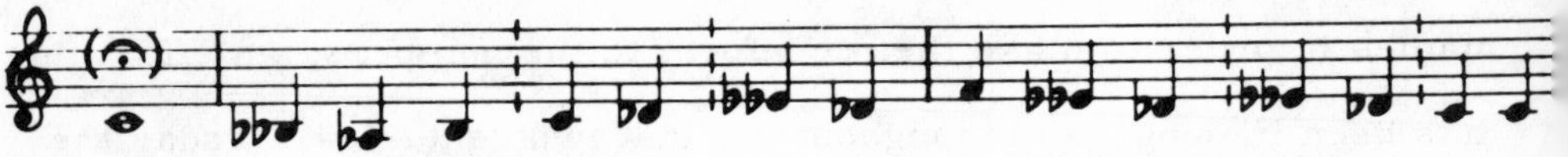

The only doubtful spot is the second SA (सा) which we transcribe as a quarter note, in order to fit it into Triputa tāla. It is, of course, possible, to lengthen the SA and shorten some of the following notes accordingly; for instance

because the notational syllables allow several interpretations as far as the rhythmic elaboration of the tāla is concerned.

The question of whether the second note (Bbb) is to be read a seventh above the first C or a second below is answered by the fact that Indian melodies, with very few exceptions, tend to use small intervallic steps.

The notational system which uses Tamil syllables is more efficient than the South Indian Nagari notation because the rhythmical features can be denoted with greater clarity. The Tamil tone syllables are:

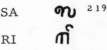

SA ஸ [219]

RI ரி

GA	க
MA	ம
PA	ப
DHA	த
NI	நி

In addition to the frequently used tone syllables a system of Telugu letters is occasionally employed. It is weak in notating rhythmical features although it uses specific letters for short and long notes. The letters of this second system are:

	Short notes (♪)	Long notes (♩)
s(a)	స	సా
r(i)	రి	రీ
g(a)	గ	గా
m(a)	మ	మా
p(a)	ప	పా
dh(a)	ధ	ధా
n(i)	ని	నీ

We shall confine our discussion to the system which employs Tamil script. Tone syllables of this system representing notes of the lowest and highest octave registers are marked with dots below or above the syllables as is done in the notational system of North India.

Although the northern mātrā and the southern laghu denote the duration of a Western quarter note, there is a difference in the concept of rhythmic unit in northern and southern music. In the North a tone syllable notated without any additional signs represents the duration of one mātrā. In the South, however, a tone syllable without any additional signs represents the duration of a "durut," a drutam, which we interpret as an eighth note. Longer note values than this rhythmic unit of a drutam have to be indicated by additional signs as shown in the following chart:

	♪	♩	♩.	𝅗𝅥	𝅗𝅥‿♪	𝅗𝅥.	𝅗𝅥.‿♪	𝅝
SA	ஸ	ஸா	ஸா,	ஸா;	ஸா;,	ஸா;;	ஸா;;,	ஸா;;;
RI	ரி	ரீ	ரீ,	ரீ;	ரீ;,	ரீ;;	ரீ;;,	ரீ;;;
GA	க	கா	கா,	கா;	கா;,	கா;;	கா;;,	கா;;;
MA	ம	மா	மா,	மா;	மா;,	மா;;	ம;;,	மா;;;
PA	ப	பா	பா,	பா;	பா;,	பா;;	பா;;,	பா;;;
DHA	த	தா	தா,	தா;	தா;,	தா;;	தா;;,	தா;;;
NI	நி	நீ	நீ,	நீ;	நீ;,	நீ;;	நீ;;,	நீ;;;

Shorter note values than an ♪ are indicated by placing short horizontal lines below the tone syllables: ரி̲ (𝅘𝅥𝅯), ரி̳ (𝅘𝅥𝅰), and so forth, or, in recent notations, by placing one or more horizontal lines above the syllables; for instance, in <u>Mela</u> <u>Dhirashankarabharanam</u> (29):

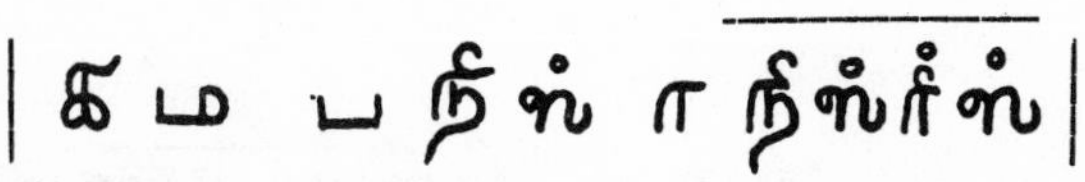

, which reads:

Rests are notated by commas and semicolons:

	Western equivalent	
,	𝄾	(1/8)
;	𝄽	(1/4)
; ,	𝄽.	(3/8)
; ;	𝄽 𝄽	(2/4)
and		
,̲	𝄿	(1/16)
,̳	𝅀	(1/32)

The notation of dotted notes uses commas:

The notation of syncopations can be observed in the following:

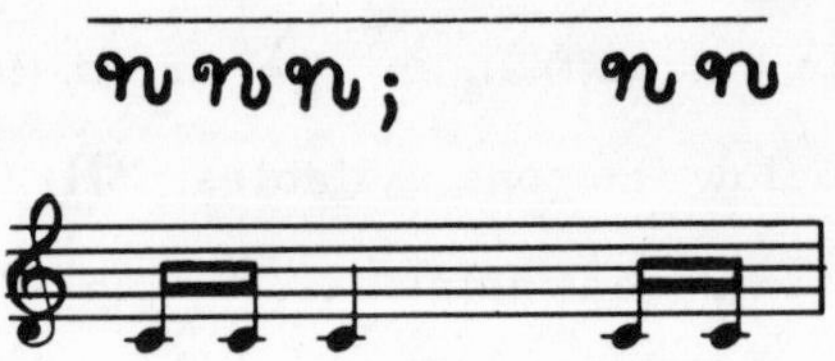

and

Figure 40, following, is the first section (pallavi) of a song in Hanumattodi, the eighth mela. Its notes are C Db Eb F G Ab Bb c, the rhythm is Āditālam, 4 + 2 + 2 (laghus), or 8 + 4 + 4 ("duruts"):

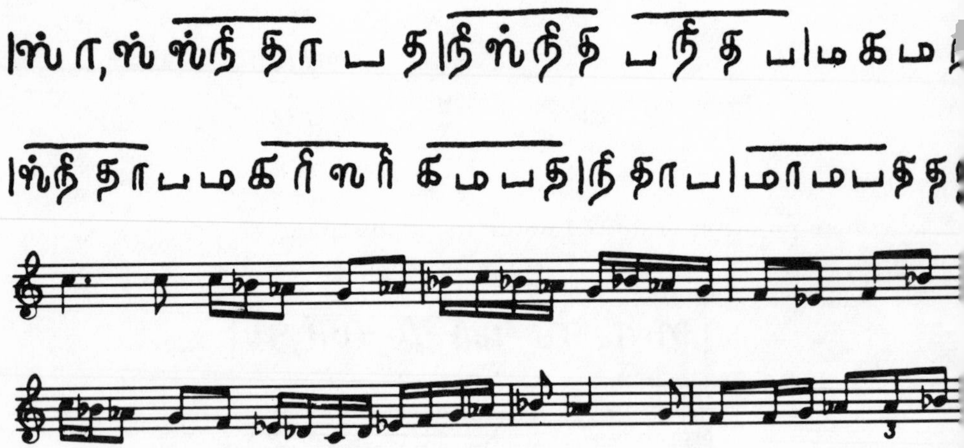

Figure 40

We know that the horizontal line above a group of notes, for instance, in $\overline{\text{ஸ்நி தா}}$, reduces the time values of the notes to half their durations. Although this group of notes could be notated as $\overline{\text{ஸ்நி}}$ தி (), South Indian musicians prefer to include the longer note in the group placed below the horizontal line by doubling its duration (தா). This method facilitates reading and avoids the risk of distorting, by misprinting, the length of the horizontal line.

If, in a subordinate rāgam, a melody uses F in descending and F# in ascending, it is notated simply as மமகரிகமபா. The notated tone syllables show no distinction between shuddha and prati MA (F#), both are indicated by ம (MA). The performer, however, knowing the required alterations, will interpret the notes in the correct manner. (In the following transcription we assume that க and ரி can be represented as E and D, respectively.)

In order to illustrate the diverse interpretations of South Indian tone syllables we show below a simple melody notated both in Nagari script (in the southern manner, without "komal" and "tīvra" indications), and in Tamil script, together with transcriptions referring to the melas Kanakāngi, Māyāmalavagaula, Hanumattodi, Harikambhoji, Kharaharapriya, Varunapriya, Dhirashankarābharanam, and Rāmapriya:

सरिगमपधपस, निधपमगरिस,

|ஸ ரி க ம ப த ப ஸ்| நி த ப ம க ரி ஸ|

Kanakāngi (1)

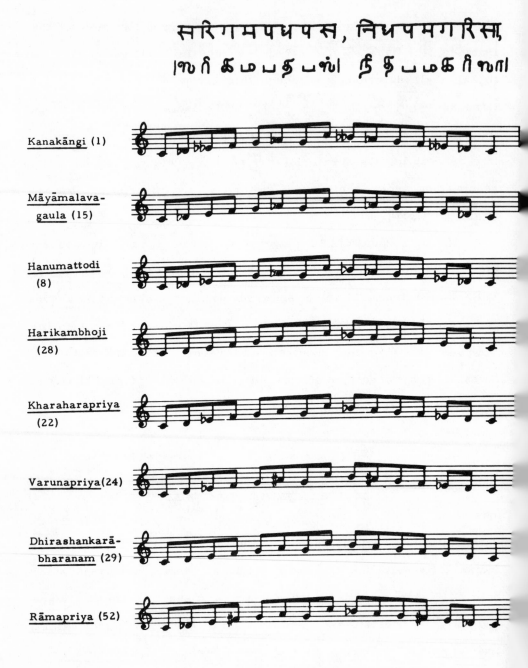

Māyāmalava-gaula (15)

Hanumattodi (8)

Harikambhoji (28)

Kharaharapriya (22)

Varunapriya (24)

Dhirashankarā-bharanam (29)

Rāmapriya (52)

Figure 41, following, is the beginning of the first part (pallavi) of a Kirtaṇam, an art song, comparable to the northern Khyāl.[220] The rāgam is Mānavati (5) and the rhythm is Āditālam. The notes of Mānavati are C Db Ebb F G A B c:

Figure 41

South Indian music theory uses separate names for three alterations of RI, GA, DHA, and NI, respectively, and two for shuddha and prati MA:

C		SA		
Db	Shuddha RI			
D, Ebb	Chatuśruti RI		or	Shuddha GA
D#, Eb	Shatśruti RI			Sādhāraṇa GA
E				Antara GA
F		Shuddha MA		
F#		Prati MA		
G		PA		
Ab	Shuddha DHA			

A, Bbb	Chatuśruti DHA	or	Shuddha NI
A#, Bb	Shatśruti DHA	or	Kaishiki NI
B			Kākali NI[221]
c		SA	

Based upon this arrangement is a procedure of altering the vowels of the tone syllables RI, GA, DHA, and NI to RA, RI, RU; GA GI, GU; DHA, DHI, DHU; and NA, NI, NU, respectively. The two MA, shuddha and prati, are denoted by MA and MI. This system is said to have had its origin with the seventeenth-century musician Govinda Dīkṣita of Tanjore. It may be of interest to note that a similar changing of the vowels was already in use in the seventh century A. D. It was found in an inscription discovered at Kuḍumiyamālai in the province of Pudukottai of the Madras Presidency.[222]

The following list demonstrates the written form of these vowel changes:

SA	ஸ			C
RA	ர			Db
RI	ரி	GA	க	D (Ebb)
RU	ரு	GI	கி	Eb
		GU	கு	E
MA	ம			F
MI	மி			F#
PA	ப			G
DHA	த			Ab
DHI	தி	NA	ந	A (Bbb)
DHU	து	NI	நி	Bb
		NU	நு	B

In treatises which use Roman letters the twelve chromatic degrees have been expressed in the following manner:

s	C
r_1	Db
r_2	D
g_1	Eb
g_2	E
m_1	F
m_2	F#

and so forth.

A note which is extended to twice the value of a tone syllable is written as a capital letter. For instance:

s r_1 G_1 m_2 r_2 S.

This would be transcribed as:

Another recent method of notating uses capital letters for the indication of the notes of mela Dhirashankarābharanam (29), which for all practical purposes is the same as the Western major scale. In this case the older basic scale of Kanakāngi is ignored and the notes of the Western major are adopted as "naturals." Chromatic alterations are shown by small letters. In this system the twelve chromatic notes are:

S	C
r	Db
R	D

Twelve Chromatic Notes (cont.)

g	Eb
G	E
M	F
m	F#
P	G
d	Ab
A	A
n	Bb
N	B

THE DRUM WORDS AND DRUM PHRASES OF NORTH INDIAN MUSIC

If we consider the term notation in its broadest sense the drum words (bols) and drum phrases (thekas) of Indian music, although not written down, may be added to the list of musical notations because the words and phrases represent a spoken and memorized system of fixed symbols which denote the various types and sequences of strokes performed by the drummers.

The drum in Indian art music has a different function from that of the drum in the West and is of infinitely greater importance. In the West the drum is used to emphasize accents or to intensify dynamic changes, or, as in Baroque music, to supply the bass part for the brass instruments. The Indian drum, however, is the "king among instruments." It accompanies the soloist (not on a subordinate level) throughout most of his performance and articulates the tāla with an amazing variety of strokes, occasionally even of great intricacy. The various drum strokes differ from each other not so much in pitch and intensity, as in quality and timbre.

Although India has produced an enormous number of drums (according to Curt Sachs, India has evolved more drums than the entire African continent), only two drum types occur in its art music: the older, the mridanga, and a type of more recent origin, the tabla pair.

The mridanga is mentioned in Sanskrit literature as early as 400 B. C. Its name means "earthen-" or "clay-drum" (Sanskrit: mṛdāṅga; Hindi: mridanga; Tamil: mritangam; Prakrit: muinga; Pali: mutingo). Legend ascribes its invention to Brahma. Ganesha, the god with an elephant head, was supposed to have played it first when Mahadeva danced to celebrate his victory over the demon Tripurasura, the heretofore invincible one.

We find the drum depicted in Buddhist sculptures in Sanchi (first century A. D.) as well as in the paintings of the Ajanta Caves (A. D. 700). The mridanga of recent and present times has a wooden corpus.[223] Tanjore in South India is the center of the mridanga makers, who use the wood of the breadfruit tree (artocarpus integrifolia) or that of the Acacia Catechu, of the pterocarpus marsupinum, and of the pterocarpus santalinum. The body of the drum has the shape of two frusta of cones linked together with their broader bases. We must add here that in most cases the profile of the mridanga is not angular but gently curved. The drum heads on both sides, of slightly unequal sizes, are held and stretched by a crisscross of leather straps. The bigger skin is tuned to SA, the basic note of the rāga to be performed, and the smaller skin may be tuned either to the upper fourth or fifth, or even to the upper octave of SA. In modern practice we often observe that the smaller skin is tuned to SA while the bigger one produces a note that has a lower pitch and is not always distinct. The tuning of the smaller (right hand) drum head is achieved by tightening the knots of the leather straps and by applying a paste consisting of flour and water[224] (āṭa) to the center of the skin, which lowers the sound to the required pitch. The larger (left hand) drum head is usually left bare; some players have the habit of occasionally applying to it a paste consisting of boiled rice, ashes, and water.

Some mridangas are provided with small, cylindrical wooden tuning blocks which are wedged between corpus and straps. By shifting the blocks up and down the pitch of the drum head can be lowered or raised, respectively.

The following, Figure 42, shows an average sized mridanga.

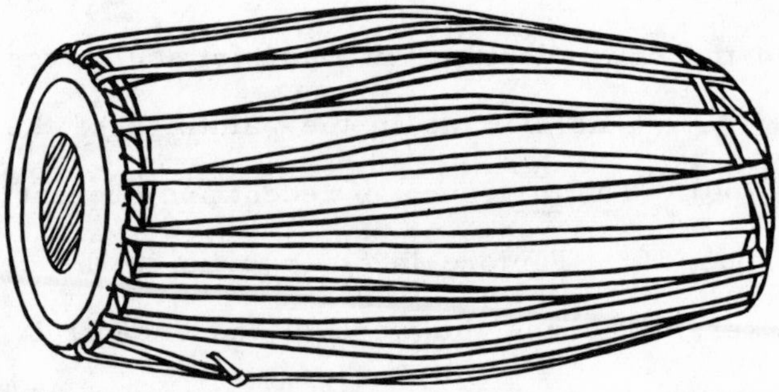

Figure 42

Today mridangas are used only in the performance of certain tālas such as Tivratāl, Sultāl, Chautāl, Dhamār Tāl, and Jhaptāl.[225] The latter tāla may be performed on the tabla pair (two small kettle drums) as well. Dhrupad[226] songs must be accompanied invariably on the mridanga, while khyāls[227] and music of lighter nature require the popular tabla pair, two small kettle drums. Both mridanga[228] and the tablas have practically the same playing technique except that the mridanga is placed horizontally in front of the drummer while the tablas stand vertically before him.

The tablas came to India with the Islamic invaders and gradually gained widespread popularity. Today they represent the most popular drum-type of India, with the exception of the southernmost districts of the peninsula, where the mridanga predominates. The prevalence of tablas, even in the South, is the reason that northern bols and thekas have found acceptance in the music of the South as well. One of the two drums, specifically called tabla[229] (Fig. 43), is played with the right hand while the other drum, called bayan ("left") or banya, is struck by the left. The corpus of the tabla is made of wood and is similar in shape to the mridanga, but smaller and shorter as shown in Figure 43.

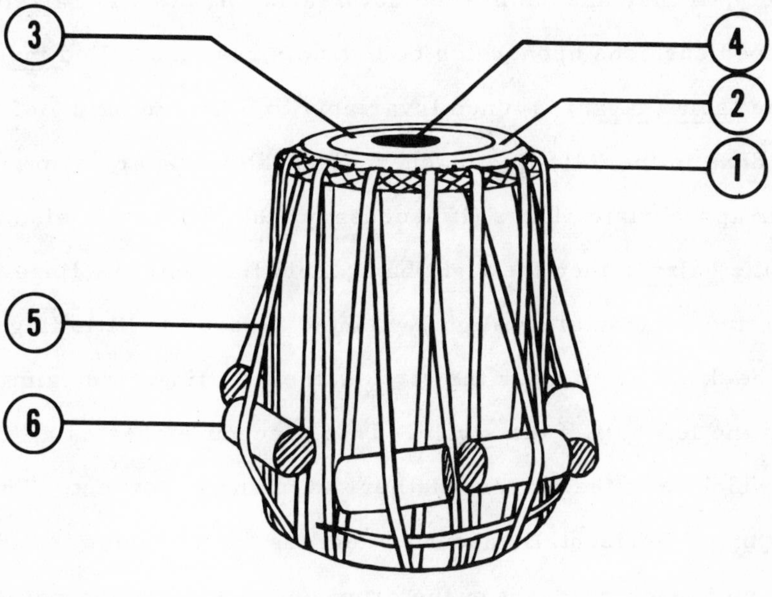

Figure 43

The drum head is called girwa or puri. The gajra (1) is a strip of leather that is twisted like a rope and holds together the tuning straps and the girwa. The got (2) is the thick leather border which covers the rim of the drum head. The rim itself is called chanti. The maidan (3) is the "open space" of the drum head, the space between the rim and the black center. The siyahi (4), which means "blackness" or "ink" is the circular patch of dried paste, more or less in the center of the drum head. The leather tuning straps (5) are the badh. The addu are six or eight small, wooden, cylindrical blocks wedged between corpus and badh. As already mentioned, the addu can be moved up and down with a hammer (usually a special hammer made of brass) in order to decrease or increase the tension of badh and drum head. (This moving of the addu is similar to the shifting of the wooden tuning blocks on some types of the mridanga.) If the addu are hammered upward, toward the drum head, the pitch of the drum is lowered and, conversely, if they are hammered downward, the pitch is raised. The ring-shaped cushions upon which both drums rest are called indhvi.

The tabla (dayan) is tuned invariably to SA. The tuning of the drum is done in the following manner: first the addus are hammered into their appropriate places (if necessary, the hammer is also applied to the gajra); then the right hand, held flat (with the fingers straight) and horizontal or slightly slanted toward the little finger, strikes the drum head; after the stroke, the fifth finger remains with its tip on the left half of the siyahi. This procedure creates a "harmonic" which tells the player whether the tuning is correct. Then the drum is turned horizontally about 90 degrees and the same testing is repeated until each quadrant of the drum head produces the correct pitch.

The corpus of the second drum of the tabla pair (bayan) has the shape of a kettle (Fig. 44). Originally it was made of clay; at the present time copper or brass is used.

If the bayan has a siyahi, the drummers place the paste (gila aṭa,

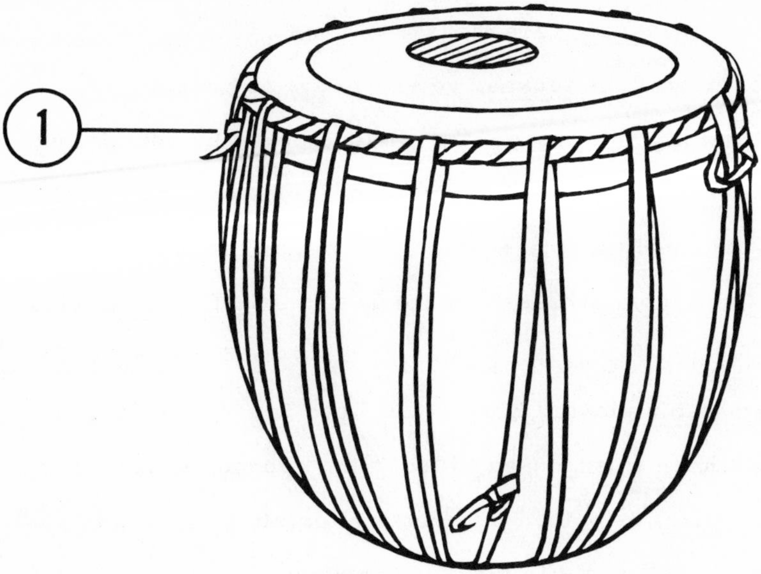

Figure 44

"wet flour") not in the center of the drum head, but slightly to one side of it. Musicians believe that the application of a small *siyahi* on the drum head of the *bayan* helps to achieve the *gunj dar*, the "echo effect." The *bayan* is tuned lower than the *tabla*; usually its sound is dull and indefinite in pitch. The *bayan* has no tuning blocks, and the tuning, if any, is done by tightening or loosening the knots in the *badh*. See (1) in Figure 44.

The tone of the two *tablas* is softer and more flexible than that of the *mridanga*. The *tālas* performed on the *tabla* pair are *Tintāl* (*Tritāl*), *Tilvada*, *Dadra*, and other popular rhythms.

As already indicated, Indian drums, with the exception of those used in primitive and folk music, are struck with one or more fingers. Some fingers may dampen the sound or create harmonics, and, in some strokes, the flat part or the heel of the hand is employed. Each drum stroke has its own name, a *bol*, and each *tāla* has its more or less fixed sequence of bols,[230] a theka. These thekas can be elaborated into numerous parands (variations).

Before describing the thekas, we shall have to consider the technique of drumming and present the various bols, the constituent elements of the thekas. We shall confine ourselves to the discussion of tabla playing because there are only a few minor differences between mridanga and tabla strokes, and today the art of tabla playing predominates by far.

The tablaji (tabla player) sits on the floor in a cross-legged fashion; the right knee is supposed to touch the ground, while the left leg (from foot to knee) is placed in a vertical or slightly oblique position. The tabla (dayan) rests in front of the right shinbone, and the bayan stands in front of the left knee of the drummer.

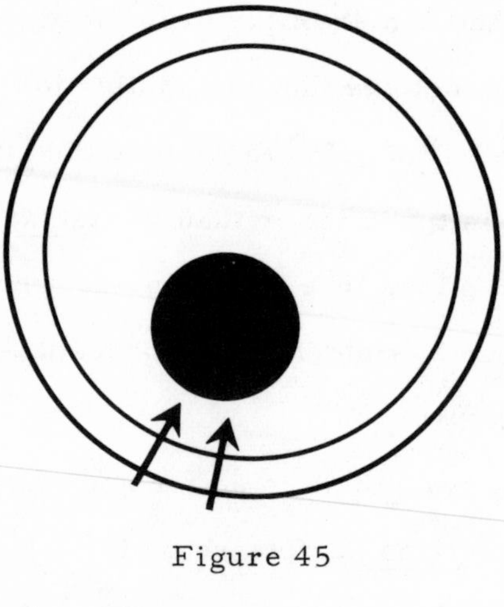

Figure 45

Two important strokes — one a version of the other — are performed on the bayan. GHE (KHE) is the bol for the so-called khula (khola) bayan, the "open bayan." It is performed by the left hand either by the second, or third finger, or by the second and third fingers held close together, striking the maidan at a spot between siyahi and chanti where the maidan is at its narrowest.

The finger (or both fingers) strikes the maidan in such a manner that the finger tip performs a movement toward the palm of the hand. The drum head is struck for a fraction of a second and then is allowed to vibrate freely. The heel of the striking (left) hand rests either on the rim of the drum, or, in a second version of GHE, it slides toward the vibrating center of the drum head and presses the maidan for a brief moment. This pressure raises the pitch of the vibrating skin. As soon as the pressure is relaxed the pitch falls. This second type of GHE is generally combined with a simultaneous stroke on the tabla.

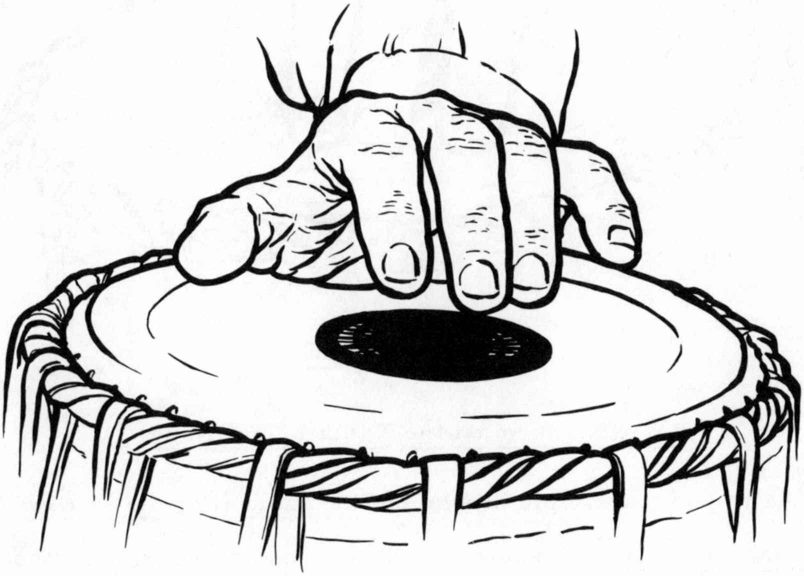

GHE

Figure 46

GE (KE), is the bol for the band bayan, the "closed bayan." The spot struck is again between siyahi and chanti (see Figure 45). When playing GE, the performer allows the heel of his left hand to remain on the rim of the drum while with his second, third, fourth, and fifth fingers slightly curved and held closely together, he strikes the maidan. All four fingers remain on the drum head after the stroke.

The thumb is bent toward the palm and thus fingers and thumb obstruct any vibrating of the drum head. The sound created is dull, dry, and "closed."

Figure 47: GE

Basic Strokes on the Tabla (Right Hand)

An important simple stroke on the Tabla (Dayan) is DIN (TIN, DIN, TIN, DI, TI). These bols all represent the same stroke. The second finger held stiffly above the drum head is thrown against the maidan and strikes it with its tip and immediately snaps back to its original position. At the same time the third finger, slightly bent, strikes the space between siyahi and maidan and remains on the drum head. The fourth and fifth fingers together with the third finger, with lesser force, fall upon the maidan and rim, respectively, and remain there. The thumb and the heel of the hand do not touch the drum.

Figure 48: DIN

TA: the tip of the second finger strikes the border line between chanti and maidan with greater force than in DIN and remains on the drum head. The third finger stays slightly lifted while the fourth and fifth fingers are set down on the maidan and rim, respectively. The heel of the hand does not touch the drum.

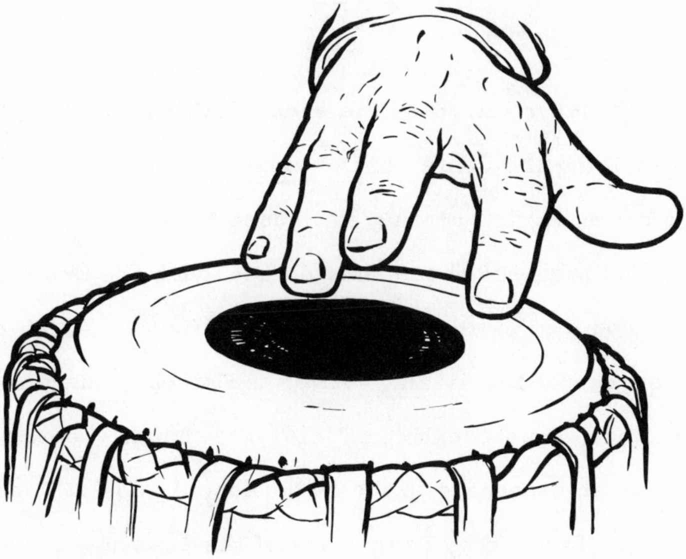

Figure 49: TA

NA is produced in the same manner as TA, but the striking force of the second finger is less marked. The tip of the straight, stiff second finger strikes only the chanti and stays there. NA is more popular with the tablajis than TA and is frequently confused with it.

NA

Figure 50

TIT (TID) is produced by the second, third, and fourth fingers jointly, all striking the center of the siyahi. These three fingers remain on the drum head, creating a "closed" (dull) sound. The thumb, fifth finger, and the heel of the hand do not touch the drum (See Fig. 51)

LA is produced by the tip of the fourth finger, which gently strikes the border of the siyahi. After the stroke, the finger remains on the drum head, thus creating a "closed" sound. Some musicians, particularly those belonging to the Delhi school, do not recognize this stroke, which is favored by drummers of the Lucknow school.

TIT

Figure 51

LA

Figure 52

DI: the flat hand is slightly curved, the fingers and the palm of the hand creating an angle of about 120 to 150 degrees. The whole hand moves in such a manner that the part of the chanti which is nearest to the player is struck by the fleshy bases of the second, third, fourth, and fifth fingers — or in some instances only by the second and third fingers. The finger tips do not touch the drum at all. The sound created is "open."

A second version of DI, performed in and around Bombay, is often called DUN (TUN) or DU (TU). It is performed in the same manner as DI except that in this version the tips of the stiffly held fingers strike the siyahi for a fraction of a second. After the stroke the drum head vibrates freely and creates a gentle, "open" sound. The bol DUN, or DU, imitates the sound very adequately.

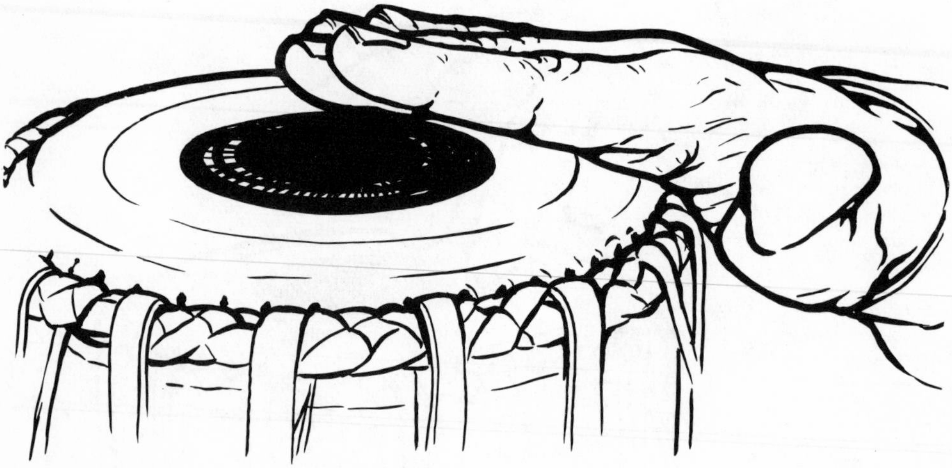

DI

Figure 53

Simple, combined strokes on the tabla and bayan are used to

produce *DHIN* (*DHIṆ*, or *DHI*). In each of these the sound is produced by a simultaneous striking of *DIN* on the *tabla* and *GHE* on the *bayan*.

DHA is produced by a simultaneous performance of *TA* on the *tabla* and *GHE* on the *bayan*.

DHIṬ (*DHID*) is produced by a simultaneous performance of *TIT* on the *tabla* and *GHE* on the *bayan*.

Special complex strokes on the *tabla* alone are used to produce the sound of *TE-ṬE*. Two strokes, each having the duration of half a

Figure 54: *TE*

mātrā (a *durut*) (♫) are required. *TE* (or *T*, त) is performed by striking the center of the *siyahi* with the tip of the third finger, which remains on the drum head for the duration of half a *mātrā*. This stroke is followed by *ṬE* (or *Ṭ*, ट), which is executed by turning the hand to the left around an imaginary horizontal axis which runs from the elbow to the tip of the third finger. While the hand turns from right to left the second finger strikes the *siyahi* with its tip. This stroke, too, has the duration of half a *mātrā*. Thumb and other fingers do not touch the drum.

TE

Figure 55

Figures 54 and 55 exaggerate the rotating movement of the hand, which is slanted to the right in TE and to the left in TE. In reality the turning is usually only a slight twist, just enough to enable the player to perform both strokes smoothly in an even tempo.

There are two other methods of performing TE-TE. One is to hold the fingers straight and rigid and roll the hand from right to left, thus allowing first the right side of the tip of the third finger, then, after the roll, the left side of the tip of the second finger to strike the center of the siyahi. The other method which must not be applied in a dugan (the fast "stretta" of a song[231]) involves rolling the hand with the rigidly held fingers from right to left, as in the previously described method, but striking the siyahi at TE with the thumb.

TE

Figure 56

TE

Figure 57

In the following bols T (त) must be performed on the siyahi:

TIT: tabla
bayan

KAT: tabla
bayan

In the following set of strokes the use of both hands on both drums is shown. Although we are still considering the strokes on the tabla, we add the bayan strokes in order to present as complete a picture as possible.

TAKAṬ: tabla
bayan

TAK: tabla
bayan

TAKA: tabla
bayan

TIRIK: tabla
bayan

TIRIKIṬ: tabla
bayan

KIṬTIK: tabla
bayan

TIṬKAT: tabla
bayan

KITIR: tabla
bayan

DHIT: tabla / bayan 

TADHIN: tabla / bayan 

TADHINNA: tabla / bayan 

TADHA: tabla / bayan 

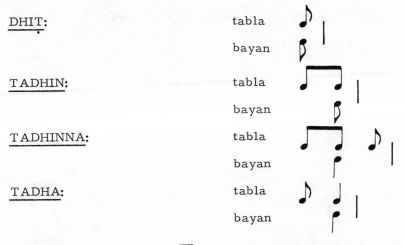

In the following bols, T (त) is to be struck on the chanti:

TIT (with two त) : the first T is to be struck on the chanti, the second on the siyahi: tabla / bayan 

TĀ: tabla / bayan 

DHADHIN: tabla / bayan 

TAG: tabla / bayan  (TA+ GE)

TIGAN: tabla / bayan 

GITA tabla / bayan 

TAT: in this bol the first T is struck on the chanti, the second on the bayan: tabla / bayan 

Whenever T (त) is followed by N (न), it is to be performed on the maidan of the tabla:

TIN: tabla / bayan

TĪN: tabla / bayan

TĪNNA (TĪNA): tabla / bayan

TINNAN: tabla / bayan

TINĪN: tabla / bayan

TINEH: tabla / bayan

TING: tabla / bayan

TINGIN: tabla / bayan

TINGAN: tabla / bayan

TINING: tabla / bayan

DỊNNA (TỊNNA): in contrast to TĪNNA (TĪNA), this bol is performed to the rhythm of two mātrās:

DI (DỊN) (Fig. 48) NA (Fig. 50)

Figure 58: *DE*

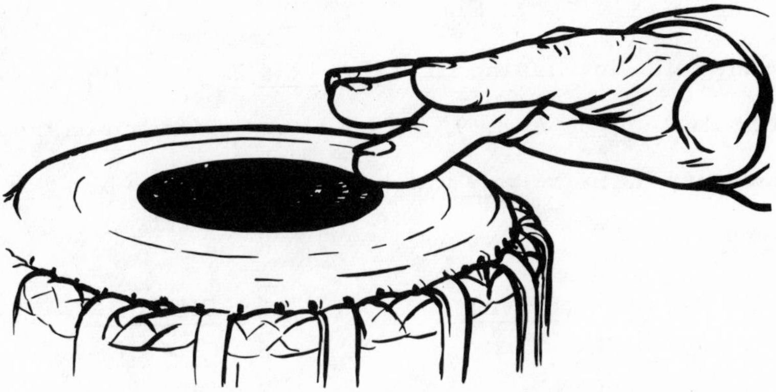

Figure 59: *NA*

DENA is performed to the rhythm of two *durut* (♫) in the following manner. First the tip of the straight second finger hits the *maidan* of the *tabla* on a spot nearest to the player in such a way that the hand, during the stroke, tilts to the left. Thus when the second finger strikes, the third, fourth, and fifth fingers are raised. As soon as the tip of the second finger has struck the maidan, it glides on the drum head to the left; then the hand tilts to the right and allows the tip of the third finger to strike the *maidan* on the same spot where the second finger had struck before. Thereby the second finger is removed from the drum head. Both phases of *DENA* are performed in a smooth, rolling movement (See above, Figs. 58 and 59).

Figure 60: TA

In the following list the first N of bols 2, 3, 4, 10, 11 and the last N of bols 1, 5, 6, 7, 8, 9, 12 are to be performed on the chanti while the other N, in the bols which have two N, is to be performed on the maidan:

1. DINA (DENA)
2. DIHIN
3. DINGIN
4. TINGIN
5. TAGIN
6. TAGHIN
7. DHAGHIN
8. GIDGIN
9. DHINA
10. DHININ
11. DHINGHIN
12. GHIDGHIN

DENENA is performed to the rhythm of three durut: DENA ♫, and NA ♪ . DENA is produced on the maidan as already illustrated, the subsequent NA on the chanti (Figs. 58, 59, and 50).

TALE is performed to the rhythm of three durut (♫ ♪) by the fifth, fourth, and second fingers in succession. First the fifth finger strikes with its tip the left side of the siyahi, then the fourth finger tip gently touches the maidan while the fifth finger is raised; after these two motions the hand rotates to the left and the tip of the second finger strikes the left side of the siyahi.

LE

Figure 61

NARE is performed to the rhythm of one mātrā and on one durut:

♩ ♪ .
NA RE

NA is produced with the tip of the second finger (Fig. 50); then RE (or RA=LA) is produced with the tip of the third finger on the edge of the siyahi (Fig. 52). The player has to keep in mind, however, that in this particular instance the third finger is to be used.

TIĪ is a variation of TIN (Fig. 48). In this bol the stroke lasts only one durut and has to be followed by a rest of one mātrā: ♪ 𝄽 |.

TIE is performed in the same manner as TIĪ but has half the duration of the former bol: 𝅘𝅥𝅯 𝄿 (Fig. 48).

TATE requires two durut: TA (Fig. 49) and TE (Fig. 54).

TATA requires two durut: TA (Fig. 49) occurs twice in succession (♫).

TATETE requires three durut: TA (Fig. 54) and TE (same as TA, Fig. 55).

DIDI requires two durut: two DI (Fig. 48) are performed in succession.

DIDINA requires three durut: DIDI (Fig. 48, twice) and NA (Fig. 50) (♫ ♪).

NANA requires two durut: NA (Fig. 50) performed twice in succession.

TADIN requires one durut and one mātrā: TA (♪ , Fig. 49) and DIN (♩ , Fig. 48).

DINANA requires three durut: DI (♪ , Fig. 48) is followed by NANA (♫ , Fig. 50, twice).

Common Combined Strokes on Tabla and Bayan

In order to simplify our explanations we place the numbers of the illustrations shown previously below the corresponding syllables of the bols:

KE NA (GE NA) tabla
47 50 bayan

TA GE tabla
49 47 bayan

NA GE tabla
50 47 bayan

KA TA tabla
47 54 bayan

(TA, the same as TE, Fig. 54, is performed without turning the hand; KA is the same as KE.)

KE TA tabla
47 49 bayan

TIN GE (DIN GE) tabla
48 47 bayan

TA GE NA tabla
49 47 59 bayan

NA GE NA — tabla
50 47 59 — bayan

TA KE TE — tabla
55 47 54 — bayan

NA KE TE — tabla
50 47 54 — bayan

TA KU — tabla
54 47 — bayan

(TA, being TE, Fig. 54, is usually performed by the third and fourth fingers jointly striking the center of the siyahi; the turning of the wrist is not required. The bol KU, the same as KE, or GE, indicates the "closed bayan," Fig. 47.)

DI GE NA (TI GE NA) — tabla
48 47 50 (or 59) — bayan

DĪ GE NA — tabla
48 47 50 (or 59) — bayan

DE NA GE NA — tabla
58 59 47 50 — bayan

TI NA GE — tabla
48 50 47 — bayan

GE DĪ — tabla
47 53 — bayan

GE DE — tabla
47 53 — bayan

DĪ GE (TĪ GE) — tabla
48 47 — bayan

DI NA GE NA (TI NA GE NA) — tabla
48 50 47 50 — bayan

KE LE DIN — tabla
47 52 48 — bayan

KE LE DI 47 52 48	tabla bayan	
KE LE TĀ NA 47 52 49 50	tabla bayan	
GE GE NA GE 47 47 50 47	tabla bayan	
KE LE 47 52	tabla bayan	
KE LE NA KE (GE LE NA GE) 47 52 50 47	tabla bayan	
TE RE KA 54 61 47	tabla bayan	

(TE and RE, the same as LE, are to be performed without the rolling movement of the hand.)

TE RE KA TA 54 62 47 54	tabla bayan	

(In this bol RE is to be performed as indicated in Fig. 62: the second finger strikes the boundary line between the siyahi and the maidan):

Figure 62: RE

KE TE 47 55	tabla bayan	

KE TE TA KA — tabla
47 55 54 47 — bayan

TE TE KA TA — tabla
54 55 47 54 — bayan

TA KA — tabla
54 47 — bayan

(TA can be substituted for TE, Fig. 55.)

TA GE — tabla
60 47 — bayan

GE TA — tabla
47 49 — bayan

GE DE GE NA — tabla
47 53 47 59 — bayan

(NA can also be performed with the fourth finger in a straight movement instead of as shown in Fig. 59, where the third finger is employed.)

GE DI NA — tabla
47 48 50 — bayan

KA DHE TE — tabla
47 54 55 — bayan
46

KE LĀ NA — tabla
47 52 50 — bayan

KE LE DHĀ — tabla
47 52 49 — bayan
46

KE LE DHA — tabla
47 52 49 — bayan
46

KE LE DHĀ NA — tabla
47 52 49 50 — bayan
46

KE LE DHIT — tabla
47 52 51 — bayan
46

KE LE ṬA KE TE
47 52 55 47 54
tabla
bayan

KE LE DỊ DỊ
47 52 48 48
tabla
bayan

KE TE RE
47 54 62
tabla
bayan

DHE ṬE
54 55
46
tabla
bayan

DHIN NĀ
48 50
46
tabla
bayan

DHỊ NA
48 50
46
tabla
bayan

DHE NE NA
58 59 50
46
tabla
bayan

DHĀ LE
49 61
46
tabla
bayan

(If DHĀLE is followed by DHITEṬE or TATEṬE, LE, Fig. 61, can be replaced by LA, Fig. 52, in order to facilitate the smooth succession of DHĀ and LA.)

DHỊ Ị̄
48
46
tabla
bayan

DHỊ E
48
46
tabla
bayan

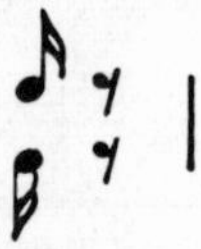

DHA TE
49 54
46
tabla
bayan

DHA DHA
49 49
46 46
tabla
bayan

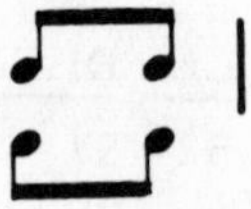

DHA TE TẸ
55 54 55
46

tabla
bayan

GHE NA
46 50

tabla
bayan

DHA GHE
49 46
46

tabla
bayan

NA GHE
50 46

tabla
bayan

DHỊ GHE
48 46
46

tabla
bayan

DHỊ̄ GHE
48 46
46

tabla
bayan

DHA GHE NA
49 46 59
46

tabla
bayan

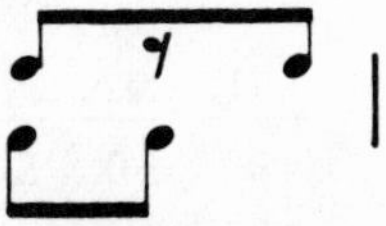

TA GHE NA
49 46 59

tabla
bayan

DHA KE TE
55 47 54
46

tabla
bayan

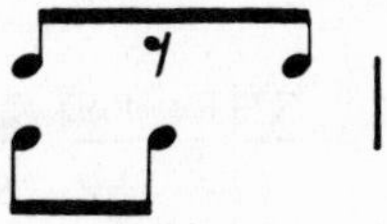

DHE GHE NA
48 46 59
46

tabla
bayan

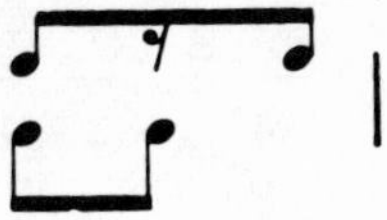

DHỊ̄ GHE NA
48 46 59
46

tabla
bayan

DHE NA GHE NA
58 59 46 50
46

tabla
bayan

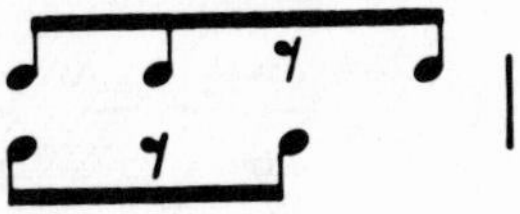

(Another method of performing DHENAGHENA is:
48 50 46 50.)
46

DHE NA GHE
48 50 46
46

tabla
bayan

GHE DE — tabla
46 53 — bayan

GHE DE GHE NA — tabla
46 53 46 59 — bayan

(NA in this bol should be performed in the same manner as in GEDEGENA; see page 243.)

KE LE DHA KE TE — tabla
47 52 55/46 47 54 — bayan

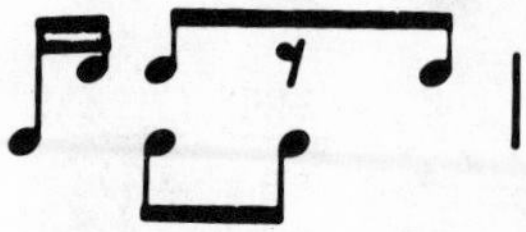

KE LE DHIN — tabla
47 52 48/46 — bayan

KE LE DHI — tabla
47 52 48/46 — bayan

DHI NA NA — tabla
48/46 50 50 — bayan

GHE GHE NA GHE — tabla
46 46 50 46 — bayan

GHE LE NA GHE — tabla
46 52 50 46 — bayan

DHE RE KE TE — tabla
54/46 62 47 54 — bayan

GHE DHĀ — tabla
46 49/46 — bayan

GHE LA NA — tabla
46 52 50 — bayan

GHE DĪ — tabla
46 48 — bayan

GHE NA GHE — tabla
46 50 46 — bayan

GHE NĀ — tabla / bayan
46 50

TA DHE NA — tabla / bayan
54 58 59
46

(TA, the same as TE, Fig. 54, is to be performed without the rotating movement of the hand.)

TA DHE NA — tabla / bayan
54 48 50
46

TA DHĀ — tabla / bayan
54 49
46

NA DHĀ — tabla / bayan
50 49
46

DHA DHIN — tabla / bayan
49 48
46 46

DHI DHI NA — tabla / bayan
48 48 50
46 46

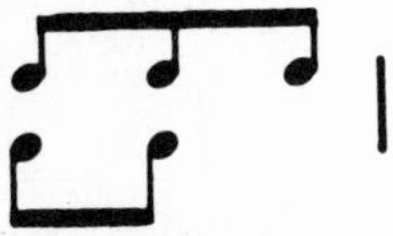

DHI DHI — tabla / bayan
48 48
46 46

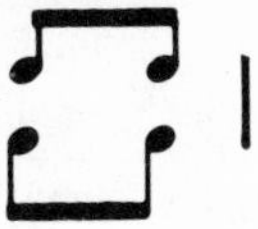

GHE NA LA NA (GHINALANA) — tabla / bayan
46 50 52 50

We may add that musicians often use the bols NA (Fig. 50) and TA (Fig. 49) in strokes which have the duration of one mātrā. TA (Fig. 60) is generally used to indicate the sām. The bols NA (Fig. 59) and TA (Figs. 54, 55, and 57) frequently occur in strokes which have the duration of one durut.

Occasionally the spellings of certain bols cause confusion: DIN may become TU+GHE, or TU alone; GA may become KA, KI, KE, and

GHE. DDHI can be GHE+ṬA (ट), or GHE+TIN; and DHA occasionally becomes NA+GHE. TTI (ति) is performed by striking the siyahi of the tabla with the tips of the second, third, fourth, and fifth fingers close together.

After these introductory remarks we are ready to consider the thekas, the "drum phrases" or chains of bols within an āvarta. In order to maintain uniformity of presentation, we shall begin each theka with the sām.

The Thekas

TINTĀL (TRITĀL, TETĀLA), on tablas:

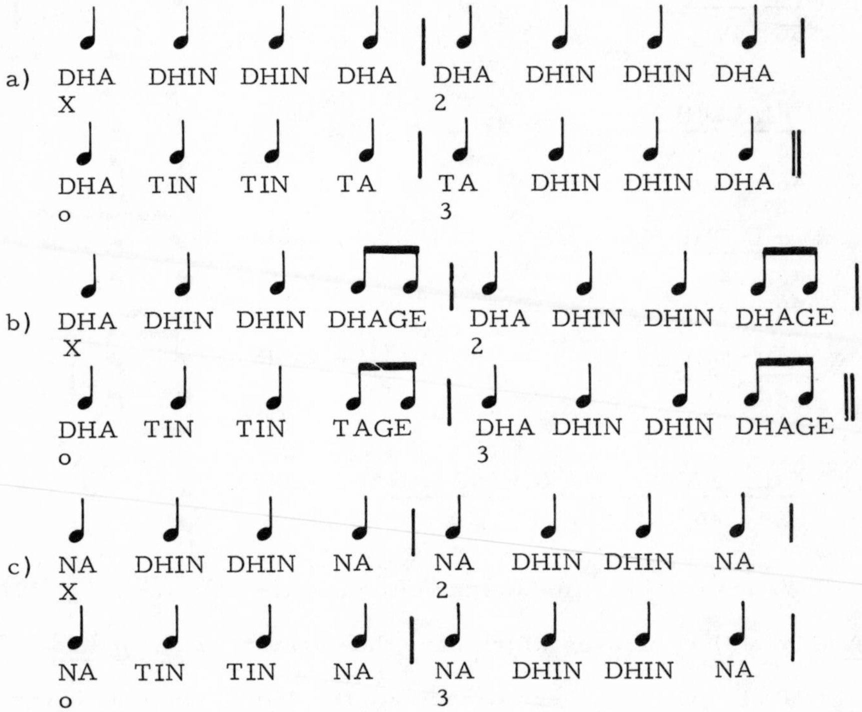

The third of these three versions, (c), is an amateurish way of drumming Tintāl. Musicians, if they wish to have a joke, order the tablaji to play his "famous" Tintāl theka of NA DHIN DHIN NA. The drummer will, of course, begin with DHA DHIN DHIN DHA.

Qaidas[232] in Tintāl (Tritāl)

A qaida is a fixed elaboration of a tāla which provides the basic material for complex variations. A very simple qaida in Tritāl is:

After having performed this qaida, the drummer returns to the original theka DHA DHIN DHIN DHA.

Occasionally two qaidas are performed in succession. The term for this procedure is dohra.[233] Thus a dohra always extends for two āvartas. The bols and rhythmic structure remain unaltered except that if the first āvarta begins with an open DHA, the second āvarta will begin with a closed TA.

A palta[234] is a variation of a dohra. It usually shows different bols only in one vibhāga, while the rest of the āvarta remains the same as in the dohra. Sometimes one can observe a palta of a palta, that is, a palta which is altered either in one or two vibhāgas.

A qaida (in Tritāl), its dohra and palta, and a palta of the palta are shown in the following examples:

QAIDA

DOHRA

DHA TEṬEKATA DHA KATA GHENA KATA GHENA KATA GHENA
X

DHA TEṬEKATA DHA KATA GHENA KATA GHENA DỊNA KENA (DHA)
o X

TA TEṬEKATA TA KATA GHENA KATA GHENA KATA GHENA
X

DHA TEṬEKATA DHA KATA GHENA KATA GHENA DỊNA KENA (DHA)
o X

PALTA

DHA TEṬEKATA DHA KATA GHENA KATA DHA KATA GHENA
X

DHA TEṬEKATA DHA KATA GHENA KATA GHENA DỊNA KENA (DHA)
o X

PALTA OF PALTA

DHA TEṬEKATA DHA KATA GHENA DINA KENA DHA TEṬEKATA DHA
X

KATA GHENA DỊNA KENA KATA GHENA DỊNA KENA
o

TA TEṬEKATA TA KATA GENA DINA KENA DHA TEṬEKATA DHA
X

KATA GHENA DỊNA KENA KATA GHENA DỊNA KENA (DHA)
o X

In addition to the numerous *qaidas* and their modifications we have to mention the *gat* and *gat paran*. The *gat* is a variation performed at twice the original speed, and the *gat paran* is four times faster than the original. Examples of two *gat* and one *gat paran* are shown below:

GAT (in *Tritāl*)

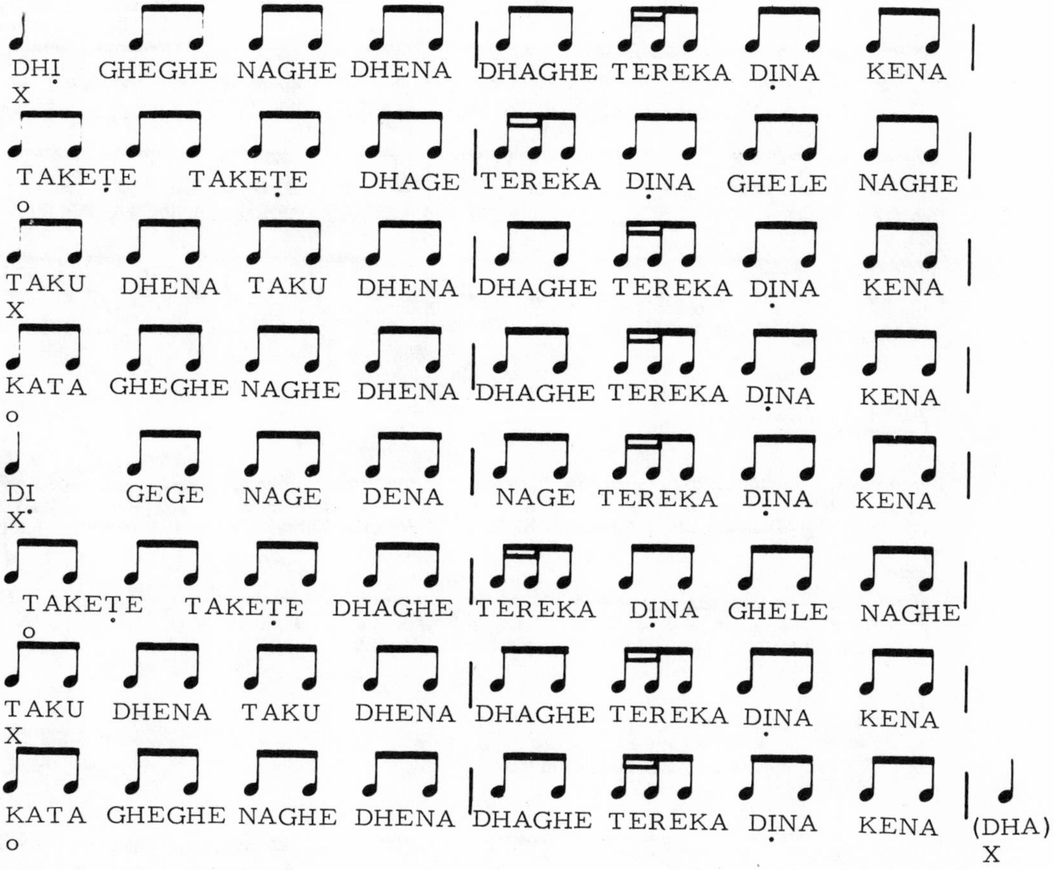

Another *gat* in *Tritāl* is:

GAT

KATA GHEGHE NAGHE DHENA DHAGHE TEREKA DINA KENA
X
DHAGHE TEREKA DHINA GHENA DHAGHE TEREKA DINA KENA
o
DIN TA KELE TA TAGE TEREKA DINA KENA
X
TENA GENA DHENAGHENA NAGENA DHAGHE TEREKA DINA KENA
o
KATA GHEGHE NA GHE DHENA DHAGHE TEREKA DINA KENA
X
DHAGHE TEREKA DHINA GHENA DHAGHE TEREKA DINA KENA
o

GAT PARAN

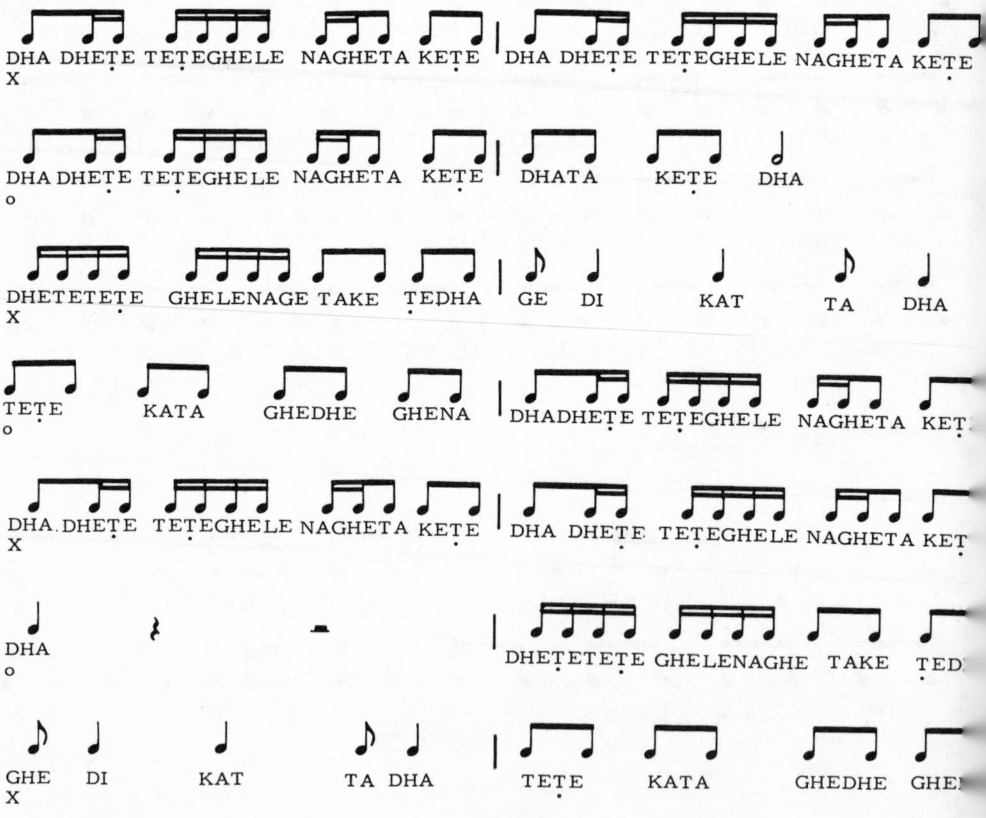
DHA DHETE TETEGHELE NAGHETA KETE DHA DHETE TETEGHELE NAGHETA KETE
X
DHA DHETE TETEGHELE NAGHETA KETE DHATA KETE DHA
o
DHETETETE GHELENAGE TAKE TEDHA GE DI KAT TA DHA
X
TETE KATA GHEDHE GHENA DHADHETE TETEGHELE NAGHETA
o
DHA DHETE TETEGHELE NAGHETA KETE DHA DHETE TETEGHELE NAGHETA
X
DHA
o
DHETETETE GHELENAGHE TAKE
GHE DI KAT TA DHA TETE KATA GHEDHE
X

DHATEṬE TEṬEGHELE NAGHETA KEṬE DHADHEṬE TEṬEGHELE NAGHETA KEṬE
o
DHA DHEṬE TEṬEGHELE NAGHETA KEṬE DHA
X
DHEṬETEṬE GHELENAGHE TAKE ṬEDHA GHE DI KAT TA DHA
o
TEṬE KATA GHEDHE GHENA DHA DHEṬE TEṬEGHELE NAGHETA KEṬE
X
DHA DHEṬE TEṬEGHELE NAGHETA KEṬE DHADHEṬE TEṬEGHELE NAGHETA KEṬE
TA TEṬE TEṬEKELE NAKETA KEṬE TA TEṬE TEṬEKELE NAKETA KEṬE
TA TEṬE TEṬEKELE NAKETA KEṬE TATA KEṬE TA
DHEṬETEṬE GHELENAGHE TAKE ṬEDHA GHE DI KAT TA DHA
EṬE KATA GHEDHE GHENA DHA DHEṬE TEṬEGHELE NAGHETA KEṬE
HA DHEṬE TEṬEGHELE NAGHETA KEṬE DHA DHEṬE TEṬEGHELE NAGHETA KEṬE
HA DHEṬETEṬE GHELENAGHE TAKE ṬEDHA
HE DI KAT TA DHA TEṬE KATA GHEDHE GHENA
HA DHEṬE TEṬEGHELE NAGHETA KEṬE DHA DHEṬE TEṬEGHELE NAGHETA KEṬE

THEKA OF ADACHAUTĀL (on tablas):

THEKA OF BRĀHMTĀL (on mridanga or tablas):

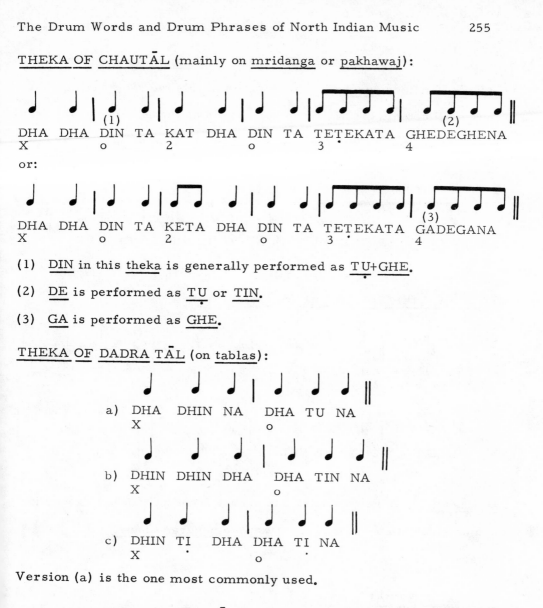

THEKA OF CHAUTĀL (mainly on mridanga or pakhawaj):

DHA DHA | DIN(1) TA | KAT DHA | DIN TA | TEṬEKATA | GHEDEGHENA(2) ||
X . . . o . . . 2 . . . o . . . 3 . . . 4

or:

DHA DHA | DIN TA | KETA DHA | DIN TA | TEṬEKATA | GADEGANA(3) ||
X . . . o . . . 2 . . . o . . . 3 . . . 4

(1) DIN in this theka is generally performed as ṬU+GHE.

(2) DE is performed as ṬU or TIN.

(3) GA is performed as GHE.

THEKA OF DADRA TĀL (on tablas):

a) DHA DHIN NA | DHA TU NA ||
X . . . o

b) DHIN DHIN DHA | DHA TIN NA ||
X . . . o

c) DHIN ṬI DHA | DHA ṬI NA ||
X . . . o

Version (a) is the one most commonly used.

THEKA OF DHAMĀR TĀL is performed mainly on mridanga and pakhawaj, although at the present time tablas are occasionally used.

a) KA DDHI TA DHI TA | TA | TA KI ṬA | KI ṬA TA ||
X . . . 2 . o . . . 3

b) KA DDHI TA DHI TA | DHA | GA TTI ṬA | TA ṬA TA ||
X . . . 2 . o . . . 3

DDHI is performed as GHE+ṬA (or ṬE, ट).

Occasionally musicians hold the view that *Dhamār Tāl* has only seven *mātrās* (fourteen *duruts*). The effect is nearly the same because the *theka* will contain the same number of *bols* as in the version with fourteen *mātrās*; the only difference is that in the seven-*mātrā theka* the *bols* are slightly altered to:

KA DHE TE DHE TE | DHA | GHE DỊ | DỊ TA
X | 2 | o | 3

THEKA OF DIPCHANDI TĀL (on *tablas*):

a) DHỊ DHỊ | DHA GA TỊ | TA TIN | DHA GHA DHỊ
X | 2 | o | 3

or

b) DHA DHIN | DHA DHA DHIN | TA TIN | DHA DHA DHIN
X | 2 | o | 3

Dipchandi Tāl is very popular and occurs frequently in light songs in conjunction with various *rāgas* – *Kafi*, *Sindhura*, *Khamaj*, *Pilu*, and others.

THEKA OF EKTĀL (on *tablas*)

The *theka* of this popular *tāla* can be represented in two different ways: (a) as shown on page 191, and (b) with four *mātrās* in each of the three *vibhāgas*, without a *khali* beat. The omission of *khali* indicates that the *theka* is used in light music where *sām* and *khali* are of little importance. Below follow three *thekas* of *Ektāl* in their common, popular forms (type b):

KAT is performed on the bayan by striking the rim opposite the player with the tips of the second, third, fourth, and fifth fingers joined. TRAKA (actually TEREKA) is performed on the tabla by striking the siyahi first with the fourth, then the third, and lastly with the second finger tip. The heel of the hand does not touch the drum:  .

THEKA OF JHAMPA TĀLA (JHAPTĀL) (tabla version):

The mridanga (or pakhawaj) theka of this tāla differs considerably from the tabla theka. It is:

GI, KI, and KA denote the same "closed" stroke on the larger drum head; DHA and TA are performed in the same manner as on the tablas.

THEKA OF JHUMRA (on tablas):

THEKA OF PANJABI TĀLA (on tablas):

This tāla is a fast variant of Tintāl (Tritāl); it is generally used in light music. The difference between Panjabi and Tintāl can be observed in the bols:

THEKA OF RŪPAK (RŪPAKA TĀLA) (on tablas):

THEKA OF SHIKAR TĀLA (on pakhawaj or mridanga):

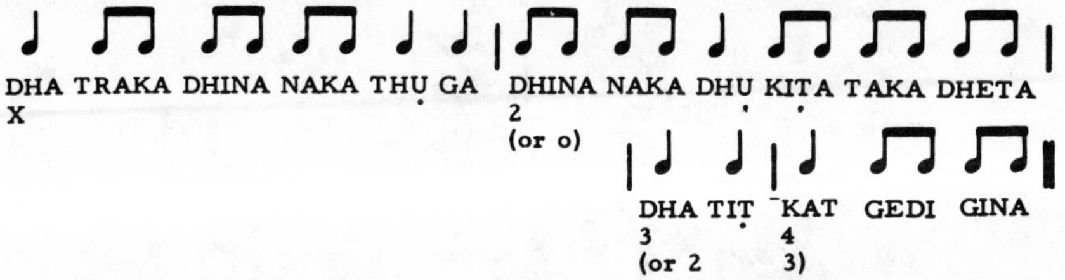

THU AND DHU are performed as TU+GHE; DHE is DHI, and GI is GE.

THEKA OF SULTĀL (on pakhawaj or mridanga):

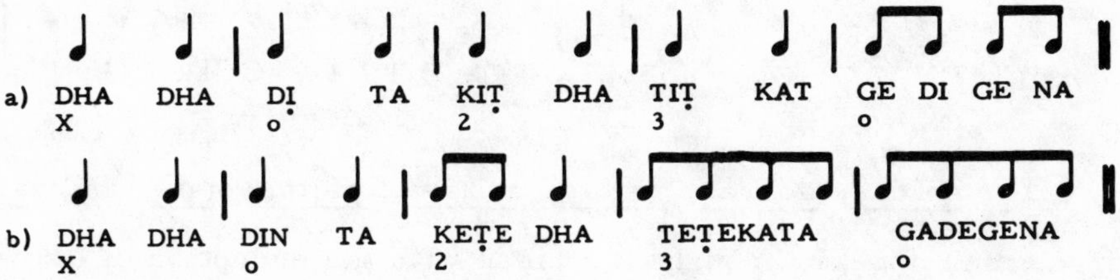

THEKA OF TILVADA TĀLA (TIRAMBA TĀLA) (on tablas):

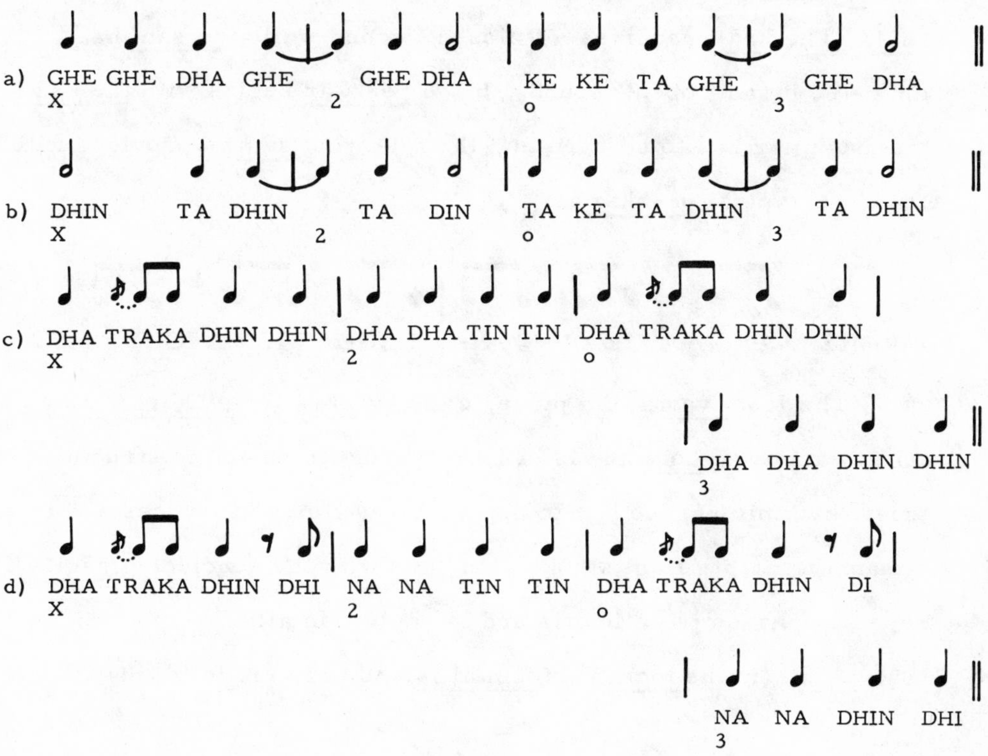

THEKA OF TIVRA TĀLA (on *tablas*):

a) DHIN DHIN DHA DHA TIN TIN NA
X 2 3

b) DHIN NA TEREKA DHIN NA TEṬE KATA
X 2 3

mridanga (*pakhawaj*) *theka*:

c) DHA DỊ TA TIT KAT GEDI GENA
X 2 3

The *qaidas*, *dohras*, *paltas*, *paltas* of *paltas*, *gats*, and *gat parans* may appear throughout a piece with the exception of its beginning and its end. The opening drum phrase, called *peshkar*, is a particular *qaida* (or half a *qaida*) which can begin with the *sām* or the *khāli*. The *khāli* requires a "closed" sound while the *sām* has to be indicated by an "open" sound. If the *peshkar* begins with the *khāli*, the drummer has to be sure that the following *sām* is provided with a DHA. A typical *peshkar* is:

DHI GHE NA DHA GHE DI NA NA TI GE NA DHA GHE DI NA NA

The last *āvarta* of a piece, called *mohra* (or *mukhra*), may contain a variety of *bols* and is of interest for its rhythmic structure: a brief rhythmic phrase has to appear three times in succession in such a manner that its final stroke coincides with the concluding *sām*. This repeated phrase is called *tia* and is applied in all *tālas*.

A *tia* (in the *mohra*) of *Tintāl* is shown in the following:

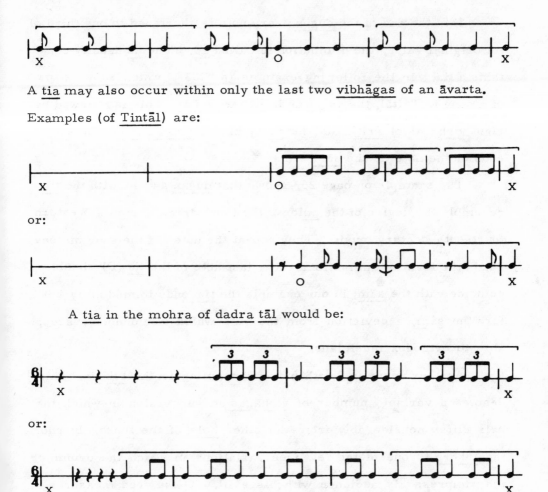

A tia may also occur within only the last two vibhāgas of an āvarta. Examples (of Tintāl) are:

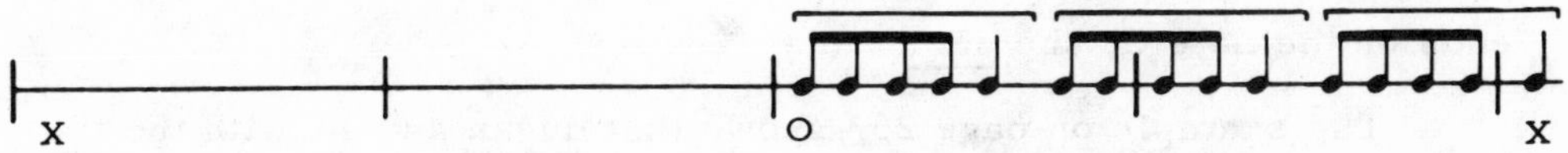

or:

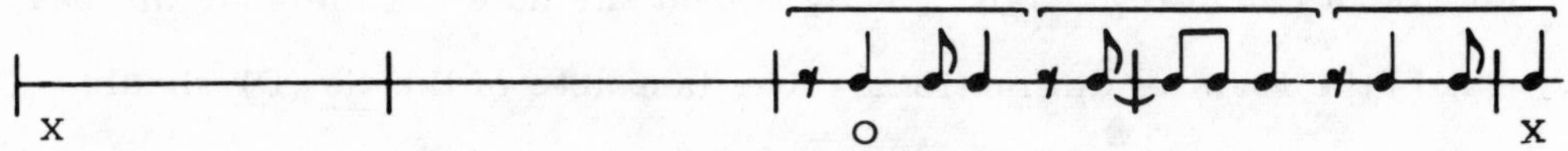

A tia in the mohra of dadra tāl would be:

or:

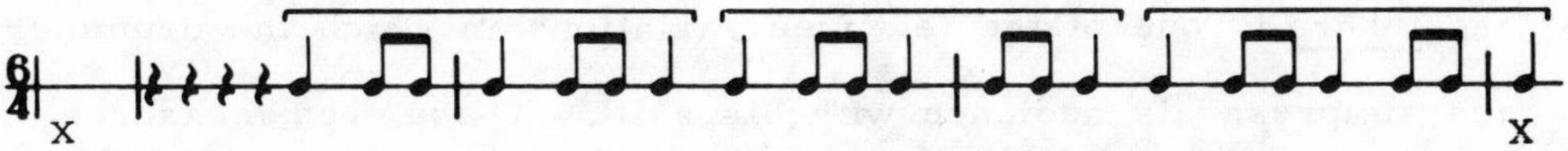

Occasionally musicians make a distinction between the terms mohra and mukhra. A mohra invariably contains a tia while a mukhra may be a qaida which concludes a piece but does not include a tia.

The closing section of many Indian art songs consists of a fast stretta, the so-called dugan, often in a different tāla than that of the preceding melody. For instance, if the song is in Dipchandi Tāl, the dugan may begin in Tritāl and close in Keherwa Tāl, a tāla consisting of eight mātrās, without a khāli beat, and having a theka such as

DHA DHIN NA TIN, TA TA DHIN NA; or DHA DHIN NA TIN, NA KA DHIN – .
X 2 X 2

If at the end of the *dugan* every note is shortened to one third of its original value, the diminution is called *aḍ*. The *aḍ* usually contains a *tia*. In the following example (p. 263), which shows a part of a song in *Tritāl*, the *dugan* is in *Keherwa Tāl*. This is followed by eight *vibhāgas* of *Tritāl* and the *aḍ* again in *Keherwa Tāl*. The song ends on the note G, the *sām*.

The example on page 263, shows that *dugan* and *aḍ* with the *tia* resemble the device of the *color* of the isorhythmic motet of Western fourteenth-century music. They repeat the notes of the song melody, but in the form of diminutions. The last note of the *tia* (D) should coincide with the *sām*; in our example the *tia* ends immediately before the *sām*, a deviation from the rule which would not be acceptable to orthodox musicians.

Another term in North Indian drumming is the *tukhra*. This denotes a variable number of *vibhāgas* in succession in which the *bols* differ considerably from the other *bols* of the *theka*. In short, the *tukhra* is one of the few free variations in which the drummer may impress his audience with his skill. These free measures may (but need not) contain a *tia*.

Laggi denotes the repetition of one *vibhāga*; it is used only in popular music where *sām* and *khāli* are of no importance.

Some of the rhythmic phrases are given picturesque names. For instance, ♩ ♪♩ is called *palankha* (palanquin); ♪♩ ♪ is called *mridanga* because the phrase has a shape similar to that of the *mridanga*; 𝅗𝅥 𝅗𝅥 𝅗𝅥 is called *gaupuchha* (cow's tail), and so forth.

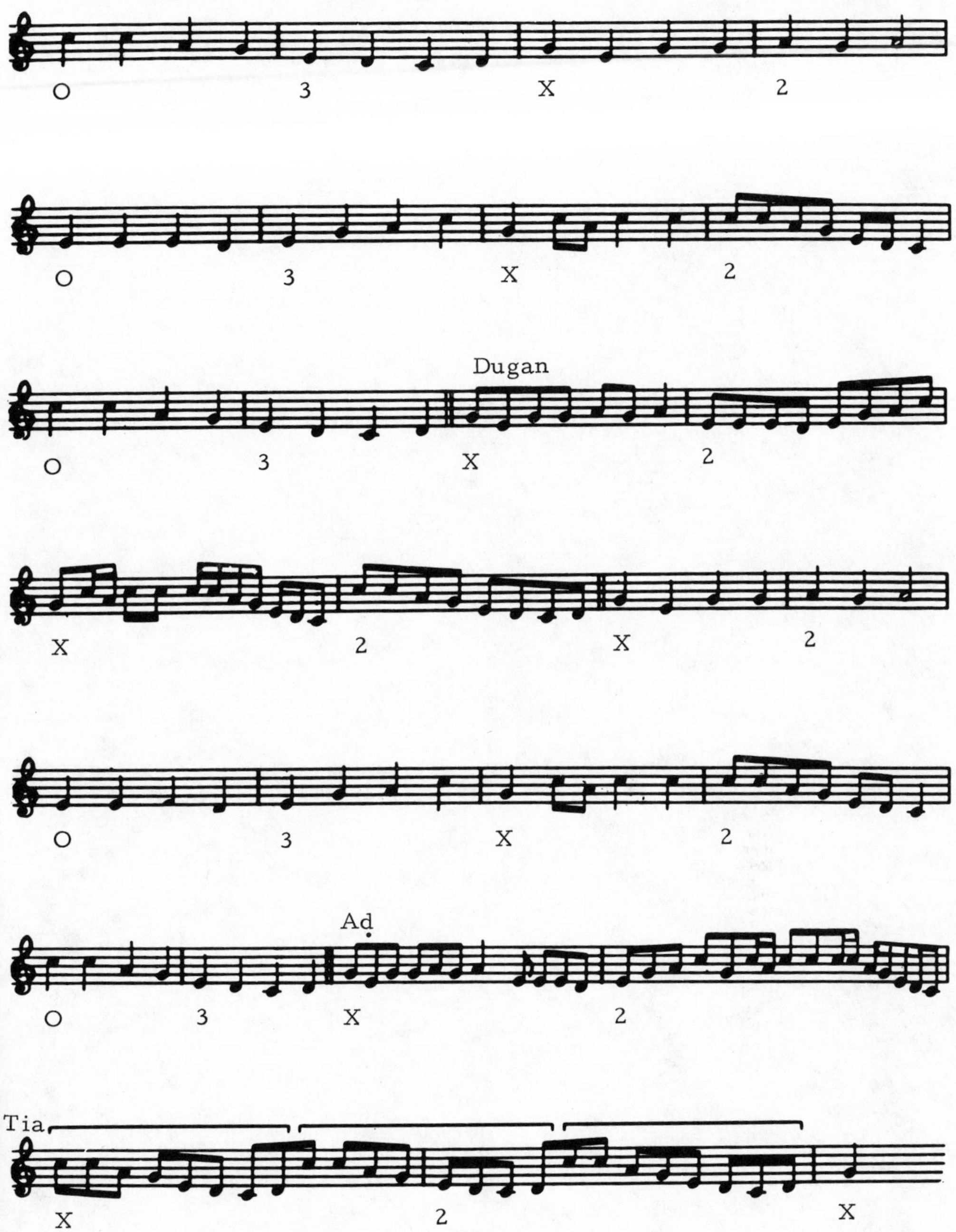
O 3 X 2
O 3 X 2
Dugan
O 3 X 2
X 2 X 2
O 3 X 2
Ad
O 3 X 2
Tia
X 2 X

III

Zither Tablatures

ZITHER TABLATURES

The distinctive and popular European lute of the sixteenth and seventeenth centuries has as its Eastern counterpart not the Asiatic lute but the zither. Similar to the three main types of European lute tablatures — those of Italy, France, and Germany — we can distinguish the three types of zither tablatures of China, Korea, and Japan.

The tablatures are more complex than pitch notations and inform the player directly about the technical procedure of playing. Thus, they offer a convenient detour around the less concrete symbols of pitch notations and their theoretical ramifications, such as scales, intervals, and so forth. Although the information given to the player by means of tablature symbols is comparatively distinct, one must remember that Oriental notations, tablatures, and other systems indicate only the skeleton of the melody, serving as a reminder to the player who already knows the melody. In short, the elaboration of music is left to the performer; and each of several performances of the same piece, by the same player, based upon the same notated music, may differ considerable in interpretation.

CH'IN TABLATURE (減字, CHIEN TZŬ)

The ch'in (琴), often poetically translated by Western writers as "lute," is the classical zither of China, the instrument of the poets, philosophers, and scholars. At the present time there are very few who still master the intricate technique of this distinguished instrument, and it is not surprising that the ch'in notation, a tablature of considerable complexity, reflects many of the subtleties that are characteristics of ch'in music.

In the distant past the ch'in was used in the ensemble music of the imperial court and in the ritual of the Confucian temple. At that time the strings were most often plucked with a plectrum. Gradually, with the growing refinement of solo-ch'in music, which required a great variety of shadings in the tone production, the plectrum was abandoned, and the strings were plucked with the fingers, thus producing a sound that was more intimate and more flexible.

The origin of the ch'in is not known to us. We have some vague information that the instrument was invented by one of the legendary emperors.[1] The ch'in-tsao (琴操), the oldest known catalogue of ch'in melodies (written without musical notations in the second or third century A. D.), states that "Fu-hsi, in addition to his interests in writing, fishing, and other arts and crafts, made the 'lute'." This emperor is supposed to have invented musical instruments, especially the two ancient zithers, the ch'in and sê (瑟). According to tradition he may have lived in the third millenium B.C.

Literary sources — for instance the Chinese Classics[2] — contain numerous references to music and musical instruments, particularly to the ch'in:

> ..when Shun was emperor...,
> he played the five stringed ch'in....[3]
>
> ..here long, there short, is the duckweed;
> on the left, on the right, we gather it.

The modest, retiring, virtuous young lady: —
with lutes, small and large, let us give her
    friendly welcome.[4]

And I will hope to grow old with you.
Your lute in your hands
will emit its quiet pleasant tones.[5]

Legge remarks that, "The superior man, according to the rules of antiquity, was never, without some urgent reasons, to be without his lute by his side.... The quiet harmony of the lute was a common image for conjugal affection."[6]

..why not daily play your lute,
both to give a zest to your joy
and to prolong the day?[7]

..when we have seen our prince,
we sit together with him, and
they play on their lutes....[8]

..I have here admirable guests
for whom are struck the lutes,
large and small....[9]

Loving union with wife and children
is like the music of the lutes....[10]

The oldest known Chinese manuscript dealing with ch'in playing is the Yu-lan-p'u (幽蘭譜, "The Refined Orchid Book")[11] which originated during the T'ang period (618-906).[12] Its extant fifth part is preserved in the Shinko-in (神光院) at Kyoto. The manuscript was copied repeatedly, principally in Japan. One of the recent publications was made in 1936 by the Commercial Press of Shanghai.

In examining the photostatic copy of the manuscript, we find that no musical notation is used. The melody, known as the "yu-lan," is indicated by means of detailed instructions which indicate which finger to use, which fret and string to stop, whether to move the finger slowly or quickly, when to make a short rest, and so forth.

Following (Fig. 63, p. 271) is a copy of the first page of this remarkable manuscript which, according to Lee, may be the earliest music book of the Orient. Below is an approximate translation of this page:

Chieh Shih Melody Introduction to Elegant Orchids:

Ch'iu Kung, known as Ming, originally came from K'uai-chi. At the end of the Liang dynasty [A. D. 502-557] he was a hermit living on the Chiu-yi hill. His work exhausted the beauty of the Ch'u tune. And in the Elegant Orchids it was especially refined and brilliant. The tune was so subtle, the theme so profound, that no one could learn and master it. In the third year of Ch'ên-ming, of the Ch'ên dynasty [A. D. 590], he taught the piece to Wang Shu-ming of Yi-tu. Ch'iu Kung died in Tan-yang canton, in the tenth year of Kai-huang of the Sui dynasty, at the age of ninety-seven. He had no son to hand down his music. Therefore the tune was abridged here.

(The fifth section of the Elegant Orchids):

Put the middle finger about half an inch on the tenth hui and produce the shang tone. The second and the middle fingers jointly handle kung and shang. Hide the middle finger, and afterwards press it on the thirteenth hui, about an inch [down], in the form of a hook. Then stop shang. Lift the second finger slowly. Maintain the tone of kung and shang in the half way. The second finger carries the shang tone. Again maintain kung and shang in the half way. Let the third finger go downward, about one inch beyond the thirteenth hui. Produce shang and chiao. At this juncture separate it into two halves. Maintain it, clasp it, lift it, and emphasize it. Make a lift then....

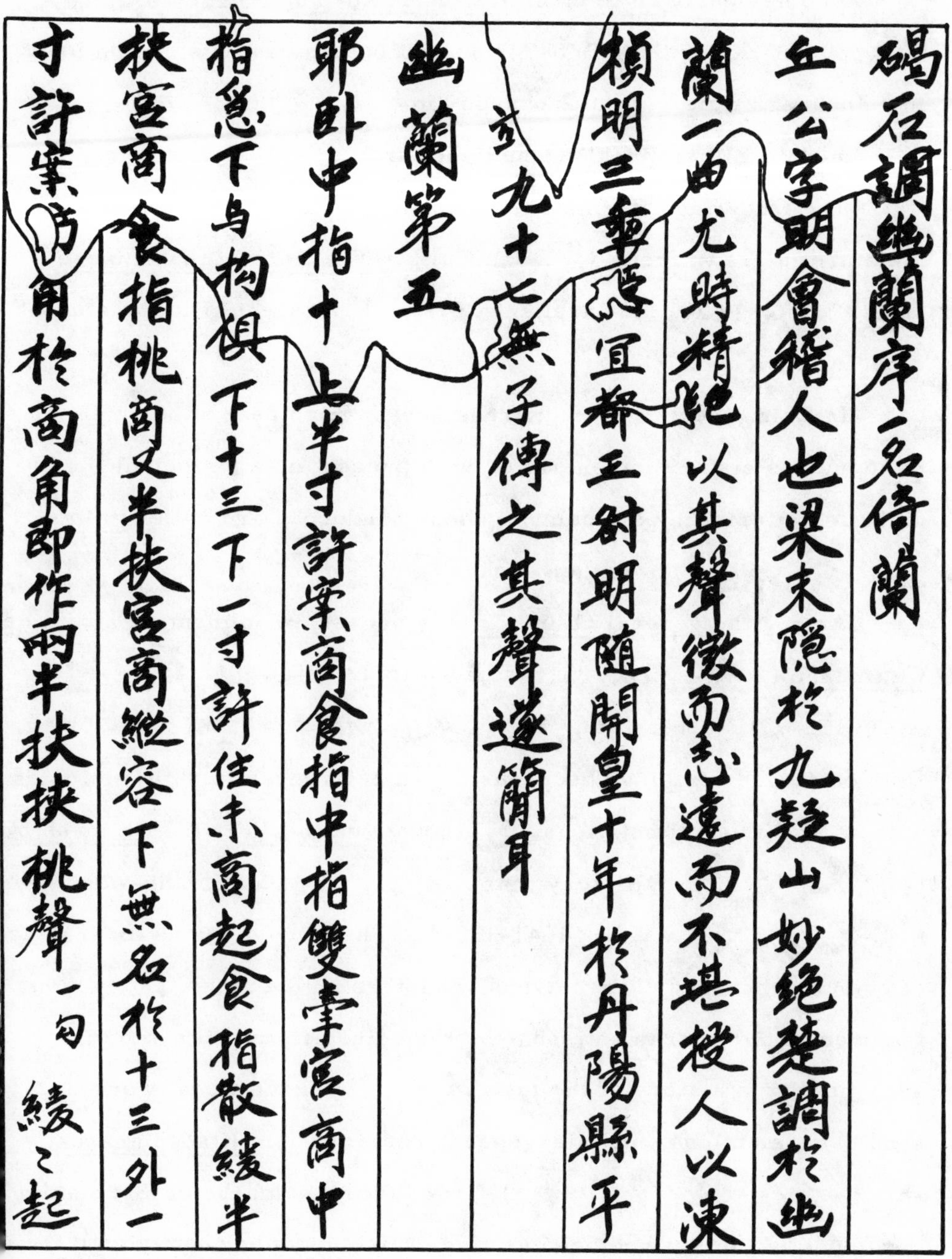
碣石調幽蘭序一名倚蘭
丘公字明會稽人也梁末隱於九疑山妙絶楚調於幽
蘭一曲尤時精絶以其聲微而志遠而不堪授人以陳
禎明三年授宜都王叔明隨開皇十年於丹陽縣卒
年九十七無子傳之其聲遂簡耳
幽蘭第五
耶臥中指十上半寸許案商食指中指雙牽宮商中
指急下與構俱下十三下一寸許住末商起食指散緩半
扶宮商食指挑商又半扶宮商縱容下無名於十三外一
寸許案商角於商角即作兩半扶挾挑聲一句 緩緩起

Figure 63

Another early ch'in book, Hui-ch'in ko-p'u (徽琴歌譜, "Hui Zither Song Book"), is lost but its contents can be found in a Japanese work called Gyoku-do kin-fu (玉堂琴譜, "Gyoku-do's Zither Book"), published in 1781.[13]

The following information concerning ch'in literature and ch'in tablature is drawn from R.H. van Gulik's The Lore of the Chinese Lute (Tokyo, 1940), an excellent work that is essential to the student of ch'in music.

In China there exist numerous books which deal either with the ch'in and its history in general or with present notated melodies and didactic material in particular. These handbooks are called ch'in-p'u (琴譜), "zither books."

Among the general ch'in-p'u it is necessary to mention again the Ch'in-tsao (琴操), ascribed to Ts'ai Yung (蔡邕, A.D. 133-92), or to K'ung Yen (孔衍, A.D. 268-320). This catalogue contains about four dozen references to ch'in melodies without any musical notations.[14] Another ch'in-p'u is the Ch'in-shih (琴史), "History of the Zither," by Chu Ch'ang-wên (朱長文, A.D. 1041-1100). The work contains biographies of over one hundred ch'in players, chapters on the notes, the various features of the instrument, scales, melodies, form and symbolism, and, finally, a history of the instrument.[15] An additional work that should be mentioned in this general category is: K'ao-p'an-yü-shih (考盤餘事), "Desultory Remarks on Furnishing the Abode of the Retired Scholar,"[16] which deals primarily with the instrument and its history. This work, in which the ch'in is discussed at the end of the second chapter, was compiled by T'u Lung (屠隆) in the sixteenth century. Other works dealing with the same subject are: Ch'in-ching (琴經), "Classical Book on the Ch'in" by Chang Ta-ming (張大命) of Fukien in the early seventeenth century that discusses the structure of the instrument and quotes a number of older ch'in works; Ch'ing-lien-fang-ch'in-ya (青蓮舫琴雅), "Elegance of the Ch'in, from the Blue Lotus Boat," compiled by Lin Yu-lin (林有麟) in the early seventeenth century; Ch'in-hsüeh-ts'ung-shu (琴學叢書), "Collected Writings on the Study of the Ch'in," a valuable series of treatises compiled by Yang Tsung-chi (楊宗稷) in 1911.[17] Of particular importance is its sixth part called Ch'in-ching, a collection of ch'in melodies notated in a system invented by the author. Ch'in-shu-ts'un-mu (琴書存目), a systematic catalogue dealing with the available ch'in literature, was published by Chou Ch'ing-yün (周慶雲) in 1914. He published a second Ch'in-shih in 1919, which was meant to serve as a supplement to Chu Ch'ang-wên's work.

The didactic ch'in-p'u were usually published in limited numbers by the ch'in masters; the quantity was just sufficient to serve the small groups of selected disciples. These books were printed on cheap paper, and only a few have survived in complete form. Generally a ch'in-p'u consists of an introductory chapter dealing with the name and history of the instrument, a theoretical section which explains the tones and their significance, and, finally, a chapter which discusses the finger technique and describes the tablature symbols. In many cases this last chapter has been separated from the booklet, or the ch'in-p'u omits it altogether. The reason for withholding this important chapter was that ch'in masters were reluctant to impart the knowledge of how to read the chien-tzŭ to unqualified people.

The oldest known of these specific ch'in-p'u is the Shên-ch'i-mi-p'u (神奇祕譜) by Chu Ch'üan (朱權), the Prince of Ning, who died in 1448. The literary name of Chu Ch'üan was Ch'ü-hsien (臞仙), "Emaciated Immortal" (lit. "crane"), hence the work was also known as Ch'ü-hsien-ch'in-p'u. Its preface is dated 1425. "The author has not been consequent in his system of notation, and...the chien-tzŭ therefore have become unnecessarily complicated. One gets the impression that the compiler purposely made the notation obscure, so that only expert players could use it... In his preface he says that properly only high officials should be allowed to occupy themselves with the lute."[18] The specific ch'in-p'u are represented by the following works: Pu-hsü-t'ang-ch'in-p'u (步虛堂琴譜), a ch'in handbook compiled by Ku I-chiang (顧挹江) in the sixteenth century, and a work that shows Taoist influences; dating from the same period is the Ch'in-p'u-ho-pi-ta-ch'üan (琴譜合璧大全), compiled by Yang Piao-chêng (楊表正); the T'ai-ku-i-yin (太古遺音), compiled by Yang Lun (楊倫), belongs in the early seventeenth century; the Wu-chih-chai-ch'in-p'u (五知齋琴譜), a very popular and easily obtainable work by the famous Hsü Ch'i (徐祺), originated in the eighteenth century; the Ch'êng-i-t'ang-ch'in-p'u (誠一堂琴譜) by Ch'êng Yün-chi (程允基) dates from the early eighteenth century;[19] the Tzŭ-yüan-t'ang-ch'in-p'u (自遠堂琴譜) by Wu Hung (吳灴), from the early nineteenth century; and, finally, the Ch'in-hsüeh-ju-mên (琴學入門) by Chang Ho (張鶴) of the same period. This latter work is a popular treatise and has been reprinted a number of times.[20]

The body of the ch'in consists of two narrow wooden boards, one placed above the other. The upper board, curved slightly convex, is made of t'ung wood (paulownia imperialis). The lower board, flat at the bottom and made of tzŭ wood (tecoma radicanus), has two rectangular or oval resonance holes. Each part of the instrument has symbolic significance. To mention only a few: the ancient ch'in had a length of $\frac{366}{10}$ inches (its width was 6.6 inches) because the year had a maximum of 366 days. The upper board, representing heaven, is frequently inscribed or engraved with the name of the zither, its owner, and the period when the instrument was built. The lower board represents earth. The names of the two resonance holes are "Dragon Pond" and "Phoenix Pool," respectively. The left side of the zither is called "Scorched Tail," and the bridge upon which the strings are attached is the "Yo Mountain," a symbol of detachedness and sturdiness. Thus, the symbolism of the various parts is expressed even to the smallest detail.

The five strings of the ancient ch'in correspond to the five elements;[21] the thickest and lowest string, the one farthest from the player, must consist of 240 silken threads; it represents the emperor. The second and fourth strings consist of 206 threads each, and the third and fifth consist of 172 threads. The seven strings of the later instrument were supposed to represent the seven days of the week.

The ancient five- and seven-tone scales of China determined the tuning of the pre-Ming (seven string) ch'in which was C D E G A c d, assuming that the lowest string was tuned to C. When the Yüan dynasty (1260-1368) came to an end and the Ming dynasty (1368-1644) was established, Chinese art, in every realm, experienced a renaissance of national sentiment. It was then that musicians and theorists endeavored to re-establish the ancient anhemitonic pentatonic scale; as stated before, all semitones were abolished as foreign, and the Ming scale, although not quite the same as the scale of ancient China, became C D F G A (or, transposed, $\underline{G}$ $\underline{A}$ C D E). Although the official scale of the imperial court underwent some modifications in subsequent periods, since the Ming period the *ch'in* tuning has remained essentially unaltered ($\underline{G}$ $\underline{A}$ C D E G A).

Occasionally, in addition to these main patterns of tuning, other tunings could occur. For instance:

C D E G A B d	mentioned in the Korean work *Shih-ak hwa-sŭng* (詩樂和聲 , lit. "Poem Music Harmonized"), written by order of Chŭng-cho (正祖 , 1777-1800), twenty-second king of the (Korean) Yi dynasty;
C D F G Bb c d C Eb F G Bb c eb C Eb F Ab Bb c eb	used by Sung composers such as Ch'iang K'uei, (Lee);
$\underline{G}$ $\underline{Bb}$ C D F G Bb $\underline{G}$ $\underline{Bb}$ C Eb F G Bb $\underline{Ab}$ $\underline{Bb}$ C Eb F Ab Bb	mentioned by Prince Chu Tsai-yü (sixteenth century);
C D E F# G A B	particularly in recent times.

The instrument is placed horizontally in front of the player in such a manner that the highest (seventh) string is nearest to him. Although the *ch'in* has no frets, we find instead thirteen small inlaid or painted studs below the outermost (lowest) string. The studs, called *hui* (徽),[22] serve a purpose similar to the frets on other instruments. We shall discuss their positions and use after we have explained the numbering of the strings.

The complexity of the *ch'in* tablature prevented its use by the common people and thus confined the elaborate *ch'in* playing to the learned musicians, poets, and philosophers.[23] The tablature system, consisting of symbols called *chien-tzŭ* (減字), "abbreviated characters," had its origin in the first centuries A. D. (according to van Gulik). Literary reports are vague about the time of its first appearance.

In order to read the tablature it is essential to be acquainted with the Chinese numerals from one to thirteen: 一 (1), 二 (2), 三 (3), 四 (4), 五 (5), 六 (6), 七 (7), 八 (8), 九 (9), 十 (10), 十一 (11, 十二 (12), 十三 (13). The seven strings of the *ch'in* in both pre-Ming and Ming (and post-Ming) periods use the same numbers but denote different pitches:

Pre-Ming:

or:

Ming and post-Ming:

In the symbols of *ch'in* tablature there appears another set of numbers (1-13), which indicates the thirteen *hui*. These *hui* are arranged in such a manner that the distances between them in both directions (to the left and to the right), beginning from a central stud (七),

become – with one or two minor exceptions – increasingly smaller. The hui are numbered from right to left; that is, the highest stopped note on each string is indicated by the first hui and the lowest stopped note (not the open string) by the thirteenth.

The following two charts illustrate the sounds produced by the open and stopped strings in both the old (pre-Ming) and the new (Ming and post-Ming) tunings:

Pre-Ming Tuning

String	Hui:	13	12	11	10	9	8	7	6	5	4	3	2	1
I	C	D	Eb	E	F	G	A	c	e	g	c'	e'	g'	c'
II	D	E	F	F#	G	A	B	d	f#	a	d'	f#'	a'	d'
III	E	F#	G	G#	A	B	c#	e	g#	b	e'	g#'	b'	e'
IV	G	A	Bb	B	c	d	e	g	b	d'	g'	b'	d''	g
V	A	B	c	c#	d	e	f#	a	c#'	e'	a'	c#''	e''	a
VI	c	d	eb	e	f	g	a	c'	e'	g'	c''	e''	g''	c
VII	d	e	f	f#	g	a	b	d'	f#'	a'	d''	f#''	a''	d
Ratio of string division	1	$\frac{7}{8}$	$\frac{5}{6}$	$\frac{4}{5}$	$\frac{3}{4}$	$\frac{2}{3}$	$\frac{3}{5}$	$\frac{1}{2}$	$\frac{2}{5}$	$\frac{1}{3}$	$\frac{1}{4}$	$\frac{1}{5}$	$\frac{1}{6}$	$\frac{1}{8}$

Ming and Post-Ming Tuning

String	Hui:	13	12	11	10	9	8	7	6	5	4	3	2
I	G	A	Bb	B	C	D	E	G	B	d	g	b	d'
II	A	B	C	C#	D	E	F#	A	c#	e	a	c#'	e'
III	C	D	Eb	E	F	G	A	c	e	g	c'	e'	g'
IV	D	E	F	F#	G	A	B	d	f#	a	d'	f#'	a'
V	E	F#	G	G#	A	B	c#	e	g#	b	e'	g#'	b'
VI	G	A	Bb	B	c	d	e	g	b	d'	g'	b'	d''
VII	A	B	c	c#	d	e	f#	a	c#'	e'	a'	c#''	e''

A third set of numbers (1-10) is occasionally used to indicate the *fên* (分): imaginary, small subdivisions between any two adjoining *hui*. As shown before, the distances between any two successive *hui* vary — for instance (in pre-Ming tuning) the interval between *hui* 6 and 7 is a major third, while the interval between *hui* 12 and 13 is only a semitone — therefore the distances between the ten assumed *fên* in each of these intervals also vary proportionally. The interval between any two successive *fên*, for instance between *fên* 6 and 7, will be one tenth of a major third, while the interval between two successive *fên* between *hui* 12 and 13 will be only one tenth of a semitone, an unlikely interval to be used in *ch'in* playing. In practice only such *fên* are employed which divide the intervals between successive *hui* into sections which generally are not smaller than semitones.

The *fên* are not marked on the instrument and have to be learned by the player. They, too, are counted from right to left, a procedure which may cause some confusion when transcriptions of *ch'in* tablatures are made. 上 ("up") means, of course, a rise in pitch (on the string, a movement of the depressing hand from left to right), while rising numbers, both for *hui* and *fên*, indicate *descending* pitches. Thus, for instance, the fourth *hui* plus the fourth *fên* will be lower in pitch than the fourth *hui* plus the second *fên*, and so forth.

In addition to the three sets of numbers there exists a wealth of notational symbols that denote technical details of playing. Of about 200 *chien-tzŭ*, we quote here only a few:[24]

Chien-tzŭ:	Name:	
卄	*San* (散)	Only the right hand is used for plucking the string.
乇	*T'o* (托)	The string is pulled in an outward

Chien-tzŭ:	Name:	
		direction (away from the player) by the right thumb.
尸	Po (擘)	The string is pulled in an inward direction (toward the player) by the right thumb (nail).
木	Mo (抹)	The string is pulled in an inward direction by the right index finger.
乚	T'iao (挑)	The string is pulled in an outward direction by the right index finger.
勹	Kou (勾)	The string is pulled in an inward direction by the right middle finger.
写	T'i (剔)	The string is pulled in an outward direction by the right middle finger.
丁	Ta (打)	The string is pulled in an inward direction by the right ring finger.
亏	Chê (摘)	The string is pulled in an outward direction by the right ring finger.
夫	Ch'üan fu (全扶)	Three strings are pulled simultaneously: one is pulled by the right index finger; the second by the right middle finger; and the third by the right ring finger.
厂	Li (歷)	Two or three strings are pulled in quick succession in an outward direction by the right index finger. This movement is also called Tu (度).
省	Shao hsi (少息)	A pause of short duration.
夏	Ju man (入慢)	Slowing down.

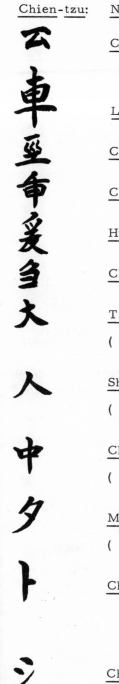

Chien-tzu:	Name:	
𠫓	Chih (至)	"Up to"; for instance it can be used in 滾六至一 , meaning k'un from the VI up to the I string.
車	Lien (連)	Smooth; legato.
巠	Ch'ing (輕)	Soft.
重	Chung (重)	Loud.
爰	Huan (緩)	Slow.
刍	Chi (急)	Very fast.
大	Ta chih (大指)	The left thumb is to be used.
人	Shih chih (食指)	The left index finger is to be used.
中	Chung chih (中指)	The left middle finger is to be used.
夕	Ming chih (名指)	The left ring finger is to be used.
卜	Ch'o (綽)	A short range glissando which starts slightly below the written note and glides up to it; it is performed by a finger of the left hand.
シ	Chu (注)	A short range glissando which starts slightly above the written note and glides down to it; it is performed by a finger of the left hand.

六	Yin (吟)	Vibrato. According to van Gulik there are numerous varieties of vibrato; the important ones are: ch'ang-yin (長吟), a wide vibrato; hsi-yin (細吟), a thin vibrato; yu-yin (遊吟), a swinging vibrato; and the ting-yin (定吟), a fine vibrato in which the finger hardly moves, and only the pulsation in the finger tip is supposed to influence the sound.
力	Jou (猱)	A broad vibrato which is more accentuated than the yin. Ch'in players pronounce this character jou, although it should be read nao – "monkey."
立	Chuang (撞)	"To strike against": immediately after the string is plucked by the right hand, the left moves quickly up and down the string to the right (above) of the indicated note.
午	Hu (滸)	The left thumb, which stops the string, glides on the vibrating string to the right to the next hui in a slow motion.
足	Kuei (跪)	"To kneel": the string is depressed with the back of the first joint of the left ring finger instead of its tip, especially in t'ao-ch'i when it is difficult to press the string with the finger tip.
色	Fan ch'i (泛起)	"Here the floating sounds begin": this is a symbol that indicates where the player has to begin using harmonics.

In addition to the manifold plucking and stopping instructions the *ch'in-p'u* occasionally contain indications concerning the various touches (timbres) of *ch'in* playing.[25] The *ch'in* masters write about light, loose, crisp, lofty, rare, and many other touches which can be ignored here because they have very little to do with the actual tablature symbols.

Each tablature symbol contains specific signs for the depressing and plucking fingers, the number of the string to be plucked, the number of the *hui* and, in some instances, the number of the *fên*. The general organization of the tablature symbols is illustrated in the following two examples:

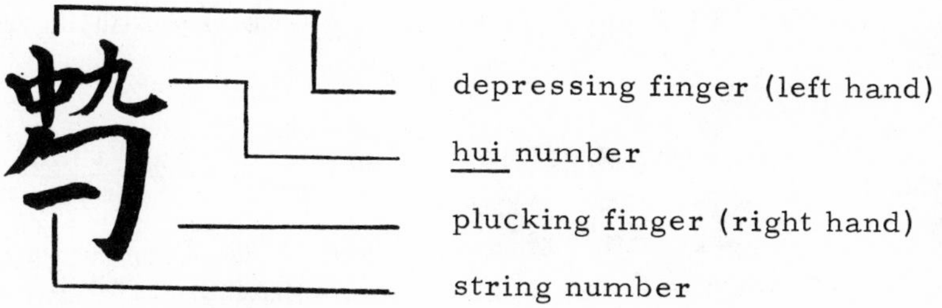

or

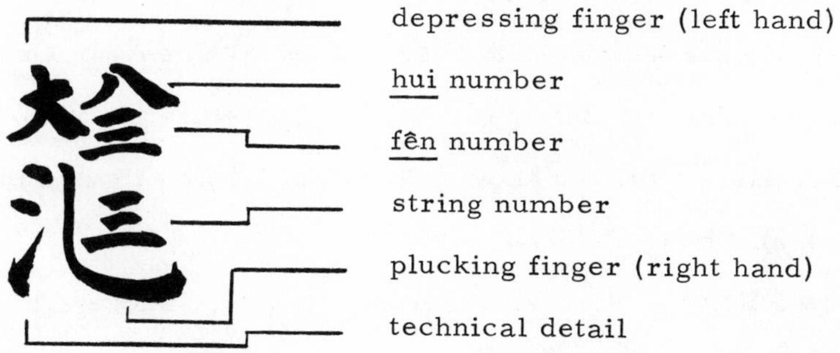

Occasionally *ch'in* tablatures use the character 上 (*shang*), "above," "up," to indicate a high alteration of a note without referring to the next higher sounding *hui* and its *fên*. For instance, if we assume that *hui* 7 produces the note G, *hui* 7 plus *fên* 7 will indicate a note lower than G, approximately the note F. But if *hui* 7 is provided with *shang* it will indicate a note becoming or being higher than G and, if not otherwise indicated, a note between *hui* 7 (G) and *hui* 6 (B). *Shang* may denote both a rising or a raised sound. We shall transcribe *shang* by a raised sound although the interpretation of rising sound is equally acceptable.

Shang is notated on top of the plucking finger symbol either in a detached form,  , or in combination with the finger symbol, 

If in certain symbols the signs for the depressing finger and the *hui* and *fên* numbers are omitted, the player is expected to apply the last notated instructions (concerning depressing finger, *hui*, *fên*, etc.) to all subsequent symbols which are without these signs until new instructions are given.

Figure 64 represents the first page of the *Ch'êng-i-t'ang ch'in-p'u* (誠一堂琴譜).[26] This work, as already mentioned, was compiled by Ch'êng Yün-chi in the early eighteenth century. The title columns inform us that Ch'êng Yün-chi came from Hsin-an, that the book was revised by his younger brother Ch'êng Yün-p'ei, that the music is in the style of Lu, the home of Confucius, and that there are fourteen strophes. As we are dealing with an eighteenth-century work we know that the ch'in will be tuned in the post-Ming manner, G̲ A̲ C D E G A.

Below follows a discussion of the symbols. These symbols provide information regarding only the notes and technical details about their production on the instrument. Meter and rhythm are practically ignored; the few signs which offer some guidance are a small circle — for instance near the fifth symbol of the first notational column — which denotes the end of a phrase, and rare instructions to perform certain passages in a slow or fast tempo. Like most *ch'in*

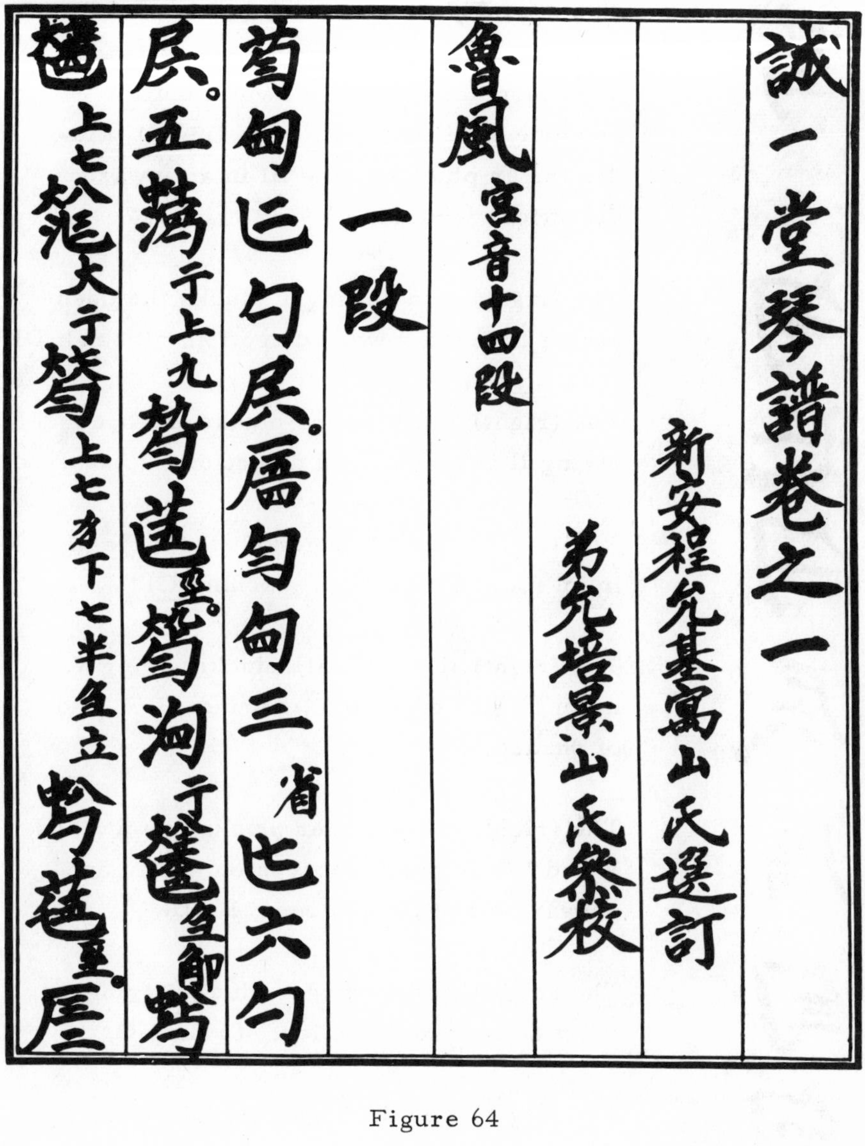

Figure 64

masters, the brothers Ch'êng expected the performer to be acquainted with the rhythmical shape of the piece before he used the notation.

The sign  indicates that only the right hand is used plucking open strings. This instruction remains valid until a new one supersedes it. The (right) middle finger plucks string III in an inward direction. (Sound: C)

The (right) middle finger plucks the open string IV in an inward direction. (Sound: D)

The (right) index finger plucks the open string II in an outward direction. (Sound: A)

The (right) middle finger plucks string I in an inward direction. (Sound: G)

The (right) thumb (nail) plucks string VI in an inward direction. (Sound: G). End of phrase.

The (right) index finger plucks two strings, V and IV, in quick succession and in an outward direction. (Sound: E, D)

The (right) middle finger plucks string III in an inward direction. (Sound: C)

The (right) middle finger plucks string IV in an inward direction. (Sound: D)

Here the plucking finger sign is not given. In such instances the previous instruction remains valid; the (right) middle finger plucks string III in an inward direction (Sound: C)

"Shao hsi," a short pause (少息).

The (right) index finger plucks string VII in an outward direction. (Sound: A)

六

The previous finger sign (乚) remains valid; the (right) index finger plucks string VI in an outward direction. (Sound: G)

勹

The (right) middle finger plucks string I in an inward direction. (Sound: G) (End of first notational column.)

The (right) thumb (nail) plucks string VI in an inward direction. (Sound: G)

五

The previous plucking finger sign remains valid; the right thumb plucks string V in an inward direction. (Sound: E)

This complex symbol instructs the player that the right middle finger (勹) plucks string I in an outward direction (丂); the left middle finger (中), starting with a short glissando from above (氵), depresses the string on hui 10. (Sound: C)

亍 ("right")
上 ("up")
九 ("9")

Annotations such as this one are inserted into Chinese, Korean, and Japanese zither tablatures. This annotation instructs the player to move the depressing finger (中) up to the right to hui 9.

The (right) middle finger plucks string II in an inward direction; the left thumb (大) depresses the string at hui 9. (Sound: E)

The sign  indicates that only the right hand is to be used. The index finger plucks (the open) string V in an outward direction. (Sound: E)

<u>Ch'ing</u>, "softly." The lowest horizontal bar of this character is missing in the manuscript. End of phrase.

The (right) middle finger plucks string III in an inward direction; the left thumb depresses the string above <u>hui</u> 9. The sign  (below 九) is <u>shang</u> (上), its lowest horizontal line being combined with the right middle finger sign. Instead of stating an exact <u>fên</u> number, the writer indicates that the spot where the string is to be depressed is above <u>hui</u> 9 (and below <u>hui</u> 8). (Sound: approximately G#)

Since we find no detailed instructions regarding <u>hui</u> or <u>fên</u>, and since no open string is prescribed, the hand position of the preceding symbol () remains valid. This note is to be started with a short glissando from above on string IV, <u>hui</u> 9, plus <u>shang</u>. (Sound: approximately A# or B)

The (depressing) hand moves to the right.

The (right) index finger plucks string V in an outward direction. At this instant the left thumb still depresses the string at <u>hui</u> 9 plus <u>shang</u>. Then, as indicated by 亍 ("right") of the preceding sign, the left thumb glides to the right to the next (8th)

hui (午), and the string is plucked again by the (right) index finger in an inward direction (木). The hui number 八 (8) appears to be combined with 午 into  . (Sound: B-c#)

 "very fast"

 "joining" (the following note 仝).

 The (right) middle finger plucks string I in an inward direction; the left middle finger depresses the string above (上) hui 八 (8). (Sound: approximately F#) (End of second notational column.)

 The (right) index finger plucks string IV in an outward direction. The left thumb depresses the string below hui 7 at fên 7. (Sound: between d and B)

 The (left) thumb moves up to hui 7.

 The (right) index finger plucks string III in an outward direction. The left thumb begins a short glide from above and ends at hui 8. (Sound: A)

 The left thumb moves to the right.

 The (right) middle finger plucks string II in an inward direction. The left thumb depresses the string below hui 7 at fên 8. (Sound: between A and F#)

上 "Up to"

七 (hui) 7

jou, a broad vibrato,

"down" (toward *hui* 8)

the left thumb glides to the right to the next *hui* (7)

"very fast"

After the string is plucked by the right hand, the left moves quickly up and down string II to the right of *hui* 7, *fên* 8. (Sound: a fluctuation between A and F#)

The (right) middle finger plucks string I in an inward direction. The left thumb depresses the string at *hui* 8. (Sound: E)

The (right) thumb plucks string V in an outward direction. The sign  instructs the player that the open string is used. (Sound: E)

"Softly." End of phrase.

Although this symbol stands at the end of the third notational column, it is the beginning of a new phrase. The (right) index finger plucks in quick succession strings III and II in an outward direction. (Sound: C, *A*) (End of third notational column.)[27]

The following *ch'in* piece (Fig. 65), called "The Three Intoxications of Yo Yang,"[28] is notated by means of *chien-tzŭ* and *kung-ch'ê* symbols. As mentioned before, during the last two centuries it has become common to facilitate reading of difficult *ch'in* tablatures b[y] combining them with a popular notation, a practice not unlike that in

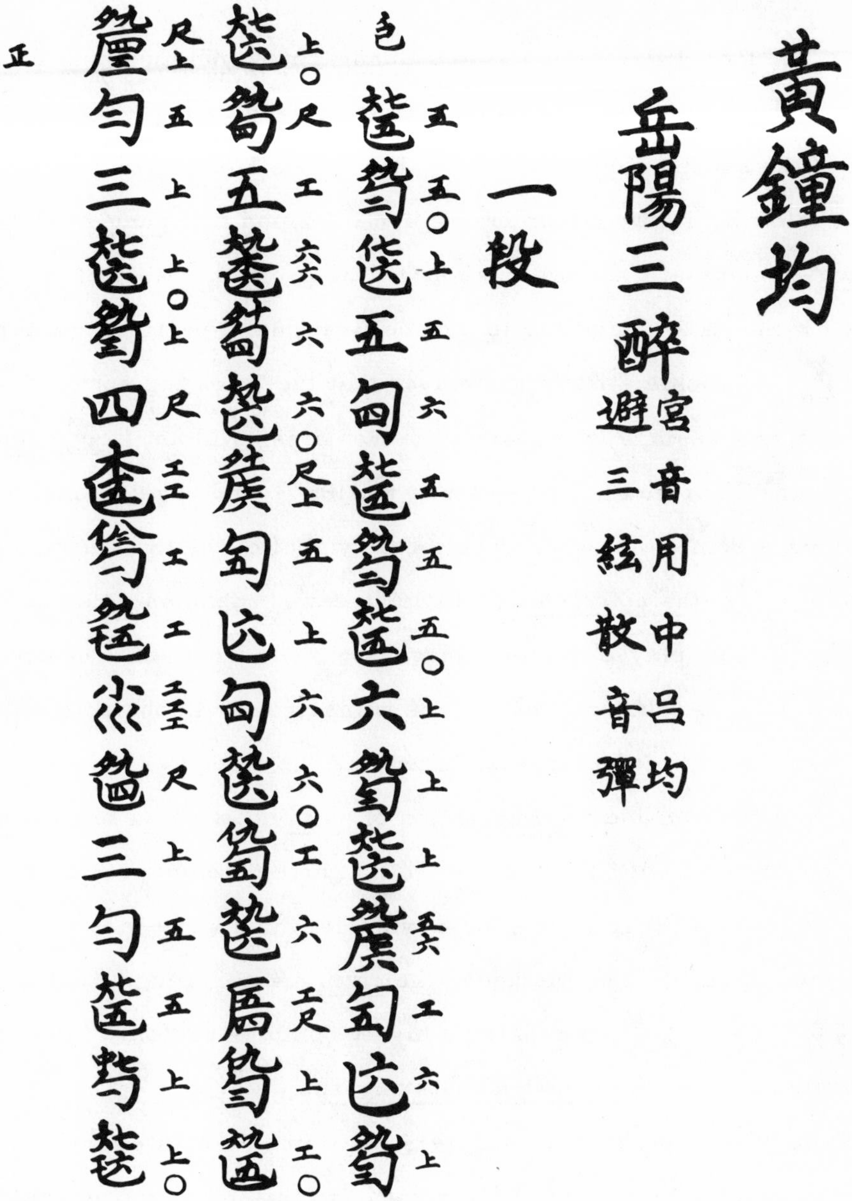
黃鐘均
岳陽三醉
宮音用中呂均
避三絃散音彈
一段

Figure 65

which European lute tablatures underwent modifications aimed at simplification.

The first title column states Huang-chung yün, meaning that the scale to be used has as its basic tone the Huang-chung. The upper half of the second column reads: "The Three Intoxications of Yo Yang," and, below it, in two columns, we are informed that kung should sound Chung-lü and that the third open string be avoided. Most of the notational symbols are familiar to us; the first one of particular interest is  , which instructs the player that the "floating sounds" – harmonics – begin. This instruction remains valid until 正 (chêng), "regular," "original," prescribes regular sounds again, and the harmonics come to an end. The tenth symbol of the third notational column,  (hsiao ch'uan), "little stream," denotes three notes (工) to be played in quick succession. The rest of the symbols present no new problems and can be transcribed without difficulty.[29]

At the end of the nineteenth century, as a counter measure against the simplification and popularization of ch'in notation, a few ch'in masters endeavored not only to re-establish the old complex tablature but to experiment with additional new symbols which were less ambiguous than the old ones. For instance, the ch'in master Yang Tsung-chi (楊宗稷) created a highly complex system of tablature symbols in his book Ch'in-hsüeh-ts'ung-shu (琴學叢書), published in Peking in 1911 and 1925, in which he notated some well known melodies by means of his notational system. He was compelled to print a multitude of explanations together with his symbols and, although Yang's instructions are comparatively clear, the reading of his notation required a considerable amount of additional study by ch'in players. For this reason the new system did not achieve any appreciable recognition.

Another experiment concerning ch'in notation was made by Wang Kuang-ch'i (王光祈) in his Fan-i-ch'in-p'u-chih-yen-chiu (翻譯琴譜之研究), published in Shanghai in 1931. Influenced by Western notation, Wang tried using notes and staves plus a number of complex special signs. None of these experiments — simplification, invention of new symbols, introduction of Western notational elements — achieved any lasting success.

Ch'in notation of ritual and ceremonial ensemble music is comparatively simple. With a few rare exceptions it avoids technical subtleties, fên, and rhythmic freedom, and limits its symbols to denoting open strings plucked either by the right index or middle fingers. This simplified ch'in tablature is combined with other Chinese notational systems, each of which denotes the music of a specific instrument. For instance, Figure 66 (p. 294) is the beginning of the middle part of the Confucian ancestral hymn,[30] a score in which four notations are used: lü, the old Five-Tone, kung-ch'ê, and simple chien-tzŭ.

The large characters at the top of the page, written in circular fields, represent the sacred text. Immediately below each textual character, written horizontally (from right to left), we find indications for the note to which each word is to be sung: below the first textual character we read, "Huang-chung acts as kung"; below the second textual character, "T'ai-ts'u acts as shang"; and so forth.[31] Below these annotations we find (in the second horizontal line) the notes prescribed for the shêng (笙) notated in kung-ch'ê symbols. The first one reads: "the shêng blows ho"; the second one, "the shêng blows ssŭ"; and so forth. The vertical notational columns, below the vocal and shêng notes and grouped into pairs, each of which belongs to one textual word, represent the accompaniment. The right hand top

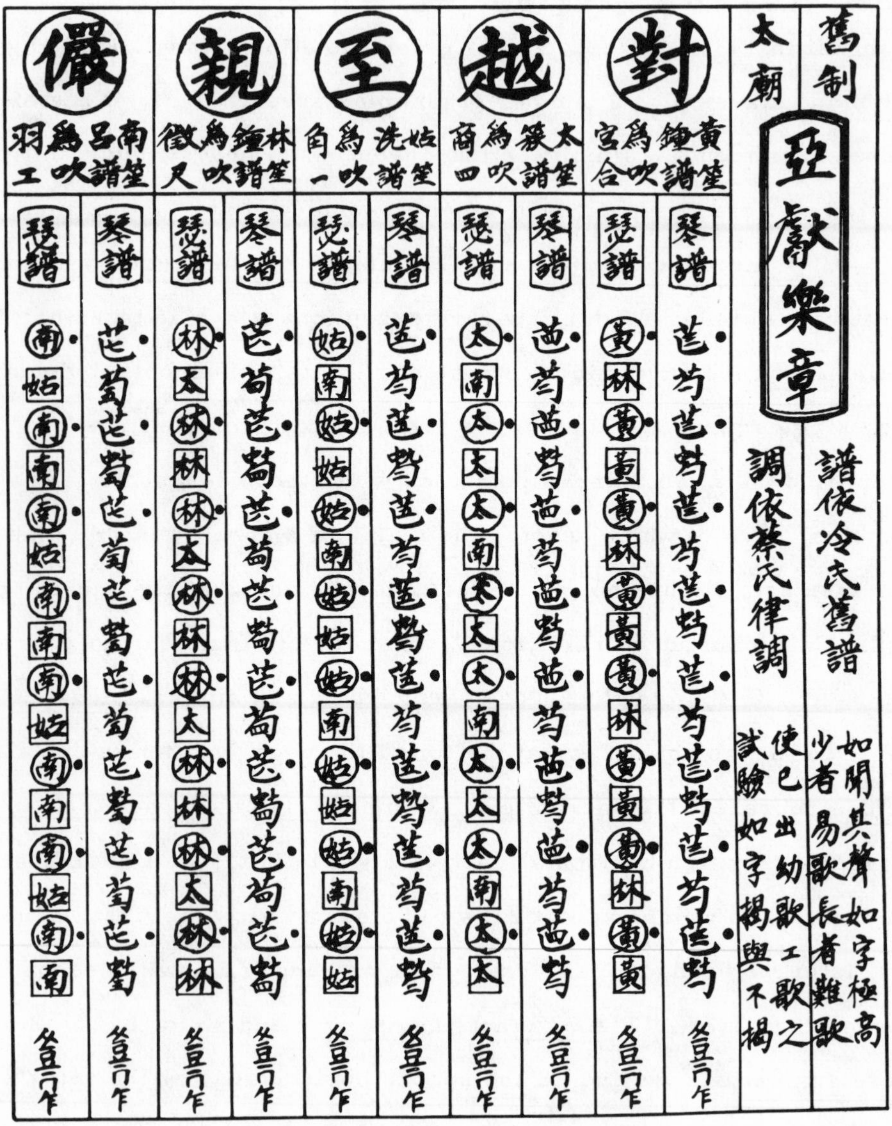
舊制
太廟
亞獻樂章
譜依冷氏舊譜
調依蔡氏律調
如開其聲如字極高少者易歌長者難歌使已出幼歌工歌之試驗如字揭與不揭
對
黃鍾為宮 笙譜吹合
越
太簇為商 笙譜吹四
至
姑洗為角 笙譜吹一
親
林鍾為徵 笙譜吹尺
儼
南呂為羽 笙譜吹工
琴譜
瑟譜

Figure 66

(written in a rectangular frame) reads: "*ch'in* notation," the left hand top, "*sê* notation."[32] The *sê* part is notated in *lü* symbols placed in small circles and squares. The circles indicate principal beats, the squares secondary beats. The principal beats are further marked with dots placed to the right of the *sê* and *ch'in* symbols.

The *ch'in* symbols can be read without difficulty; a sequence of four symbols is repeated throughout each column. In the first one we find:

open string III	C
open string I	$\underline{G}$
open string III	C
string I, *hui* 10	C

If we compare *ch'in* and *sê* notes we find that both instruments perform in unison. The annotations at the bottom of each column indicate repetitions.

SÊ TABLATURE

Ensemble *sê* music is notated with *lü* and occasionally with *kung-ch'ê* symbols. Solo *sê* music, besides using the aforementioned systems, is sometimes notated in a simple form of tablature which is derived from the *chien-tzŭ*.

Before we consider this tablature, a few remarks about the *sê* are indicated.

The *sê* (瑟), like the *ch'in*, is a Chinese zither, the origin of which has been ascribed to the mythical emperor Fu Hsi. Since both ch'in and sê are frequently mentioned together in the Confucian Classics[33] we may assume that they date from approximately the same era. The sê is larger than the ch'in and consists of a long board (the sizes vary — the longest measures 81 inches) which is more curved than the upper board of the ch'in. It resembles the upper half of a wooden cylinder. Along the curved surface 25 strings are strung, tuned most often in an anhemitonic pentatonic, less frequently in a heptatonic order.

According to legend the instrument originally had 50 strings, but this number had been reduced to 25 at the time of the legendary emperor Huang Ti. The Êrh Ya[34] reports that one day a Miss Su played the sê, and the emperor was so overwhelmed by the mournful sound of the instrument that he issued an order to reduce the number of strings from 50 to 25 in order to reduce the saddening effect. The number of strings varied from one instrument to another. The so-called "Great Sê" used to have 27, the "Elegant Sê" 23 (or 19), and the "Praise Sê" 23 strings.

In contrast to the ch'in the sê has no hui but uses movable bridges Each string has its own bridge and each group of five bridges is painted in a different color: blue, red, yellow, white, and black. The instrument is always played in octaves; that is, two open strings are plucked simultaneously.

During the later Chou period the sê disappeared as a solo instrument,[35] and only in the nineteenth century, after more than a millennium of neglect, did it become popular again. Several factors may hav contributed to this revival: the movable bridges allow a number of differing tunings, the sê is relatively easy to play since only open strings are used, and its tablature is remarkably simple.

In order to read this tablature we list below the Chinese numbers from 1 to 25 which represent the 25 strings together with their pentatonic tuning:

In sê tablature each number is placed in an abbreviated kou (勹), and two strings tuned an octave apart are always plucked simultaneously. The following pairs are in use:

The number of the right represents the lower note of the octave; the one on the left, the upper note. The following (Fig. 67, p. 299) is the sê part of the Hymn to Confucius.[36] This form of sê tablature was also applied to the notation of music of other Chinese zithers (e. g., the Chêng).

Following (Fig. 68, p. 300) is one page of a Sê-p'u (瑟譜)[37] by Hsiung P'êng Lai (熊朋來), a composer who lived during the Yüan period. The title column at the right reads: "sê-p'u, second book." The second column informs us that it is a poem with old notation; the third column is the title of the poem, "Deer Calling, III." The text which follows, in columns four and five, is one of three stanzas of a famous ode of the Shih Ching. The English translation of this stanza,[38] as far as it is shown in Figure 68, is as follows:

> Yu, yu, cry the deer
> Nibbling the black southernwood in the fields.
> I have a lucky guest.
> Let me play my zithern, blow my reed-organ,
> Blow my reed-organ, trill their tongues,
> Take up the baskets of offerings.
> Here is that man that loves me
> And will teach me the ways of Chou. . . .

The notation of the melody appears twice: lü symbols in column six, kung-ch'ê symbols in column seven. The reading of both notations causes no difficulties. We observe that the tone material is C D E F# G A B c d, which shows the sê tunings were not always pentatonic.

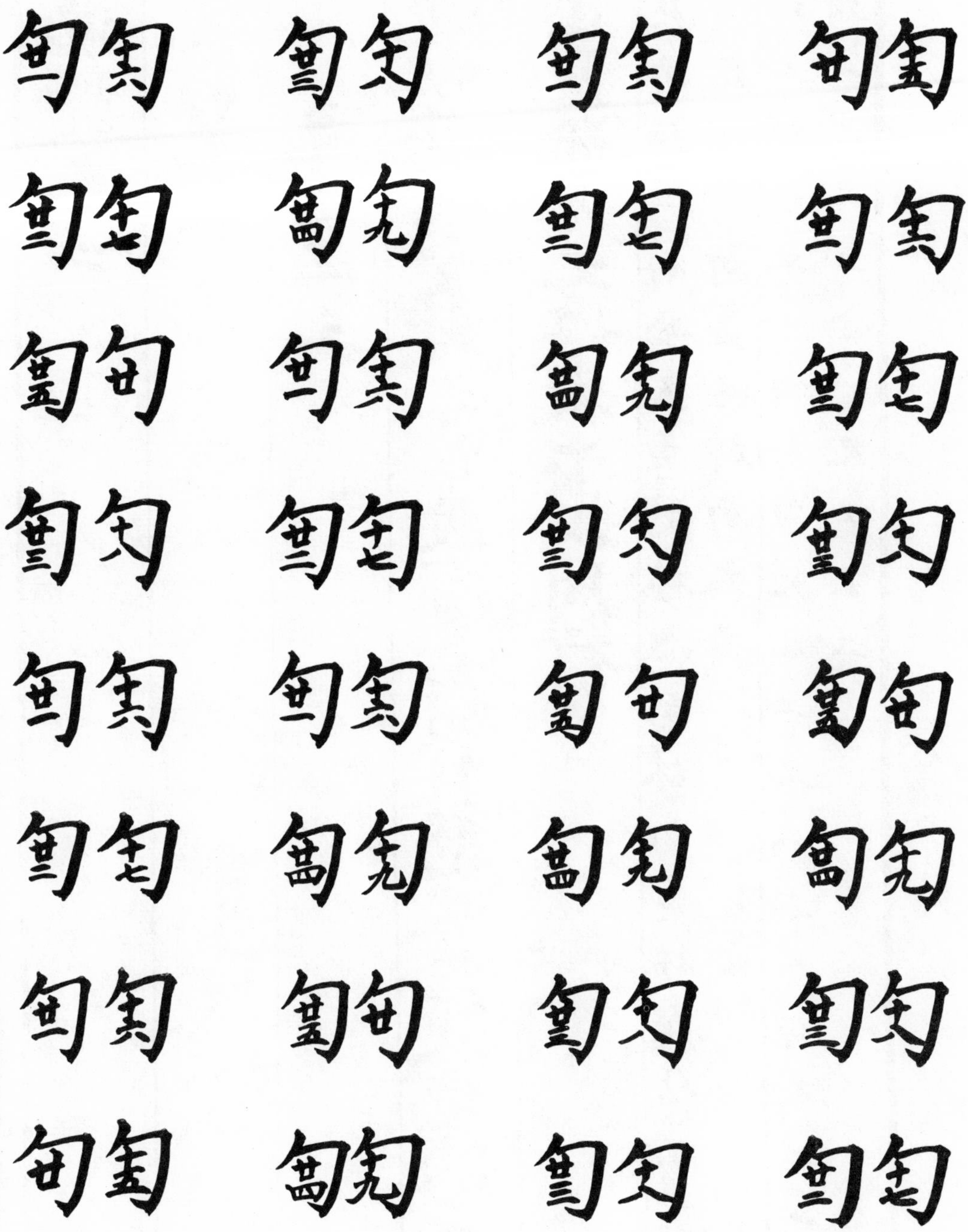

Figure 67

Figure 68

瑟譜卷二

詩舊譜

鹿鳴之三

呦呦鹿鳴食野之苹我有嘉賓鼓瑟吹笙吹笙鼓簧承
筐是將人之好我示我周行
黃南蕤姑南姑太黃蕤林應南林南黃林蕤林南姑應
黃姑南林南黃姑林南太黃
六工勾一工一四合勾尺凡工尺工六尺勾尺工一凡
六一工尺工合一尺工五六

KOREAN ZITHER TABLATURE
(HAP-CHA-PO, 合字譜)

All East Asiatic zithers have their origin in China; some have retained the features of their Chinese prototypes while others have developed along individual lines. Korea possesses a number of zithers,[39] but only one approximates the nobility and distinction of the Chinese ch'in. This instrument is the hyŭn-kŭm (玄琴), a zither often freely and poetically translated as "black lute." Eckardt writes[40] that it is possible that the Korean general term for zither, kŭmunko (usually pronounced komunko, 거문고), is derived from the "black zither," because kŭmunko or komunko means "black ko." The syllable ko may have been the ancient Sino-Korean kŭm, a sound that is still recognizable in the Chinese ch'in and the Japanese koto.[41]

Although legend relates[42] that the kŭm was invented in the fifth century A. D. in Kokuryo,[43] and that the description "black" is explained by a story in which a group of black storks danced around the inventor after he had completed the zither, there is no doubt that the kŭm had its origin in China. In contrast to the Chinese ch'in, which has seven strings and no frets, the hyŭn-kŭm has six strings and is fretted. A further difference is that the strings of the Chinese ch'in are usually plucked with the fingers while the strings of the hyŭn-kŭm are generally plucked with a small rod called suttae (숫대), which the player holds in his right hand.

The hyŭn-kŭm has approximately the same shape as the Chinese ch'in. The chief characteristics of the Korean zither are its sixteen frets and six strings, of which the first, fourth, fifth, and sixth remain open while the second and third are strung across frets. It must be noted that although the frets extend below the fourth string, this string is never depressed against the frets but always remains open. Contrary to the hui of the Chinese ch'in, the frets of the hyŭn-kŭm are numbered from left to right.

The first information about the appearance of a kŭm type in Korea can be found in the oldest Korean historical document, the Samkuk-saki (三國史記),[44] the "History of the Three Kingdoms,"[45] written by Kim Pu-shik (金富軾) at the order of In-chong, King of Korea, about 1145. In the ak-chi (樂志), the chapter on music in the Samkuk-saki, one reads that a man brought an instrument with seven strings from Tsin (晉) China (265-420) to Kokuryo, but that no one was able to play it. The Samkuk-saki contains no musical notations but mentions the titles of a number of pieces[46] written by a musician called Ok Po-ko (玉寶高), who lived in the kingdom of Silla. The information given in the Samkuk-saki that a zither had been imported from China which could not be played by Korean musicians is repeated in a Japanese work called Tai-ho ryō (大寶令) — its full name is Tai-ho ritsu-ryō — written in A. D. 701 under the auspices of Emperor Mommu Tennō (697-707). It states that although students were studying the kŭm, they were unable to perform music on it.[47]

In 1370 the first ruler of the Chinese Ming dynasty, Tai Ts'ou (太祖), sent a number of instruments to Korea. Among them were stone chimes (with sixteen stone slabs), bell chimes (with sixteen bells), a Chinese shêng (Korean: saeng), a kŭm, a sŭl (the Chinese sê), and others. A year later, in 1371, several Korean students went to Ming China to study the art of kŭm playing. In the fifteenth century, too, instruments were sent from China to Korea and treated with great respect. According to the Ak-hak-koe-pŭm[48] these imported instruments were used only by court musicians who had learned how to master them. The kŭm and sŭl were used in the ritual of the ancestral temple (Chong-myo, 宗廟) and, according to the ceremonial order of this period,[49] six kŭm were used in the temple and another six in the orchestra of the imperial court.

It is not known when the specifically Korean form of the hyŭn-kŭm (six strings and frets) evolved and when solo kŭm music became popular in Korea. We can assume that this evolution occurred after the fifth and before the tenth centuries A. D.

The hyŭn-kŭm tablature is called hap-cha-po (合字譜), "combined letter notation." Indications concerning its first appearance can be found in the Ak-hak-koe-pŭm. This work relates that hap-cha-po was used for notating music of the various zithers (hyŭn-kŭm, kaya-kŭm, etc.) and lutes (T'ang- and Hyang p'i-pa). Sŭng Hyŭn, the author of the Ak-hak-koe-pŭm and of a second work, the O-chu-yŭn-mun (五洲衍文, "Five States Travel Report"),[50] was given the honorary title "Inventor of Hap-cha-po." It is more likely, however, that hap-cha-po was already in use in the fifteenth century, and that Sŭng Hyŭn's contribution was more one of recording than of inventing. If he had been the inventor of hap-cha-po, one would expect to find some notational examples of hap-cha-po in his work, but neither the Ak-hak-koe-pŭm nor the O-chu-yŭn-mun contain any.

Figure 69 (p. 304) illustrates how the first kŭm tuning was notated in the Ak-hak-koe-pŭm. The work discusses five tunings, of which only the first was in use. We observe the old Chinese Five Tone Notation[51] in the left column, the definition of pitches expressed by lü symbols[52] in the middle column, and the numbering of the seven strings in the right column.

宮	黄	一絃
商	太	二絃
角	姑	三絃
徵	林	四絃
羽	南	五絃
小宮	潢	六絃
小商	汰	七絃

Figure 69

The *lü* symbols in Figure 69 inform us explicitly that the seven strings are to be tuned to C[53] D E G A c d. This tuning refers to the Chinese *ch'in* at the time when it was imported into Korea and musicians began to use the instrument. The Korean *kŭm* tunings eventually underwent changes which make them differ considerably from the Chinese types.[54]

The earliest zither books came from China. It is probable that manuscripts such as the *Yu-lan-p'u*,[55] with detailed playing instructions, were favored by Korean musicians because they enabled them to learn zither playing without any detours to study notational symbols. We know (Lee) that the original *Hui-ch'in ko-p'u*[56] (in Korean: *Hwi-kŭm ka-po*) had been preserved in Korea by the late Dr. Yun Yong-ku until it was lost recently during the Korean War.

There are numerous zither books which represent the Korean art of *kŭm* playing; particularly important are two works from the sixteenth and seventeenth centuries respectively: the *An-sang kŭm-po* (安瑺琴譜), the "*Kŭm* Book of An-sang," written in 1572, and the *Yang-kŭm shin-po* (梁琴新譜), "Yang's New *Kŭm* Book," written in 1610. The name in this title must not be confused with the name of the (Korean) zither with fourteen strings, called *yang-kŭm* (洋琴). Both books are collections of zither pieces, some of which are original and some of which are songs arranged for the instrument.

The *An-sang kŭm-po*[57] contains eleven pieces, among which we find the famous *Man-tae-yŭp* (慢大葉), *Yŭ-min-ak* (與民樂), *Po-hŭ-cha* (步虛子), and *Sa-mo-kok* (思母曲), which will be discussed later in this chapter. The author and compiler of the *Yang-kŭm shin-po*[58] was Yang Tŭk-soo (梁

德壽), a Korean court musician of the seventeenth century. As a result of the Japanese invasion (Hideyoshi) Yang fled to Namwon and was ordered by Kim Tu-nam, the ruler of the province of Im-sil, to compile a book of zither music in order to preserve the important melodies of his time. For this work Yang Tŭk-soo has been referred to as the inventor of hap-cha-po, an ascription which is, as we know, erroneous because hap-cha-po had been mentioned one hundred years earlier in the O-chu-yŭn-mun. The Yang-kŭm shin-po contains nine pieces, all notated in hap-cha-po and none of which is an original composition of Yang's. They all are Sok-ak (俗樂), "popular music," which usually is not performed officially at the royal court. If we consider that sok-ak pieces were collected by Yang, a court musician, they must indeed have been well known to be deemed worthy of being recorded by him. The titles of all nine pieces are: a) Man-tae-yŭp (慢大葉), lit. "Wandering Big Leaf"; b) Puk-chŭn (北殿), lit. "North Palace"; c, d, e, f, g) Chung-tae-yŭp (中大葉), lit. "Middle Big Leaf"; h) Cho-ŭm (調音), a tuning piece; i) Kam-kun-ŭn (感君恩), lit. "Appreciating the King's Favor."

Chung-tae-yŭp (pieces c, d, e, f, g), written in several modes which will be discussed later, has been described as the oldest-known Korean melody. These five versions are notated for the first time in the Yang-kŭm shin-po; the other four items can be found in other collections as well.

The importance of Chung-tae-yŭp is evidenced by the fact that it is included in another collection which contains only ceremonial music, the Tae-ak hu-po (大樂後譜), lit. "Great Music, Later Book," published in 1759.[59] The pieces of this collection are called Cho-ak (朝樂), "Palace (Morning) Music," which were performed at the Cho-hoe (朝會), the official morning audience at the royal palace.[60]

Following a Chinese custom similar to one of medieval Europe, the writers of the An-sang kŭm-po and the Yang-kŭm shin-po placed the symbols of hap-cha-po side by side with those of one or more other notations. The most frequent combination is hap-cha-po and yuk-po (肉譜)[61] in parallel columns. This particular combination gradually led to a modification of hap-cha-po which will be discussed below. At the present time hap-cha-po is used only for notating music of the hyŭn-kŭm.

The Tuning of the Hyŭn-kŭm

The tunings of the imported Chinese ch'in[62] underwent changes in Korea, especially between the time of the Ak-hak koe-pŭm and the time of the great zither books, the An-sang kŭm-po and Yang-kŭm shin-po. Instead of using all strings for performing the melody, the hyŭn-kŭm usually confines the playing of the melody to two strings while the other four remain open. This practice necessarily led to changes in tuning which we shall endeavor to describe.

The six silken strings of the hyŭn-kŭm are numbered in such a manner that the first is nearest the player and the sixth is farthest from him. The first, fourth, fifth, and sixth strings are always open, while the second and third are depressed against the sixteen frets of the instrument. The following chart (Fig. 70) illustrates the board, strings, and frets (in our subsequent descriptions of hap-cha-po we shall again number the strings with Roman numerals, the sixteen frets with Arabic numerals):

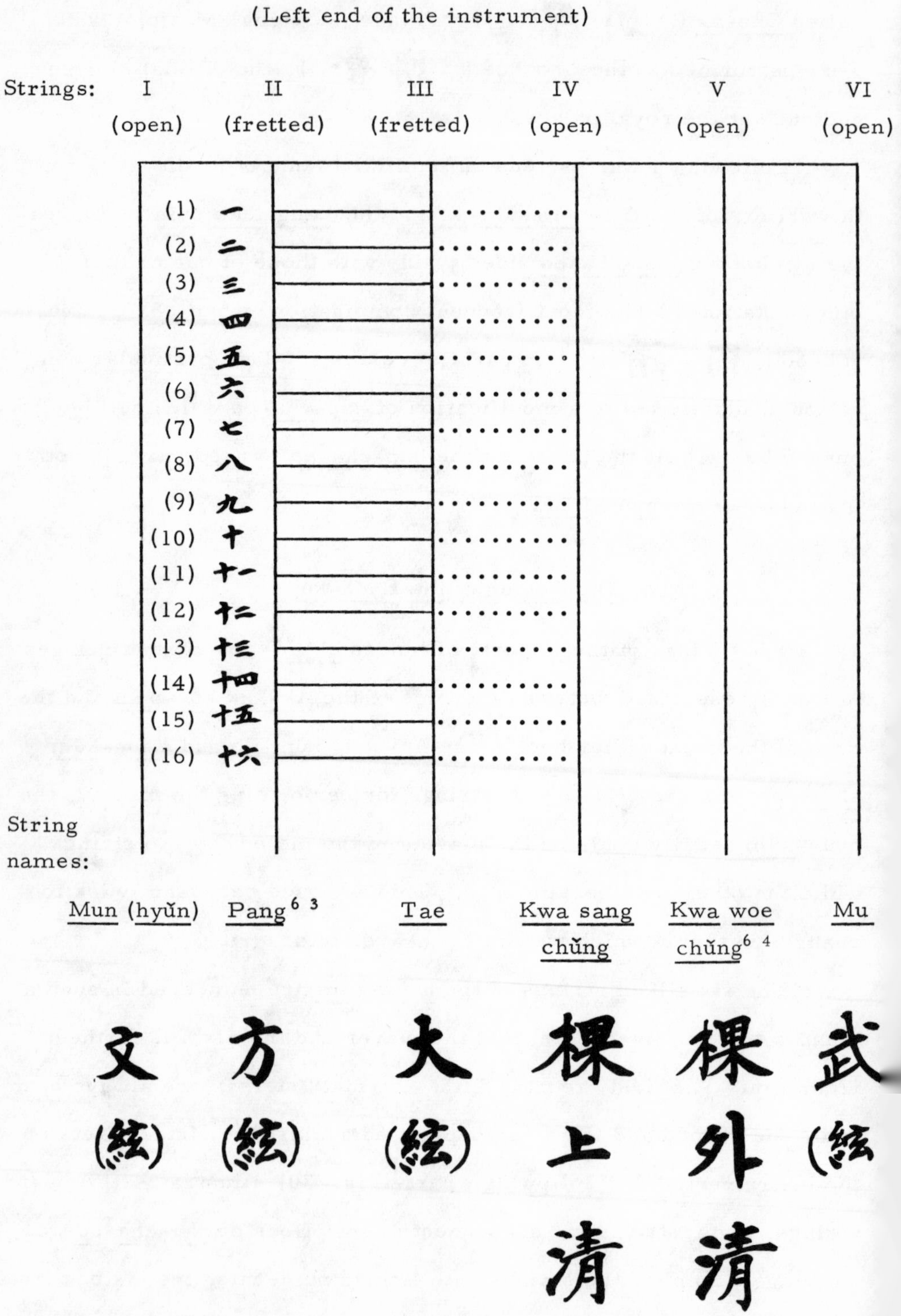
(Left end of the instrument)
Strings: I II III IV V VI
(open) (fretted) (fretted) (open) (open) (open)
(1) 一
(2) 二
(3) 三
(4) 四
(5) 五
(6) 六
(7) 七
(8) 八
(9) 九
(10) 十
(11) 十一
(12) 十二
(13) 十三
(14) 十四
(15) 十五
(16) 十六
String names:
Mun (hyŭn) Pang[63] Tae Kwa sang chŭng Kwa woe chŭng[64] Mu
文(絃) 方(絃) 大(絃) 棵上清 棵外清 武(絃

Figure 70

It is remarkable that the open second and third strings are indicated by "fret one," that is, the strings are not depressed if fret one is notated. The strings have names: I is called the Mun (hyŭn), the "civil" (string); II, the Pang (hyŭn), "play" (string); III, the Tae (hyŭn), the "big" (string); IV, the Kwa sang chŭng, the "clear one above the frets"; V, the Kwa woe chŭng, the "clear one outside the frets"; and VI, the Mu (hyŭn), the "military" (string). Strings IV, V, and VI are often played in quick succession with a sweeping arpeggio stroke. The word chŭng, "clear," "high," used in the names of strings IV and V indicates that they are tuned an octave higher than string VI.

Before turning to the tuning of the instrument we have to consider the four modes (cho) of Korean Ah-ak; all four are anhemitonic pentatonic. There is no adherence to absolute pitches; the instruments are tuned either to accommodate the requirements of the singer or, if used in ensembles, according to stone or bell chimes, in which instances pitches are fixed. The chimes, however, are not always in tune and vary in pitch from one set to another. The lowest string is usually tuned to the note Bb (or Eb), a procedure which we shall adopt. The four modes of Ah-ak are:

a) Pyong-cho (平 調):[65]
Bb C Eb F G Bb

b) U-cho (羽 調):
Eb F Ab Bb c eb

c) Pyong-cho-kae-myon-cho (平 調 界 面 調):
Bb Db Eb F Ab Bb

d) U-cho-kae-myon-cho (羽 調 界 面 調):
Eb Gb Ab Bb db eb.

Both *pyong* modes begin with the note *Bb*, and both *U-cho* modes, beginning with Eb, are transpositions a fourth higher than the *pyong* forms. *Pyong-cho* is believed to represent the tranquil and peaceful voice of justice and wisdom; *U-cho*, the open, virile moods; and the *kae-myon* modes represent the peacefully pathetic and the virile pathetic moods, respectively.

The introductory chapter of the *Yang-kŭm shin-po*, which explains the tuning of the instrument, offers the following instructions: the strings IV and V are to be tuned to *kung* (宮)[66] in the *pyong* modes. String VI has to be tuned to *chok kung* (蜀宮), also called *tak kung* (濁宮), "cloudy kung," both terms indicating a note an octave below that of strings IV and V:

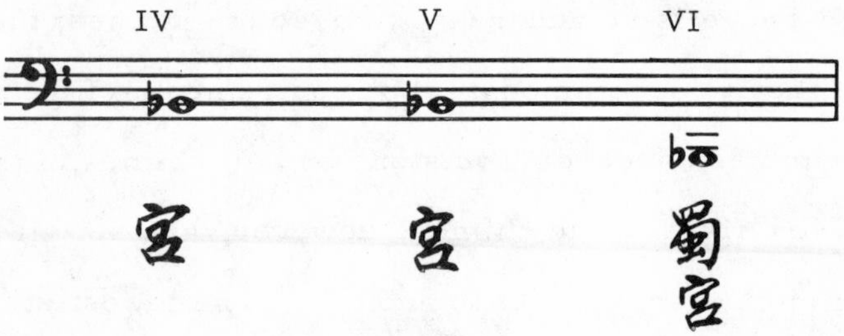

In the *U-cho* forms, where the *kung* is a fourth higher (Eb), the tuning of strings IV, V, and VI is:

Even though the instructions concerning the tunings of the *hyŭn-kŭm*, as we find them in the *Yang-kŭm shin-po*, are somewhat involved, we shall discuss them because they provide an interesting view of how Korean *kŭm* masters of the seventeenth century dealt with the problem

Before we consider these instructions we have to remember that "fret one" always indicates the pitch of the open string. Thus "fret two" will be the first one to alter the pitch of the string. Another unusual feature is the instruction "lightly depressed." If, for instance, the string is to be "lightly depressed" on the third fret, the finger touches the string in such a manner that it is stopped not by the third but by the next taller fret — the second one. In short, the pitch will be lower than if it were produced by the third fret, yet it is notated by means of the third fret symbol. If we read that a string is to be "lightly depressed" on fret two it means that fret one (the open string) is intended. The reason for this practice is that it can suggest a change of hand position on the instrument and, in certain cases, may facilitate (or confuse) notation.

Pyong-cho Tuning:

The pitch of string III is indicated by an indirect instruction: fret six of string III when "lightly depressed" should produce the same note as that of the open string IV. Fret two of string II, if "lightly depressed," should again produce the same pitch as that of the open string IV, and the open string I should be tuned to the pitch produced by fret two of string III.

U-cho Tuning:

Strings II and III retain the same tuning as in Pyong-cho. String II on fret one or on fret two, "lightly depressed," has to have the same pitch as string IV; string III on fret six, "lightly depressed," has to produce the same pitch as string IV. In contrast to the Pyong-cho tuning, string I has to produce the same pitch as string III on fret two "lightly depressed" (which means open string), and which is also the pitch of string VI.

Yang's involved tuning method can be reduced into two short formulas:

Pyong-cho: (宮 is Bb)

I, 1 = III, 2 (徵 is F)

II, 2 (lightly depressed) = IV, V (宮 , Bb)

III, 6 (lightly depressed) = IV, V

IV }
V } = 宮 (Bb)

VI = 宮 (lower Bb)

U-cho: (宮 is Eb)

I, 1 = III, 2

II, 2 (lightly depressed) = IV, V (徵 , Bb)

III, 6 (lightly depressed) = IV, V (Bb)

IV }
V } = 徵 (Bb)

VI = III, 2 = I (宮 , Eb)

We must add that several notes on both strings are never performed but may occasionally be used as bases for alterations. In practice, III, 3 is never used. It represents the note G (natural), which does not occur (in that position) in any of the four modes. How ever, it can become important as a low alteration of III, 3.

Below is a list of the notations of the pitches commonly produce on strings II and III, irrespective of the alterations in the kae-myon modes. The notes on string II are notated with "pang" (方), c string III with tae (大). The fret numbers are written below the pang and tae symbols.

String II

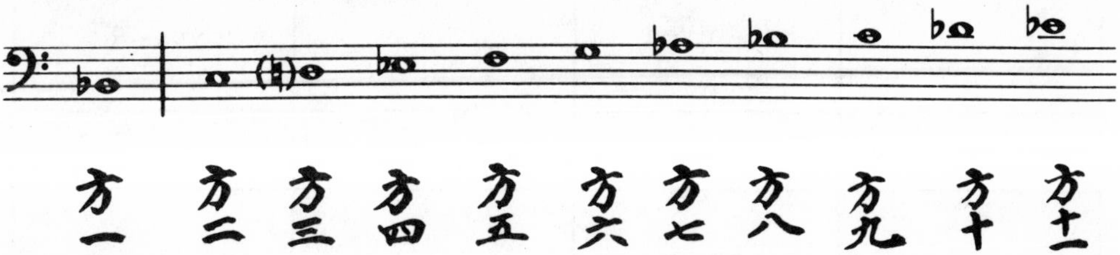

String III

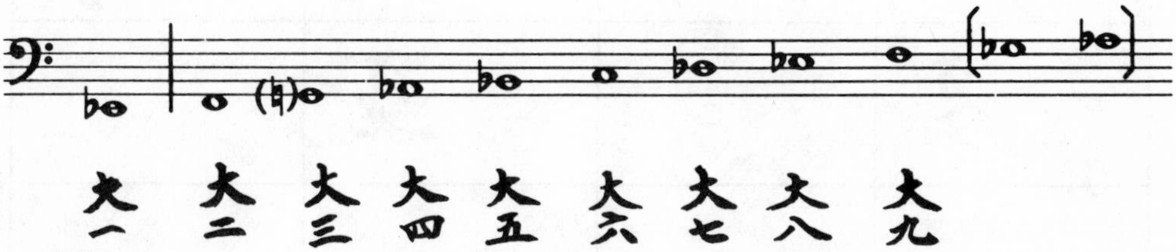

The "big string" (III) is never played higher than the ninth fret. The open "play string" (II), invariably tuned a fifth higher than the "big string," corresponds to the pitch of III, 5. Since the *kae-myon-cho* forms require alterations of notes, notes which in *Pyong-cho* and *U-cho* can be produced by merely stopping the strings on the rigid frets, the player has to apply pressure against the string with his left hand in order to modify the sounds. For instance, in *U-cho*, II, 5 produces the note F; *U-cho kae-myon-cho*, however, requires Gb (and omits F), and here the player has to apply pressure to the string in order to change F to Gb. This procedure is notated with the symbol 力 , which is placed below the fret number, e.g. 方五力 , and will produce the required Gb in *U-cho kae-myon-cho*. The symbol 力 is called *yok* ("strength") in Korea.[6] [7]

The following chart shows the commonly-used notes of all four modes notated with basic *hap-cha-po* symbols:

Pyong-cho	Pyong-cho kae-myon-cho	U-cho	U-cho kae-myon-cho
Bb	(方八)	eb	(方五)
	Ab 方六力		db 方九力
G 方六		c 方九	
F 方五	F 方五	Bb 方八	Bb 方八
Eb 方四	Eb 方四	Ab 方七	Ab 方七
	Db 大六力		Gb 方五力
C 大六		F 方五	
Bb 大五	Bb 大五	Eb 方四	Eb 方四

In Pyong-cho kae-myon-cho the notes Db and Ab, and in U-cho kae-myon-cho the notes Gb and db, are notated with yok. These four notes are produced by applying pressure to the notes C and G of Pyong-cho and F and c of U-cho.

The opposite effect of yok is created by the "lightly depressed" sign, ス.[68] As already mentioned this sign instructs the player to touch the string on the prescribed fret so lightly that the next lower sound is produced. For instance, in U-cho, we may find 大五 大五ス, which will sound 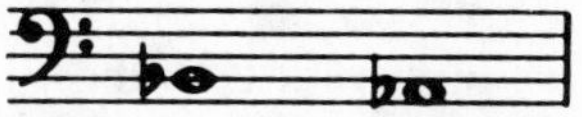 ; it could be notated in a less complex manner by 大五 大四. Or, in Pyong-cho kae-myon-cho, the following could be written: 大四 大三ス which will sound  ; 大三, denotes that the note G (natural) cannot be used in this mode. We could, however, notate 大四 大三ス as 大四 大二.

In the introductory part of the Yang-kŭm shin-po[69] we read that fret six of string III when "lightly depressed" should produce the same pitch as the (open) string IV. We know that successive frets produce a diatonic sequence of notes; thus, if we assume that fret six of string III produces Bb (the same as the open string IV), all we have to do is count in reverse, or better, down the scale until we reach fret one. Before we do this we have to keep in mind that the "lightly depressed" fret six produces the same pitch as fret five, hence counting down the scale must start from Bb. If fret five produces Bb, fret one (the open string) will produce Eb.[70] Similarly, if we endeavor to ascertain the pitch of string II we again have to remember that the "lightly depressed" fret two of string II produces the same pitch as the open string (fret one). This has to produce the same pitch as the open string IV (Bb). String I should be tuned to the pitch produced when depressing fret two of string III. The open string III produces Eb, hence fret two will produce F, one diatonic degree higher.

The Yang-kŭm shin-po still refers to movable bridges placed below the open strings (I, IV, V, VI). These bridges are no longer in use; when they were they served only as tuning devices. The famous kŭm-po states that in the tuning of Pyong modes the bridge of the Mun string (I) should be moved in such a manner that the pitch of the string (I) becomes the same as that produced by string III when "lightly depressed" on fret three. We read further that in the tunings of the U modes the "big string" (III) and strings IV and V should be tuned in the same way as in the Pyong modes, but that the Mu string (VI) should be raised to Eb and the bridge of the Mun string (I) should be moved in such a manner that the pitch becomes a whole-tone lower than that in the Pyong mode tunings, namely Eb.

Figures 71 and 72 (pp. 317-18), taken from the Yang-kŭm shin-po, illustrate the tuning of the old hyŭn-kŭm in both Pyong and U modes. Both charts shown in these figures are provided with the symbols of the old (Chinese) Five-Tone Notation, which are applicable to any specific five-tone tuning.

The first chart informs us (outer right column) that we are dealing with the hyŭn-kŭm; the second column from the right mentions that this is the Pyong-cho sang-hyong ("scattered form") tuning. Below it we read that the mode is a five-tone form in which the notes kak (角) and chih (徵) are used. In the second chart, which deals with the U-cho tuning, the corresponding annotation states that the notes U (羽), kung (宮), and sang (商) are used. These two annotations refer to the Eb - F location in both mode in Pyong-cho (Bb C Eb F G), with the appropriate Bb as kung, the

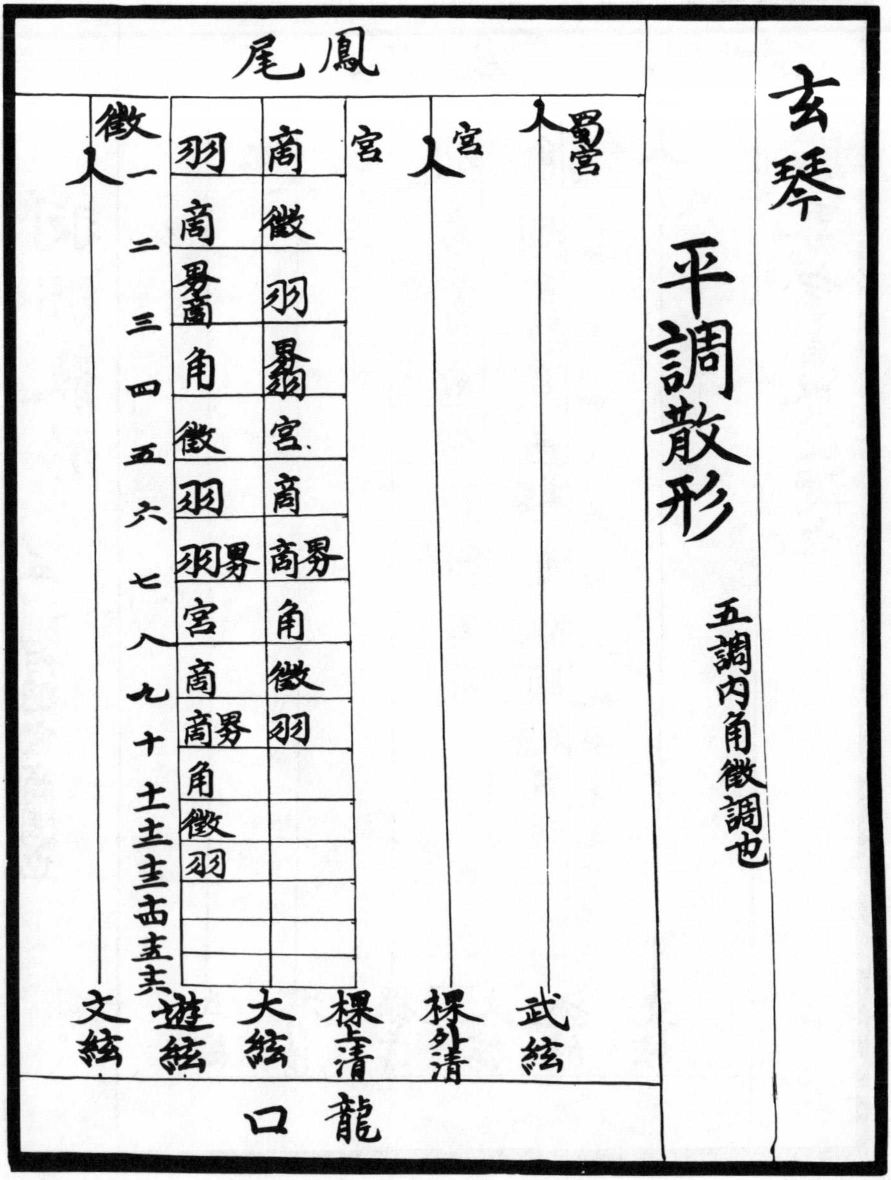

Figure 71

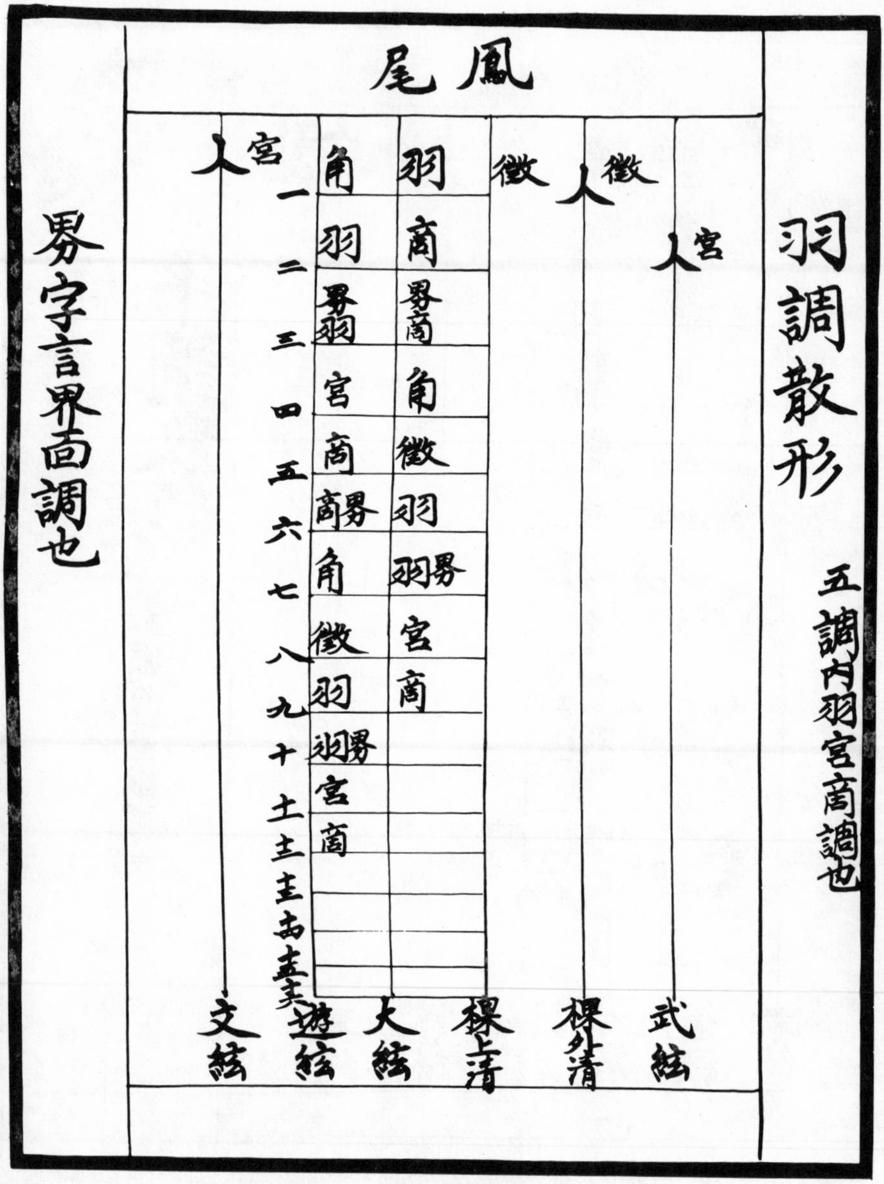

Figure 72

notes Eb and F are kak and ch'ih; in U-cho (Eb F Ab Bb c), with the required Eb as kung, the notes Eb and F are kung and sang, and, furthermore, the preceding U is given. This is helpful because in both modes the upper three notes progress by whole-tone steps. Hence the position of U, kung, and sang is a determining factor; the interval between sang and kak becomes that of a minor third.[71]

At the top of both charts stands "Phoenix Tail" and at the bottom "Dragon Mouth" – terms for the two ends of the board of the hyŭn-kŭm. At the outer left side of the U-cho chart (Fig. 72) is an indication that the symbols provided with 界 appear only in the kae-myon-cho forms where sang and U have to be raised by a semitone (to 商界 and 羽界). This remark applies also to the Pyong-cho chart.

Somewhat puzzling are the relative pitch indications for strings II and III. The charts show that the two strings, when open (fret one), are supposed to produce the pitches U and sang respectively, each of which is a fourth lower than the pitches produced when the strings are depressed at fret two. Instruments built during the last two centuries show that the interval between open string and fret two has become that of a major second.

Upon examining the prescribed relative pitches on strings II and III, beginning with fret two, we find that the charts are in accordance with our previous statements except that fret three would produce a note which is a semitone higher than sang (fret two) on string II and would also produce the note U, which is a whole tone higher than the preceding chih on string III. This is technically impossible because the frets are rigid, and the distance between frets two and three cannot produce an interval of a semitone on string II and one of a whole tone on string III. The charts show these unequal intervals because string II is never used below fret four, hence the carefree approach to notation found in the two charts, though most puzzling to a person who tries to study the subject without the help of a *kŭm* master, is of no consequence to the initiated. In short, a certain amount of secrecy, perhaps even purposeful misleading of the uninitiated, can be detected in these charts.

We shall now leave the charts of *Yang* and turn to basic string and fret signs, assuming that the distance between fret one and two creates the interval of a major second. In order to save the reader the bother of checking the four modes as notated in the charts, we list the notes once more:

Pyong-cho

Bb C Eb F G (宮 商 角 徵 羽)

Pyong-cho kae-myon-cho

Bb Db Eb F Ab (宮 商界 角 徵 羽界)

U-cho

Eb F Ab Bb c (宮 商 角 徵 羽)

U-cho kae-myon-cho

Eb Gb Ab Bb db (宮 商界 角 徵 羽界)

The following illustrates the notes of the four modes notated in *hap-cha-po*. As some notes can be performed either on strings II or III, the common alternatives are shown:

Pyong-cho

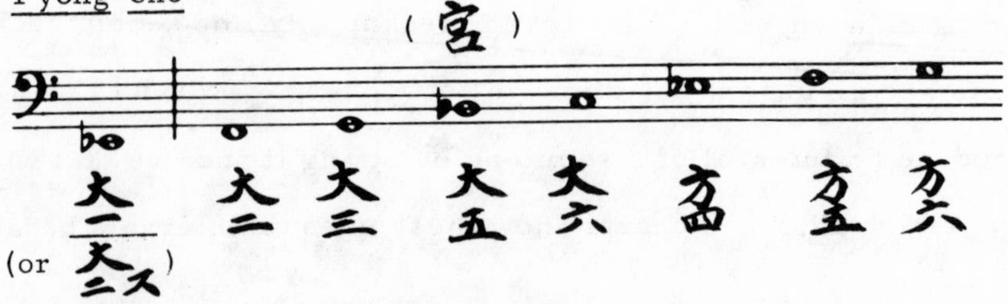

Pyong-cho kae-myon-cho

U-cho

U-cho kae-myon-cho

Occasionally writers omit the yok sign and notate only the string symbol and the number of the fret. If the note produced by this particular fret does not appear in the mode prescribed (this can happen only in one of the two kae-myon-cho forms), the fret number will then represent the note as if it were raised by a yok sign. For instance, if a writer wishes to notate Db in U-cho kae-myon-cho, he may do this by writing  or by omitting the yok sign and writing only . In Pyong-cho and U-cho  represents the note C, but since the piece is in U-cho kae-myon-cho the writer assumes that the player knows that the symbol cannot possibly denote C and expects him to perform Db, the correct note appropriate for the kae-myon-cho forms.

The organization of hap-cha-po symbols differs from that of the Chinese chien-tzŭ. The Korean symbol places the fret number below the string sign and any other instructions regarding the plucking finger, direction of plucking, arpeggio, and others are placed to the left or right of the string-fret combination. The Korean symbols do not number the strings because only two strings are employed for melody playing (大 and 方). In Chinese chien-tzŭ the plucking finger sign is the central feature of the complex symbol; in hap-cha-po the central feature is the string-fret combination:

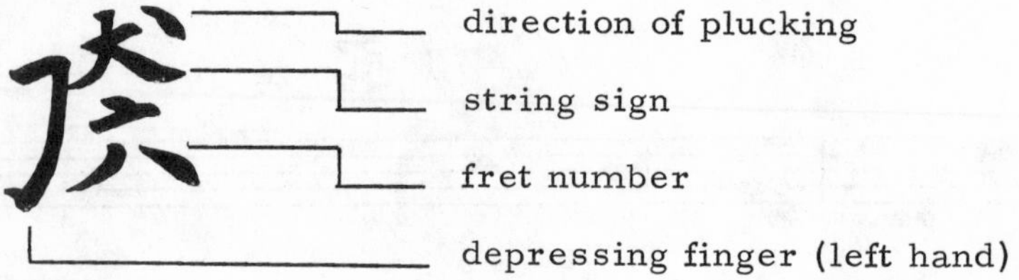

In contrast to the Chinese ch'in tablature Korean hap-cha-po does not use any signs for the plucking of strings because, as mentioned before, a small rod is employed. However, the Ak-hak koe-pŭm of the fifteenth century reports that two kinds of (finger) plucking were in use: 勾 (ku), the right middle finger plucking in an inward direction, and 挑 (cho), the right middle finger plucking in an outward direction. Since the great zither masters of Korea used the small rod (suttae), no plucking finger instructions are given in their books except the two comma-shaped signs placed to the right and left of the notational symbol, which denote the direction of the plucking movement. Technical details are indicated by:

ㄱ — the left thumb depresses the string; the sign is an abbreviation of 母 ("thumb").

人 (亻) — the left index finger depresses the string; it is an abbreviation of 食 ("index finger").

レ — the left middle finger depresses the string; it is an abbreviation of 長 ("middle finger").

タ — the left ring finger depresses the string; it is an abbreviation of 名 ("ring finger").

丨 — denotes an appoggiatura; the ornamental note has to be performed by the rod on the open <u>Mun</u> string (I) and can be followed by a note on string II or III. The succeeding note is notated in the symbol while the ornamenting note is indicated by the vertical line; for instance,  is transcribed as

 .

丿 — at the <u>left</u> side of the notational symbol; indicates that the string is to be plucked in an outward direction away from the player.

丶 — at the <u>right</u> side of the notational symbol; indicates that the string is to be plucked in an inward direction toward the player.

Some of the foregoing signs may be combined:

フ and 丨 may be notated: 卩

フ and レ may be notated: ヲ

丨 and タ may be notated: 阝夕

Frequently we find annotations such as 上同 (or 仝), "the same as above," which mean that the preceding note is to be repeated and performed in the same manner as before. We may also find 上同ス which indicates that ス is to be applied when the preceding note is being repeated. For instance, 大三上同 may be transcribed as

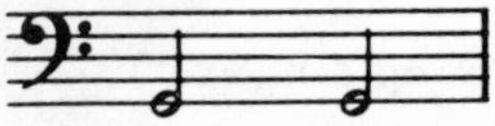

, but 大三上同ス must be read

.

The sign 乚 indicates an arpeggio across the open strings. It usually begins with string I and, avoiding strings II and III, extends to one of the strings IV, V, or VI. Avoiding strings II and III is not difficult because the open strings are strung slightly higher than are the two fretted strings.

The following shows two typical annotations in which the use of 乚 is illustrated:

乚

至 chi ("up to")

棵 kwa-

外 woe-

清 chŭng

This means that an arpeggio, which always begins with string I, is performed up to the kwa-woe-chŭng string (V).

ㄴ

乃 nae (namely'')

至 chi (''up to'')

武 mu-

絃 hyŭn

The second annotation indicates an arpeggio beginning with the Mun string (I) and ending with the Mu string (VI).

Occasionally the symbol ㄴ, and particularly the words kae chŭng (皆 清), ''all chŭng,'' indicate the succession of strings IV, V, and VI without string I. This generally occurs when the arpeggio becomes the concluding feature of a phrase or a piece.[72]

The rarely-used sign ○ indicates a full arpeggio across all six strings. The sign ミ indicates a shake or a vibrato. 厶 denotes a lateral push of the string after it has been plucked — the left hand depresses the string at a prescribed spot, the right hand plucks, and then the left hand pushes the vibrating string laterally whereby the pitch is raised. For instance:

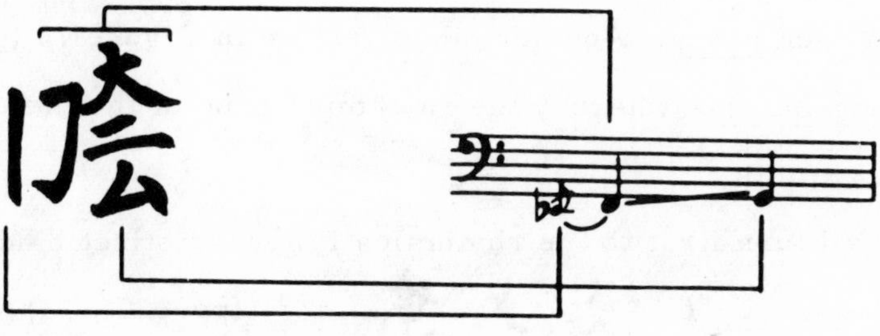

The left ring finger depresses only the pang string (II), the middle finger the tae string (III), and the left index finger and thumb can thus be used on both strings II and III. If the symbol does not contain any signs for the depressing finger and if the note is to be produced on an open string, the plucking can be done by either the middle finger, the index finger, or the thumb of the left hand.

Hap-cha-po is frequently combined with the (Chinese) Five Tone Notation, the two being written in parallel columns side by side. In such instances the Five Tone Notation shows a "new" symbol (界) which is added to represent the raised sang and U (the hap-cha-po combinations with yok) in the modes of Pyong-cho kae-myon-cho and U-cho kae-myon-cho. For instance, if Bb is kung, C is sang in Pyong-cho. In Pyong-cho kae-myon-cho, where sang becomes Db, the symbol is denoted by 界
商 (or 商界). The same applies to the note Ab, the raised U in the two kae-myon-cho forms: 界
羽 (or 羽界).

While ch'in tablatures show very little rhythmic organization, leaving most of it to the player's memory and invention, we find that hyŭn-kŭm tablatures show some clarity in rhythmic matters by using the chŭng-kan-po.[74] The division of a "measure" (haeng) into six kang and each kang into two or three chŭng-kan may be observed in many kŭm books.

The piece shown in Figure 73 (p. 327) has two haeng in each column without showing a detailed organization of the required eight beats within each haeng. Another piece, shown in Figure 75 (p. 347), utilizes chŭng-kan-po, whereby the rhythmic shape of the melody becomes fully explicit.

We shall turn first to the rhythmically less-distinct piece, the famous Man-tae-yŭp (慢大葉)[75] (pp. 327-34) by

Figure 73

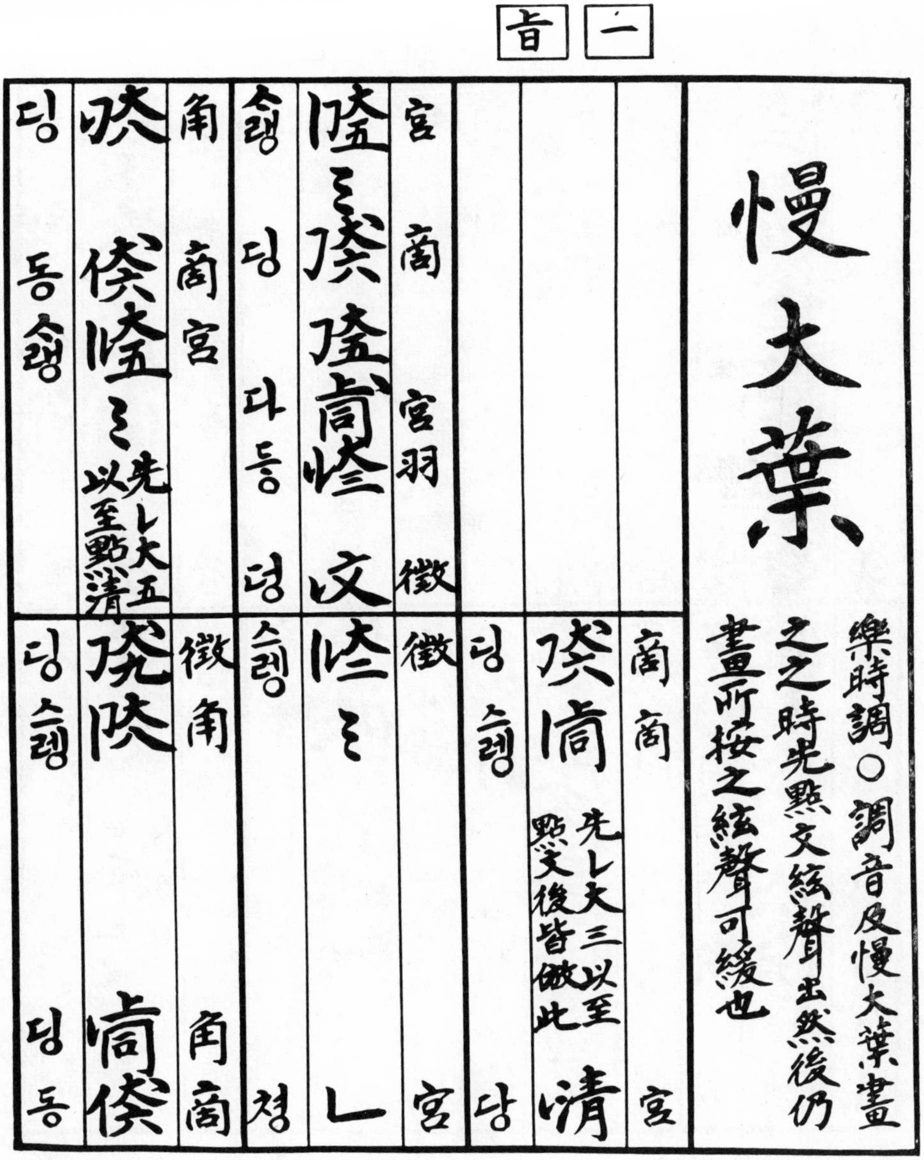

Figure 73 (cont.)

Figure 73 (cont.)

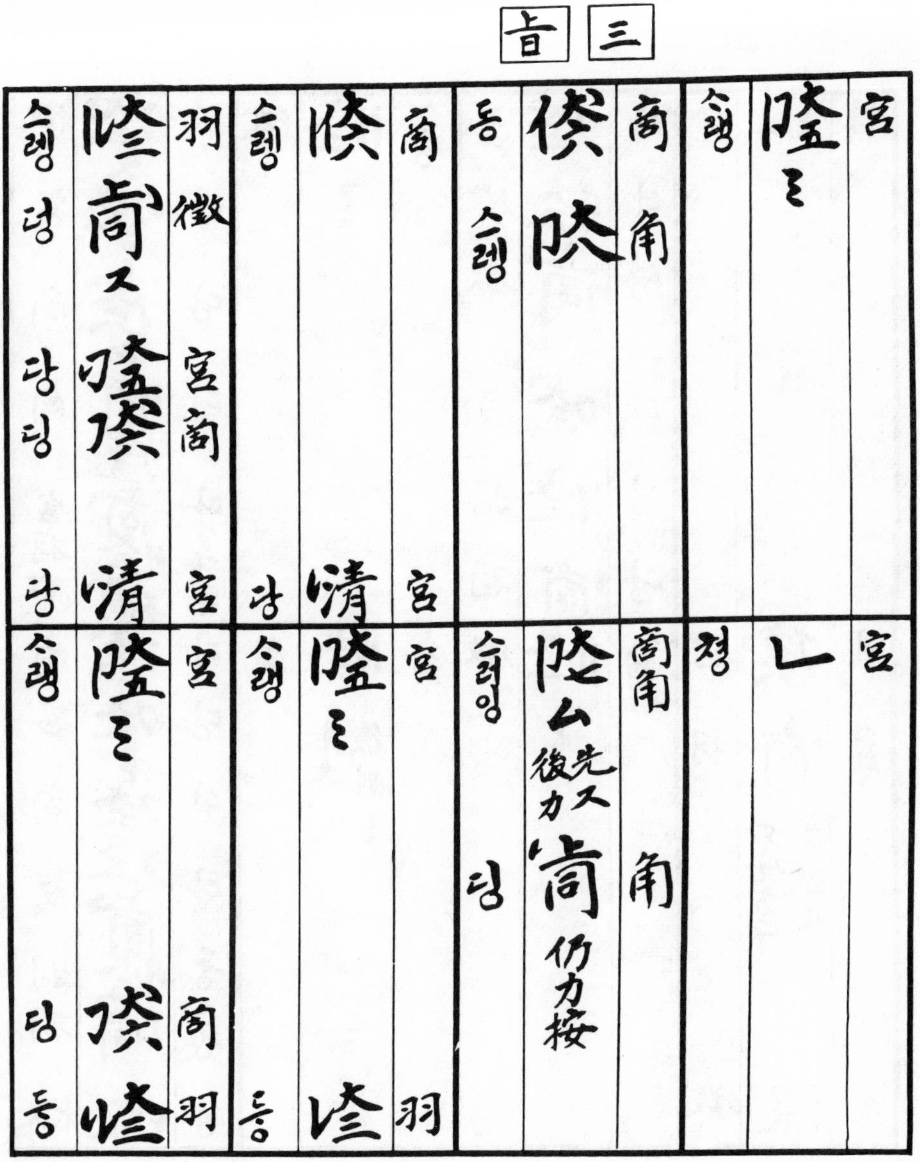

Figure 73 (cont.)

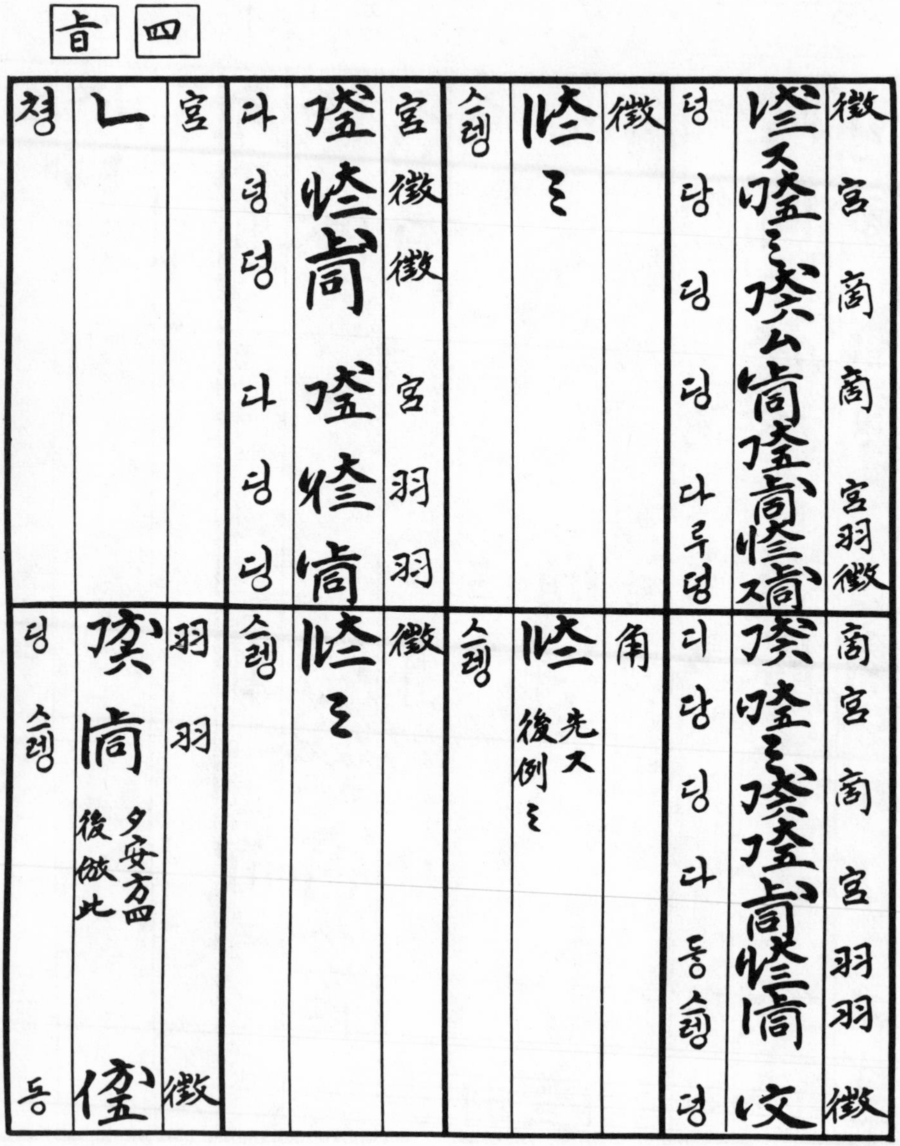

Figure 73 (cont.)

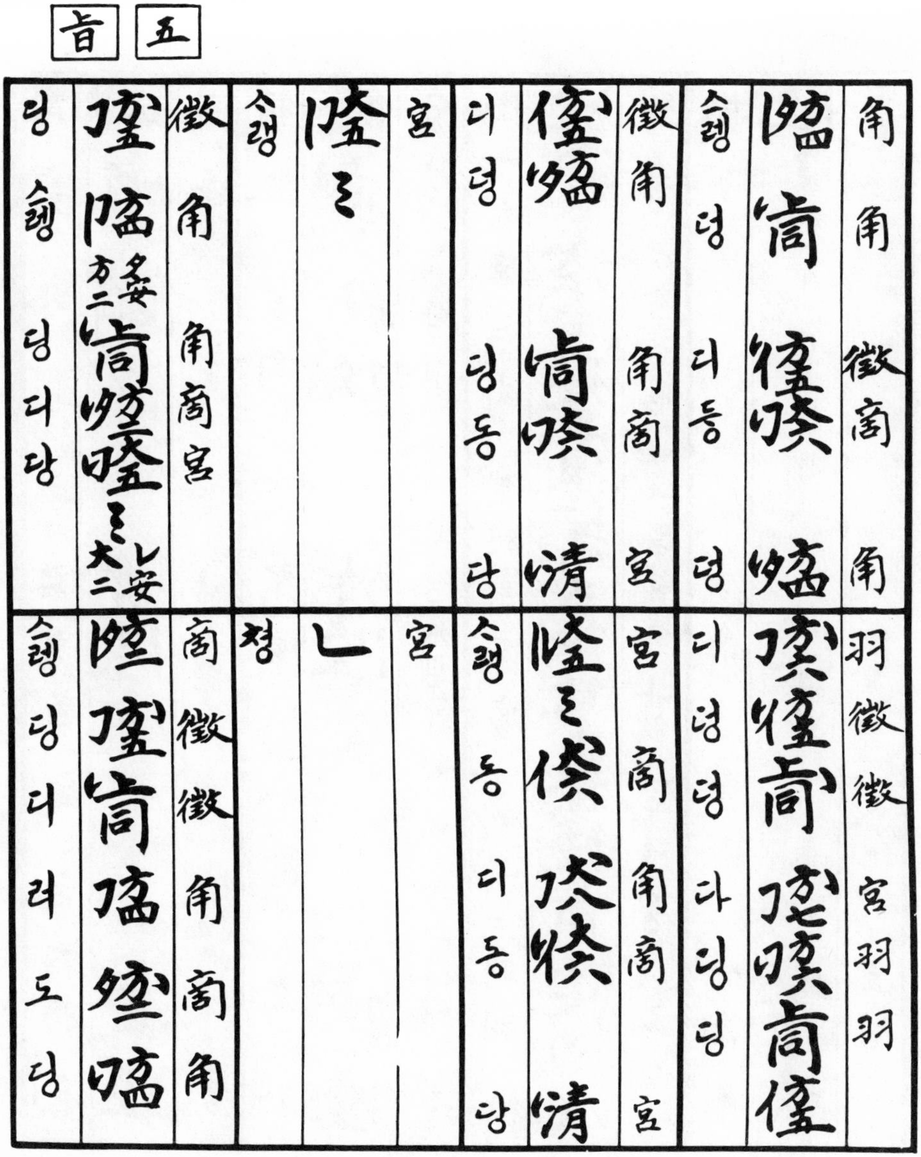

Figure 73 (cont.)

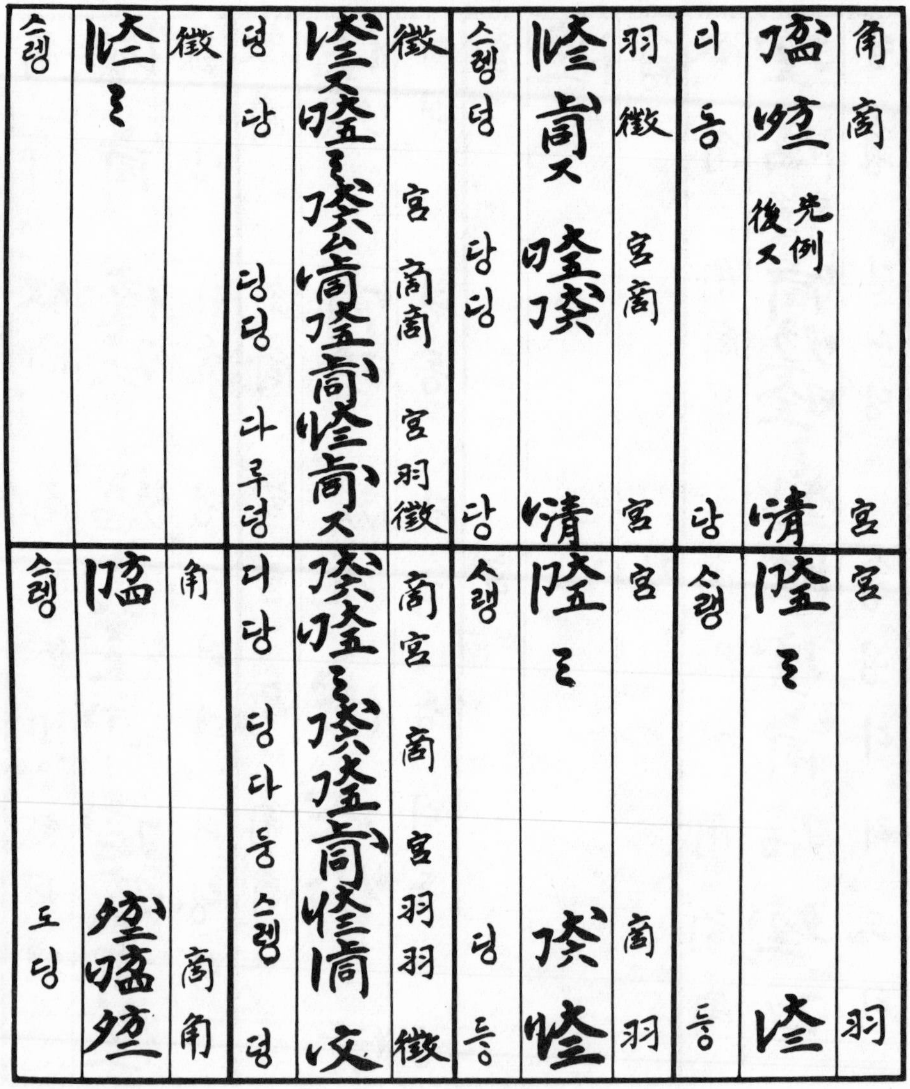

Figure 73 (cont.)

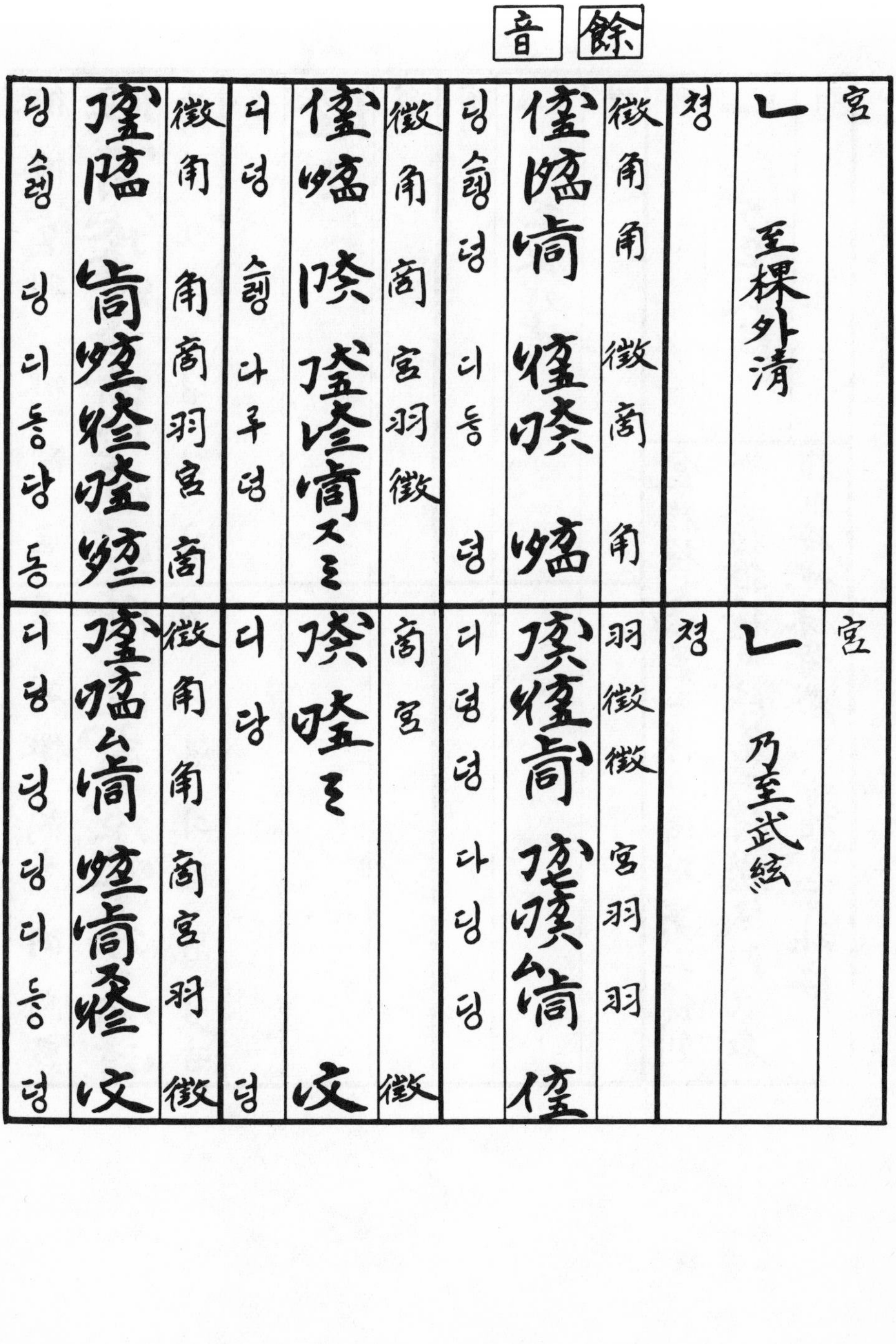

Figure 73 (cont.)

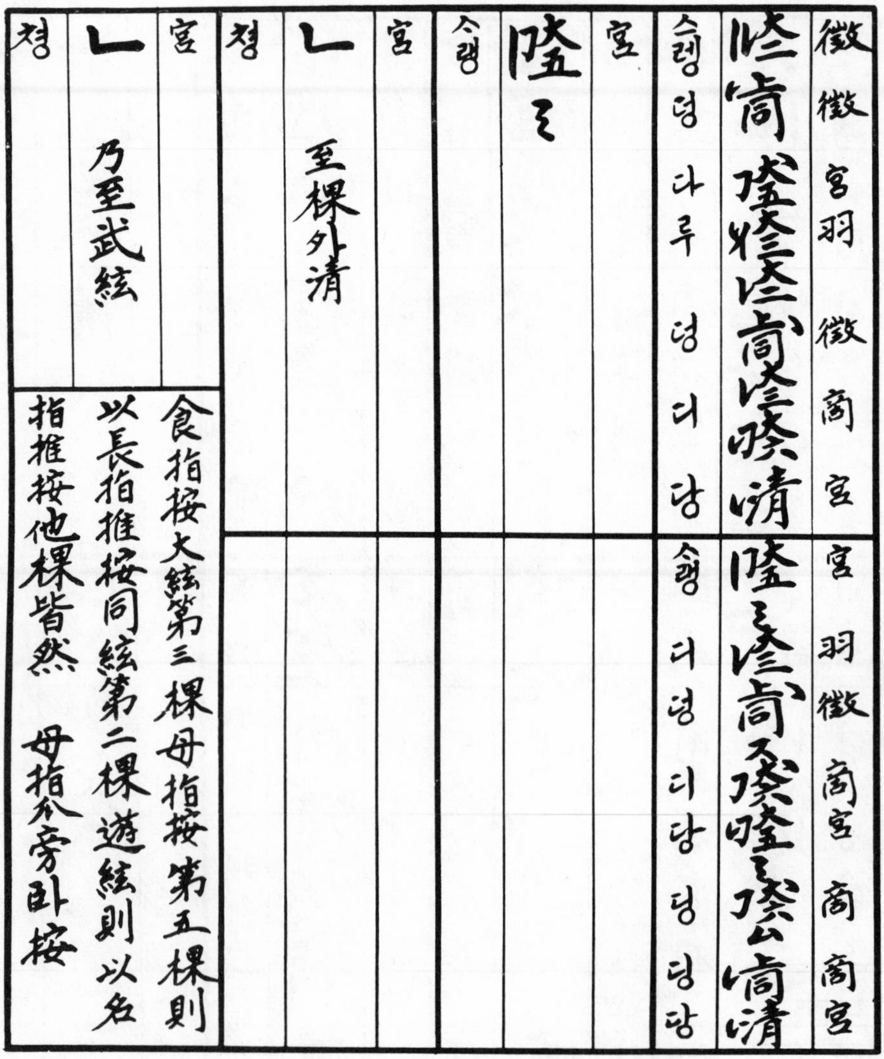
徵
徵 宮羽 徵 商 宮
宮 羽 徵 商 宮 商 商 宮
슬렝 덩 다 루 덩 디 당
슬렝 디 덩 디 당 덩 덩 당
宮
宮
청
至棵外清
宮
청
乃至武絃
食指按大絃第三棵母指按第五棵則
以長指推按同絃第二棵遊絃則以名
指推按他棵皆然

Cho-sŭng (趙晟) of the fifteenth century, as notated in the Yang-kŭm shin-po. For easier reading the pages of this copy are arranged in the Western manner — in a left to right sequence. However, each page is to be read in the Korean way, that is, each (big) column from top to bottom and the columns on each page from right to left. The title Man-tae-yŭp appears in large characters in the outer right column of page 327. The annotation below the title informs us that the melody is in Ak-shi-cho[76] (樂時調), which is another term for Pyong-cho. The rest of the annotation offers advice in tuning, a procedure we have discussed before in detail.

The hap-cha-po symbols begin with the second column. We observe that each column is divided into two haeng. As in Chinese solo ch'in music the player has considerable freedom concerning the duration of the notes. However, in hap-cha-po he must observe the basic eight (or sixteen) beats within each haeng, and, whenever possible, he must endeavor to maintain the $\frac{3+2+3}{4}$ meter.

The example shows the combination of three notational systems: the center column contains hap-cha-po symbols, the left side shows the melody notated in yuk-po,[77] and to the right are the symbols of the Chinese Five-Tone Notation. At present we shall confine our attention to the hap-cha-po and the Chinese Five-Tone symbols.

First measure (second column from the right, lower half):

String III is depressed on fret 6 by the left thumb; the string is plucked (scooped) in an outward direction. As we have transcribed kung as Bb, the Chinese Five-Tone symbol substantiates our finding: III, 6 and 商(商) denote C.

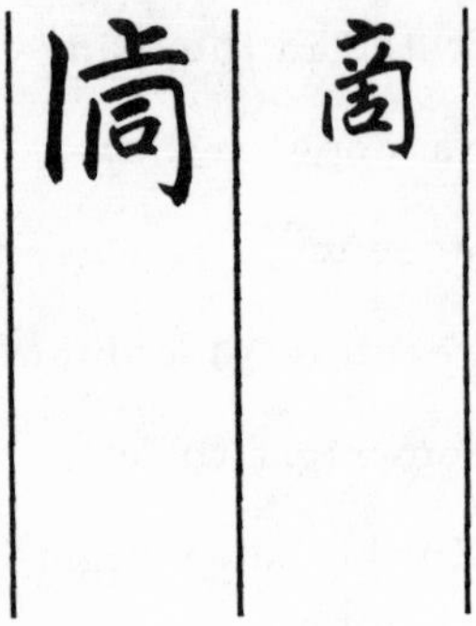

The second character in the hap-cha-po column is , meaning "the same as above." Included in the symbol is , which means that the note must be preceded by an appoggiatura beginning with the Mun string (I):

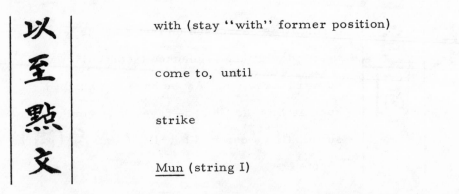

What follows now is characteristic of numerous East Asiatic tablatures: the musical notation is interrupted and an annotation is interpolated instructing the player about technical details – mainly about the required position of his left hand.

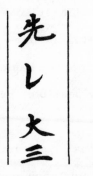

先	At first
レ	(left) middle finger
大	tae string (III)
三	fret 3

The meaning of this portion of the annotation is "at first the left middle finger depresses fret 3 of string III." This implies a basic hand position on the hyŭn-kŭm in which the left index finger and thumb are ready to depress the string on frets 5 and 6.

以	with (stay "with" former position)
至	come to, until
點	strike
文	Mun (string I)

This portion of the annotation means "maintain the hand position (described in the previous paragraph) until string I (<u>Mun</u>) is struck." In order to understand this we must consider briefly the <u>hap</u>-<u>cha</u>-<u>po</u> symbols in the second measure (the upper rectangle of column three). There we find that frets 5, 6, and, again, fret 5 of string III are to be depressed by the left thumb (), and, below, fret 3 is to be depressed by the middle finger (). This fingering cannot be executed unless the previously indicated hand position is maintained. A change from this position is shown by the first symbol of the second rectangle of the third column (), where the middle finger has shifted from fret 3 to fret 2. In short, up to  the original hand position remains unaltered. The rest of the annotation is:

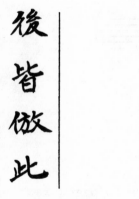

後	afterwards
皆	all
倣	imitate
此	this

These last four characters of the (first) annotation instruct the player that "after the plucking of string I at the end of the first rectangle of the third column, all other symbols of the tablature refer to the new hand position assumed at  at the beginning of the lower rectangle of the third column."

We now return to the lower rectangle of the second column. The symbol below the (first) annotation at the end of the lower rectangle is

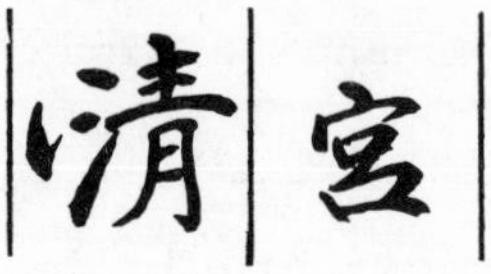

, meaning that strings IV and V are to be scooped in succession in an outward direction.

The rhythmic shape of the first measure remains vague except that we know that the total number of beats in each rectangle must be eight. The basic grouping of the beats should be 3+2+3, but the position of the annotation after the second symbol seems to indicate that this is the note of longest duration. We may transcribe this measure as:

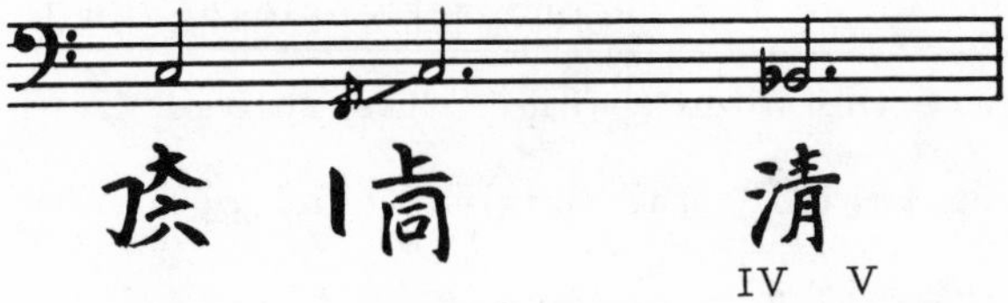

or as:

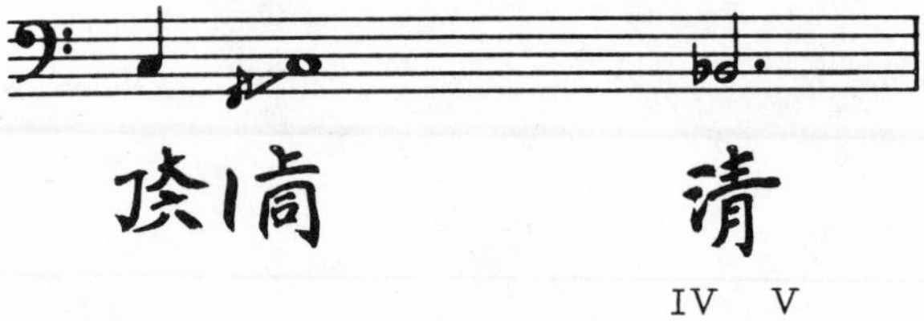

Second measure (top of third column):

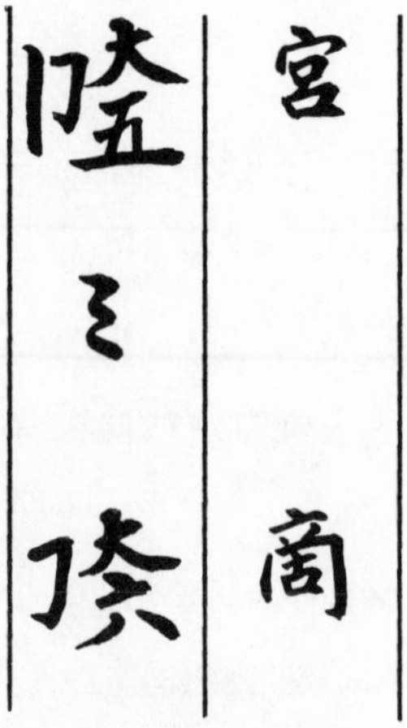

III, 5 depressed by left thumb; appoggiatura from string I:

The wavy line indicates that the note is to be held – its duration is determined by the total of durations of the other notes in this measure.

III, 6 depressed by left thumb:

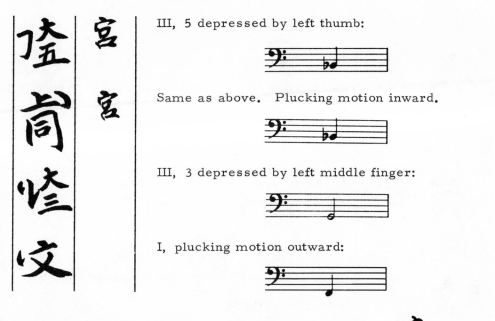

III, 5 depressed by left thumb:

Same as above. Plucking motion inward.

III, 3 depressed by left middle finger:

I, plucking motion outward:

As we are aiming at the basic 3+2+3 rhythm we extend  to the duration of a half note in order to get

Third measure (bottom of third column):

II, 2 appoggiatura from I

The wavy line again indicates that the note is to be held. This is the point at which the position of the left hand is changed.

This is a "cadential" arpeggio in which the open strings IV, V, and VI are played in succession:

Fourth measure (top of fourth column):

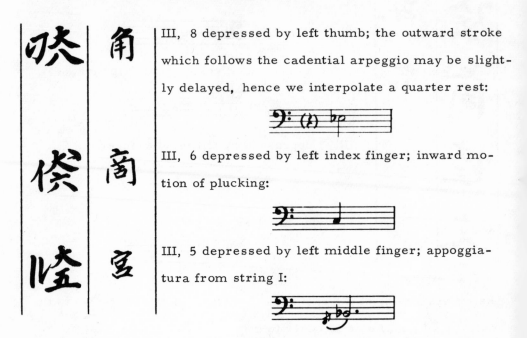

角 III, 8 depressed by left thumb; the outward stroke which follows the cadential arpeggio may be slightly delayed, hence we interpolate a quarter rest:

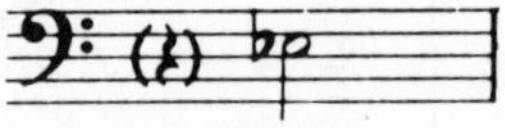

商 III, 6 depressed by left index finger; inward motion of plucking:

宮 III, 5 depressed by left middle finger; appoggiatura from string I:

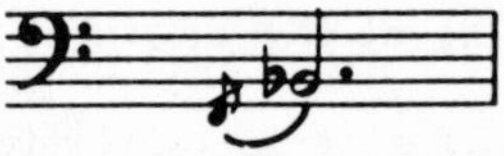

The annotation that follows again deals with the position of the left hand; the right hand column of the annotation reads:

先	first
レ	middle finger
大	tae string (III)
五	fret 5

This means that the (left) middle finger moves to fret 5 of string III. The left hand column of the annotation reads:

以	herewith
至	continue

點	strike
清	<u>chŭng</u> string

This means that the middle finger of the left hand maintains its position on fret 5 of string III until the <u>chŭng</u> string is struck (at the end of the sixth measure — second page of the manuscript, first column, top).

Fifth measure:

徵 — III, 9 depressed by left thumb; inward motion of plucking:

角 — III, 8 depressed by left thumb; appoggiatura from string I:

角 — Same as above; outward motion of plucking:

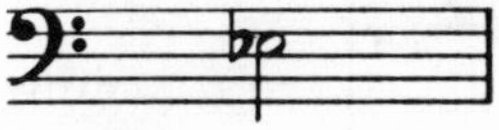

商 — III, 6 depressed by left index finger; inward motion of plucking:

Sixth measure (first column, second page of manuscript):

宮 — III, 5 depressed by left middle finger; appoggiatura from string I:

亻六	商	III, 6 depressed by left index finger: 
大八	角	III, 8 depressed by left thumb; inward plucking motion. The quick succession of Eb and C (next symbol) results from the inward-outward strokes (). 
㐅亻六	商	III, 6 depressed by left index finger; outward plucking motion: 
乚清	宫	The left middle finger plucks the open chŭng string: 

The beginning of the seventh measure is:

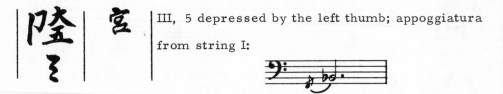

陸 ミ	宫	III, 5 depressed by the left thumb; appoggiatura from string I: 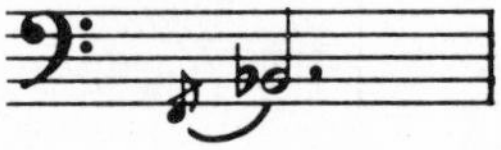

This is followed by the annotation:

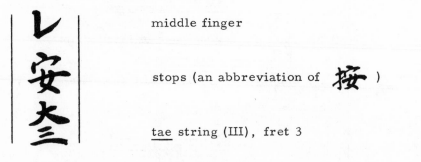

乚	middle finger
安	stops (an abbreviation of 按)
大三	tae string (III), fret 3

and, at the left, the annotation continues with:

後 afterwards

倣 like

此 this

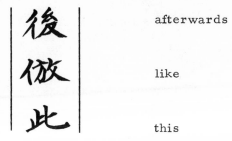

which means that the following remains unchanged. The complete seventh measure reads:

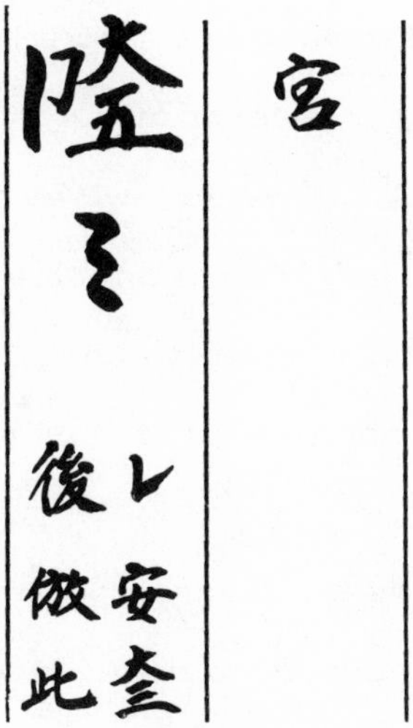

Eighth measure (second column, top, second page of manuscript):

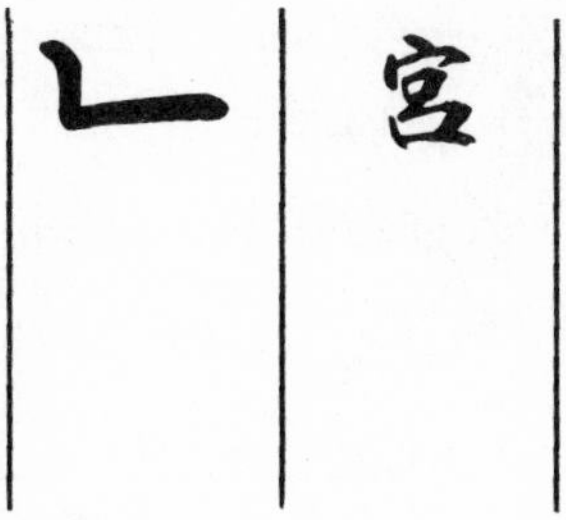

The arpeggio has to fill the whole measure, hence the characteristic 3+2+3 grouping of beats.

The ninth measure begins with:

III, 6 depressed by left index finger; inward motion of plucking.

III, 8 depressed by left thumb; appoggiatura from string I.

The following annotation has the same meaning as the one found in the seventh measure except that the middle finger () has to move up to fret 5 of string III.

There is no necessity for us to continue this analysis. The transcription of the melody is comparatively easy because most of the symbols discussed before occur over and over again. Moreover, we have mentioned previously that occasional annotations including the lengthy one at the end of the piece deal with technical details (mainly hand positions) which have no direct bearing upon the notation and transrip-tion of the melody.

The following, Figure 74 (pp. 345-46) shows the transcription of *Man-tae-yŭp* in its entirety.[78] The reader is advised to transcribe the entire piece and to compare his result with Lee's transcription. This comparison will show that in terms of rhythm, several interpretations are possible.[79]

In ensemble music the *hyŭn-kŭm* tablature, like that of the Chinese *ch'in*, becomes simplified, and the rhythmic organization become more explicit than in solo pieces. The following, Figure 75 (p. 347) represents an excerpt of *Yŭ-min-ak*[80] as notated in the *An-sang-kŭm-po*.[81] At the right side the melody is notated in *o-ŭm-yak-po*,[82] the column next to it is *hap-cha-po*, the third column contains the text, anc the outer left column the symbols for the *chang-ko* (drum) part. The use of *chŭng-kan-po*[83] enables the performer to get a clear rhythmica

Figure 74

Figure 74 (cont.)

Figure 75

與民樂

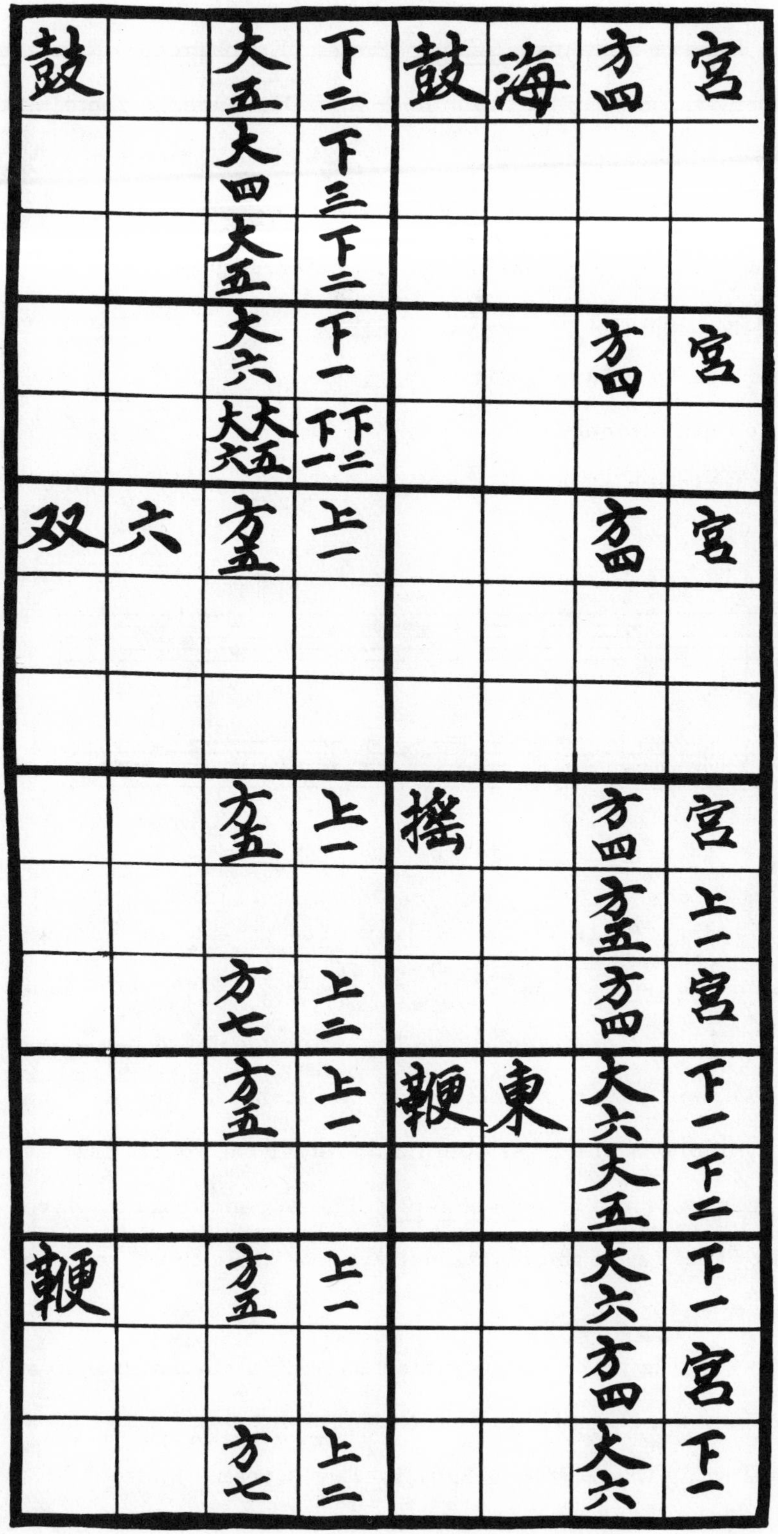

outline. There are two haeng in each column. Each haeng shows the characteristic division into 3+2+3 chŭng-kan. Our excerpt contains only three textual characters. They are: 海, hae, "ocean"; 東, tong, "east"; and 六, yuk, "six." The chang-ko signs are: 鼓, ko "drum," which indicates that the hand-beaten skin of the drum is to be used; 搖, yo, "roll"; 鞭, pyŭn, "whip," the stick-beaten side of the drum is to be used; and 双, sang, "both," both sides are to be beaten simultaneously.

The transcription of the four haeng of Yŭ-min-ak is shown below in Figure 76:

Figure 76

The following, (Fig. 77, p. 349), is Yŭ-min-ak as notated in the Shin-sŭng kŭm-po (申晟琴譜), "Shin-sŭng's Zither Book."[84] The example shows the combination of hap-cha-po and yuk-po. Three textual characters are written near the first and penultimate symbols of the first column and near the fourth last symbols of the second column of hap-cha-po. The second textual character is placed to the left of the notational symbol while the other two are written to the right.

It is remarkable that this specimen shows no rhythmic indication Nevertheless, the reading of this version of yŭ-min-ak causes no difficulties. Following (Fig. 78, p. 350) is Lee's transcription[85] together with the hap-cha-po symbols.

Figure 77

申晟琴譜 所載 與民樂

당소랭당소랭 스랭 딩 소랭동 당 스랭 동 당 스랭 당

方海四上同上同 大六方五 方五大六方四己 方七方五方四己 東大六 清

스랭딩 당 동 스랭 동 덩 소랭딩 덩 동 스랭 당 소랭 동 딩

大六方五方四大六 大五大四大五 大七大六大五大四 大二力 六清 大二上同力 大四

註

方四(潢)。 大六(南)。 方五(汰)。

方七(沖)。 大五(林)。 大四(仲)。 大二(太)。

Figure 78

Beyond the left edge of Figure 77 we find an annotation (註) which informs the performer about the pitches in relation to <u>hap-cha-po</u> symbols. (潢) means that II, 4 should produce the <u>Huang-chung</u>, here notated as 潢 , with the <u>ch'ing</u> sign denoting the higher octave.

In our discussion of the <u>lü</u> (Part I) we transcribed this symbol as the note C. Lee, however, uses the note Eb, as may be observed in his transcription. The entire annotation reads (left to right):

II, 7	(Ab)	II, 4	(Eb)
III, 5	(Bb)	III, 6	(C)
III, 4	(Ab)	II, 5	(F)
III, 2	(F)		

In the introductory pages of the <u>Anthology of Korean Traditional Music</u> (민 속 악 보)[86] are given a few symbols that are variants of the ones shown above. In addition, the work presents a few symbols which concern notations of the kaya-kŭm (kaya-ko)[87] and hae-kŭm (奚琴)[88] music. As they may be of some interest, we present a few of them here.

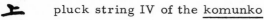

ㄱ pluck string I of the komunko

 strike or pluck a string of the komunko with the left hand

> strike or pluck a string of the komunko or the kaya-ko with a small stick

上 pluck string IV of the komunko

下 pluck string V of the komunko

大 pluck string VI of the komunko

○ "putting the nail of the fore-finger on the inside of the thumb, forming a circle, strike the string of the . . . kaya-ko"

8 "in the same way, strike the strings of the . . . kaya-ko successively with the nails of small finger, ring finger and middle finger"

天 move the left forefinger down to the place of the middle finger (hae-kŭm)

ㅎ move the left forefinger down to the place of the small finger (hae-kŭm)

ㅗ return the left index finger to where it had started moving (hae-kŭm)

IV

The Notations of the Buddhist Chant (Tibet)

THE NOTATIONS OF THE BUDDHIST CHANT (TIBET)

With the exception of the Japanese shōmyō, which we shall discuss in a second volume, information about musical notations of Buddhist chant of the continent of Asia is meager and vague; and information particularly relating to Indian Buddhist chant is practically non-existent. Buddhism in India came more or less to an end when the Muslims invaded the land, particularly Bihar and Bengal at the close of the twelfth century. At that time the monks were expelled or killed and monasteries and libraries were destroyed. Today there exist only some very small scattered Buddhist communities, and they possess no notational system of their own.

In China, where Buddhism flourished, and a multitude of sects, schools, and a wealth of translations of Indian Buddhist scriptures appeared, there exists to our knowledge no characteristic Buddhist notational system. Notations used were mainly the lü, the Five Tone, and kung-ch'ê systems.

Of some interest may be the notation or notations of Tibetan liturgical chant. Buddhism made its first appearance in Tibet during the reign of King Srong-tsan gam-po in the sixth century A. D., but it was not until the year 750 that the saintly Indian Padma-Sambhava widely propagated the new religion and incorporated into it numerous rites of the ancient Bön religion. These ancient rites, dealing with magic, demon cult, and devil dances, made Buddhism appear more formidable as well as more enticing to the Tibetan people. During Padma-Sambhava's lifetime monasteries were built and the various orders of monks established. Sacred Buddhist texts, which had been imported from India across the Himalayas, were gradually translated into Tibetan, and there is little doubt that with the texts sacred images and Buddhist melodies came into Tibet.

Most of the Tibetan melodies are anhemitonic pentatonic and in strict meter. This can be noticed in indigenous folk songs, in secular music — influenced by Chinese stylistic elements, particularly Chinese opera — and in the liturgical chant of monasteries.[1] In order to illustrate this pentatonic character we show Figure 79, a short, religious song performed by school children at the monastery school in Ghoom near Darjeeling.[2] Part A of the song is repeated several times. In Part B a feature appears that resembles the organum of the medieval West. That is, the lower voice in the second part, which uses the material G A B D E, runs strictly parallel with the upper voice, which uses C D E G A. Similar phenomena appear in China and, occasionally, in the Buddhist chant of Japan.

Tibetan Buddhist prayer-songs, hymns, presentations of offerings to the Buddha and other deities, mystery play songs, and so on, like the plainsong of the West, are generally performed by monks in the lowest attainable register in unison, but, unlike the chant of the Roman Catholic Church, Tibetan chant is metrical and is accompanied by a drone produced by two, long, telescope-shaped copper trumpets (rag-dung)[3] and one or more drums. The use of these instruments is illustrated in the following example, Figure 80 (p. 358), which represents a fragment of a liturgical melody as performed in the monastery

Figure 79

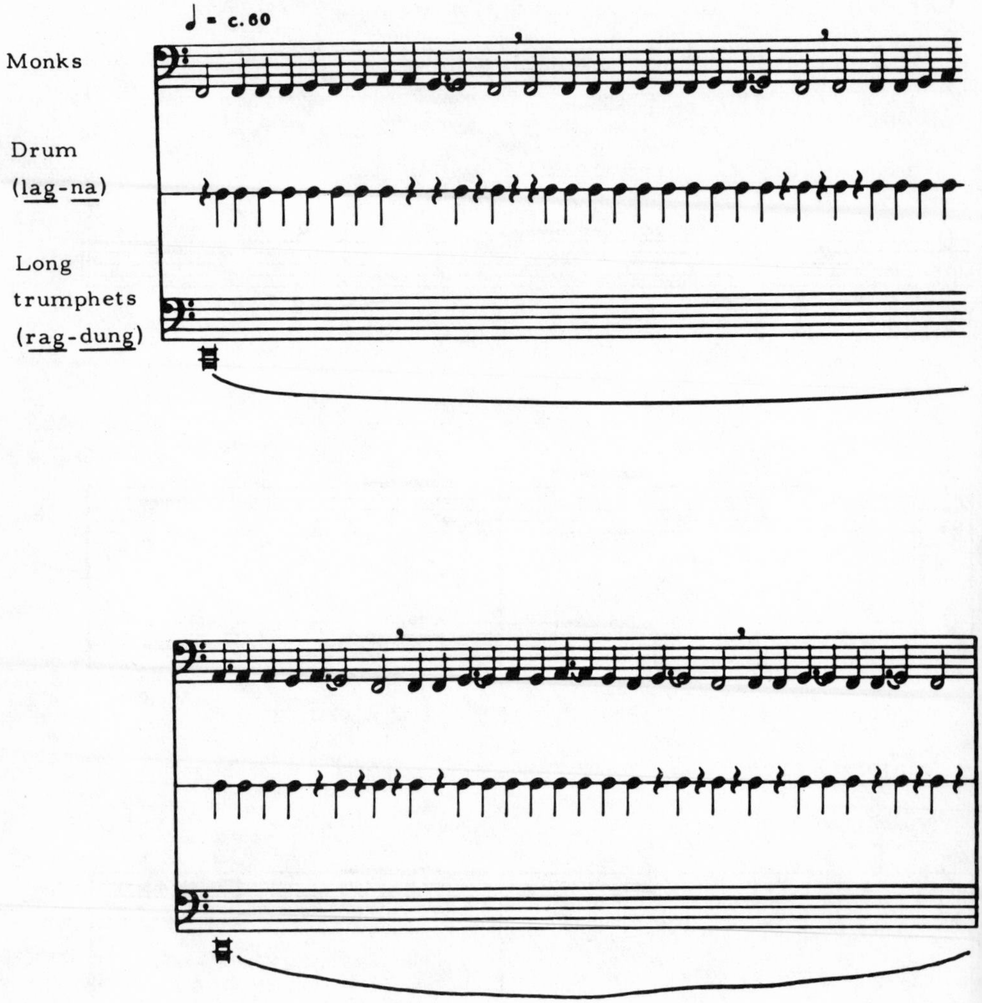
♩ = c.60
Monks
Drum
(lag-na)
Long
trumphets
(rag-dung)

Figure 80

of Gyantse. The latter melody (Fig. 80) also shows pentatonic character.[4]

Recordings of some Tibetan melodies convey the impression that semitones and, occasionally, microtonal intervals are in use. While we have to agree that the sounds produced do show complex intervallic steps, we must point out that the basic tone-material of these melodies is predominantly anhemitonic pentatonic. This writer, who had numerous opportunities to listen to these chants performed in Ladakh and in eastern Tibet, came to the following conclusion: the liturgical melodies have to be chanted by the monks in as low a range as possible, and the massed bass voices produce a sound that indeed becomes tremendously impressive and unforgettable to the Western listener. However, only a few of the choir usually are able to sing the very low notes correctly. The majority of the choir, who cannot perform these low notes, incline to intone them a little higher; the difference between the intended note and that actually produced by the "baritone" voices being a semitone, or even a whole tone. Often the majority of the voices are somewhat out of tune, hence unusual intervals result. For instance, if the actual melody is to be F G A C C A G, we hear the majority of the monks chanting F# G# A C C A G#, or similar alterations generally affecting the lowest notes. Occasionally singers having intoned the lowest notes somewhat higher remain in that higher "key" until the rest of the voices either join them in the higher key or until some powerful voices pull them back into the original key. These differences do not occur only in liturgical chant where they are clearly noticeable but also in folk music. In folk melodies, occasionally, Indian influences (semitones, different intervals in the rising and descending scale) become apparent, and the same may happen in liturgical chants when a choir master, who is acquainted with Indian music, introduces some complex intervals; but, as a rule, folk music and liturgical chant of Tibet have predominantly pentatonic character. The range of the liturgical melodies rarely exceeds the interval of a fifth except at syllables such as PHAT, when nga ("strong voice") is to be performed.[5]

It is not known when the notational system (or systems) of Buddhist Chant in Tibet was first used. This writer was informed by Tibetan monks that the song books, called yang-yig, are "very old and have been copied over and over again for a long time."[6] The available manuscripts show two related types of neumatic notation; one with short, simple hooks and curves, the other with large, florid symbols. Both forms are written from left to right, and each curve is placed to the right or above the textual syllable.

Although we have no proof, we may conjecture three possible sources of these neumes: it is possible that they are an indigenous Tibetan product; there is some slight possibility that the neumes originated in the mysterious hand positions and patterns of small wooden sticks of Vedic India; but a much more plausible assumption is that the use of neumes for notating important melodies was imported by the Nestorians and by other Christian missions in their remarkable eastward movement.

Although Mazdaism was the state religion in Persia, Christianity under Constantine (306-337) had become the official religion of the Roman Empire and had found its way into Mesopotamia and Persia. However, Christians were so severely persecuted by the Persians that they finally broke their relationship with the church of Antiochia and eventually established a center in Edessa (the modern Urfa) which joined with the followers of Nestorius. Under the reign of the great Persian warrior king and patron of the arts, Khosru I (531-579), this Nestorian church began to flourish and expand. Its missions spread the gospel not only in Syria, Armenia, and Persia but moved to the East into India, Central Asia, and parts of China.

In the year 1625 Jesuit priests discovered a marble slab at Singanfu on the Yellow River. The inscription of the tablet in Syriac and Chinese reports the events of a Syrian mission and gives the name of a missionary called Olopan who had come from Judaea to China in the year 636. The tablet also tells of how the emperor ordered a church to be built; how, after great favors were bestowed upon the mission, persecution of the Christians began in 699; and how, later, Christianity was tolerated again, and so forth.[7]

The Syrian church, which had been carried by the Nestorians into Persia, India, Central Asia, and China, had also spread between the fourth and seventh centuries to the West as far as Verona and Ravenna; to some extent its influence could be felt even in Germany and England. In short, members of the Syrian church had ample opportunities for learning the numerous types of musical notations not only of Asia Minor but of Europe as well. A comparison between the neumes of Tibetan liturgy and those used in the fragments of the New Testament and in the Manichaean hymns with texts written in Syriac characters[8] in Soghdic — a middle Persian dialect — shows no apparent similarities. The Nestorian notation consists of dots, the Tibetan of hooks and curves.

We do know that the Soghdic dialect[9] was used by Buddhists, Manichaeans,[10] and Nestorians for the propagation of their respective religions in Central Asia. The notational dots, although not directly related to the Tibetan signs, deserve our attention: they are placed above or below the textual line and occasionally they appear in pairs, triplets, and quadruplets. According to Wellesz[11] the meaning of some of these dots is as follows:

 (dot above the line), the voice rises;

 (dot below the line), the voice falls;

 rise and fall of the voice.

The doubling of dots intensifies the rise or fall; similarly a tripling partially indicates further intensification. Of interest is the grouping of four (or more) dots to form the sign , which denotes the end of a section. According to Wellesz the sign which has the function of the *teleia* (+) in Greek evangelistaria often appears after headings such as: "Jesus said," "Thus He spoke," "Jesus spoke to the disciples." Later, when we examine the Tibetan manuscript, this sign can be found again in the form of 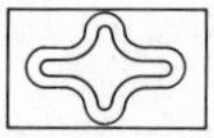 (and other, corresponding ones), where it has a similar function. Similarly we may find Tibetan parallels to the *oxeia*, *bareia*, and the *syrmatike*, and, probably, to other neumes not necessarily of West Asian origin.

Tibetan neumes show no Chinese features at all. If we consider that in the Yüan period the Chinese *kung-ch'ê* system became widely popular and that the Confucian temples still adhered to the *Lü* and the old Five and Seven-Tone Notations, it is remarkable that neither during the Yüan period nor in the subsequent dynasties of their culturally-productive neighbor, nothing concerning musical notation came into Tibet.

Notational influences seem to have been confined to the West and, perhaps, to some degree, to the South. We know that at the time of Marco Polo there existed considerable cultural exchange between West and East, and there is not the slightest doubt that caravans brought to the East missionaries and manuscripts, and not necessarily only those of the Syrian church.[12] We can assume that several notational systems from the West may have found their way into Tibet and, perhaps, even into Chinese Buddhist monasteries. The monks may not have retained the original significance of the neumatic symbols which they found in the imported manuscripts but may have imitated the symbols and adapted them to their own requirements. For instance, a <u>quilisma</u> of the West may have had a different meaning than its corresponding symbol in the Tibetan neumes. The wriggly part of the symbol would possibly represent some form of vibrato in both notations, but the intervallic characteristic of the symbol, which concerns a minor third in the West, may be interpreted quite differently in Tibet.

Without taking into consideration their musical significance, we list below a number of neumatic symbols.[13] By merely viewing their shapes we find that  and   in Syriac, Byzantine, and Armenian notations, or 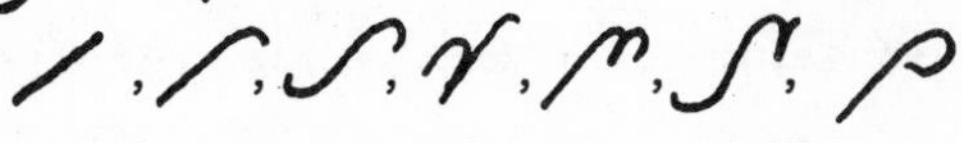 of St. Gall, appear in one form or another in the Tibetan system.

Throughout the centuries leading up to recent times, a great deal of music was used in Tibetan monasteries. The chanting was accompanied or interrupted by the sound of conch shells, trumpets, cymbals, drums, and other instruments. The <u>yang-yig</u>, used by the choir leaders,[14] contains neumes and instructions as to the use of the various instruments.

The following, Figure 81 (pp. 365-80), is a part of such a yang-yig, showing a photographic reproduction of a manuscript fragment from the monastery at Phyang. The pages shown below represent the beginning of an old text common to all sects of Tibetan Buddhism, an invocation of Shri He-ru-ka, Lord Heruka, the patron saint of Sikkim. Heruka, "unclad," is the title given to Lha-tsün ch'en-po, "The Great Reverend God," who was born in 1595 in southeastern Tibet. In the middle of the seventeenth century Lha-tsün appeared in Lhasa where he became famous and gained the high esteem of the Grand Lama. The latter part of his life was spent in Sikkim where he founded the monastery of Dub-de. The building of the monasteries of Tashiding, Pemiongchi, Sa-nga-ch'öling, and others is ascribed to him, although not proven. The date of his death is not known. Lha-tsün supposedly had many miraculous powers, particularly the power of being able to fly. He is depicted almost naked (hence: Heruka), with a dark blue complexion, and seated on a leopard skin. He is adorned with human skulls, his left hand holding a skull cup filled with blood, his right hand performing a teaching gesture. His personal belongings became sacred relics and were preserved and worshipped in the monastery of Pemiongchi; later the relics were removed to the monastery of To-lung.[15]

Although we do not know where the manuscript was written, we can assume that it originated in Sikkim. Described as "very old," it may date back to the end of the seventeenth century, the period following the death of Lha-tsün, which was a time of intense religious activity in Sikkim.

MANUSCRIPT I

Figure 81

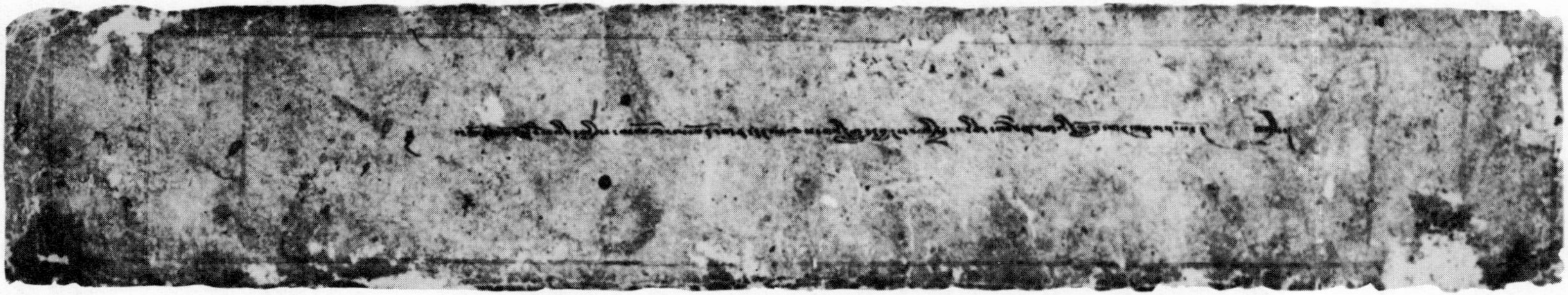

Sheet 1a

Figure 81 (cont.)

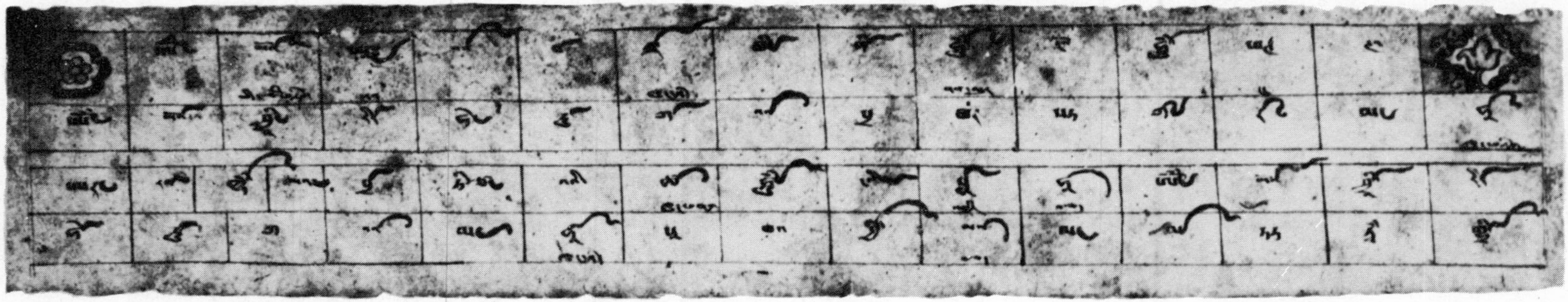

Sheet 1b

Figure 81 (cont.)

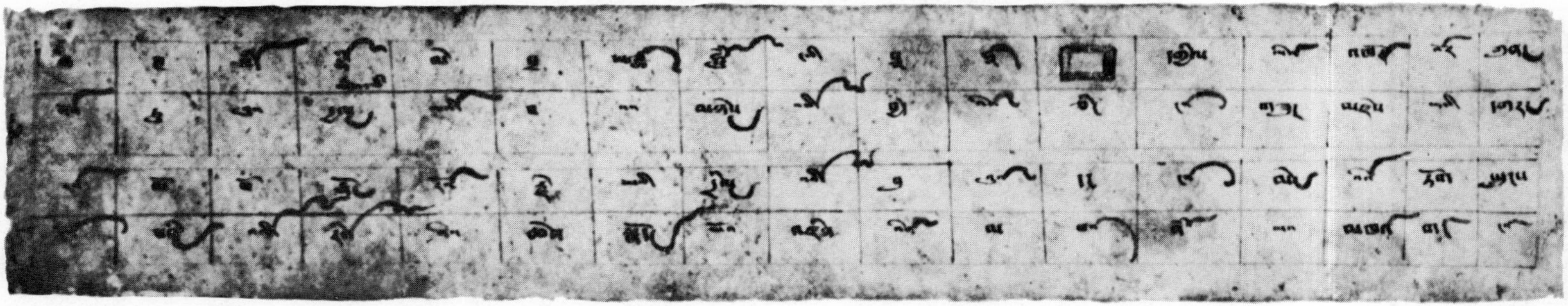

Sheet 2a

Figure 81 (cont.)

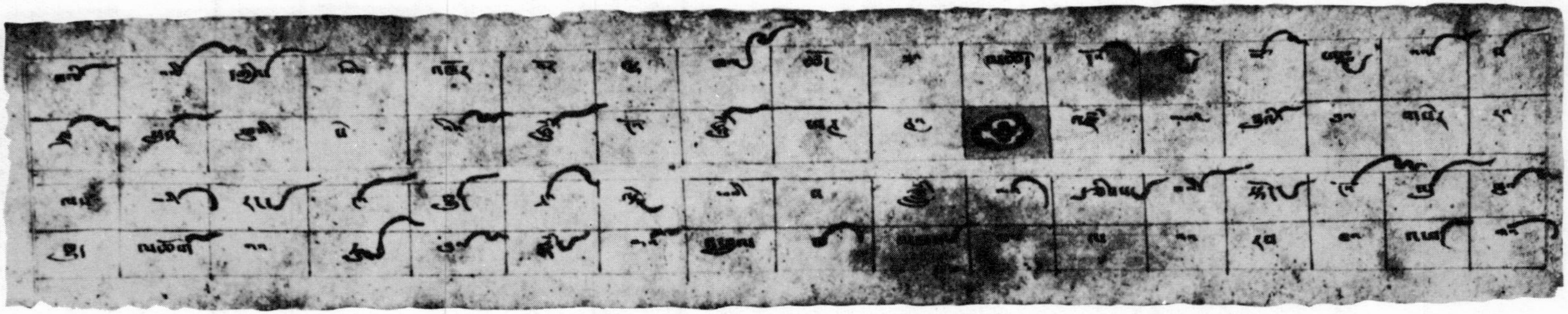

Sheet 2b

Figure 81 (cont.)

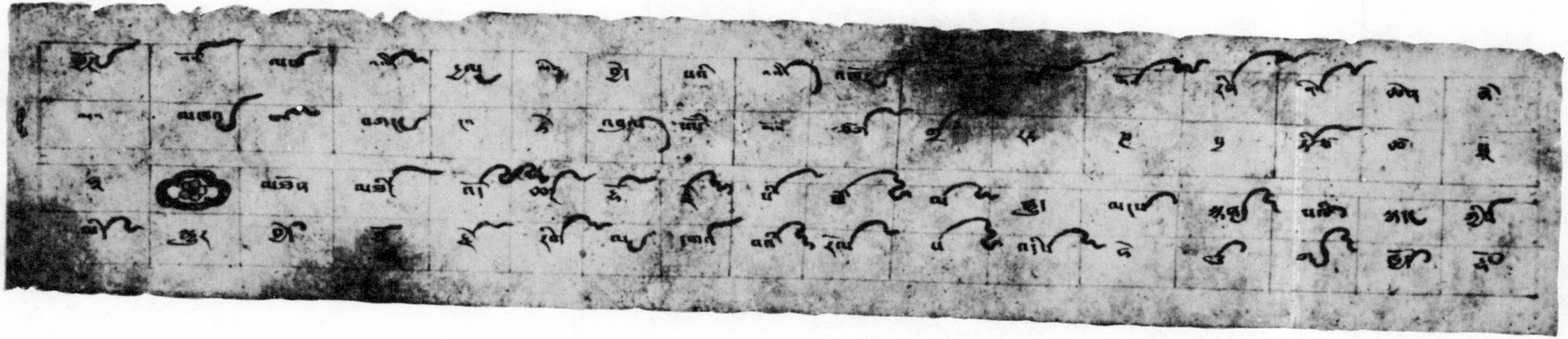

Sheet 3a

Figure 81 (cont.)

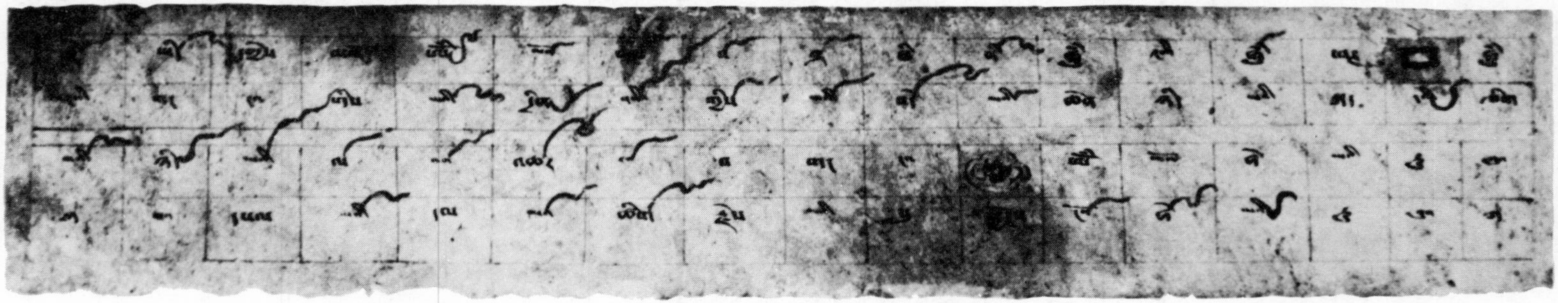

Sheet 3b

Figure 81 (cont.)

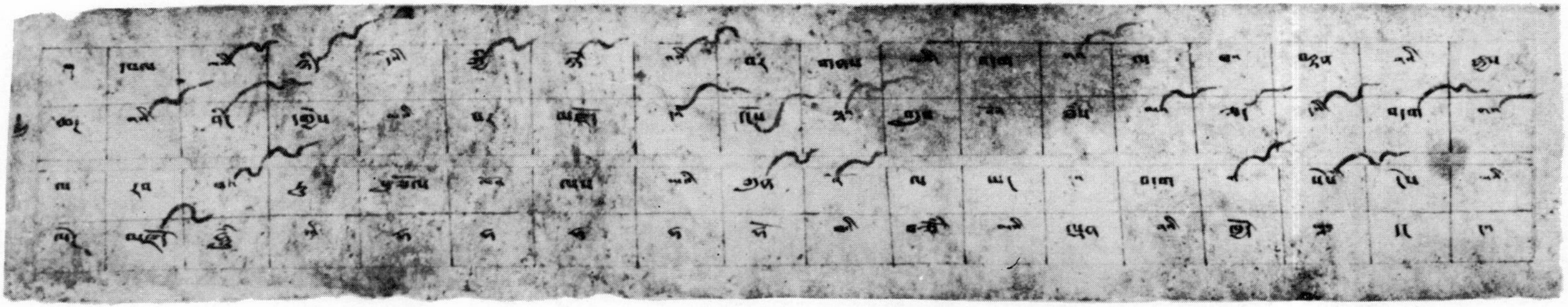

Sheet 4a

Figure 81 (cont.)

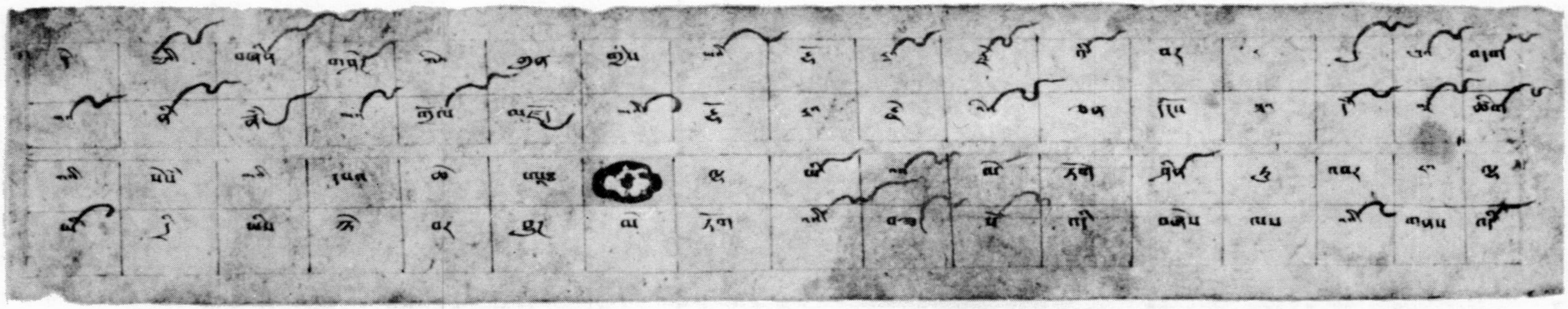

Sheet 4b

Figure 81 (cont.)

Sheet 5a

Figure 81 (cont.)

Sheet 5b

Figure 81 (cont.)

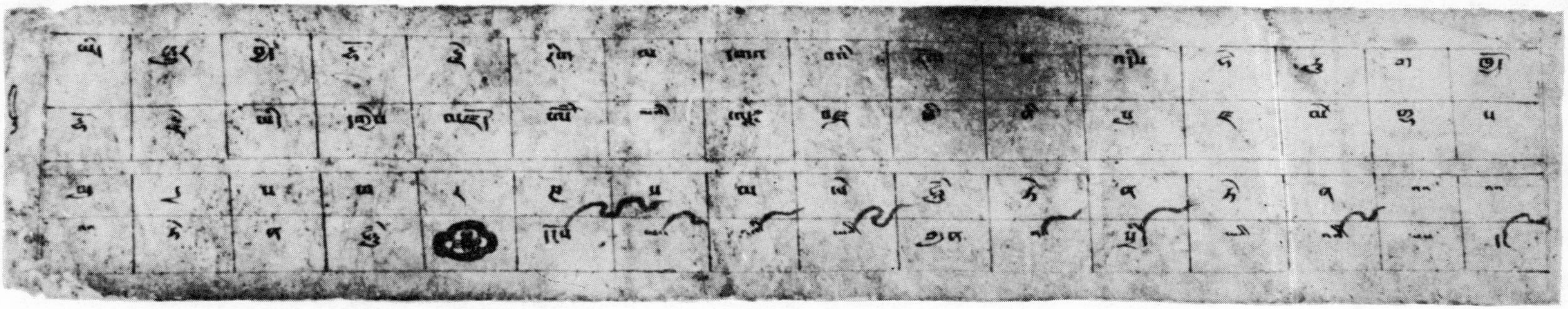

Sheet 6a

Figure 81 (cont.)

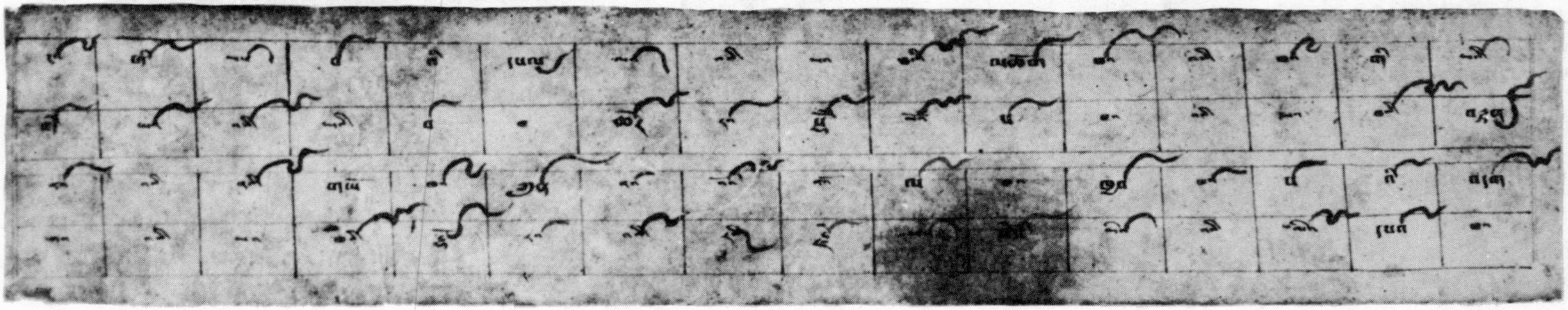

Sheet 6b

Figure 81 (cont.)

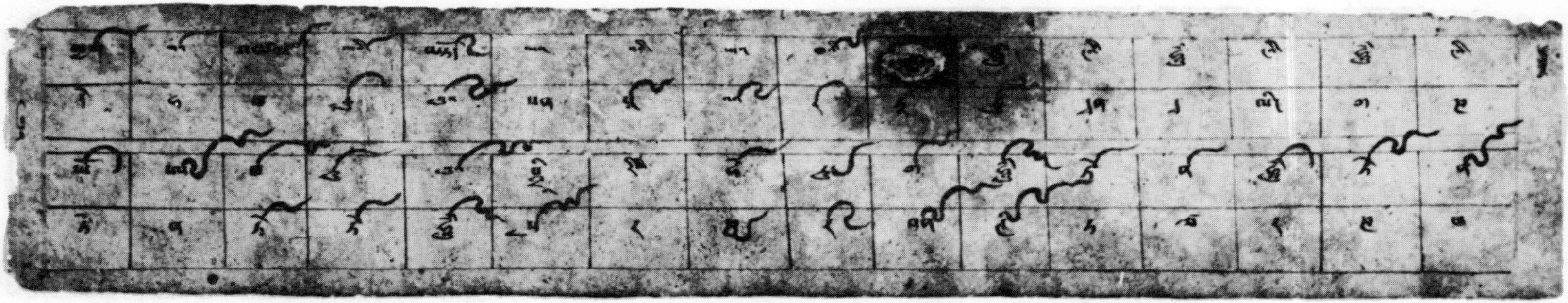

Sheet 7a

Figure 81 (cont.)

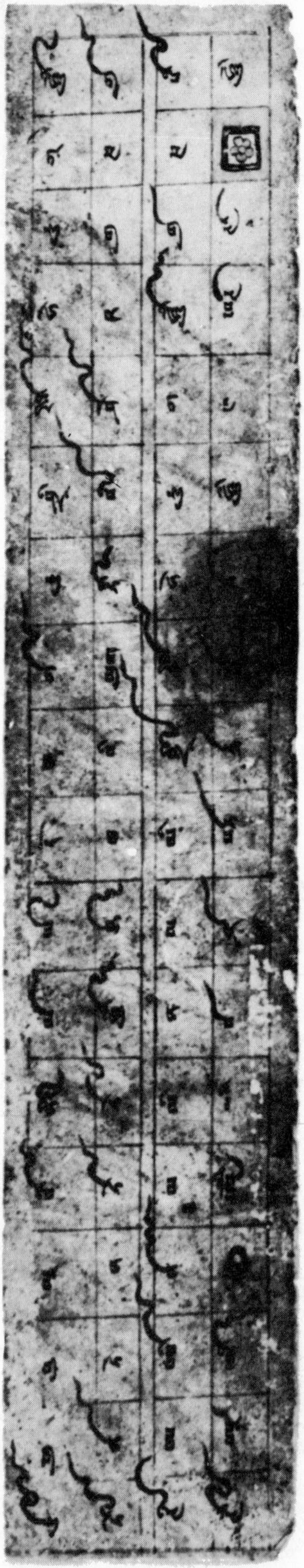

Sheet 7b

Figure 81 (cont.)

Sheet 8a

Figure 81 (cont.)

Sheet 8b

Before turning to a consideration of the notational symbols and annotations, we shall present the text both transliterated[16] and translated, together with a few explanatory remarks. Each sheet consists of four horizontal lines (read from left to right) which will be identified with Roman numerals (I-IV). The small subdivisions appearing in each of these four lines will be identified with Arabic numerals (1-15, 16, etc.) In the transliteration the textual words are printed in capital letters. Between them, in small letters, appear Tibetan "phonetics" which are used to continue preceding words (and notes) or to join them to the following words. Below the text, and extending and joining the phonetics, we find at a few specific points instructions for the singer, which are shown in italics. The text is interspersed with Sanskrit syllables which are rendered in Tibetan phonetics. These have not been translated because to bring these phonetics back into their original Sanskrit form would require lengthy considerations which would unnecessarily delay our already extended presentation. Moreover, these phonetics are prayer formulae which have no direct bearing on our subject.

Sheet la (title sheet):

'KHOR LO SDOM PA'I DKYIL MCHOG MCHOD GAR DANG
Wheel of binding to cycle ritual dance together

BCAS PA'I GLU DBYANGS KYI DRA YIG MEI NA KA'I
with sacred song of diagram lettered Mei-na-ka's

ZLOS GAR BZHUGS SO BKRIS.
dance this book contains — Blessings.

<u>Sheet</u> <u>1b</u>:

I.

1	2	3	4	5	6	7	8
○	OM	mo'o	ĀH	'a'a	BA	DZRA	WI
		yid tsam bteg				cung shod	

9	10	11	12	13	14	15
NI	HŪM	ngo'o	HŪM	PHAT	ta'a	○
	nab myur			nga		

II.

1	2	3	4	5	6	7	8
OM	mo'o	SHRI	ri'ri	HE	RU	KA	a'a

9	10	11	12	13	14	15
PRA	WAR	SAT	KA	RA	MA	HĀ
						cung bteg

III.

1	2	3	4	5	6	7	8
AR	ra'a	GHAM	ma'a	PRA	TITS	'a'i	TSHA
							cung bnan

9	10	11	12	13	14	15	16
HŪM	nga'a	SWA	HĀ	OM	mo'o	SHRI	ri'ri
			bcad				

IV.

1	2	3	4	5	6	7	8
HE	RU	KA	'a'a	MA	HĀ	SĀ	wa'a
					cung shod		

9	10	11	12	13	14	15
DYAM	ma'a	MA	LA	TAT	TWAM	GHRI
	bcad					

Sheet 2a:

	1	2	3	4	5	6	7	8	9
I.	HA	Ṇ A	SI	DHI	ME	PRA	YATSTSHA	HỤ̄M	nga'a
			bteg	cham					

10	11	12	13	14	15	16	17
SWA	HĀ	○	DKYIL	le'e	'KHOR	'or	KUN
			mandala				all

	1	2	3	4	5	6	7	8	9
II.	'o'o	TU	'u'a	RGYAL	la'i	BA	'a'a	MNYES	'a'i
		"over"		victorious				veneration	

10	11	12	13	14	15	16	17
BYED	'e'e	CING	nga'a	GZUGS	MDZES	ya'i	DKAR
to		and		form	beautiful		white

	1	2	3	4	5	6	7	8	9
III.	ra'a	PO	wo	RDO	ro'o	RJE	ya'i	DRIL	'a'i
					thunderbolt			bell	

10	11	12	13	14	15	16	17
BU	'u'a	DANG	nga'a	ME	'e'e	TOG	SPUNGS
		and		flowers			heaped

	1	2	3	4	5	6	7	8	9
IV.	ngu'a	PA'I	'a'i	RIN	ne'a	CHEṆ	SNOD	yo'o	'DZIN
		of		jewelled			receptacle		

10	11	12	13	14	15	16	17
'en	MA	wa'a	NAM	ma'a	MKHA'	GANG	nga'a
			heavens			fills	

Sheet 2b:

I.

1	2	3	4	5	6	7	8
BA'I	'a'i	DKYIL	le'e	'KHOR	'or	LHA	wa'a
which		mandala				gods	

9	10	11	12	13	14	15	16	17
TSHOGS	swa'a	MCHOD	do'o	OṂ	mo	ĀḤ	'a'a	BA
assembly		veneration	to					
			bcad					

II.

1	2	3	4	5	6	7	8	9
DZA	PUṢH	wu'i	PE	'e'e	HŪṂ	ngo'o	HŪṂ	PHAṬ

10	11	12	13	14	15	16	17
ta'a	◯	'DZAM	ma'a	BU'I	'u'a	GSER	ra'a
		world		of		gold	

III.

1	2	3	4	5	6	7	8
LAS	ya'i	RANG	nga'a	BYUNG	ngwa'a	LTE	ya'i
from				emerging		middle	

9	10	11	12	13	14	15	16	17
BA	ZLUM	ma'a	RTSIBS	ba'i	STONG	ngo'o	MU	wu'a
axle	circle		spokes		1000		rim	

IV.

1	2	3	4	5	6	7	8
KHYUD	MCHOG	ga'a	TU	'u'a	RNAM	ma'a	'PHRUL
	great				parts		divided into

9	10	11	12	13	14	15	16	17
wa	MKHA'	wa'a	LA	'a'a	RAB	ba'a	'PHAGS	ga'a
	heavens		in		most		exalted	

<u>Sheet</u> <u>3a</u>:

	1	2	3	4	5	6	7	8
I.	PHYOGS	'o'o	LAS	'a'i	RGYAL	le'e	BYED	PA'I
	over all	directions			victorious		is	which

9	10	11	12	13	14	15	16	17
'a'i	'KHOR	'or	LO	'o'o	RIN	ne'e	CHEN	NAM
	wheel				precious			heavens

	1	2	3	4	5	6	7	8
II.	ma'a	MKHA'	wa'a	BGANG	nga'a	TE	'BUL	OṂ
				honor			offer to	

9	10	11	12	13	14	15	16	17
mo'o	TSAG	KRA	RAT	NAṆ	PRA	TITS	TSHA	SWA

	1	2	3	4	5	6	7	8
III.	HĀ	◯	MTHON	MTHING	'OD	CHAGS	RDO	RJE
			high	blue	light	producing	thunderbolt	

9	10	11	12	13	14
PI	WAM	MA	RGYUD	MANGS	SNYAN
p'i-pa				("harp", "zither")	sweet (sounding).

15	16	17
PA'I	SKAD	KYIS
of	voice	by

	1	2	3	4	5	6	7	8
IV.	YID	SGYUR	BYED	RDO	RJE	RIG	MA	DGA'
	mind	diverted	be	thunderbolt		mudra		joy

9	10	11	12	13	14	15	16	17
BA'I	ROL	PA	'DIS	HE	RU	KA	KHOD	RDO
of	dance		by this		He-ru-ka		your	adamantine

Sheet 3b:

I.

1	2	3	4	5	6	7	8
RJE	YID	DGYES	MDZOD	OM	mo’o	ĀH	BA
	mind	pleased	made				

9	10	11	12	13	14	15	16	17
DZRA	WI	NI	HŪM	nga’i	HŪM	PHAT	○	HŪM

II.

1	2	3	4	5	6	7	8	9
nga’i	GANG	nga’a	GIS	ya’i	DRIN	na’i	GYIS	ya’i
	“your”				grace		by	

10	11	12	13	14	15	16	17
BDE	ya’i	CHEN	NYID	ya’i	SKAD	da’i	CIG
happiness		great	itself		word		one
						(in one instant)	

III.

1	2	3	4	5	6	7	8	9
ga’i	NYID	ya’i	LA	’a’a	‘CHAR	ra’a	BA	GANG
	itself				realized			“all things’

10	11	12	13	14	15	16	17
nga’a	○	OM	mo’o	HE	ya’i	RU	’u’a

IV.

1	2	3	4	5	6	7	8
KA	wa’a	DPAL	ya’i	DAM	ma’a	TSHIG	RJES
		great		vows			follow

9	10	11	12	13	14	15	16	17
ya’i	SU	SKYONGS	ngo’o	HE	ya’i	RU	’u’a	KA
		one who protects						

<u>Sheet</u> <u>4a</u>:

I.

1	2	3	4	5	6	7	8	9
ya	DPAL	ya'i	NYID	da'i	KYI	LTE	'a'i	BAR
	magnificence		itself			center		

10	11	12	13	14	15	16	17	18
GNAS	ya'i	BDAG	ga'a	LA	wa'a	BRTAN	na'i	RGYAS
abides		Lord		to		attachment		expansive

II.

1	2	3	4	5	6	7
CHAGS	ga'i	SHING	DGYES	ya'i	PAR	MDZOD
produce		and	joyfulness			"let there be"

8	9	10	11	12	13
da'a	DNGOS	swa'a	GRUB	bo'o	THAMS
	siddhi (perfections)				all

14	15	16	17	18
ma'a	CAD	da'i	BDAG	ga'a
			me	

III.

1	2	3	4	5	6	7	8	9
LA	RAB	ba'a	TU	STSOL	lo'o	LAS	ya'i	KUN
on	generously			bestow		deeds		all

10	11	12	13	14	15	16	17	18
na	LA	YANG	nga'a	BDAG	ga	SEMS	NGES	ya'i
	in	also		my		mind	true	

IV.

1	2	3	4	5	6	7	8	9	10
LEGS	MDZOD	HŪṂ	nga'i	HA	HA	HA	HA	HO	wa'i
do	be								

11	12	13	14	15	16	17	18
BCOM	ma'i	LDAN	na'i	KHYOD	ya'a	DANG	nga'a
victorious		one		you		and	

Sheet 4b:

I.

1	2	3	4	5	6	7	8
DE	ya'i	BZHIN	GSHEGS	ge'e	KUN	GYIS	ya'i
Tathagatas					all	by	

9	10	11	12	13	14	15	16	17
RDO	rwa'a	RJE	'I	BAR	ra	DU	'u'a	BDAG
adamantine				space				me

II.

1	2	3	4	5	6	7
ga'a	NI	RNAM	ma'a	GROL	MDZOD	ya'i
	"as for"	deliver		from	circle	of existence

8	9	10	11	12	13	14	15
RDO	rwa'a	RJE	e'e	CAN	DNGOS	swa'a	DAM
thunder	-	bolt		like	true		vow

16	17
ma	TSHIG

III.

1	2	3	4	5	6	7	8	9
ga'i	SEMS	ma'i	DPA'	CHE	AH	◯	LHA	YI
	mind		brave	great			gods	of

10	11	12	13	14	15	16	17
'a'a	ME	TOG	SHIN	TU	'BAR	ra'a	LHA
	flowers		most		radiant		gods

IV.

1	2	3	4	5	6	7	8	9
YI	DRI	YIS	LTE	BAR	BYUGS	ME	TOG	'a'i
of	fragrance	by	center		anointed	flowers		

10	11	12	13	14	15	16	17
BZANG	PO	'DI	BZHES	LAS	'a'i	GNAS	'DI
		these	accept	"and"			this

Sheet 5a:

I.

1	2	3	4	5	6	7	8	9
NYID	DU	BZHUGS	SU	GSOL	OṂ	ma'i	ĀḤ	BA
itself	"in"	remain	to	beseech				

10	11	12	13	14	15	16
DZRA	PUṢH	PE	PRA	TITSTSHA	HŪṂ	ngo'o

II.

1	2	3	4	5	6	7	8	9
SWA	HA	◯	E	MA	'a'a	BDE	MCHOG	ga'a
			Listen			happiness	great	

10	11	12	13	14	15	16
SGYU	MA'I	yi'i	LONGS	SPYOD	dwa'a	RDZOGS
illusion	of		use			perfected

III.

1	2	3	4	5	6	7	8
PA'I	'PHRUL	'la	E	MA	PI	WAM	nga'i
who	emanation		listen		p'i - pa,		

9	10	11	12	13	14	15	16
GLING	BU	wu'a	RNGA	ZLAM	mo	DZA	RNGA
	(flute)		(drum)				(drum)

IV.

1	2	3	4	5	6	7	8
MA	wa'i	◯	HŪṂ	nga'a	BCOM	mo	LDAN
					victorious		one

9	10	11	12	13	14	15	16
MGON	PO	DPA'	BO'I	DBANG	PHYUG	NI	ya'i
protector		heroic		might		"as far"	

Sheet 5b:

I.

1	2	3	4	5	6	7	8
BSKAL	PA'I	ME	CHEN	LTA	wa'i	BUR	RAB
world destruction	of	fire	great	like			greatly

9	10	11	12	13	14	15	16
wa'i	TU	BAR	○	OM	ma'i	BA	DZRA
				·			
		radiate					

II.

1	2	3	4	5	6	7	8	9
LĀ	'a'a	SYĀ	MĀ	'a'i	LI	GIR	TI	'i

10	11	12	13	14	15	16
NRI	TE	HŪM	nga'a	PHAT	ta	OM
		·		·		·

III.

1	2	3	4	5	6	7	8
ma'i	BDZRA	LA	'a'a	SYA	MA	'a'i	LI

9	10	11	12	13	14	15	16	17
GIR	TI	'i	NRI	TI	HUM	nga'a	PHAT	ta

IV.

1	2	3	4	5	6	7	8	9
○	MTHON	MTHING	'OD	CHAGS	RDO	RJE	PI	WAM
	high	blue	light	producing	thunderbolt		p'i-pa	

10	11	12	13	14	15	16
MA	RGYUD	MANGS	SNYAN	PA'I	SKAD	KYIS
	("harp")		sweet sounding	of	voice	by

Sheet 6a:

I.

1	2	3	4	5	6	7
YID	SGYUR	BYED	RDO	RJE	RIG	MA
mind	diverted	be	thunderbolt		mudra	

8	9	10	11	12	13	14	15	16
DGA'	BA'I	ROL	PA	'DIS	HE	RU	KA	KHYOD
joy	of	dance		by this		He-ru-ka		your

II.

1	2	3	4	5	6	7
RDO	RJE	YID	DGYES	MDZOD	OṂ	ma'i
adamantine		mind	pleased	made		

8	9	10	11	12	13	14	15	16
AH	BDZRA	WI	NI	SU	DZA	ME	GHA	SA

III.

1	2	3	4	5	6	7	8	9
MU	DRA	SA	YA	RA	ṆA	SA	MA	YE

10	11	12	13	14	15	16
HŪṂ	TE	NA	TE	NA	'a'e	'a'a

IV.

1	2	3	4	5	6	7	8
'a'a	TE	NA	HŪṂ	○	DNGOS	ya'a	'a'i
					samsara		

9	10	11	12	13	14	15	16
ya'i	KUN	na'a	SRID	ya'i	'a'i	yas	DANG
							and

Sheet 6b:

I.	1	2	3	4	5	6	7	8
	nga'a	ZHI	ya'a	BA	'I	DPAL	la'a	a'i
		nirvana				exalted one		

	9	10	11	12	13	14	15	16
	ya'a	wa'i	MCHOG	wa'a	a'i	wa'a	GI	ya'i
			most excellent				of	

II.	1	2	3	4	5	6	7	8
	BDE	ya'a	a'i	ya'i	BA	wa	CHER	ra'a
	happiness						greatly	

	9	10	11	12	13	14	15	16
	SDOM	mo'o	PA	wa'a	'a'i	ya'a	wa'i	BRTAN
	binds							moving

III.	1	2	3	4	5	6	7	8
	na'a	'a'i	na'i	G. YO	wa'a	KUN	na'a	'o'o
				things		all		

	9	10	11	12	13	14	15	16
	no'o	LA	wa'a	KHYAB	wa'a	PA	'I	BDAG
				embraces		who		master

IV.	1	2	3	4	5	6	7	8
	ga'a	'a'i	ya'a	wa'i	RDO	ra'a	'a'i	ra'i
					thunderbolt			

	9	10	11	12	13	14	15	16
	RJE	ye'e	SEMS	me'e	a'i	me'e	DPA'	wa'a

Sheet 7a:

I.

1	2	3	4	5	6	7
PHYAG	ga'a	'TSHAL	la'i	BSTOD	ya'a	'a'i
make		obeisance				

8	9	10	11	12	13	14	15	16
ya'a	wa'i	○	HỤ̄M	nga'i	HỤ̄M	nga'i	HỤ̄M	nga'i

II.

1	2	3	4	5	6	7	8
DE	HA	WA	TU	'u'a	SAN	PĀ	'a'a

9	10	11	12	13	14	15	16
RA	TĀ	TU	DWAN	DWA	LING	KA	NẠ

III.

1	2	3	4	5	6	7	8	9
YO	A	WA	TU	'u'a	SHRĪ	ri'i	HE	RU

10	11	12	13	14	15	16
KA	HỤ̄M	TE	NA	HỤ̄M	TE	NA

IV.

1	2	3	4	5	6	7	8
TE	NA	TE	TE	HỤ̄M	SU	RA	NA

9	10	11	12	13	14	15	16
RA	BAN	TỊ	TA	TSA	RA	NA	WA

Sheet 7b:

I.

1	2	3	4	5	6	7	8	9
TU	KU	SU	MA	BI	NIR	MĀ	YA	RO

10	11	12	13	14	15	16	17	18
WA	KA	RU	SHRI	ri'i	HE	RU	KĀ	HŪṂ

II.

1	2	3	4	5	6	7	8	9
TE	NA	TE	NA	TE	TE	HŪṂ	BHA	WA

10	11	12	13	14	15	16	17	18
PI	MUG	TI	BE	SHE	KA	GU	ṆA	KU

III.

1	2	3	4	5	6	7	8	9
ṬI	A	I	NA	MA	MI	NA	MA	MI

10	11	12	13	14	15	16	17	18
SHRĪ	ri'i	HE	RU	KA	HŪṂ	GU	ṆA	SI

IV.

1	2	3	4	5	6	7	8	9
ṬAM	A	I		OṂ	ma'i	BA	DZRA	STWA

10	11	12	13	14	15	16	17	18
TWA	?	?	HŪṂ	nga'a	PHAṬ	ta'a	◯	HŪṂ

Sheet 8a:

I.

1	2	3	4	5	6	7	8	9
nga'i	YE	SHES	BSKAL	PA	ME	LTAR	'BAR	ra'a
	divine	wisdom	universe		fire	like	blazes	

10	11	12	13	14	15	16	17	18
BA	'I	'OD	ya'a	'a'i	ya'a	MA	RIG	'DOD
which		light				ignorant		desire

II.

1	2	3	4	5	6	7	8
PA'I	MUN	KHAMS	THAMS	ma'a	CAD	ya'a	BSGREGS
of	dark	regions	all				consume

9	10	11	12	13	14	15	16	17	18
'a'a	'a'i	ya'a	○	OṂ	ma'i	GZI	BRJID	ya'a	CHEN
						great	splendid	one	

III.

1	2	3	4	5	6	7	8	9
na'a	'a'i	wa'i	PO	wa	ME	YI	'a'i	wa'i
					fire	of		

10	11	12	13	14	15	16	17	18
wa'i	'a'i	LHA	wa'i	wa'a	LAS	KYI	ya'a	DON
		god			activity	of		objects

IV.

1	2	3	4	5	6	7	8	9	10
na'a	'a'i	wa'i	KUN	na'a	BSGRUB	PA	'a'i	wa'i	wa'i
			all		fulfills	one			

11	12	13	14	15	16	17	18
'a'i	PO	wa'i	wa'a	SNYING	RJES	ya'a	SEMS
	who			compassion		(through)	mind

Sheet 8b:

I.	1	2	3	4	5	6	7	8
	'a'a	'a'i	wa'i	CAN	na'a	DON	MDZAD	'a'i
				creatures		for the benefit of	act	

9	10	11	12	13	14	15	16	17	18
wa'i	wa'i	'a'i	PHYIR	ri	'a	'DI	NYID	ya'a	DU
			because			to	this very place		

II.	1	2	3	4	5	6	7	8	9
	wa'a	'a'i	wa'i	NI	ya	NYE	BAR	'a'i	wa'i
				"as for"		close			

10	11	12	13	14	15			
wa'i	'a'i	MDZOD	ya'i	ya'a	○	○	○	○
		remain						

The general translation of the text is as follows:

Sheet 1a: This book contains the dance of the Mei-na-ka, the lettered diagram of sacred song together with the ritual dance cycle of 'KHOR LO SDOM PA – blessings.

Sheet 1b: contains only Tibetan phonetics of Sanskrit syllables.

Sheet 2a: I, 1-12: Tibetan phonetics of Sanskrit syllables.

2a, I, 13 to 2b, I, 12: Veneration to DKYIL 'KHOR KUN TU RGYAL BA and veneration to the assembly of gods, the mandala[17] which fills the heavens, the jewelled receptacle of heaped flowers, the bell, the thunderbolt,[18] and the white beautiful form.

The first mantra[19] ends with the syllable PHAṬ (1b, I, 13; see also 5b, III, 16 and 7b, IV, 15), a sound full of mystic power. Other mantras often end with SWA HĀ, "I offer" (for instance: 1b, III, 11 and 13; 2a, I, 10-11; 3a, II, 17 to 3a, III, 18; 5a, II, 1-2). The syllables OṂ and HŪṂ are the first and last of the sacred opening salutation OṂ MANI PADME HŪṂ, "OṂ, the jewel in the lotus, HŪṂ." OṂ corresponds to the Indian AUM, the representation of the triad: Creator, Preserver, and Destroyer. These four words have exceedingly involved significances; for instance OṂ may represent the world of gods, HŪṂ that of the purgatory, and even the form of the letters which are employed to write these sacred words receive manifoldly profound interpretations.

2b, I, 13 to 2b, II, 10: Tibetan phonetics of Sanskrit syllables.

2b, II, 12 to 3a, II, 7: Offer to and honor the heavens, the precious wheel which is victorious over all regions, most exalted in the heavens, divided into parts, the great rim, the thousand spokes, the axle, self-emerging from the gold of the world.

3a, II, 8 to 3a, III, 2: Tibetan phonetics of Sanskrit syllables.

3a, III, 3 to 3b, I, 4: MTHON MTHING 'OD CHAGS RDO RJE, let your mind be diverted by the voice of the sweet sounding pi-wa-ma, the rgyud mangs.[20] May your adamantine mind, Heruka, be pleased by the joyful dance of the RDO RJE RIG MA.

3b, I, 5 to 16: Tibetan phonetics.

3b, I, 17 to 4a, IV, 2: HŪṂ. Through your grace all things are realized in an instant of great happiness. OṂ, Heruka. DPAL DAM TSHIG RJES SU SKYONGS, let there be joyfulness and expansive attachment to Heruka, the Lord who abides in the center of magnificence itself. Bestow generously on me all siddhi (perfections). Let my heart beat true in all deeds.

4a, IV, 3 to 10: Tibetan phonetics.

4a, IV, 11 to 5a, I, 5: BCOM LDAN, you and all the Thatagatas, deliver me from the circle of existence unto the adamantine space. RDO RJE CAN DNGOS DAM TSHIG SEMS DPA' CHE ĀḤ. I beseech you to remain in this very place and to accept these good flowers which are the most radiantly divine flowers anointed by the fragrance of the gods.

5a, I, 6 to 5a, II, 3: Tibetan phonetics.

5a, II, 4 to 5b, I, 11: Listen! You who are an emanation who has perfected the use of illusion, listen! The pi-wa, gling-bu, rnga-zlam, dza rnga[21] HUM BCOM LDAN MGON PO DPA'A BO'I DBANG PHYUG, radiate greatly like the great conflagration of the universe.

5b, I, 12 to 5b, III, 16: Tibetan phonetics.

5b, IV, 1 to 6a, II, 5: MTHON MTHING 'OD CHAGS RDO RJE, let your mind be diverted by the voice of the sweet sounding pi-wa-ma rgyud mangs. May your adamantine mind, Heruka, be pleased by the joyful dance of the RDO RJE RIG MA.

6a, II, 6 to 6a, IV, 4: Tibetan phonetics.

6a, IV, 6 to 7a, I, 5: I make obeisance to RDO RJE SEMS DPA', master who embraces all moving things, he who binds himself greatly to the most excellent happiness, he who is the exalted one of samsara and nirvana.

7a I, 6 to 7b, IV, 17: Tibetan phonetics.

7b, IV, 18 to 8b, II, 15: HŪṂ. The light of divine wisdom which blazes like the conflagration of the universe, consumes all the dark regions of ignorant desire. OṂ. GZI BRJID CHEN PO, ME YI LHA, he who fulfills all objects of activity, through compassion for the benefit of sentient creatures, remain close to this very place.

The text at the bottom of *sheet 8b* is difficult to read – many words are faded, hence no satisfactory transcription and translation can be offered. The readable parts contain sentences such as:

> I make obeisance to RDO RJE SEMS DPA', master who embraces all moving things, he who binds himself greatly to the most excellent happiness, he who is the exalted one of samsara and nirvana.

and:

> Having seen creatures oppressed by the five poisons, abolish all misery.

The last sentence is:

> Obeisance to the leader of the circle of the assembly of DPA' 'O NA RO MA, . . . great happiness arising from the Five Buddhas.

Some of the neumes of the manuscript are provided with the following annotations:

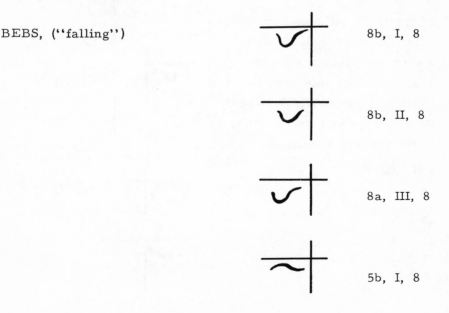

BEBS, ("falling")

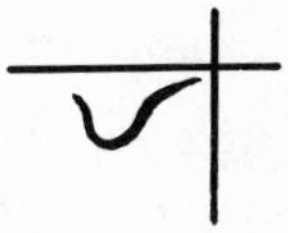

8b, I, 8

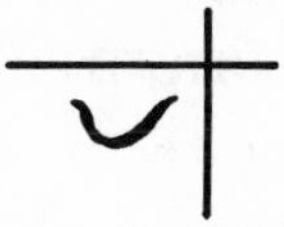

8b, II, 8

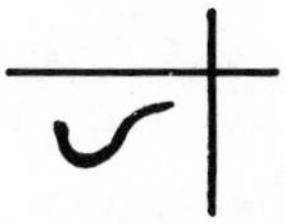

8a, III, 8

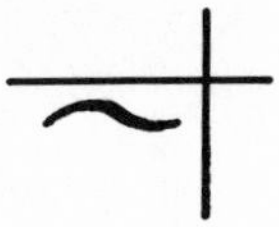

5b, I, 8

BCAD, ("cut")[22] 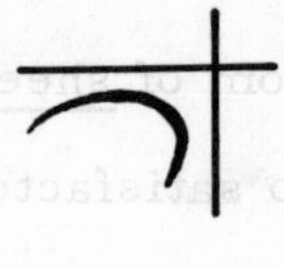 1b, III, 12

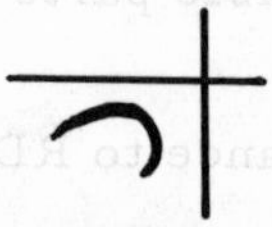 1b, IV, 10

BTEG CHAM ("short rise") 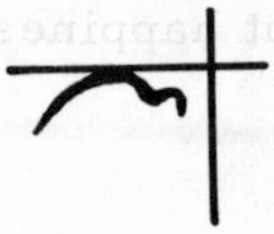 2a, I, 4

BTEG TSAM ("raised voice")  8a, IV, 10-11

This neume seems to be the same as NAM BTEG TSAM (8a, III, 10-11).

CUNG BNAM ("tighten voice") 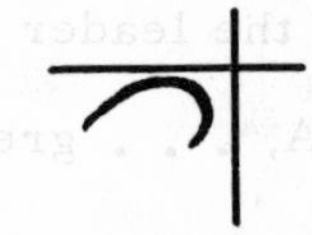 1b, III, 8

This neume may have the same significance as BCAD (1b, III, 12 and 1b, IV, 10).

CUNG BTEG ("raise voice a little") 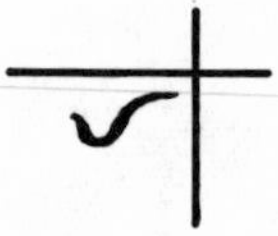 8b, I, 2; 8b, II, 2; 8a, III, 2; 8a, IV, 2

There is no noticeable difference between the shapes of this neume and the one denoting BEBS. The reason why we interpret BEBS as "falling" and CUNG BTEG as "raising the voice a little" is due to the Tibetan annotations.

but also (?): 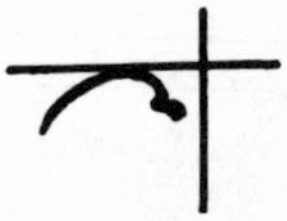 1b, II, 15

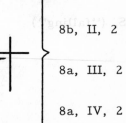

CUNG SHOD ("little louder"?) 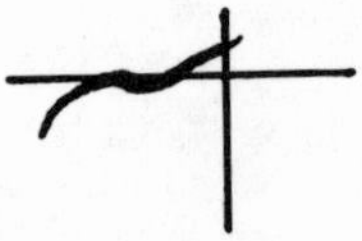 1b, I, 7

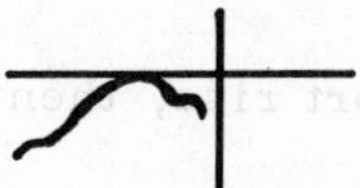

lb, IV, 6

DEGS ("lift")

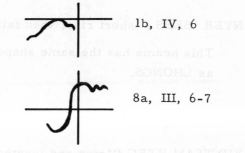

This neume probably has the same significance as BTEG TSAM.

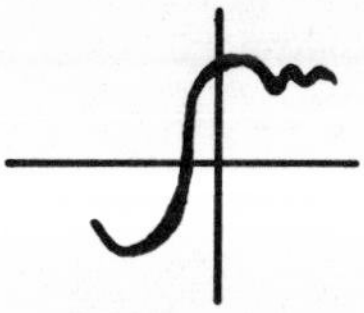

8a, III, 6-7

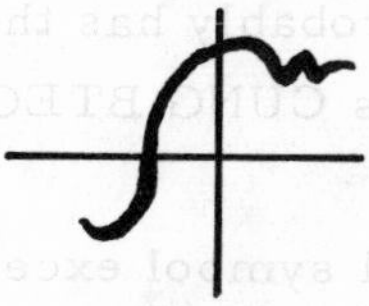

8b, I, 6-7

8b, II, 6-7

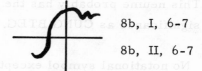

LHONGS ("relaxed voice")

8a, IV, 5-6

8b, I, 5-6

8b, II, 5-6

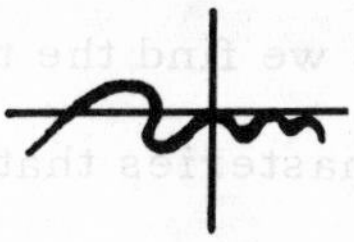

8a, III, 5-6

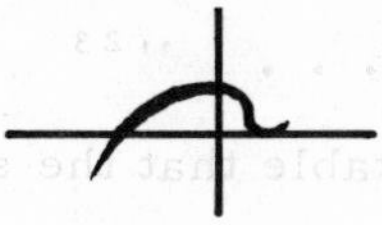

5b, I, 7

NAB MYUR ("up and quickly come down")

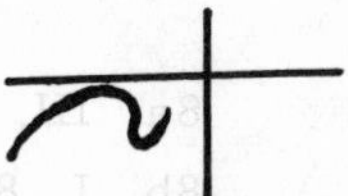

lb, I, 10

NAM BTEG ("raise voice high")

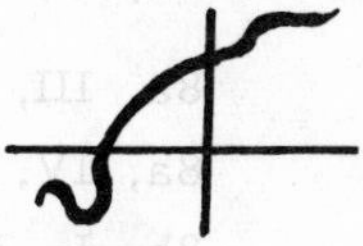

8b, II, 10

NAM BTEG TSAM ("raise voice and stay high")

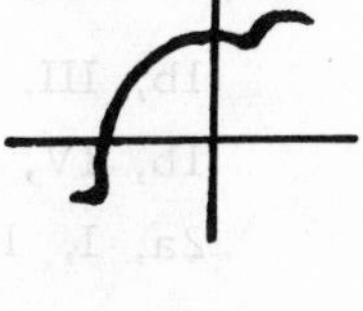

8a, III, 10

NYER 'BEBS ("short rise, then fall")

This neume has the same shape as LHONGS.

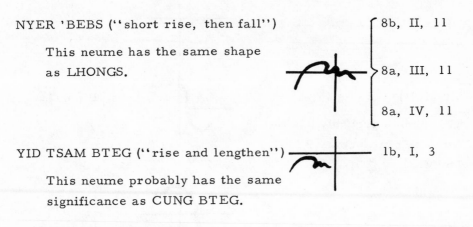

8b, II, 11
8a, III, 11
8a, IV, 11

YID TSAM BTEG ("rise and lengthen")

This neume probably has the same significance as CUNG BTEG.

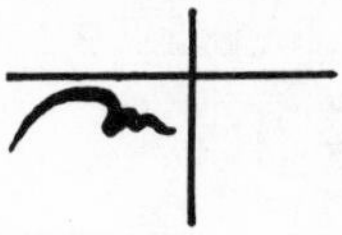

1b, I, 3

No notational symbol except the annotation nga is added to the mysterious syllable PHAT at 1b, I, 11 (nga meaning "strong voice").

The annotation in a different handwriting at 5b, IV, 9 means the same as the text: PI WAM MA.

At 1b, I, 1-3 we find the text word AR-GHAM. There exists a rule in certain monasteries that "at the word Argham the cymbals are held horizontally and struck with mid-finger erect. On Pargham, held below waist and the upper cymbal is made to revolve along the rim of the lowest . . . . "[23]

It is remarkable that the same notational symbols now and then recur at the same spots within the lines. For instance,

BEBS occurs at	8a, III, 8 with 'a'i
	8b, I, 8 with 'a'i
	8b, II, 8 with 'a'i
CUNG BTEG at	8a, III, 2 with wa'i
	8a, IV, 2 with 'a'i
	8b, I, 2 with 'a'i
	8b, II, 2 with 'a'i
BCAD at	1b, III, 12 with HA
	1b, IV, 10 with ma'a
	2a, I, 11 with HA

2a, II, 13 with nga'a
2a, III, 13 with nga'a
2a, IV, 12 with wa'a
2b, I, 12 with do'o
(2b, II, 11 [])
2b, III, 11 with ma'a
2b, IV, 9 with wa

MYER BEBS at 8a, III, 11 with 'a'i
8a, IV, 11 with 'a'i
8b, II, 11 with 'a'i

LHONGS at 8a, III, 5 with wa
8a, IV, 5 with na'a
8b, I, 5 with na'a
8b, II, 5 with ya

The recurrence of the same symbol at approximately the same spot in nearly every line of a page of the manuscript occurs mainly in conjunction with the extension sounds 'a'i, wa'i, nga'a, and others. Only occasionally is the recurrence of a symbol combined with a proper textual word such as:

DEGS at 8a, III, 6-7 with ME YI
8b, I, 6-7 with DON MDZAD
8b, II, 6-7 with NYE BAR

or, as already shown:

1b, III, 12 with HA
2a, I, 11 with HA

and so forth.

The meaning of these frequent recurrences is not known to us. We cannot speak of some endeavor to create rhymes by this procedure because the four lines of each manuscript page do not necessarily represent four separate "verses" or sections so that, for instance, spot

8 in a line would rhyme or otherwise correspond to spot 8 in another line. The literal translation shows that sentences can be shorter or longer than a line of the manuscript pages and generally do not fit into the 15, 16, 17, or 18 syllables allotted to each line.

The recurrent syllables, mainly of a "liquescent" nature and linking textual syllables or words, are performed to the same or similar melismas as shown by the corresponding neumes. For instance, the syllable <u>'a'i</u> is notated mainly by the neumes BEBS, CUNG BTEG, and NYER BEBS, curves which indicate a short melodic movement: a small descent, a small ascent, and a short rise and fall, respectively.

The syllables <u>ma'a</u>, <u>nga'a</u>, <u>wa</u> are notated mainly by BCAD and LHONGS, symbols which indicate "cut," a vaguely delineated cadential descent, and "relaxed voice," either a held note or a slight descent, both with a cadential character.

This feature can also be observed in instances when there are no recurrences of neumes at specific spots. For instance: YID TSAM BTEG, CUNG BTEG, and NAB MYUR are combined with the linking syllables <u>mo'o</u>, <u>ngo'o</u>, <u>ro'o</u>, and <u>wo</u>; CUNG BTEG, BCAD, BEBS, and NAB MYUR with <u>ra'a</u>, <u>ma'a</u>, <u>nga'a</u>, <u>ngwa'a</u>, and <u>wa'a</u>. We notice that there is some ordering principle in the use of Tibetan neumes and their textual syllables. A complete clarification of this principle will be possible only when more material becomes available for analysis.

The following two sheets (Fig. 82), although not directly related to the first manuscript are, however, a part of the same group of seven or eight volumes of which the entire text (including the first manuscript) supposedly consists.[24] The two sheets contain chants used during offering ceremonies and neumes written by a different person than those of the first manuscript.

MANUSCRIPT II

Figure 82

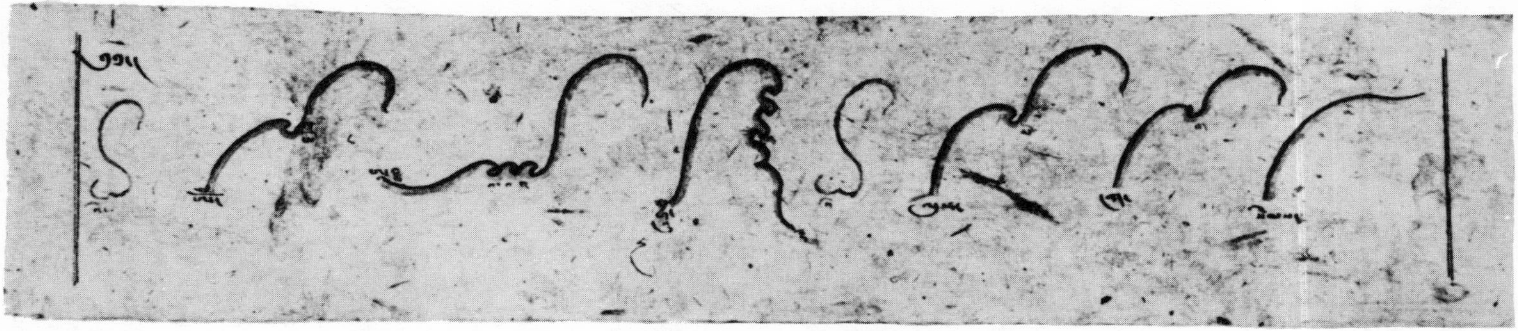

Sheet 1

Sheet 2

The first offering chant (sheet 1) is complete; the longer, second one (sheet 2) is not — one or two pages are probably missing. According to the Lama Geshe Nornang this text, when chanted, is accompanie by a dance performed by two monks.

The text is as follows:

<u>Sheet 1</u>:

'o	OṂ	o	AH	'a'a'a	HŪṂ	'o	LUS	sa	NGAG	ga	SEMS
	OṂ		AH		HŪṂ;		body		speech		mind.

Below the HŪṂ neume we read <u>rnga</u>, "drum." A general translation of the text is the same as the literal translation.

<u>Sheet 2</u>:

ME	'e'e'e	LA	'o	ya	ya	'a'a'a	GNAS	'a'a'a	PA'I
Fire		"in"					reside		"who"

'o	BGEGS	ga	KYI	'a'a'a	TSHOGS	KUN	no	NGA	ba
	demons		of		assembly	all		me	

LA	ba	'a'a'a	NYON
to			listen.

The general translation of this text reads: Listen to me, assembly of demons who reside in the fire.

Not shown in the photographic reproduction of this manuscript is the fact that it is written in three colors: the text (in our presentation shown in capital letters) is written in black, as are the notational curves; the extensions of, or links between, the text syllables or words ('a'a'a, and others — in our presentation shown in small print) and the curves  (first and fifth of sheet 1, third of the first line and first of the second line of sheet 2) are in blue; and the word rnga ("drum") in red.[25] The colors are used to facilitate the reading. Whether or not they have any symbolic or mystic significance is uncertain and subject to differing opinions. The word rnga appears below LA and GNAS in the first line and below TSHOGS in the second line of sheet 2.

We shall now consider the neumes, starting from the beginning of sheet 1. The first small curve (), written in blue, represents a brief introductory sound on 'o before the first regular text word OṂ is intoned. This habit of chanting, occasionally humming, an introductory note to the sound of a following sacred syllable can also be observed in the manuscripts and performances of Japanese shōmyō.

The notational curve of the word OṂ, written in black, consists of two parts: the first, immediately above the word OṂ, and the second, continuing the first, above the letter 'o (written in blue), which extends and, following the outline of the curve, raises the sound:

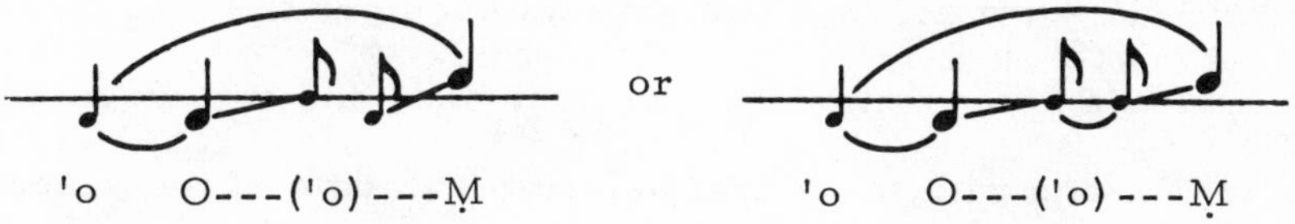

This is followed by ĀḤ (black) — 'a'a'a (blue). The "quilisma" at the end of the first half of the curve is performed to the three 'a'a'a extensions of ĀḤ; the second half of the curve raises the sound:

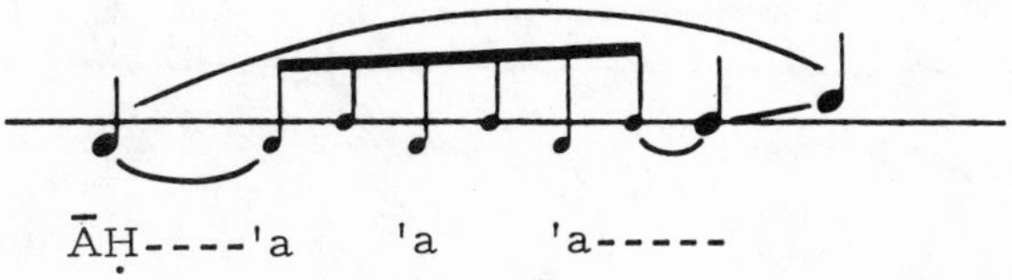

The following curve written above HŪṂ (black) represents the end of the formula OṂ ĀḤ HŪṂ. With this temporary halt we can expect a descent of the voice which seems to be indicated by the wriggly right-hand side of the curve. Below the word HŪṂ stands <u>rnga</u> (drum) written in red ink:

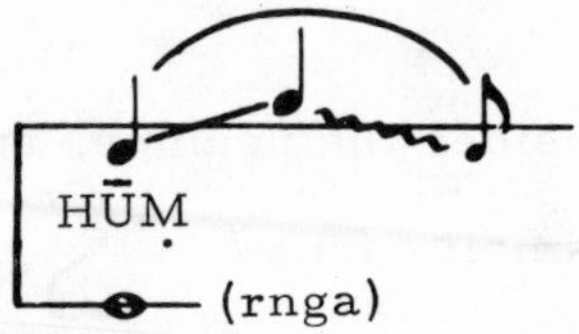

The next curve (blue) again denotes an introductory or a linking sound, chanted to 'o, aiming at the next word LUS. LUS has the same notational curve as ŌṂ; the upper part of the curve is chanted to sa (blue), forming the extension of LUS. NGAG-ga, too, is performed in the same manner as ŌṂ and LUS. The last curve on sheet 1, above SEMS, is comparatively simple. It resembles the <u>virga</u> of the West (as in the several St. Gall manuscripts) and the <u>oxeia</u> of Byzantine neumes, and may have had a similar function.

Sheet 2 contains two rows of neumes, most of which have been considered in sheet 1. The two unusual ones are the long curve above GNAS 'a'a - 'a, (penultimate of the first line) and the curve above TSHOGS (the one with the spiral before the middle of the second line).

The GNAS curve consists of  and 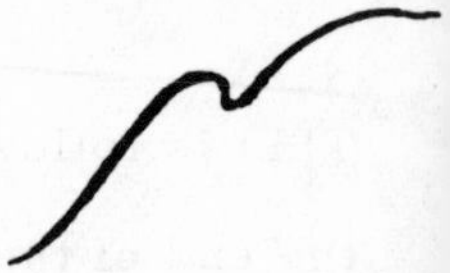

both of which are more or less "known" to us:

At the beginning of GNAS, below the text word, stands *rnga* (in red).

The TSHOGS curve resembles in shape the Western *cephalicus* or *ancus* without having the function of a liquescent neume. As mentioned before, TSHOGS too is annotated with *rnga*.

Each of the notational curves of manuscript II, with the exception of  and the sign for the introductory sound (), consists of two parts. The first part usually indicates the note or notes of the text word, while the second part assumes a function which resembles that of Western liquescent neumes. For instance, in sheet 1 we find

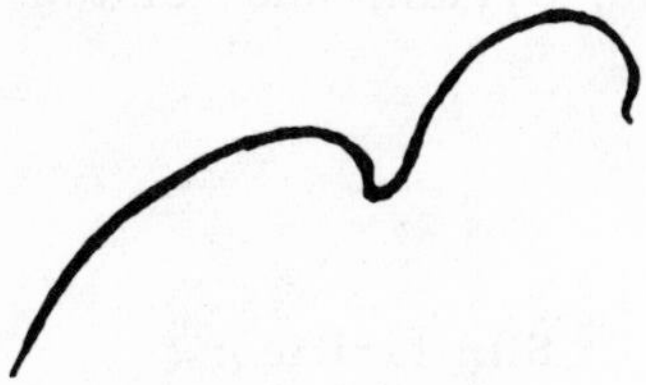

OM 'o (blue)

AH 'a 'a 'a (blue)

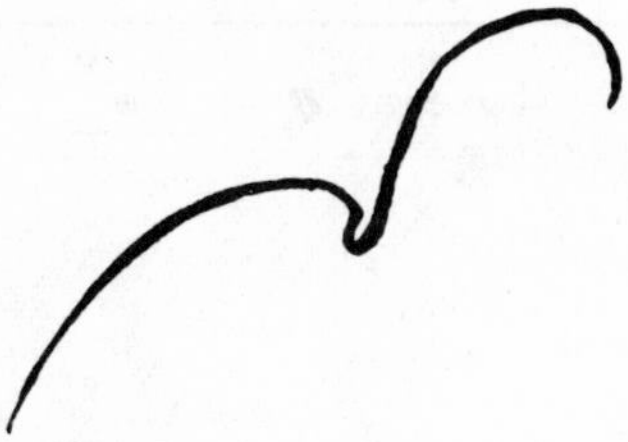

LUS sa (blue)

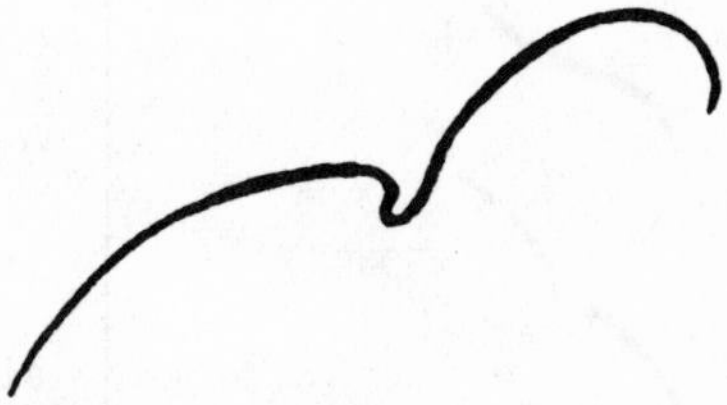

NGAG ga (blue)

and so forth.

Sheet 2 contains two unusual sequences of neumes. The first one beginning with LA (first line, second curve) is:

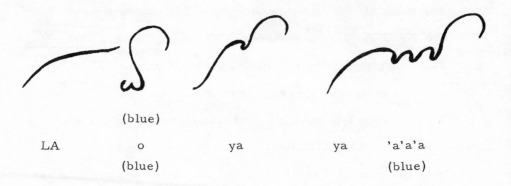

	(blue)			
LA	o	ya	ya	'a'a'a
	(blue)			(blue)

Below are listed the neumes which occur most frequently in these manuscripts and also commented upon are their similarities to other neumatic signs that possibly had found their way at one time or the other into Tibet. The names of Byzantine, Syrian, and related neumes[26] are shown in brackets:

MS. I:	MS. II:		Similarities:
			virga (Ban. tav. I); [oxeia, ___•]
 		CUNG SHOD "little louder" indication to intensify the sound	[oxeia, // ; ___•˙]
	 	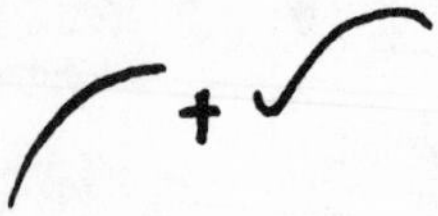 NYER 'BEBS "short rise and fall" 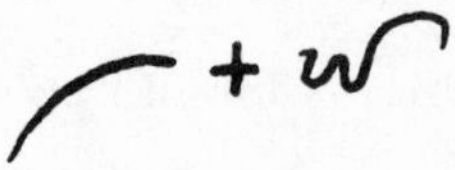	virga and clivis

MS. I:	MS. II:	Similarities:
	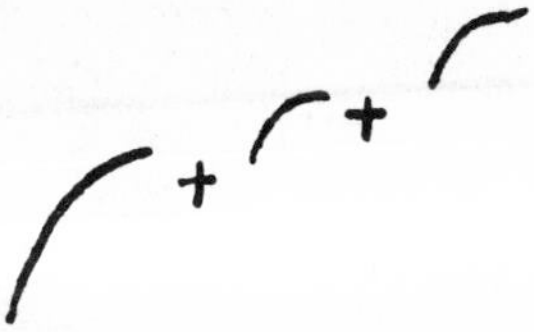	Scandicus (?)
	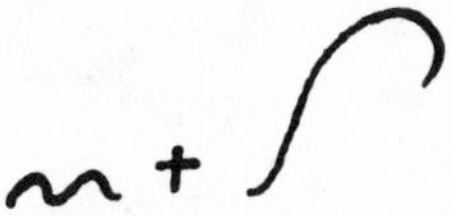	(Scandicus, Ban. tav. IV)
	CUNG BNAN "tighten voice"	Clivis; (Flexa, Ban. IV) [bareia; apostrophos, elaphron?; —•]
	BTEG CHAM "short rise"	(Pes flexus, Ban. tav. III)
		(Pes flexus, Ban. tav. III)
	BCAD "cut"	Clivis; (flexa, Ban. tav. IV; cephalicus ?)
	NAB MYUR "(up) and quickly down"	Clivis, (flexa, Ban. IV) [apostrophos ?]
	YID TSAM BTEG  ("raise and lengthen")	(Pes, Ban. tav. II) combination of  and LHONGS.

MS. I:	MS. II:	Similarities:
	LHONGS ("relaxed")	(Punctum, Ban. tav. I) [oligon]
		Porrectus (?)
		(Flexa resupina, Ban. tav. V)
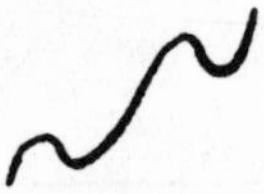		Torculus resupinus (?)
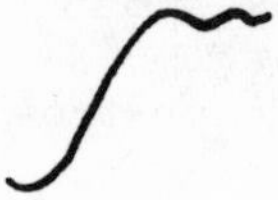	BTEG TSAM ("raise voice")	Podatus (Pes, Ban. tav. II)
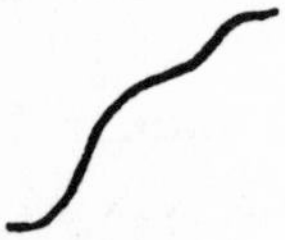	NAM BTEG ("raise voice high")	Podatus (Pes, Ban.)
	CUNG BTEG ("raise a little")	Podatus (Pes, Ban.) [Petaste; pelaston]
	BEBS ("falling")	(Flexa resupina, Ban. tav. V, exs. e, f, g) [synemba (?)]
	BEBS (?)	[syrmatike; ]
 		Torculus, (Pes flexus, Ban. tav. III)
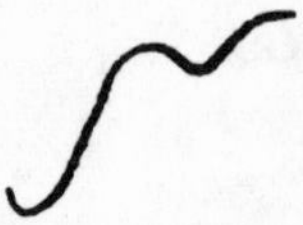	NAM BTEG TSAM ("raise voice and stay high")	Podatus, (Pes, Ban. tav. II) [oxeia; pelaston (2)]

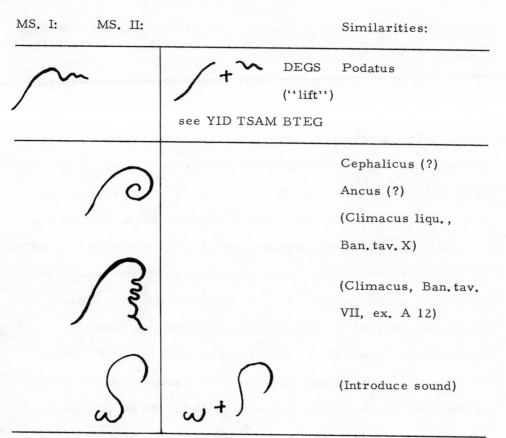

MS. I:	MS. II:		Similarities:
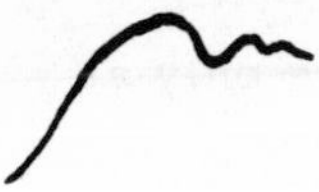	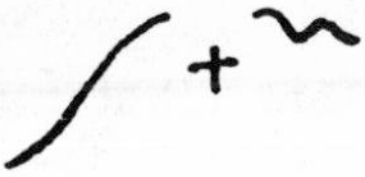 see YID TSAM BTEG	DEGS ("lift")	Podatus
			Cephalicus (?) Ancus (?) (Climacus liqu., Ban. tav. X)
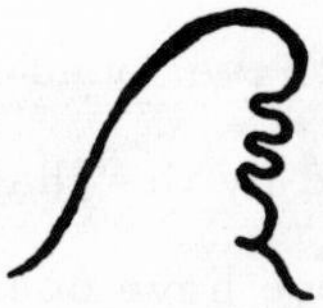			(Climacus, Ban. tav. VII, ex. A 12)
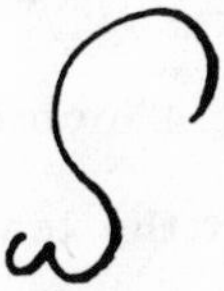	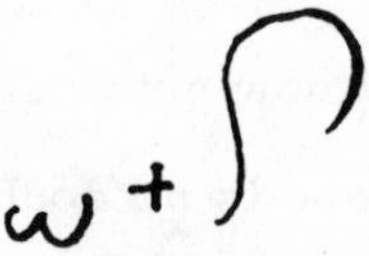		(Introduce sound)

Another fragment of a manuscript can be found in Waddell's The Buddhism of Tibet,[27] which shows the same or similar symbols as the ones presented in Figures 81 and 82. The reproduction of Waddell's score is not distinct enough to enable us to read the important annotations. The example consists of three sheets printed on one page. The upper one contains triple curves such as  , probably choir neumes; the middle and lower ones show curves similar to the ones we have observed in Figures 81 and 82. The lowest notation, perhaps an instrumental part, contains in its lower right corner the drawing of a conch shell, indicating the use of the tun, the conch-shell horn. This instrument produces an unusually deep sound which is generally combined with that of the si-nen (written: sil-smyan), a pair of large cymbals.

In summing up we may say that Tibetan neumes serve only as mnemonic aids to the music masters and choir leaders who know the melody. This writer was informed that the same notation may receive different interpretations in different monasteries. Thus, even if we had notations and recordings from one particular place we would still be in doubt as to how the same notations were read in other places.

It is possible for us to reconstruct a vague outline of the notated melody by depending upon the few instructions we have found in manuscript I and by following the rise and fall indicated by the shapes of the neumatic curves, but the limited information we have does not suffice to enable us to make a clear transcription.[28]

As already mentioned we know nothing about a musical notation of Buddhist chant in China. There is no doubt that the learned monks used one or more notational systems because the complexity of Buddhist service, the singing of the office, the chanting of hymns and responses, the strictly prescribed use of drums, bells, gongs, cymbals, "wooden fish," and other instruments, are unthinkable without some form of musical score.[29]

Buddhism began to appear in China in the first century A. D., during the reign of Han Ming Ti, an emperor of the Eastern Han period who ruled during the latter part of the Han dynasty (25-220). Tradition relates[30] that the emperor had a dream about a mighty deity in the West. He sent ambassadors to India who returned with sacred texts and images and probably also with melodies of Indian Buddhist chant. The texts were translated into Chinese and chanted in the Chinese manner; that is, the chanting was based upon the anhemitonic pentatonic scale with the occasional use of the two less important pien[31] notes. Any Indian characteristics, such as complex scales and ornaments, were completely ignored. By the year A. D. 500, after several comparatively mild persecutions instigated mostly by the Taoists, Buddhism prevailed over the whole of China.[32] During the T'ang period (618-906) Buddhism became fully adjusted and modified to the various Chinese beliefs and customs and, although it never gained any political power, it attained a permanent place in Chinese culture.

Although no information exists regarding a definite Buddhist chant notation in China, we must assume that some type of notational system was employed.[33] If a melody was notated, non-Buddhist notations borrowed from the imperial court or from secular music[34] were used. Even in Japan, where definite Buddhist notations can be found, we occasionally discover the use of koto, biwa, and flute tablature signs, a habit that may very well have had its origin in China. We may, however, assume that one or more definite Buddhist notations must have existed in China — and in Korea, too — because, we are informed, eleventh-century Japan saw the "invention" of meyasu-hakase,[35] a notational system based upon the medium of curves similar to the one used in the Lāmaist liturgy of Tibet. It is unlikely that the notational curves of Tibet, although modified, would appear in Japan without ever having appeared in China, whose culture was the most important of East Asia. Moreover, scales, melodies, formulae, and instruments which had come from the West always appeared in China before they found their way into Japan.

The following, Figure 83,[36] shows a typical Chinese Buddhist melody. With one exception (measure 15) it is purely pentatonic. It is sung at the Incense Offering ceremony.

Figure 83

The melody shown in the foregoing example strongly resembles a popular Chinese operatic aria. The light-hearted quality of this piece, characteristic of most Chinese Buddhist melodies, stands in noticeable contrast to the heavy dignity of Tibetan Buddhist chant melodies.

Notes
Bibliography
Index

NOTES*

Introduction

1. A Chinese chancellor and chronicler of the third century B. C.

2. A famous Chinese historian who lived between 163 and 85 B. C. His monumental work, the *Shih Chi* (史記), deals with history, geography, literature, astrology, divination, the calendar, biographies of important persons, and music. See Burton Watson, *Records of the Grand Historian of China* (New York, 1961), II, 55, 397.

3. Abū Naṣr Muḥammed b. Muḥammed b. Ṭarkhan b. Uzalāgh al-Fārābī (870-950); famous for his works on ethics, politics, philosophy, mathematics, and music. See *MGG*, I, 315.

4. Abū Yūsuf Ya'qūb b. Isḥāq al-Kindī (790-874), the "Philosopher among the Arabs," was famous for his works on music and its relation to other fields.

5. 429-347 B. C. See, e. g., H. Albert, *Die Lehre vom Ethos in der griechischen Musik* (Leipzig, 1899).

6. 384-322 B. C. See *MGG*, I, 631. See also W. Vetter, "Die antike Musik in der Beleuchtung durch Aristoteles," *AfMW*, I (1936), 2-41.

7. 305-285 B. C. See *MGG*, III, 1614-15. See also H. Menge, *Euclides Opera Omnia* (Leipzig, 1916), Vol. VIII.

8. A. D. 46?-120? See *Plutarchi De Musica*, ed. Ricardus Volkmann (Leipzig, 1856).

9. Concerning the Quadrivium see H. Abert, "Die Stellung der Musik in der antiken Kultur," *Die Antike*, II (1926), 136-54.

* Throughout the Notes the running heads refer to corresponding pages of text. Wherever a note is expanded by a following full-page example of Chinese text, the reader is referred by a subheading at the top of the example to the note that is being commented on.

10. See Eta Harich-Schneider, "Japanische Impressionen," *Musica*, IV (1949), 129 ff.

Part One

1. See Wang Guang Ki (also written Wang Kuang-ch'i), "Ueber die chinesischen Notenhandschriften," *Sinica*, III (1928), 110 ff.

2. See p. 106.

3. Since the earliest times, Chinese authors have left a wealth of information about music. Among these works are the *Chinese Classics* (or *Confucian Classics*) which, although not necessarily confined to the actual teachings of Confucius (551-479), were written and preserved by Confucian scholars. The first, the *Shu Ching*, is a book of historical documents which dates back to to the Chou period (1050-221). The work which was known to Confucius is simply called *Shu* in the *Analects*, and 400 years after the death of Confucius the compilation of the *Shu Ching* was ascribed to him. In later times the book was severely altered, especially during the Han period (206 B.C.-A.D. 220). The original text, supposedly discovered in a wall of the house of Confucius, is called the "Old Text," while the changed work is called the "Modern Text." Most of this text is in prose, with a small part in verse. In addition to valuable historical facts, the *Shu Ching* offers information regarding music. In Part II, Book I ("The Canon of Shun") we are informed about the standard pitch pipes and the "five instruments of gem"; in the same book, paragraph 13, we read that "all within the four seas, the eight instruments [these are the eight materials producing the eight sounds: instruments made of metal, stone, silk, bamboo, gourd, earth, leather, and wood] were stopped and hushed." In Book IV, paragraph 4, we read about the songs of the period; in paragraphs 9 and 10 indirect reference is made to the "lutes" (the famous Chinese zithers); and so forth.

The second of the *Classics* is the *Shih Ching*, the "Book of Odes." It must not be confused with the *Shih Chi*, an important historical work by the Han historian Ssŭ-ma Ch'ien (145-86). The *Shih Ching*, also called "The Three-hundred," contains 305 rhymed ballads — poems that originated in a pre-Confucian era. Although Confucius expressed admiration for them and later writers credited him with compiling the poems, doubts concerning this have arisen. A passage in the Li Chi (another of the Chinese Classics) exists which suggests the true origin of the poems (see J. Legge, trans., The Chinese Classics [London, 1871], IV, i [Prolegomena]; II, 23-24): "Every fifth year, the son of Heaven made a progress through the kingdom, when the grand music-master was commanded to lay before him the poems collected in the States of the several quarters, as an exhibition of the manners of the people." This means that according to the quality of the poems the emperor would judge how the princes had ruled the various states and would then reward or punish them accordingly. Although none of the melodies to which the poems were sung have survived, the rare and simple beauty of these odes shows how impressive the songs must have been.

The third Chinese Classic is the I Ching, the "Book of Changes." This pre-Confucian work, probably the oldest of the Classics, consists of two texts which in later periods were joined to make one book. The first of these consists of omen-texts in rhyme dealing with the pa-kua, the eight mysterious trigrams (hexagrams), used for divination. The I Ching has been ascribed to Wên Wang, the father of Wu Wang, who was the first emperor of the Chou dynasty (1027-256).

The fourth Chinese Classic, the Li Chi ("Book of Rites"), is a collection of tractates of varying dates written sometime between the fourth and second centuries B.C. Some parts of the work, especially chapters three and four, are perhaps older than the rest and may go back to the time of Confucius. The Li Chi was compiled by an uncle and his nephew named Tai during the first and second centuries B.C. The uncle, Tai Teh (or Ta Tai), shaped the work into 85 sections, and his nephew, Tai Shêng (or Hsiao Tai), shortened it to 46. Although the Li Chi was not written by Confucius, it reflects Confucian thinking and in A.D. 175 became an official part of the Confucian Classics. Section 27, Yüeh-chi, "Record of Music," is of considerable importance to the musicologist. See J. Legge, trans., Sacred Books of China (Oxford, 1885), Vol. XXVIII; also Richard Wilhelm, trans., "Das Buch der Sitte," Li-Gi (Jena, 1930), chap. "Yo-ki."

Another Chinese Classic, the Chou Li, "The Rites of the Chou Period," was added to the Li Chi during the Han dynasty (202 B.C.-A.D. 220). It was written during the first century B.C. and deals mostly with ritual and constitutional matters of the Chou period. It contains information about the pitch-pipes (lü), the stone-chimes, and the kau-ku — a twelve-foot-long drum used at imperial hunting parties — but offers no remarks about the famous Chinese zither, the ch'in.

The Ch'un-ch'iu, "The Annals of Spring and Autumn," another Classic (not to be confused with the Lü-shih-ch'un-ch'iu, "Spring and Autumn of Lü Pu Wei"), is a history of the state of Lu from 722 to 481 B.C. It contains brief entries about victories, murders, treaties, and natural phenomena and, as was the custom, adds to the date of each entry the season when the event occurred — hence the title, "Spring and Autumn." According to Mencius (372-289? B.C.) this was a work which Confucius believed would make him known in the future. As with the Shih Ching, later writers tried to read hidden meanings into its text. Linked with the Ch'un-ch'iu is the important Tso Chuan, Tso Ch'iu-ming's Commentary on the Ch'un-ch'iu, which was written about 300 B.C. Both works contain numerous references to music and musical instruments, and in the Tso Chuan we note that a clear distinction has already been made between the musical styles of North and South China.

A work that does not belong to the Chinese Classics (certain doubts have been raised about its importance and value) is the Lü-shih ch'un-ch'iu, the "Spring and Autumn of Lü Pu Wei" (third century B.C.), which offers some information about the early periods of Chinese history and music.

The monumental collection of the Confucian Classics has been translated into English by James Legge under the title of The Chinese Classics: Li Ki (Li Chi) (Oxford, 1885); She King (Shih Ching) (London, 1871); Shoo King (Shu Ching) (Hongkong, 1865); Yi King (I Ching) (Oxford, 1882). See also Sacred Books of the East, ed. Max Müller (Oxford, 1897-1927). Of considerable importance is Notes of Chinese Literature by A. Wylie, published in Shanghai in 1867. This work contains information about 2000 Chinese works, including the Classics, history, philosophy, and other fields.

4. *Yin-hsü wên-tzŭ chui-ho* (殷虛文字綴合), publ. by Chung-kuo k'o-hsüeh-yüan k'ao-ku-yen-chiu-so (中國科學院考古研究所) (Peking, 1955).

5. Ch'ên Shou-yi, *Chinese Literature* (New York, 1961), p. 5.

6. For further information on bronzes see Kuo Mo-jo (郭沫若), *Liang-chou chin-wen tz'ŭ ta hsi t'u-lu k'ao-shih* (兩周金文辭大系圖錄考釋) (Peking, 1956).

7. Ch'ên Shou-yi, op. cit., p. 6.

8. The manuscript is preserved in the Bibliothèque nationale, Collection Pelliot, No. 3808.

9. See Arthur Waley, *Ballads and Stories from Tun-Huang* (London, 1960).

10. Ibid., p. 242.

11. See Richard Wilhelm, *Fruehling und Herbst des Lü Bu We* (Jena, 1928), esp. book five, chap. two; see also above, n. 10. (Chinese editions: *Ssu-pu ts'ung-k'an*, first series, Shanghai, 1920-1922; third series, 1935).

12. The twelve pitches were grouped into six male (律 , "laws") and six female (呂 , "pipes"); both words are pronounced *lü*, but the former is pronounced in the high-falling tone, and the latter in the low-rising tone and, of course, are written differently.

13. J. van Aalst, *Chinese Music* (Shanghai, 1884; repr. Peking, 1933).

14. Maurice Courant, "Essai sur la musique classique des Chinois avec un appendice relatif a la musique Coreenne," in *Encyclopédie de la musique*, ed. A. Lavignac (Paris, 1913), Vol. I.

15. V. Ch. Mahillon, *Annuaire du Conservatoire de Bruxelles* (Ghent, 1886, 1890).

16. Père Amiot, *Mémoire sur la musique des Chinois tant anciens que modernes* (Paris, 1779).

17. Curt Sachs, *The Rise of Music in the Ancient World* (New York, 1943), pp. 116-17. See also Georges Soulié, *La Musique en Chine* (Paris, 1911). Soulié transcribes the *Huang-chung* with A# below the middle C.

18. See *Li Ki* (*Li Chi*), "Book of Rites," chapter on music; trans. J. Legge in *The Sacred Books of China*, ed. F. M. Müller (Oxford, 1885), Vol. XXVII.

19. Cf. A. Daniélou, *Introduction to the Study of Musical Scales* (London, 1943), pp. 75-82.

20. "Exposé de la musique des Chinois," in *L'Echo musical* (Brussels), October 12, 1890.

21. Cf. E. Faber, "The Chinese Theory of Music," *China Review* (1873), p. 388. See also Laurence Picken, "Chinese Music" in *Grove's Dictionary of Music and Musicians*, 5th ed. (New York, 1959), II, 230.

22. *Chinesische Musik* (Kassel, 1956), pp. 79-82.

23. A dictionary showing the characters of the ancient script is *Shuo-wên chiai-tzŭ chên-pên* (說文解字眞本) by the Han author Hsü Shên (許慎) (Shanghai, n. d.).

24. The thought underlying the organization of the *lü* is the principle of the union of the male and female in procreation. Similar doctrines can be found throughout the Orient, especially in the Jewish Cabbalah. According to the Cabbalists, God the Infinite Being, far removed and beyond all mundane existence, and God the Active Being, who influences creation and life, represented a paradox which the Cabbalists resolved in the Sefirot, the ten spheres of divine manifestation — luminous rays in which God emerges from the concealed Infinite and Incomprehensible. The Sefirot, described as male and female, arose from the first Sefirah, the Keter (Crown), an absolute primeval unity from which the two other male and female Sefirot emerged — a male called Chochmah (Wisdom), and a female called Binah (Intellect); together these formed the "Father and Mother." The remaining seven Sefirot were the result of the union of Chochmah and Binah.

25. The excerpt on page 427 is taken from a copy of the *Chou Li*, Book 37 of the *Ssŭ-pu-pei-yao* edition (Shanghai, n. d.). A rough translation of this excerpt reads as follows:

> Ta Shih (the name of a musical official) is in charge of the six *lü* and their six companions. The former represent the sounds of *yang*,

(Refers to Note 25)

大師掌六律六同以合陰陽之聲陽聲黃鍾大蔟姑
洗蕤賓夷則無射陰聲大呂應鍾南呂函鍾小呂夾鍾

consisting of Huang-chung, T'ai-ts'u, Ku-hsi, Jui-pin, I-tsê, and Wu-i, and the latter (the six companions) represent the sounds of yin, consisting of Ta-lü, Ying-chung, Nan-lü, Han-chung (函鐘), Hsiao-lü (小呂), and Chia-chung.

Remarkable are the names Han-chung and Hsiao-lü, which are used here instead of the usual Lin-chung and Chung-lü.

Another excerpt (p. 429), taken from a copy of the Kuo Yü (國語 , "Episodes of State"), Vol. III, is a work attributed to Tso Ch'iu-ming, the author of the Tso Chuan, who adds four principles to the yang and yin and elaborates the extramusical connotations of the lü. Roughly translated this excerpt reads:

> In ancient times a learned blind musician (Shên Ku) examined the central tone and established it as the basis of a system of tones. Rules (to this effect) were postulated which were used by numerous government officials. He (Shên Ku) established three tones (representing heaven, earth, and men), then he divided (split) them into six and then, from six into twelve (which included the yang and yin tones). Six is the central number between heaven and earth. Yellow is the central color among all colors, hence the first tone was called Huang-chung ("Yellow Bell") and was employed to harmonize with the six principles (yin, yang, wind, rain, cloudiness, and clearness) and the nine te (water, fire, metal, wood, earth, grain, virtue, resources, and industry). The second tone (after the Huang-chung) is T'ai-ts'u, which fosters growth and does away with all tardiness. The third tone, Ku-hsi, assists in the cleansing of all objects under the sun, honors the gods and welcomes guests. The fourth tone, Jui-pin, pacifies both people and spirits and encourages friendship. The fifth tone, I-tsê, praises the harvest and calms the people. The sixth tone, Wu-i, announces the virtues of the sages in order to guide the people in the correct ceremonies.
>
> There are also six chien ["spaces," "intervals"] which harmonize with the former six lü: Ta-lü assists the Huang-chung in the completion of its task. Chia-chung harmonizes the weather of all seasons. Chung-lü presents the universal law. Lin-chung supervises deeds and prevents fraud. Nan-lü assists the yang lü in order to make the world prosperous. Yin-chung maintains the most effective functioning of both officials and objects.

26. See p. 39.

(Refers to Note 25)

古之神瞽考中聲而量之以制度律均鍾百官軌儀
紀之以三平之以六成於十二天之道也夫六中之
色也故名之曰黃鍾所以宣養六氣九德也由是第
之二曰太蔟所以金奏贊陽出滯也三曰姑洗所以
修潔百物考神納賓也四曰蕤賓所以安靖神人獻
酬交酢也五曰夷則所以詠歌九則平民無貳也六
曰無射所以宣布哲人之令德示民軌儀也爲之六
間以揚沈伏而黜散越也元間大呂助宣物也二間
夾鍾出四隙之細也三間仲呂宣中氣也四間林鍾
和展百事俾莫不任肅純恪也五間南呂贊陽秀也
六間應鍾均利器用俾應復也

27. The ancient Chinese vertical flute was made of bamboo and had five holes above and one below. It was used in the music of the Confucian temple.

28. See p. 69.

29. See van Aalst, Chinese Music, p. 20.

30. Maurice Courant, "Chine et Corée," in Encyclopédie de la musique, ed. A. Lavignac (Paris, 1913), I, 126. It may be of interest to study the following example (p. 431); it represents another setting of the first ode in lü notation and is quoted from Wang Kuang-ch'i (王光祈), Chung-kuo yin-yüeh-shih (中國音樂史, "History of Chinese Music"), published in Taipei in 1956.

Below follows the transcription of the heptatonic melody:

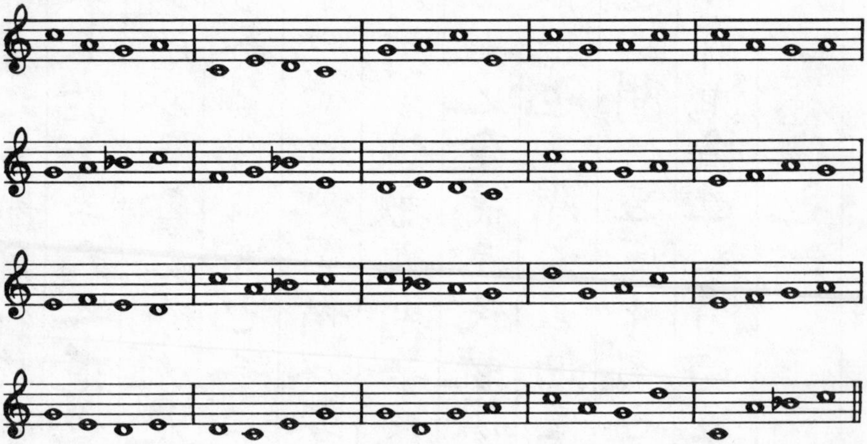

31. Although not prescribed in the score of this ode music, the po-fu player can perform three different beats:

(扎) means that both hands beat both skins of the drum,

(鼕) the right hand beats the right skin of the drum,

(鼓) the left hand beats the left skin of the drum.

32. The t'ao-ku (鞉鼓) is a small barrel-shaped drum (or two or more drums tied together), the corpus of which is pierced by a wooden handle.

(Refers to Note 30)

關雎

關 黃清	參 黃清	求 黃清	參 黃清	參 太
關 南	差 南	之 南	差 無	差 黃
雎 林	荇 林	不 林	荇 南	荇 姑
鳩 南	菜 南	得 南	菜 林	菜 林
在 黃	左 林	寤 姑	左 太清	左 林
河 姑	右 南	寐 仲	右 林	右 姑
之 太	流 無	思 南	采 南	芼 林
洲 黃	之 黃清	服 林	之 黃清	之 南
窈 林	窈 仲	悠 姑	窈 姑	窈 黃清
窕 南	窕 林	哉 仲	窕 仲	窕 南
淑 黃清	淑 無	悠 姑	淑 林	淑 林
女 姑	女 姑	哉 太	女 南	女 太清
君 黃清	寤 太	輾 黃清	琴 林	鐘 黃
子 林	寐 姑	轉 南	瑟 姑	鼓 南
好 南	求 太	反 無	友 太	樂 無
逑 黃清	之 黃	側 黃清	之 姑	之 黃清

Setting of First Ode in Lü Notation

Strings are attached to the middle of the corpus, on both sides, with freely swinging balls at their ends. When the drum is turned to and fro, the balls strike against the two drum skins. In Confucian temples one t'ao-ku is placed at the east side, the other at the west side. At the present time the instrument is also used by traveling vendors and beggars. An illustration of the t'ao-ku can be found in van Aalst, p. 77.

33. The text, as far as it is shown in Fig. 1 reads: Kuan, kuan, chü chiu tsai ho chih chou; roughly translated the words mean: "Kuan, kuan, cry the fish-hawks from the island in the river . . . ."

34. The pien-ch'ing (編 磬), a stone-chime, consists of sixteen L-shaped stone slabs hung in two rows of eight slabs each, from a wooden frame. All slabs are equally long but differ in thickness. The slabs are tuned to the twelve lü in the following manner:

Upper row (yang lü):

wu i jui ku t'ai huang pei-wu pei-i

Lower row (yin lü):

ying nan lin chung chia ta pei-ying pei-nan

The ancient instrument had sixteen slabs; in the Han period (202 B. C. -A. D. 200) nineteen; in the Liang period (502-556), twenty-one; in the Wei (220-581), fourteen; and in the Ming period (1368-1644), twenty-four. The instrument was used only in ritual and ceremonial music of the temple and imperial court. In the Confucian temple the pien-ch'ing corresponds to the t'ê-ching (see below, n. 35). The latter stands at the east side and the former at the west side of the Moon Terrace.

35. The t'ê-ch'ing (特 磬 , "single musical stone") is a single L-shaped slab made of black calcareous stone or jade (hence it is often de-

scribed as the "gem") which is hung on a wooden frame. It is placed at the left side of the Moon Terrace of the Confucian temple. Usually at the end of every verse of a hymn the longer part of the slab is struck once with the cushioned end of a wooden mallet. The t'ê-ch'ing produces a clear deep sound which intones the kung, the basic note of the melody. We read in the Analects (XIV, 42) that Confucius frequently uttered his approval of this instrument because its sound was not influenced by climatic changes. Occasionally the instrument is called li-ch'ing (離磬), "separate (distant) ch'ing." (W. E. Soothill, The Analects of the Conversations of Confucius . . . [London, 1937]).

36. See van Aalst, p. 50.

37. This is only an assumption. In reality the Huang-chung was considered to be a yin sound; hence the note A would be a degree of the yang row.

38. Cf. Yüeh-lü ch'uan-shu (樂律全書), a work in nineteen volumes by Prince Chu Tsai-yü (朱載堉); Imperial Catalogue, ch'üan 38, p. 5. The work was written during the last decennium of the sixteenth century.

39. The sounds of the vocal part and of the pien-ch'ing would be as follows:

voice

pien-ch'ing

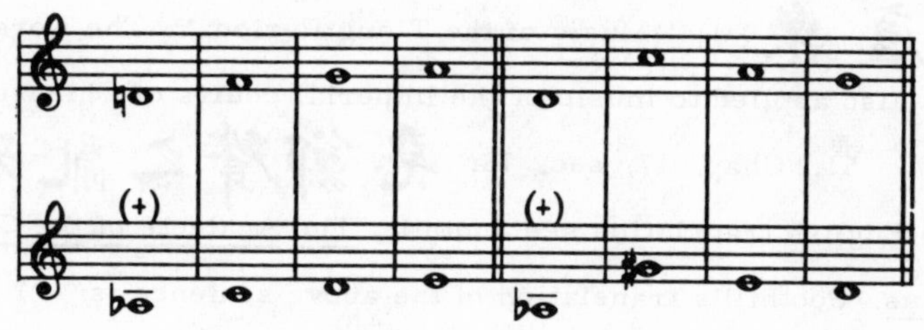

The instruments other than the pien-ch'ing would perform the lower part and "double" it in an anhemitonic pentatonic manner using the notes A and G.

40. Koreanische Musik (Tokyo, 1930), p. 30.

41. See p. 53.

42. Van Aalst, p. 23.

43. The notations of Chiang K'uei (姜夔) are extant in the Pê Shih Tao Jen Ko Ch'ü (白石道人歌曲), Official History of the Sung Dynasty (Shanghai, 1936), Vol. 2037, p. 6. See also p. 177 and p. 456 (n. 174).

44. John Hazedel Levis, *Foundations of Chinese Musical Art* (Peiping, 1936), pp. 174-75.

45. Also called *Kambhojika*, *Kambhoja*, or *Kambhoji* is a popular rāga of North India. Its tone-material is C E F G A Bb c in the rising, and c Bb A G F E D C in the descending scale.

46. The word *hu* (胡 , "irregular") was used to denote foreigners, especially Mongol and Tartar tribes.

47. Transcribed by Laurence Picken in *New Oxford History of Music* (New York, 1957), I, 109.

48. Ibid., p. 110.

49. The *Ak-hak-koe-pŭm* was reprinted several times, e.g., in 1610 by Rhee Chung-koo of the Ak-su-chŭng (樂書廳), and again during the reign of King Yung-cho (1724-1776). A photographic reproduction of this important work was published in 1933 in Seoul by the Ko-chŭn kan-haeng hoe (古典刊行會), or, as the company's name is often pronounced in Japanese, by the Koten kanko kai of Keijo (Seoul). See also Courant, "Chine et Coreé," in *Encyclopédie de la musique*, I, 212.

50. Korean musicians called imported music from China *T'ang-ak* (唐樂), "Music of the T'ang Period." The Korean term *T'ang-ak* was also applied to music of the imperial courts of Chinese pre-T'ang periods.

51. Chap. 17, sec. 18: 惡鄭聲之亂雅樂也
For English translation see Soothill, *The Analects of the Conversations of Confucius*. Soothill's translation of the above sentence is: "I hate the way the airs of Chêng pervert correct music."

52. Ibid., chap. 7, sec. 13:

子在齊聞韶。三月不知肉
味。曰不圖為樂之至於斯也。

The literal translation by Soothill is: "When the master was in Ch'i [Chê] he heard the Shao music and for three months was unconscious of the taste of meat.

'I did not imagine,' said he, 'that music had reached such perfection as this' " (pp. 62-63). The character 韶, pronounced Shao in Chinese (in Korean it is So), is the name of the music of the legendary emperor Shun (舜, in Korean pronounced Sun), who supposedly ruled from 2255-2205. In addition shao also means "harmonious," "excellent," "beautiful."

53. Tōyō-rekishi-dai-jiten (東洋歷史大辭典) ("Dictionary of Oriental History") (Tokyo, 1937), V. 432.

54. The titles of the musical items (ak-po) contained in the Sae-chong shillok are:

a) Ah-ak-po (雅樂譜)

b) I-yae kyŭng-chŭn t'ong-hae (儀禮經傳通解)

c) Won-cho im-u tae-song ak-po (元朝林宇大成樂譜)

d) Chŭng-tae-ŭp ch'i mu-ak-po (定大業之舞樂譜)

e) Po-tae-pyong ch'i mu-ak-po (保太平之舞樂譜)

f) Pal-sang ch'i mu-ak-po (發祥之舞樂譜)

g) Chŭn-in-cha (前引子)

h) Yŭ-min-ak-po (與民樂譜)

i) Ch'i-hwa-pyong po (致和平譜)

j) Chwi-pung-hyong po (醉豐亨譜)

k) Hu-in-cha (後引子)

l) Pong-hwang-ŭm (鳳凰吟)

m) Man-chŭn chun (滿殿春)

55. The work contains the following twelve pieces notated in yul-cha-po and chŭng-kan-po:

a) *Po tae-pyŭng po* (保太平譜)

b) *Jŭng-tae-ŭp po* (*in*) (定大業譜一仁)

c) *Mu-an wang myo-che ak po* (武安王廟祭樂譜)

d) *Kyŭng-mo-kung che-ak kae-hi-un-po* (景慕宮祭樂 啓熙運譜)

e) *Po-ryung-ŭn po* (報隆恩譜)

f) *Yŭ-min-ak* (*man*) (與民樂一慢)

g) *Nak-yang-chun* (*ye*) (洛陽春一禮)

h) *Yŭ-min-ak* (*kwan-po*) (與民樂一管譜)

i) *Po-hŭ-cha* (步虛子)

j) *Yŭng-san hwae-sang* (靈山會相)

k) *Yŭ-min-ak* (*hyŭn-po*) (與民樂一絃譜)

l) *Po-hŭ-cha* (*ji*) (步虛子一智).

The original of this work is preserved in the former Imperial Library of Seoul.

56. Lee Hye-ku, *Han-kuk ŭm-ak yon-gu* (韓國音樂研究) (Seoul, 1957).

57. See p. 124.

58. There are several Confucian hymns (and strophes) which have identic beginnings. Compare this example, for instance, with the one shown on p. 58.

59. See "Hymne pour le sacrifice à Confucius," in Courant's article "Chine et Corée," in *Encyclopédie de la musique*, I, 103 ff.

60. To be discussed in Volume II.

61. To be discussed in Volume II.

62. See Walter Kaufmann, "The Forms of the Dhrupad and Khyal in Indian Art Music," *The Canadian Music Journal*, Vol. III, No. 2, (1959), p. 26.

63. To be discussed in Volume II.

64. See Part I, n. 3 (p. 424).

65. The correct writing of shang is 商 ; Korean authors and occasionally a few Chinese musicians use instead the character 啇 (which actually reads ti).

66. Four other pentatonic scales were derived from the linear permutations of the kung scale:

Kung	Scale
kung	(C)
shang	(D)
chiao	(E)
chih	(G)
yü	(A)

Shang	Scale	Chiao	Scale	Chih	Scale	Yü	Scale
shang	(D)	chiao	(E)	chih	(G)	yü	(A)
chiao	(E)	chih	(G)	yü	(A)	kung	(c)
chih	(G)	yü	(A)	kung	(c)	shang	(d)
yü	(A)	kung	(c)	shang	(d)	chiao	(e)
kung	(c)	shang	(d)	chiao	(e)	chih	(g)

The five basic notes (kung, shang, chiao, chih, and yü) were called chêng (正, "principal"); additional notes, which will be discussed later, were called huo (or ho, 和 , "to harmonize").

67. For further information see Wm. Theodore de Bary, ed., Sources of Chinese Tradition (New York, 1960), pp. 214 ff.

68. See p. 45.

69. See Part I, n. 3 (p. 424).

70. See Liu Chin Tsao, Yüeh-kao ch'ing-chao hsu-wên-hsien-tung-kao (Shanghai, 1936), CXC, 201.

71. According to the Yüeh-lü ch'uan-shu, V, 191 (See Part I, n. 38 [p. 433]).

72. Ibid.

73. Courant, "Chine et Corée," I, 156.

74. See p. 69.

75. For further details about Chinese scales see Koh Nie Kuh, "A Musicological Study of the Important Tonal Systems of the T'ang Dynasty" (dissertation, School of Education, New York University, 1942).

76. In Korea the *pien* notes were called *pyon-chih* and *pyon-kung*. The notational symbols were the same as in China.

77. See p. 69.

78. 氵 is an abbreviation of 清 (*ch'ing*) and actually means "clear"; in this context however, 氵 means "higher." Correctly written C# should be expressed with 清宮 .

79. To be discussed in Volume II.

80. Occasionally an alternative for *hen* (the Chinese *pien* 變) is used; it is the symbol 变 . Thus 变宮 means the same as 變宮 . The same applies to *hen-chi*.

81. According to Japanese custom we interpret *kyū* (宮) as the Western note D.

82. *Ongaku Jiten* (音樂事典), "Music Dictionary," ed. Shimonaka Yasaburo (下中彌三郎), 12 vols. (Tokyo: Heibon-sha, 1955-57). Article on notation, III, 87, fig. 2-13.

83. See p. 63.

84. For *saibara* examples transcribed into Western notation see Shiba Sukehiro (芝 祐泰), *Gagaku* (雅樂) (Tokyo, 1955-56), II, 23.

85. Ise, near the southern coast of central Japan on the Bay of Ise (Ise Wan), is famous for its ancient shrines, which are frequently visited by pilgrim

86. See Volume II.

Part Two

1. The characters *kung* (工) and *ch'ê* (尺) are not to be confused with *kung* (宮) and *chih* (徵) of the old Chinese Five and Seven-Tone Notations. The "ancient" *kung* (宮) always represents the starting note, the basic tone of the scale, while the "new" *kung* (工) denotes the sixth diatonic degree of a heptatonic scale.

2. A. Lavignac, ed., *Encyclopédie de la musique* (Paris, 1913), Vol. I

3. See p. 59.

4. Shên Kua lived from A. D. 1030-1096. A recent edition of this work (2 vols.) was published by the Chunghwa Bookstore (Shanghai, 1960). See also Donald Holzman, "Shên Kua and his Meng-ch'i pi-t'an," *T'oung Pao*, XLVI (1958), pp. 260-92.

5. A musical system based upon four basic scales. It is discussed by the T'ang scholar Tu Yu (735-812) in his work *T'ung Tien* (VII, 766), a rich source of information on economy, examinations, rites, music, etc. There are several publications of this work, the most recent by the Commercial Press (n. d.). The scales are also mentioned by the Sung scholar Chang Yen in the *Tz'u Yüan* (I, 3). The *Tz'u Yüan* is the earliest dictionary dealing with Chinese phrases, etc. The work was compiled by Lu Erh-k'uei and published by the Commercial Press in 1915. See also Koh-Nie-Kuh, "A Musicological Study of the Important Tonal Systems of the T'ang Dynasty," (dissertation, School of Education, New York University, 1942).

6. The correct names of the ascending chromatic scale degrees of *kung-ch'ê-p'u* after the time of Shên Kua are discussed below.

7. There are hundreds of works in which the *kung-ch'ê* symbols, their proper sequence, and affixes are discussed. One of the early sources is a work called *Sê-p'u* (瑟譜 , "Sê [zither] – notation") by Hsiung P'eng-lai (熊朋来), an author of the Yüan dynasty (1260-1368). The work, which consists of six parts and was reprinted by the Commercial Press, Shanghai, in 1936 (edited by Wang Yün-wu 王雲五), offers the following comparison (p. 440) between *lü* and *kung-ch'ê* symbols. The right hand column states *Ya lü t'ung su p'u li* (lit. "Refined *lü* comparison with common notation usage"). The reader will have no difficulties recognizing in the other three columns the *lü* characters (abbreviated) in large size; below them, in smaller size, are the complete names; and to the left of the *lü* names are the corresponding *kung-ch'ê* symbols. Wang Yün-wu transcribes the *huang* with *ho*, (黄=合), a method which we adopt in subsequent pages.

8. As already mentioned, the range of three octaves can also be observed in Indian music and Japanese *shōmyō*.

(Refers to Note 7)

雅律通俗譜例

黃 黃鍾 合　大 大呂 四下　太 太簇 四上　夾 夾鍾 一下　姑 姑洗 一上　仲 仲呂 上　蕤 蕤賓 勾

林 林鍾 尺　夷 夷則 工下　南 南呂 工上　無 無射 凡下　應 應鍾 凡上　黃 黃鍾清 六　大 大呂清 五下

太 太簇清 五上　夾 夾鍾清 五緊

9. E.g., ya-yüeh (雅樂), "classical category"; sung-yüeh (頌樂), "hymn category"; su-yüeh (俗樂), "vulgar category"; yen-yüeh (燕樂), "banquet category"; ch'ing-yüeh (清樂), "pure [Chinese] category"; and others.

10. A popular fiddle with two strings tuned to a fifth. The corpus can be made of coconut, bamboo, etc. The hair of the bow passes between the two strings.

11. A two-stringed fiddle, built and tuned like the êrh-hsien, with a cylindrical corpus covered on one side with snakeskin.

12. For further information see Koh-Nie-Kuh, "A Musicological Study of the Important Tonal Systems of the T'ang Dynasty."

13. We present only five of a larger number of scales.

14. The literary names of the transposing scales are:

chêng-t'iao (正調), "principal scale," for yi-fan-t'iao;

chi-liang-t'iao (寂凉調?), "plaintive scale," for shih-kung-t'iao;

hsien-so-t'iao (絃索調?) "string instrument scale," for ho-ch'ê-t'iao;

p'ing-t'iao (平調) "even scale," for fan-shang-t'iao;

pei-kung-t'iao (倍宮調), "reversed kung scale," for kung-yi-t'iao;

mei-hua-t'iao (梅花調), "plum blossom scale," for ch'ê-wu-t'iao;

tzŭ-mu-t'iao (子母調), "son and mother scale."

15. For further information see Ch'iu Hao-ch'ou, Kuo-yüeh-hsin-shêng (國樂新聲).

16. See also above, Part II, n. 12.

17. Generally êrh-huang is written 二簧 ; the character 簧 de-

notes the "reed" tongues (made of metal) of the shêng (笙), the Chinese mouth organ. (The top of the character ⺮, indicates "bamboo"). However, there are some Chinese scholars who object to the use of 簧 and insist that the character 黃 (huang, "yellow") be used. Their argument is that êrh-huang supposedly has originated in certain districts of China which are called "yellow slope," and "yellow mound," and that the operatic style is named after these places and has to be written 二黃. See Liu Ch'eng-fu (劉誠甫) in Yin-yüeh-tz'ŭ-tien (音樂辭典, "Music Dictionary") (Shanghai: Commercial Press, 1936). See also Wang Kuang ch'i (王光祈), Chung-kuo-yin-yüeh-shih (中國音樂史, "History of Chinese Music") (Taiwan, 1956).

18. See below, n. 27 (p. 443).

19. See p. 79 (shêng).

20. Hsiao (簫), a vertical flute with five holes on the top and one at the bottom, originated during the Han period (202 B.C.-220 A.D.). It was made of bamboo, occasionally also of jade, marble, or copper, and was admitted into the Confucian temple music during the Yüan period (1260-1368). J.A. van Aalst, (Chinese Music [Shanghai, 1884; repr. Peking, 1933], p. 70), states that "at Confucian ceremonies there are six hsiao, placed immediately outside the hall, on the 'Moon Terrace.' The music which they perform is exactly the same as that of the other instruments, but it is noted in a different manner."

21. Ti (笛) is the Chinese transverse flute with six fingerholes and another hole covered with a fine reedy membrane. The tube is wrapped in waxed silk and ornamented with tassels. Contrary to the hsiao, the ti is not a "transposing" instrument.

22. The 合 of ti notation actually sounds or approximates e; in our simplified version the note c is used.

23. According to van Aalst in Chinese Music, 尺 of the hsiao actually sounds d, and 六 of the ti sounds a' (902 vibrations per second).

24. "Moon-ch'in," a guitar with a circular, flat corpus and a short neck with five to ten frets. The instrument has four silken strings tuned in pairs; strings 1 and 2 are tuned a fifth higher than strings 3 and 4. Modern

tunings differ from the tuning in pairs; one tuning in frequent use is: e a d' g'. The strings are plucked with the fingers or a plectrum.

25. "Three-strings," a guitar with a small, flat, cylindrical corpus and a long neck with three lateral pegs. The top and bottom of the body are covered with snakeskin. Most of the *san-hsien* have no frets, but there are a few exceptions. The three strings are of silk (occasionally of metal) and are tuned to 1 4 8, or 1 5 8, or 1 2 6.

26. See Volume II.

27. Lit. "Western drum (skin)" — one of the important Chinese operatic styles. *Hsi-p'i* dramas deal with events of civilian middle-class life and are of a quieter nature than those of the related *êrh-huang* style. In the latter, rhythms begin with down beats, while *hsi-p'i* rhythms begin with up beats. Both *êrh-huang* and *hsi-p'i* evolved from the *pang-tzŭ* (梆子) style which came into existance during the reign of Emperor Kang Hsi (1662-1722). *Pang-tzŭ* indicates "drum sticks" (wood-block) and illustrates the prevalence of percussion instruments. The roots of *pang-tzŭ* reach back into the Yüan period when it became customary to set great heroic plots to music in a crude and noisy manner. This type of theater with its grandiose pantomimic battle scenes was performed only outdoors because of the overwhelming noise. The *êrh-huang* style appeared during the reign of Emperor Yung Cheng (1732-1735) as a welcome relief after the noisy *pang-tzŭ*. *Êrh-huang* and *hsi-p'i* employ string instruments, especially the *hu-ch'in* (See Part II, n. 11 [p. 441]). In *hsi-p'i* the two strings of the *hu-ch'in* are tuned a whole tone higher than in *êrh-huang*. For further information see Xia Ye, "Zur Entwicklung der chinesischen Opernstile," in *Beiträge zur Musikwissenschaft*, Vol. III (Berlin, 1961).

28. See pp. 31 ff.

29. Van Aalst, p. 27. For translation of the text, pp. 34-35.

30. See p. 119.

31. Maurice Courant, "Chine et Corée," in *Encyclopédie de la musique*, ed. A. Lavignac (Paris, 1913), I, 133.

32. The transliteration of the text can be seen in the transcription of the hymn, Figure 15, p. 82; a general translation may be found in Courant, "Chine et Corée," I, 135 n.

33. The real *ying-ku* is larger, but its name is frequently applied to the smaller *tsu-ku*, a drum which is placed upon a wooden stand on the west side of the "Moon Terrace" of the Confucian temple, and beaten in response to the larger drum. In our transcription *ku* represents the large and *ying* the small drum.

34. Van Aalst, p. 26, describes the March as follows: "the way from the first gate to the centre of the temple is left open for the passage of the emperor or his deputy, with his suite of princes, dignitaries, and attendants. At the second gate the emperor leaves his sedan and walks to the temple at a slow, stately pace; a band of fourteen musicians and eleven ensign and umbrella bearers precedes him, while . . . the Guiding March is played."

35. The Chinese mouth organ (the Japanese *shô*) symbolizes the *Fêng-huang*, the wonderful bird Phoenix. Supposedly invented in the third millenium B.C., it came into use about 1100 B.C. Its body, the wind chest, was made originally of gourd, but later wood was used. It has seventeen thin cane pipes, mounted into the top of the wind chest, which are arranged in such manner as to depict the tail of the bird Phoenix. Each sound-producing pipe (pipes 1, 9, 16 and 17 are silent) has at its lower end a small brass tongue and a ventage outside which must be stopped by the player's finger in order to produce a sound. The pipes are tuned diatonically. See also Alex. J. Ellis, "Ueber die Tonleiter verschiedener Voelker," in *Sammelbaende fuer vergleichende Musikwissenscha* I (Munich, 1922), 58.

36. See Part II, n. 21 (p. 442).

37. See Part II, n. 20 (p. 442).

38. A set of ten little brass gongs suspended in a wooden frame. All the gongs have the same diameter but vary in thickness; they are tuned diatonica ly. For tuning see A. Ellis, op. cit., pp. 58-59.

39. See p. 31.

40. *Chinesische Musik* (Kassel, 1956), p. 184.

41. *Chinese Music*, p. 26.

42. See p. 79.

43. See p. 104.

44. Van Aalst, p. 19.

45. See Wang Kuang-ch'i, "Ueber die chinesischen Notenhandschriften" in Sinica, III (1928), 110-23.

46. E.g., in hsi-p'i style; see Part II, n. 27 (p. 443).

47. See Laurence Picken, "The Music of China," in The New Oxford History of Music (London, 1957) I, 115-17. See also Reinhard, op. cit., p. 211, examples 22 and 23 (a rhythm which symbolizes "night").

48. See Part II, n. 17 (p. 441).

49. See Part II, n. 27 (p. 443).

50. Lao yüan, one of the few preserved works, has been reprinted in Ch'ing-jên-tsa-chü (清人雜劇, "Dramatic plays of the Ch'ing people"), a work consisting of twelve volumes, published by Chêng Chên-to (鄭振鐸) in 1934. A copy of this work is preserved in the library of Indiana University.

51. The general translation of the text is:

Ah, my hair has turned half gray,
Look, my frosted temples.
Though I would still hold that I am strong and vigorous,
Yet age is creeping in and my feeling tells me so.
Roaming through the big cities amidst laughter and excitement,
I try to lessen my growing melancholy.
But as I look at my battle horse, pitiful animal;
Swaying his tail which is bare of all tender and soft hair,
He toddles along like a brindled ox.
Yes, he is only fit to plough now until dusk comes.

52. See R.H. Mathews, Chinese-English Dictionary (Cambridge, Mass., 1956), p. 1178.

53. Ibid., p. 1070, character 7187.

54. Ibid., p. xiv.

55. Conversational Chinese (Chicago, 1947), p. 2.

56. See John Hazedel Levis, Foundations of Chinese Musical Art (Peiping, 1936), pp. 11 ff.

57. See Part I, n. 3 (p. 422).

58. "In his autobiography he [Shên Yüeh] writes, 'The poets of old,

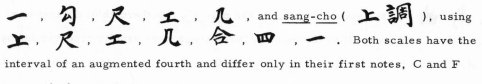

一, 勾, 尺, 工, 几, and sang-cho (上調), using 上, 尺, 工, 几, 合, 四, 一. Both scales have the interval of an augmented fourth and differ only in their first notes, C and F respectively.

75. See p. 124.

76. Ongaku Jiten, (Tokyo, 1950), V, 3068 ff.

77. Ibid.

78. The only copy of this work is preserved by the National Court Music Association (Ku-wang kung ah-ak-pu, 旧王宮雅樂部); in addition to this "later" collection, there existed an earlier one, called Tae-ak chŭn-po (大樂前譜, "Great Music Former Notation"), edited in 1653 and/or 1759. The melodies contained in the Tae-ak chŭn-po were originally collected by order of King Sae-cho; the first editor was Pak Yŭn (朴堧), 1378-1453. The work contained:

雅樂樂歌	步虛子管
定大業	桓桓曲
醉豐亨	水龍吟
致和平	憶吹簫
鳳凰吟	夏雲峰
與民樂慢	小抛毬樂
步虛子	五雲開端朝
洛陽春	會入仙
前引子	千年萬歲
後引子	折花
與民樂絃	衆仙會
與民樂管	

The Tae-ak chŭn-po, which had been preserved by the Royal Music Department (chang ak-won, 掌樂院), at Seoul, is lost. The texts of five pieces are preserved in Koryo-sa ak-chi (高麗史 樂志 , "Music Chapter of the History of the Koryo Dynasty"). See also Naito Konan (内藤湖南), Sogaku to Cho-sen gaku (宋樂と朝鮮樂 , "Sung Music and Korean Music"), in Shina gaku (支那學), "Study of Chinese Music"), in Japanese.

79. See p. 127.

80. See section on hap-cha-po, beginning on p. 301; Chung-tae-yŭp can be found in the Yang-kŭm shin-po, a famous zither book of 1610 (See p. 305).

81. See section of hap-cha-po, beginning on p. 301.

82. Pyong-cho and u-cho are sol-modes; pyong-cho kae-myon-cho and u-cho kae-myon-cho are la-modes.

83. The two pieces are: Chong-myo chae-ak (宗廟祭樂 , "Imperial Temple Music") and Pung-an chi-ak (豐安之樂 , "Music of Abundant Ease").

84. Serious music imported from China.

85. Lit., "Well-between Notation" — the name refers to the openings of water wells which are surrounded by four tree trunks placed horizontally in the form of a 井 . Metrical and rhythmic features in chŭng-kan-po are indicated by means of a chart which consists of horizontal and vertical lines.

86. See Part I, n. 54 (p. 435).

87. In addition to the Sae-chong and Sae-cho shillok, chŭng-kan-po is referred to and used in numerous works: for instance in the collection Yŭng-sŭng-so-mu-po (靈星小舞譜 , "Small Dance Notation of Yŭng Sŭng") of the sixteenth century; in the eighteenth-century collection of Ku-kung-tae-sŭng-po (九宮大成譜 , lit., "Nine Palaces Great Achievement Notation"); in Nap-sŭ-yŭng-kok-po (納書楹曲譜 , "Song notation of Nap-sŭ-yŭng"); in Pan-mok-pu-ho (板眼符號 , "Heavy and Light Beats Notation"); in the Japanese works Kin-kyoku shi-hu (琴曲指譜 , "Zither Music Didactic Notation"), of 1764 (using thirty-two chŭng-kan in each haeng); and in Kin-kyoku tai-i-sho (琴曲大意抄 , "Zither Music Summarizing Selection") of 1779 (using the rhythmic signs ◎ and ○).

88. See p. 171.

89. Such exceptions can be found in the Sae-cho shillok and in the An-sang kŭm-po (安瑺琴譜), a zither book of 1572, preserved as a national treasure in Seoul in the care of Mr. Sŭng Kyŭng Lin.

90. See section on hap-cha-po, beginning on p. 301.

91. Most modern Korean song melodies begin with the third chŭng-kan.

92. Yŭ-min-ak (與民樂, lit., "Grant People Music").

93. Nak-yang-chun (洛陽春, "Spring of the Royal City").

94. See also A. Eckardt, Koreanische Musik, (Tokyo, 1930), pp. 55-58.

95. See p. 144.

96. Opinions are divided — Po-hŭ-cha may have been of Korean origin.

97. By Chiang K'uei (the "White stone priest"); see section on Sung notation, beginning on p. 174. See also below, p. 456 (n. 174).

98. See Part III, n. 57 (p.475).

99. See Part I, n. 55 (p.435).

100. See Lee, pp. 16, 94.

101. A later version of Po-hŭ-cha was published by the National Court Music Association of Seoul; date of publication is unknown.

102. See Eckardt, p. 59.

103. Po-hŭ-cha when performed as an instrumental piece — with or without dancing — is called Chang-chun pul lo chi-kok (長春不老之曲, "Never Ageing Song").

104. Lee, pp. 101-4.

105. There are different settings of the text of Po-hŭ-cha: in the An-sang-kŭm-po textual characters appear at comparatively regular intervals of about ten chŭng-kan. The first word is extended over eleven chŭng-kan, the second over ten chŭng-kan, and so forth. In the Tae-ak hu-po a character appears with nearly every haeng of sixteen chŭng-kan; while in the Sok-ak won-po each word is held for about twenty chŭng-kan.

106. Lee, p. 105.

107. The character 與, "to grant," could, perhaps, have been 興, "to prosper"; however, Lee uses exclusively 與, hence we are following his manner of writing.

108. The chang-ko (杖鼓) is a drum used mainly for the accompaniment of vocal music. It has the shape of an hour glass and a corpus made of metal, the left side of which is covered with skin. The left hand beats this skin, producing a low, gentle sound ("drum-side"), while the right hand, using the "whip," a small stick, beats against the other end of the corpus. The skin can be tuned to some extent by manipulating the leather straps which encircle the drum in a criss-cross pattern. The chang-ko is probably of Chinese origin. We find its characteristic hour-glass shape depicted in a seventh-century (A. D.) tomb (number 17 of Chipan-Koguryo-kobun, 輯安高句麗古墳, in Manchuria) and in an engraved bell of the Silla period (57 or 37 B. C. -A. D. 935). The bell is now preserved in the shrine Usa-hachiman-goo (宇佐八幡宮) in the Oita district of Japan.

The drum-side beats are basic beats which occur at the beginning of any kang. The whip-side beats, however, can be performed on any chŭng-kan. In addition to the old Korean drum words (ko, pyŭn, yo, sang) "modern" symbols are used, always in conjunction with chŭng-kan-po. These symbols are: ⦶ , or ◐ — the latter symbol appears also in notations for kalko (羯鼓, the Chinese chieh-ku, or the Japanese kakko), a chang-ko with two drum skins. This symbol, called hap-chang-tan (합장단 , "both hands together"), is performed by both drum hand and whip hand simultaneously. The hap-chang-tan always indicates the beginning of a rhythm with the basic sequence of 3, 2, 3, 3, 2, 3 chŭng-kan in one haeng. Modifications, beyond the scope of this discussion, occur if the piece does not begin with the first chŭng-kan. The ancient Korean symbol for hap-chang-tan is 雙 (ssang). Other symbols are: ○ , puk-pyŭn (북편 , "drum-side"), with the drum hand beating the drum (this is also notated with the ancient character 鼓 , ko); | , chae-pyŭn (채편 , "whip-side"), commonly called ki-tŭk, with the whip hand beating the drum (ancient symbol: 鞭 , pyŭn). Occasionally we find the symbol ˋ| , particularly in kalko parts, indicating that the whip hand beats twice in succession.

109. See p. 120.

110. See p. 130

111. In 1443 by order of King Sae-chong, the Korean phonetic alphabet (*hangŭl*) was devised; see below, n. 122.

112. The six flying dragons imply six royal ancestors of King Sae-chong.

113. See Part II, n. 84 (p. 449).

114. See p. 48.

115. Lee, p. 123

116. *Man* and *yŭng* types appear in only three pieces: *Yŭ-min-ak*; a song called *Yŭng-san-hoe-sang* (靈山會相); and supposedly *Po-hŭ-cha* (Lee).

117. See Eckardt, p. 42.

118. See p. 145.

119. Lee, facing p. 128.

120. Ibid., p. 126.

121. Lee, after p. 124, examples 7/1-5. If the reader wishes to compare the three *Yŭ-min-ak* types shown above with others he may consult the notations of the *An-sang-kŭm-po* and *Shin-sang-kŭm-po* in the section on *hap-cha-p* on pp. 347, 349.

122. *Hangŭl*, originally called *Hun-min chŭng-ŭm* (訓民正音), the indigenous Korean alphabet invented by order of King Sae-chong in the fifteenth century, enables the less educated Korean to put in writing any form of colloquial speech. In contrast to Chinese characters, the letters of *hangŭl* can be learned without much effort, and their shapes supposedly represent the human organs of speech. The alphabet is indeed the world's most complete system of phonetic letters. Several scholars endeavored to derive the letters of *hangŭl* from foreign systems, but with no success. *Hangŭl* is an original creation of King Sae-chong and his learned helpers. The letters of *hangŭl* never displaced the Chinese characters, which remained the scholarly medium of writing. Even today learned treatises in Korea (and Japan) are still written in Chinese characters, while common matters are written in *hangŭl*.

123. See pp. 24, 54; see also Part I, n. 24 (p. 426).

124. See p. 301.

125. See pp. 305 f.

126. Ibid.

127. See Lee, p. 15.

128. Ibid., p. 8; occasionally yuk-po has been called Cho-sŭng-po (趙晟譜) after the zither book of Cho-sŭng.

129. See p. 301.

130. A long Korean zither with twelve strings and twelve movable bridges.

131. Generally it is the T'ang p'il-lyul (唐觱篥), a heterophonic double-reed instrument with seven holes; it is related to the Japanese hichiriki.

132. The largest Korean flute; it has six finger holes, one covered with a membrane.

133. For string names, tunings, frets, etc., of the hyŭn-kŭm see pp. 307 ff.

134. In u-cho kae-myon-cho (mode) see p. 309; for Man-tae-yŭp, Chung-tae-yŭp, Sak-tae-yŭp see Part II, n. 140 (p. 454).

135. Han-kuk ŭm-ak yon-gu.

136. 二度弱

137. A few kaya-kŭm have only ten strings.

138. Eckardt, Koreanische Musik, p. 42. We implement Eckardt's information with the following kaya-kŭm tunings as stated in the Ak-hak-koe-pŭm, VII, 25 ff. Written in the old Five-Tone Notation and in yul-cha-po, read horizontally from left to right:

宮	商	徵	羽	宮	商	角	徵	羽	宮	商	角
南	應	姑	蕤	南	應	大	姑	蕤	南	應	大
商	角	羽	宮	商	角	徵	羽	宮	商	角	徵
南	應	姑	林	南	應	太	姑	林	南	應	太
羽	商	角	徵	羽	宮	商	角	徵	羽	宮	商
南	太	姑	蕤	南	應	太	姑	蕤	南	應	太
羽	商	角	徵	羽	宮	商	角	徵	羽	宮	商
南	太	姑	林	南	潢	太	姑	林	南	潢	太
商	徵	羽	宮	商	角	徵	羽	宮	商	角	徵
應	姑	蕤	南	應	大	姑	蕤	南	應	汰	姑

139. The word *yang* (洋) in *yang-kŭm*, which means "foreign," must not be confused with the name *Yang* (梁) of the famous seventeenth-century zither book, the *Yang-kŭm shin-po*.

140. *Man-tae-yŭp* (慢大葉), lit., "Slow big leaf," *Chung-tae yŭp* (中大葉), lit., "Middle big leaf," and *Sak-tae-yŭp* (數大葉), lit., "Fast big leaf," originally were song types (*kagok*, 歌曲, "vocal music") which, similar to the *canzon francese* of sixteenth- and seventeenth-century European music, were performed by instrumental ensembles or solo instruments. Of the three types mentioned only *Sak-tae-yŭp* (also called *chad-ŭn-han-ip*, 잣은 한닢, lit., "Frequent big leaf," or *Kŭ-sang-ak*, 擧床樂, lit., "Awakening music,") is used at the present time. Real *kagok* pieces use short lyrical poems usually consisting of five verses as text. Each piece contains a prelude played by an ensemble (*hyŭn-kŭm*, *kaya-kŭm*, *hae-kŭm*, *chŭt-tae*, etc.), an interlude (*chung-yŭŭm*, 中餘音) between the third and fourth verses, and a postlude (*tae-yŭŭm*, 大餘音) after the fifth verse. The melodies are first performed in the mode of *u-cho*, then followed by *u-cho kae-myon-cho*. (These modes are explained on p. 309).

141. See pp. 327 ff.

142. See p. 301.

143. Although the symbols of the Five Tone Notation and *yuk-po* do not indicate the durations of the notes, we show them — derived from the *hap-cha-po* symbols (see p. 301) — in staff notation. The reader will be able to examine the whole piece as shown in Figure 74 on pp. 345 f.

144. They are the open strings IV, V, and VI; see p. 308.

145. See Lee, facing p. 82.

146. See p. 147.

147. Ibid.

148. Op. cit., pp. 82 ff.

149. According to Chu Hsi.

150. See Ch. S. Keh, *Die Koreanische Musik* (Strassburg, 1935), Appendix, example 3.

151. See p. 131; see also Lee, p. 82.

152. Lee, p. 82.

153. Ibid.

154. 內譜가 音階名을 表示한 것이라고(도) 볼수없다 (Lee, p. 9).

155. This line represents an excerpt of a version of Sak-tae-yŭp as notated by Cho-sŭng.

156. For instance:

Japan:	Korea:
Tsuru (ツル)	Ttul (뜰)
Ten (テン)	Tŭng (덩)
Tsun (ツン)	Tung (둥)
Ton (トン)	Tong (동)

157. Songs with texts originating in the middle Javanese language period, performed at temple festivals. See E. Schlager, "Bali," MGG, I, 1110.

158. Gendér is a metallophone, consisting of ten (or twelve) metal slabs which are placed horizontally upon a net of cords. Below each slab is a bamboo resonator; both are tuned to the same pitch.

159. See Colin McPhee, "The Balinese Wayang Koelit and Its Music," Djawa, XVI, (1936).

160. MGG, I, 1111.

161. We are using the Chinese term lü instead of the Korean yul.

162. 趙晟, a Korean court musician under King Myŭng-chong (明宗, 1546-1567).

163. We quote the example with slight modifications from Lee, p. 3.

164. The notation of the Heike biwa will be discussed in Volume II.

165. See Lee, p. 15. See also below, pp. 172 ff.

166. Ibid.

167. "Chine et Corée," op. cit., pp. 156-57.

168. For further information see C.P. Fitzgerald, *China* (London, 1954), pp. 427-29.

169. A famous figure of twelfth-century China. He was a commentator on the Confucian canon, a historian of the utmost importance, a prolific writer, and a musician who composed songs using as texts the odes of the *Shih Ching*.

170. "Chine et Corée," p. 157.

171. "Ch'in Sounds (music) Commentary" is a part of the collected works of Chu Hsi (also called Chu Wên Kung, 朱文公); see also Hsia Ch'êng-ch'ou, "A Study of the Musical Notations of Chiang K'uei's Songs," *Yenching Journal of Chinese Studies* (Peiping) (December 1932), pp. 2559-89.

172. Column 4, see Courant, loc. cit., column 7, according to Hsia Ch'êng-ch'ou. Liu-ch'êng-fu (劉誠甫) in his *Yin-yüeh-tz'ŭ-tien* (音樂辭典), a music dictionary published by the Commercial Press (Shanghai, 1936), states that the *Tz'ŭ-yüan* was reprinted by the Peking University Press (n.d.), edited by Wu Mei (吳梅).

173. Published by Yeh (葉) in Chêng-tu, Szechuan. See also Hsia Ch'êng-ch'ou.

174. Chiang K'uei is often referred to as the "White Stone Hermit." A reprint of the White Stone Songs was made by the Chung-hua-shu-chü (中華書局), Shanghai, 1900.

175. 越 here refers to the old state of Yüeh, which today is the province of Chekiang. 九歌 (*chiu-ko*, "Nine Songs") was a form of ritual music supposedly used in the time of Emperor Yü of the ancient Hsia dynasty (third millenium B.C.).

176. The second character can also be 製, *chih*, "to make," "to construct." This latter version is preferred in Korea and Japan.

177. Other songs composed during the Sung period survived as fragments in *Chin-lien-yüeh-chang-tzŭ-yeh* (金奩樂章子野), and in *P'ien-yü* (片玉).

178. According to the Heibon-sha *Oriental History Dictionary* (Tokyo, 1941), IV, 434, the *Shih-lin-kuang-chi* was republished several times: (1) in

1325, editor unknown, in four volumes (50 chapters), with one copy preserved in the Cabinet Library in Tokyo; (2) in 1496, editor unknown, in six volumes (6 chapters); (3) a later edition, date of publication and editor unknown, in six volumes (29 chapters); the second part of Appendix II contains musical notations. The work is preserved in the Toyo Library (東洋文庫 , _Toyo bunko_), Tokyo.

179. _Foundations of Chinese Musical Art_, p. 91; the symbols are quoted from Hsia Ch'êng-ch'ou.

180. See Bibliography.

181. An author of the Ch'ing dynasty. According to Ts'ao Ch'ou-shêng (曹惆生), _Chung-kuo-yin-yüeh, wu-tao Hsi-ch'ü jên-ming tz'ŭ-tien_ (中國音樂舞蹈戲曲人名詞典), Dictionary of Chinese Music, Dances, etc., (Peking: Commercial Press, 1959), p. 157.

182. Polite form of referring to Chu Hsi, used in works of the Ming period. For instance in _Ch'in-lü-shuo_ (琴律說).

183. According to T'ang Lan ㄣ can be an abbreviation of 亣 . In the _Tz'ŭ-yuan_ 亣 can be used interchangeably with 上 . "This, too, is doubtful" (Hsia Ch'êng-ch'ou).

184. Hsü Hao (徐灝), a scholar of the Ch'ing period. He wrote only one work, called _Shêng-lü-k'ao_ (聲律考 , "Study of Vocal Sounds"); see Ts'ao Ch'ou-shêng, _Chung-kuo-yin-yüeh, wu-tao_ . . ., (Peking, 1959), p. 137.

185. In the songs _Yü-mei-ling_ (玉梅令), lit., "Jade-plum Verse," and _Chüeh-chao_ (角招), lit., "Horn Call."

186. 唐蘭 , T'ang Lan, a music theorist born in 1796, is the author of _P'ang-p'u-k'ao_ (旁譜考), a work which deals with the musical notations of Chiang K'uei.

187. E.g., in _Sung-shih-yüeh-chih_ (宋史樂志).

188. In _p'i-pa_ playing the raising of some notes can be effected by pulling the string; in certain instances by pulling the string across the adjoining string.

189. See p. 39.

190. See Part II. n. 188. Chê is usually not a rhythmic sign but indicates a microtonal alteration. See p. 39.

191. The "Kuang Book" is the Shih-lin-kuang-chi. See Part II, n. 178 (p. 456).

192. Therefore 尖一 is the same as 下一, and 下五 (in the "Kuang Book") is notated with 尖五.

193. Shih-lin-kuang-chi.

194. The character 住 (chu) actually denotes a pause; hence 大住 (ta-chu) means a long (big) pause and 小住 (hsiao chu) a short (small) pause.

T'ang Lan, in an epilogue to Hsia Ch'êng-ch'ou's article, remarks that the following additions may clarify Hsia's text:

Lü	Kung-ch'ê	Pê-shih-tao-jên-ko-ch'u	Shih-lin-kuang-chi	Tz'ŭ-yüan
清黃	六	久 夂	(夂) 六	幺 六
清大	下五		(丂) 五	丂 下五
清太	五	ゆ	(丂) 高五	(ゆ) 五
清夾	一五	丂	(丂) 尖五	(丂) 高五

T'ang Lan summarizes thus: 六 should be 夂, as notated by Chiang K'uei; 下五 should be (ゆ); both the Tz'ŭ-yüan and the Shih-lin-kuang-chi are wrong; 五 should be ゆ, as used by Chiang K'uei; and 一五 should be 丂. Here, too, both Tz'ŭ-yüan and Shih-lin-kuang-chi are incorrect.

195. Pê-shih-tao-jên-ko-ch'ü, IV, 2.

196. See Koh-Nie-Kuh, "A Musical Study of the Important Tonal Systems of the T'ang Dynasty."

197. Śrutis (from Sanskr., śru, "to hear") microtones or microtonal intervals. North and South Indian Music theorists of the past employed these twenty-two (on a few occasions, twenty-four) intervals within the octave in the determination of their various (basic) seven-scale degrees.

198. There are a few exceptions which will be discussed at the end of this part.

199. South Indian term for *rāga*.

200. Lit. "group maker"; parent-scales.

201. See pp. 203 f.

202. See, e.g., Pandit V. N. Bhatkhande, "A Short Historical Survey of the Music of Upper India," reprint of a speech delivered by Bhatkhande at the First All-India Music Conference, Baroda in 1916; (Bombay, 1934), pp. 16 f.

203. See Walter Kaufmann, "The Classification of Indian Ragas," in *Asia and the Humanities*, Indiana University: Comparative Literature Committee, 1959, pp. 131-45.

204. Six volumes in Hindi and Marathi (Bombay, 1934-1937).

205. The terms for octave are *saptaka* ("set of seven"), occasionally also *sthāyī* ("section"), or *sthāna* ("register," or "voice").

206. As previously mentioned, the same organization can be found in the notational system of Japanese *shōmyō*; to be discussed in Volume II.

207. For instance, P. Sambamoorthy, *South Indian Music* (Madras, 1935), I, 46.

208. Ancient Indian music theory distinguished three important notes in the scale of the *rāga*: the *graha*, the starting note; the *aṃśa*, the predominant; and the *nyāsa*, the "finalis," the terminal note. Neither the *graha* nor *nyāsa* are in practical use at the present time. The *aṃśa*, better known today as *vādī*, however, still plays an important role. The *vādī* (and the lesser important *saṃvādī*, "consonance," usually a fourth or a fifth apart from each other) is the "king" of the *rāga*. Musical phrases usually end on it (or on the *SA*). The position of the *vādī* is one of the indications of the time when the *rāga* is to be performed: if the *vādī* stands in the lower tetrachord of the scale, the *rāga* is mostly performed in the evening or at night; conversely, if the vādī stands in the upper tetrachord it is usually performed in the morning or during the early part of the day. Indian books on music always state first the tone material of the *rāga* together with the *vādī* and *saṃvādī*.

209. See W. Kaufmann, "The Forms of the Dhrupad and Khyal in Indian Art Music," *The Canadian Music Journal*, III, No. 2 (1959), p. 26.

210. Ibid.

211. South Indian Music, I, 33.

212. See Kaufmann, "The Forms of the Dhrupad and Khyal," p. 28.

213. Pandit V. N. Bhatkhande, Hindusthani Sangit Paddhati (Bombay, 1941), II, 223.

214. For further information see Kaufmann, "The Forms of the Dhrupad and Khyal," p. 30.

215. For further information see Kaufmann, "The Classification of Indian Rāgas."

216. As a matter of fact, Veṅkaṭamakhin lists only 55 rāgams and expresses the opinion that they could be classified under the headings of 19 melakartas, which he describes in detail.

217. Madras, 1938.

218. (Madras, 1953), III, 40.

219. സ is not a Tamiḷ but a Malayalam letter derived from the Grantha sign ஸ (Sa).

220. See Kaufmann, "The Forms of the Dhrupad and Khyal."

221. Chatuśruti, "four śrutis"

Shatśruti, "six śrutis"

Sādhārana, "twilight"

Antara, "interval"

Prati-, "counter-"

Kaishiki, "hair's breath"

Kākali, "low"

222. See P. R. Bhandarkar, "The Kuḍimiyāmalai Inscription of Music," Epigraphia Indica, XII (1913-14), 226-37.

223. Occasionally the name khol is used, particularly if the corpus is made of clay.

224. The mixture may contain a number of substances such as iron or manganese dust, boiled rice, tamarind juice (if available), modern factory-made ink, and so forth.

225. Jhaptāl is another name for Jhampa Tāla.

226. See Kaufmann, "The Forms of the Dhrupad and Khyal."

227. Ibid.

228. We must add here the Pakhawaj (pakh, "wing", awaz, "sound"), a comparatively recent member of the mridanga family. It usually is smaller than the mridanga but has the same shape as the ancient drum.

229. Occasionally it is called dayan, "right."

230. The pronunciation of the drum words varies to some extent from one place to the other. We adopt the north Indian forms as used by Hindustani-speaking musicians.

a is pronounced as in the English word lark

e, as in tell

i, as in sing

u, as in root

Long vowels, indicating strokes of extended notes, are indicated by a horizontal line above the vowel, e.g., ā.

ṭ is produced by placing the tip of the tongue between the teeth and roof of the mouth (ट)

ṇ is a nasal sound as in the n in the French name Jean

ị, ẹ, ụ are pronounced with a slight tinge of ṇ

As is customary in Urdu, vowels are not always clearly indicated; GE, GI, KE, KI, GA, KA, may denote the same stroke, and so forth.

231. See p. 261.

232. qaida, "rule," "regulation," "custom."

233. dohra, from dohrana, "to fold," "to double."

234. palta, from palna, "to nourish."

Part Three

1. The origin of Chinese music is ascribed to heavenly and legendary emperors, figures who represent extensive periods of Chinese history. The first of these sovereigns was Fu Hsi (about 2852 B.C.). He was succeeded by Nü-kua and Shen-nung. Ssŭ-ma Ch'ien, the famous Chinese historian (136-85),

ignores these early rulers, and lists as first Huang Ti, the "Yellow Emperor" (about 2697 B.C.).

Dr. R.H. van Gulik in his The Lore of the Chinese Lute (Tokyo, 1940), p. 9, presents an interesting theory for the determination of the age of the ch'in (and the sê) from a paleographic point of view, which deserves careful study by persons who wish to pursue the matter of the history of the ch'in.

2. See Part I, n. 3 (p. 422).

3. James Legge, trans., Sacred Books of China (Oxford, 1885), Vol. XXVIII.

4. Shih Ching, Part I, Book I, ode 1, stanza 3; James Legge, trans. Chinese Classics (London, 1871), IV, Part I. This famous ode originated during the Western Chou period (1122-770).

5. Ibid., Book VII, ode 8, stanza 2.

6. Ibid.

7. Ibid., Book X, ode 2, stanza 3.

8. Ibid., Book XI, ode 1, stanza 2.

9. Ibid., Part II, Book I, ode 1, stanza 3.

10. Ibid., ode 4, stanza 7.

11. The copy in possession of this writer is called Chieh shih tiao yu-lan-p'u (碣石調幽蘭譜), the Chieh shih Melody Introduction to Elegant Orchids. Chieh Shih was a piece of music based on the text by Emperor Wu (Wei). The piece consisted of four sections: the first mentioned the emperor's travel eastward to Chieh Shih and the vastness of the ocean from which sun and moon rose and into which sun and moon set; the second mentioned how, after work in the fields was accomplished, the merchants became active; the third explained how the shape and climate of a region influence its inhabitants; the fourth was in praise of the brave man.

12. See Hayashi Kenzo in Tōyō ongaku kenkyu (東洋音樂研究, "Journal of Oriental Music Research") (Tokyo, 1954), II, chap. 4; and Kishibe Shigeo in Tōa ongaku shi kō (東亞音樂史考, "Thoughts on Oriental Music") (Tokyo). Kishibe believes that the work originated as early as the sixth century.

13. Lee Hye-ku, in *Han-kuk ŭm-ak yon-gu* (Seoul, 1957), mentions a fourteenth-century work called (in Japanese) *Kin-fu dai-jen* (琴譜大全, "Zither-book Complete Collection").

14. The work was reprinted in 1799 in Ku Hsiu's collection *Tu-hua-chai-ts'ung-shu* (讀畫齋叢書), and again, in another collection of texts, compiled by Sun Hsing-yen (孫星衍, 1753-1808) called *P'ing ts'in-kuan-ts'ung shu* (平津館叢書). Further reprints appeared in Japan in the nineteenth century. Detailed information about this and subsequent works can be found in van Gulik, op. cit., pp. 167 ff.

15. A recent reprint appeared in the *Tung-t'ing-shih-êrh-chung* (棟亭十二種) (Shanghai, 1921).

16. A reprint of this popular work appeared in Japan in 1803, edited by Hayashi Jussai (林述齋, 1768-1841).

17. The work was expanded in 1925.

18. Van Gulik, p. 170.

19. See p. 285, Figure 64, and Part III, n. 27 (p. 464).

20. For additional *ch'in-p'u* and for further information see van Gulik, op. cit.

21. Earth, metal, wood, fire, and water.

22. The Korean pronunciation of *hui* is *hwi*.

23. In the nineteenth century, *ch'in-p'u* authors endeavoured to simplify the reading of the *ch'in* tablature by adding to the *chien-tzŭ* the much less complex *kung-ch'ê* symbols. The two notations are placed side by side in parallel columns.

24. As already indicated before, we lean heavily upon van Gulik's *The Lore of the Chinese Lute*, pp. 120 ff., where a larger number of *chien-tzŭ* is shown.

25. See L. Laloy, *La Musique chinoise* (Paris, n.d.), p. 71; this concerns the second of the twenty-four articles called *Ch'in-k'uang* (琴況) by the *ch'in* master Hsü Hung (徐谼). The Chinese text was first published in the seventeenth century in the *Ta-huan-ko-ch'in-p'u* (大還閣琴譜). See also van Gulik, pp. 105 ff, for a translation of the *Ch'in-*

sheng-shih-liu-fa (琴聲十六法 , "Sixteen Rules for the Tones of the Ch'in") by Lêng Hsien (冷仙), fourteenth to fifteenth century.

26. See p. 274.

27. In order to enable the reader to examine a larger part of this ch'in-p'u we present a copy containing strophes 1-14 (pp. 465-73).

28. Georges Soulié, La Musique en Chine (Paris, 1911), p. 36.

29. A detailed explanation of the notational symbols is given by Soulié, pp. 37-41.

30. See Chu Tsai-yü, Yüeh-lü-ch'üan-shu (reprinted Shanghai, 1934), II, 87. See also Maurice Courant, "Essai historique sur la musique classique des Chinois," in Encyclopédie de la musique, ed. Lavignac (Paris, 1913), I, 13
the Chinese text of the hymn can be found in the same work on p. 221 (A, k) and the transliteration and translation of the text on pp. 130-31.

31. Courant transcribes all lü a major third higher than we do.

32. A specific sê tablature will be described below.

33. See p. 269; "lutes large and small" indicates the larger sê and the smaller ch'in.

34. "Nearing the Standard" (爾雅), a scholarly work which may have been written as early as the twelfth or as late as the fourth century B. C., is a dictionary which deals with the correct use of a variety of terms.

35. See van Gulik, op. cit., p. 7.

36. J. A. van Aalst, Chinese Music (Shanghai, 1884), p. 64.

37. The work was reprinted by the Commercial Press, Shanghai, in 1936

38. Arthur Waley, The Book of Songs (New York, 1960), p. 192, ode 18

39. For instance, the tae-cheng (大箏), the "big chêng," a zither with fifteen strings, derived from the Chinese chêng and related to the Japanese yamato koto, wagon, (大和琴); the sŭl (瑟), a zither with twenty-five strings, derived from the Chinese sê (the Koreans call it the "big komunko" the yang-kŭm (洋琴), a zither with fourteen wire strings, derived from the Chinese yang-ch'in; the kaya-kŭm, or kaya-ko, (伽倻琴), a zither with seven strings and without frets. It had the name hwi-kŭm (徽琴), the "hui-kŭm" in Korea.

(Refers to Note 27)

Ch'êng-i-t'ang ch'in-p'u

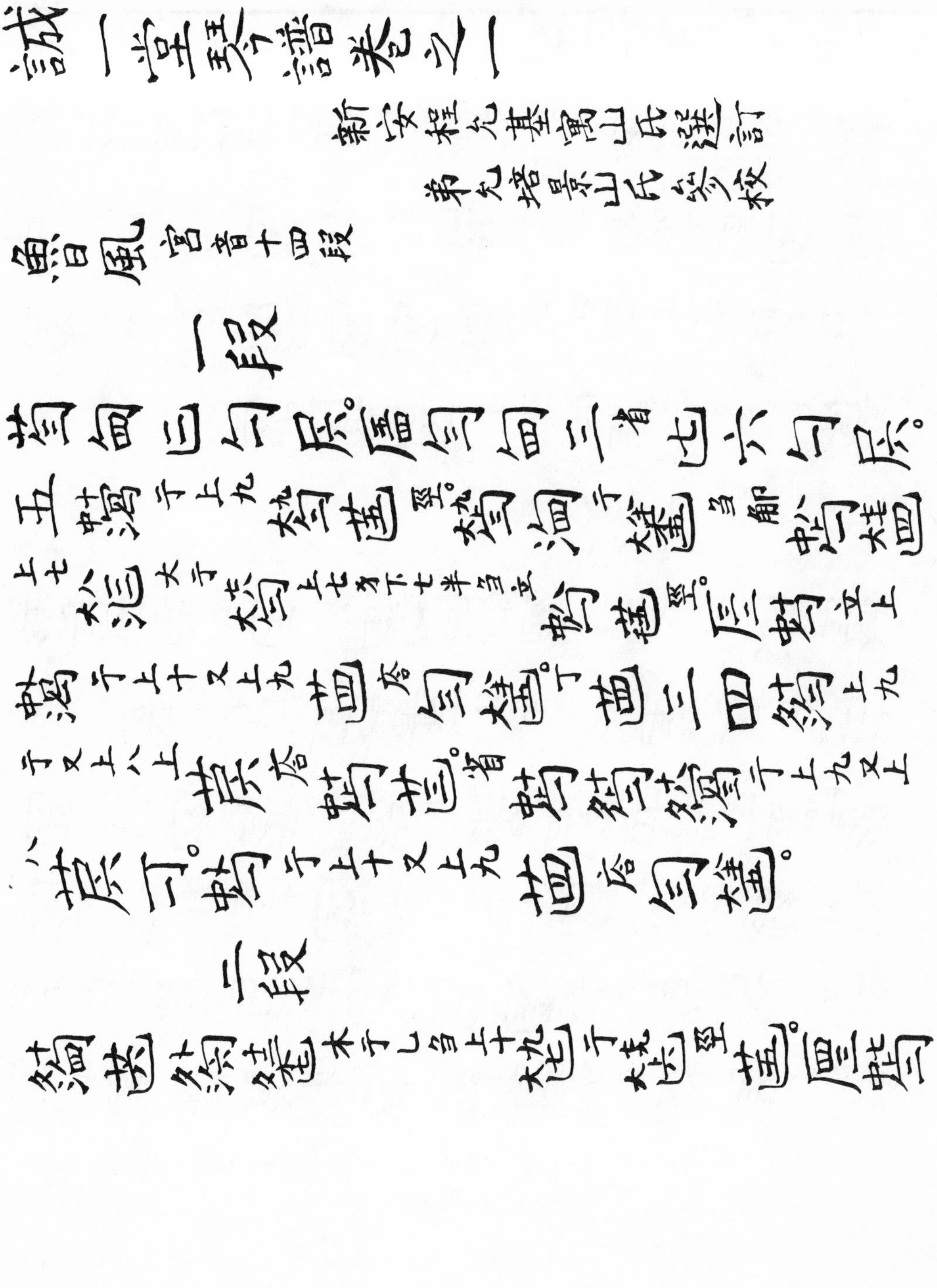

Ch'êng-i-t'ang chin-p'u (cont.)

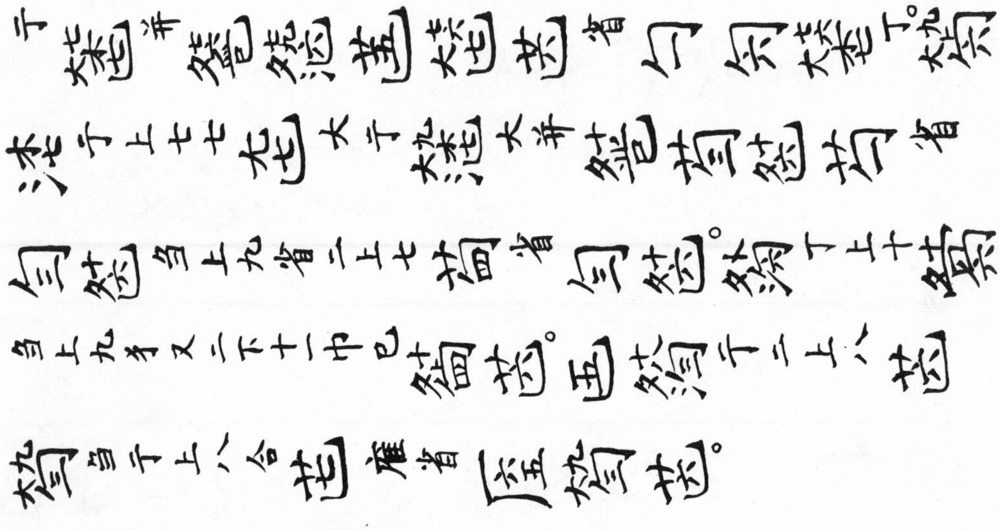

二段

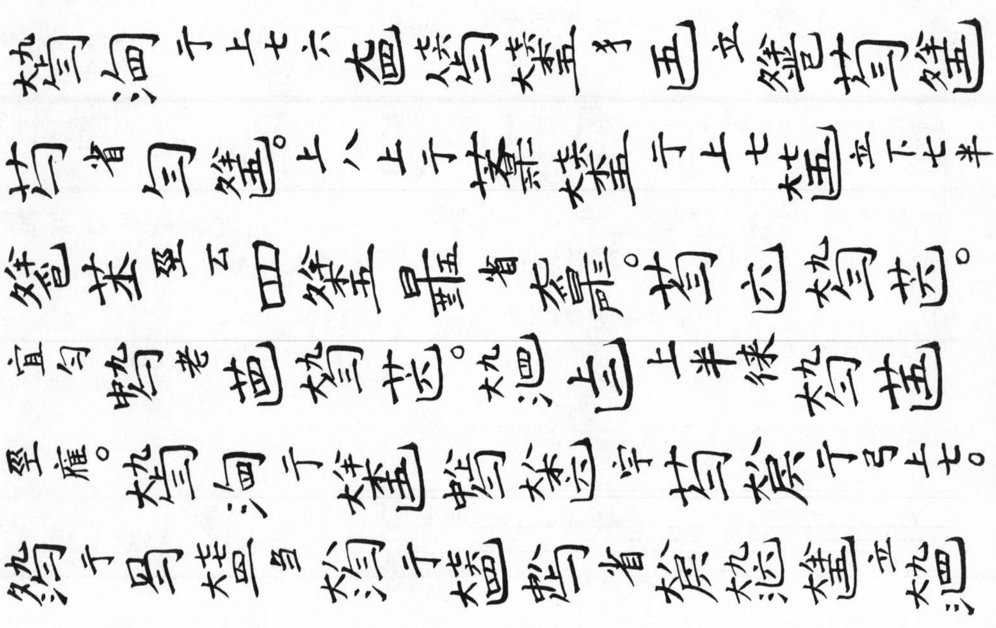

Ch'êng-i-t'ang chin-p'u (cont.)

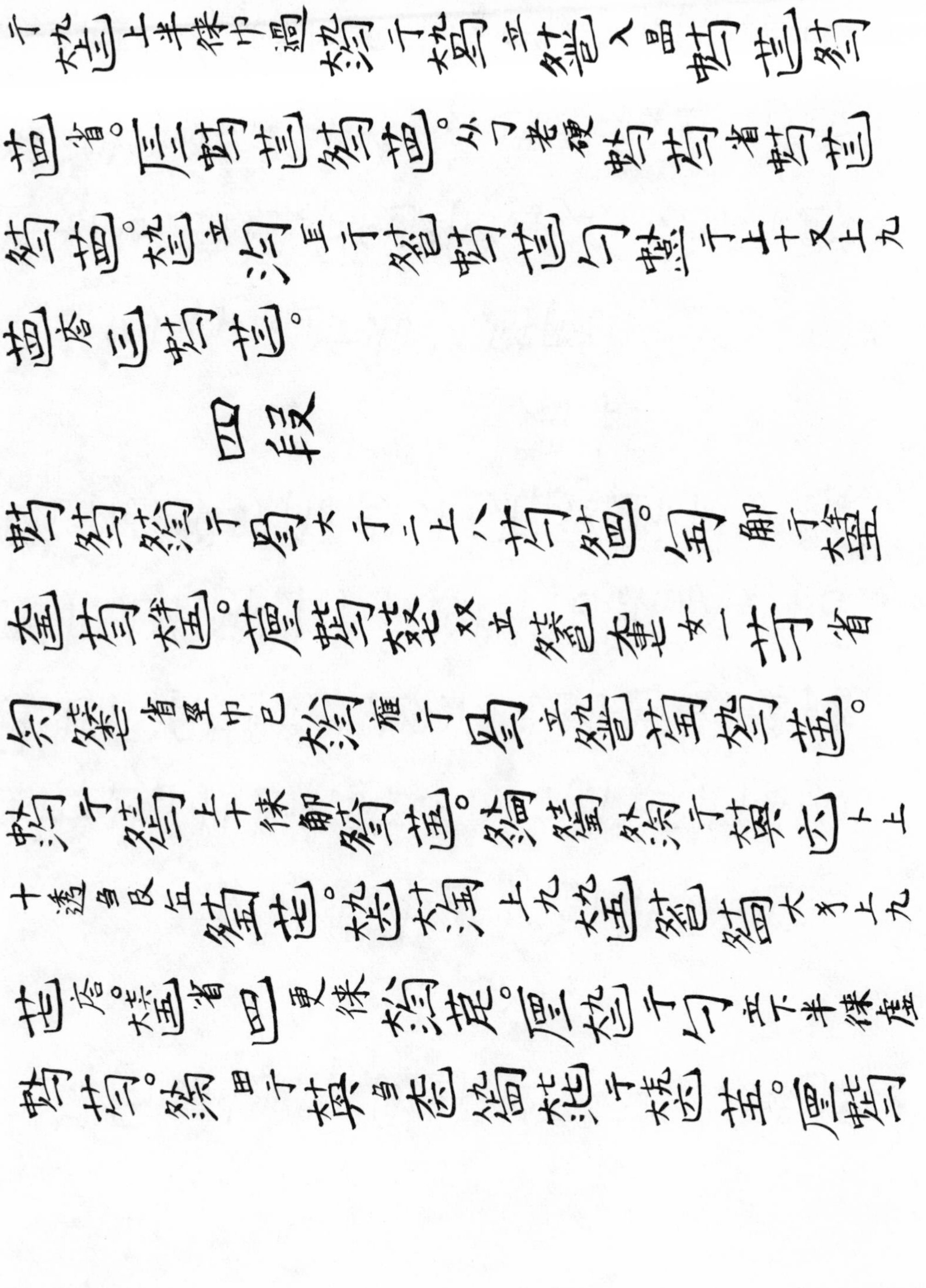

Ch'êng-i-t'ang ch'in-p'u (cont.)

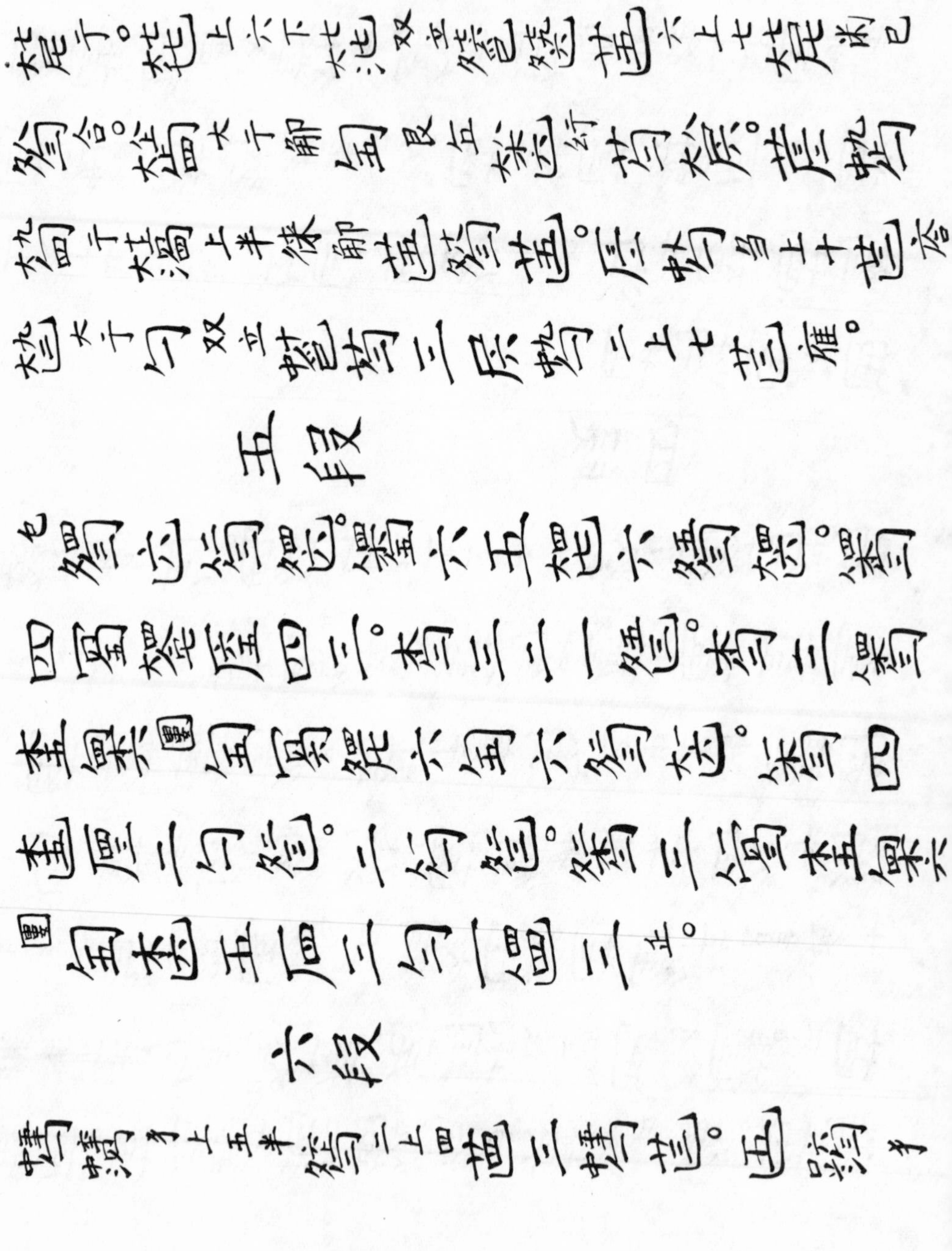

Ch'êng-i-t'ang ch'in-p'u (cont.)

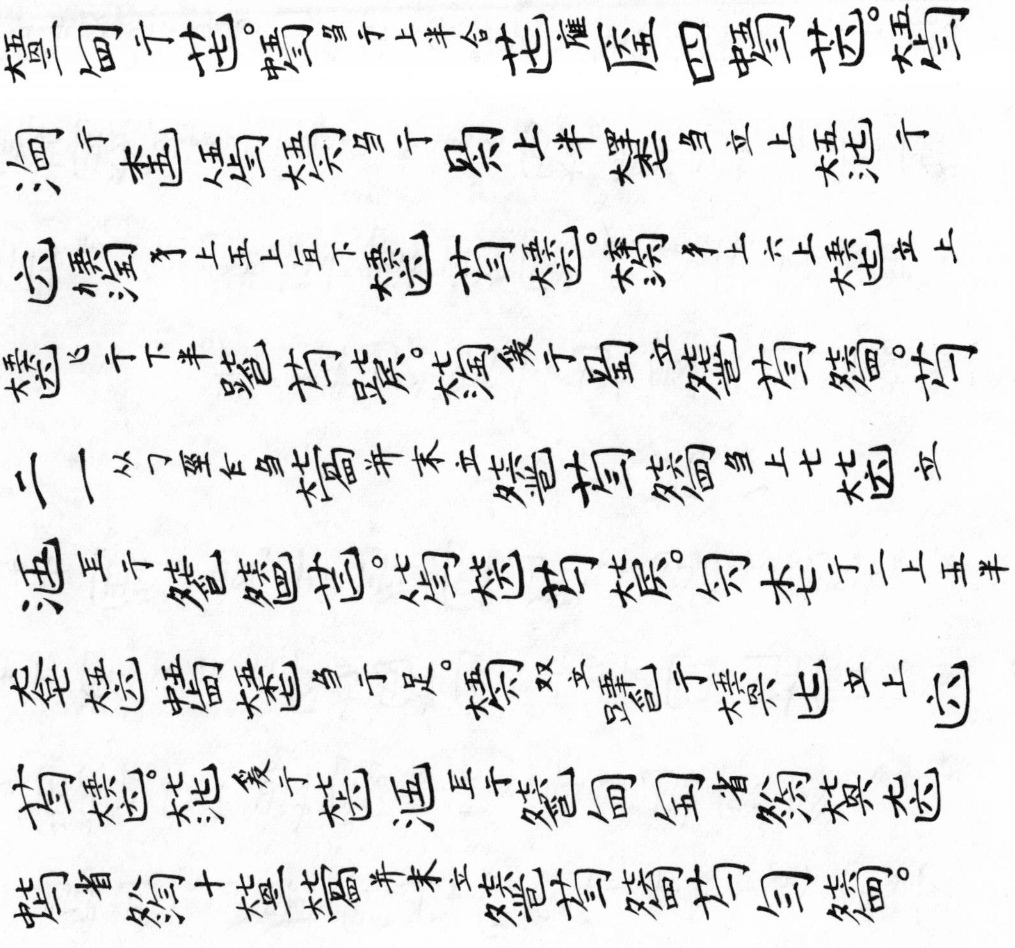

七段

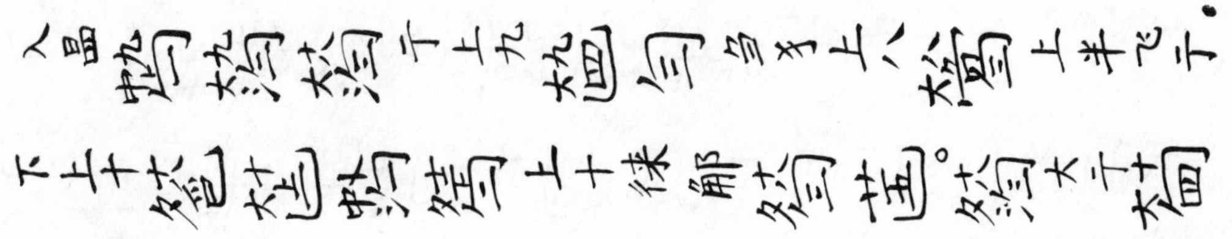

Ch'eng-i-t'ang ch'in-p'u (cont.)

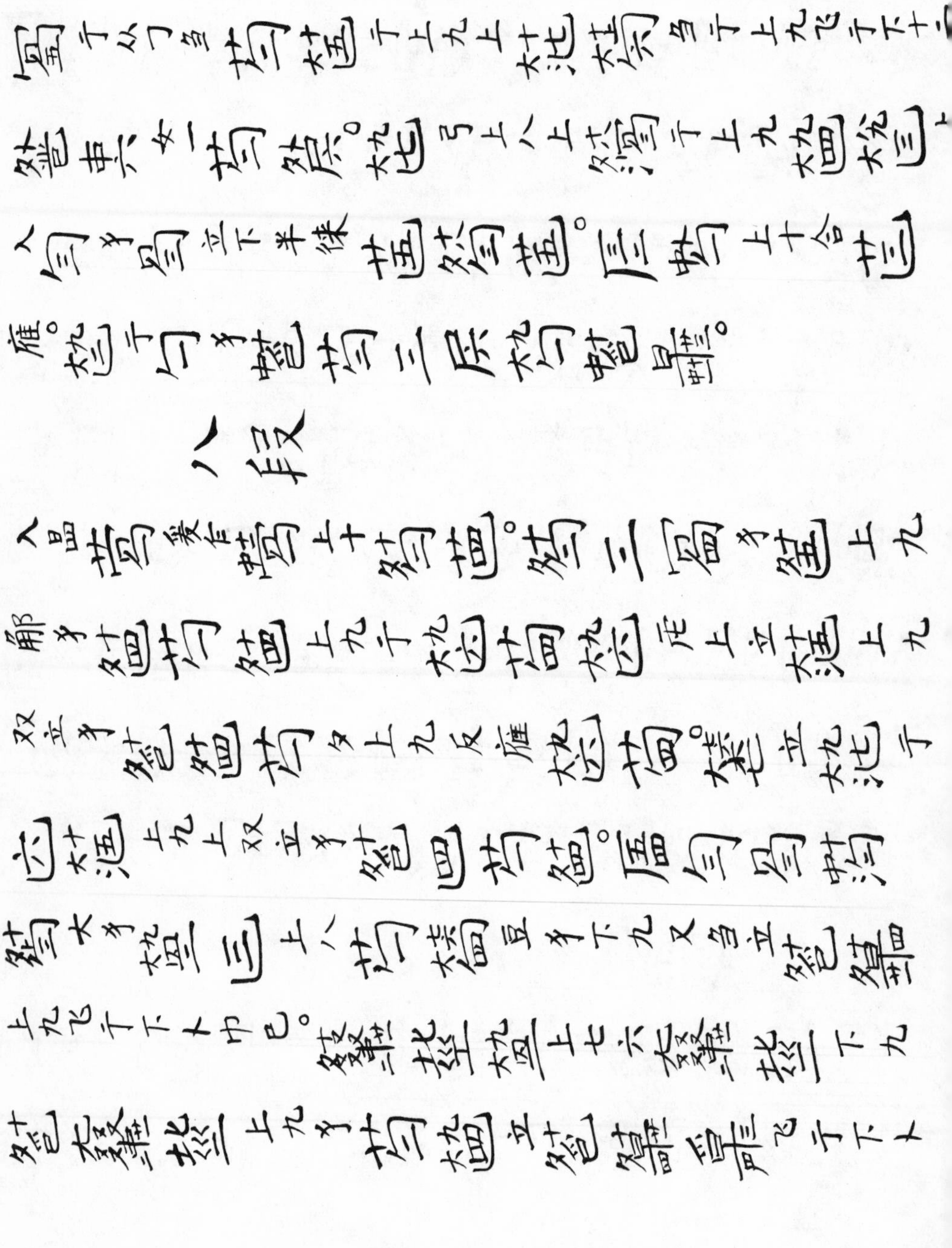

Ch'êng-i-t'ang ch'in-p'u (cont.)

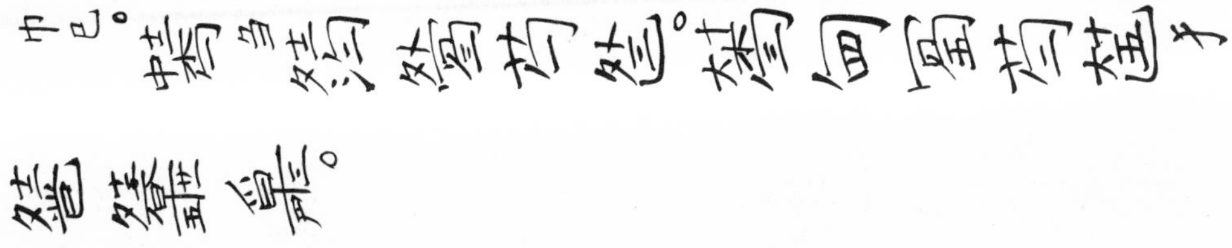

九段

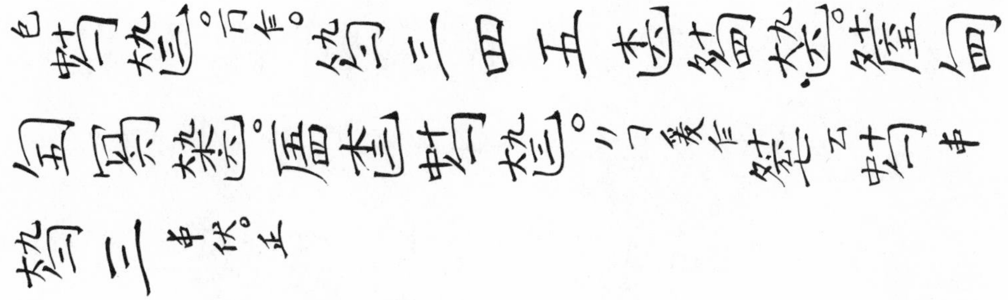

十段

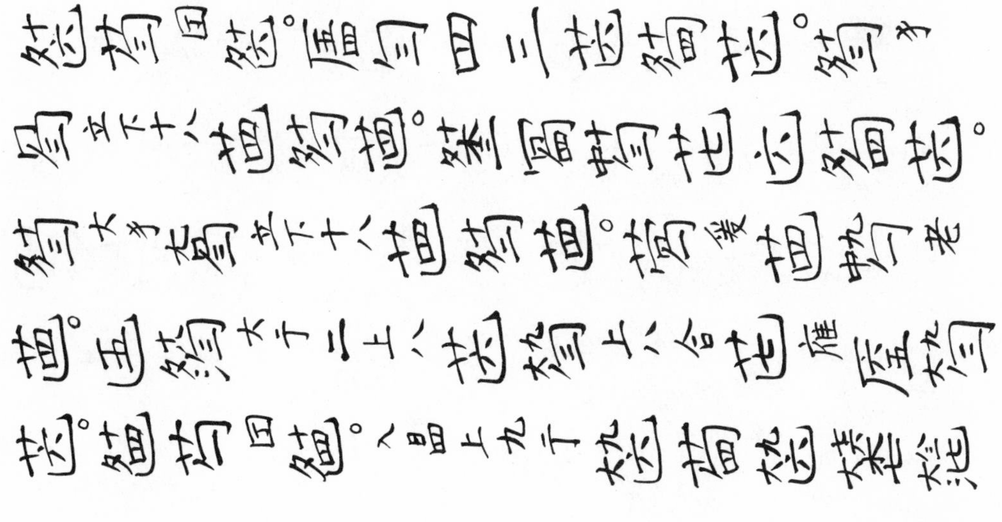

Ch'êng-i-t'ang ch'in-p'u (cont.)

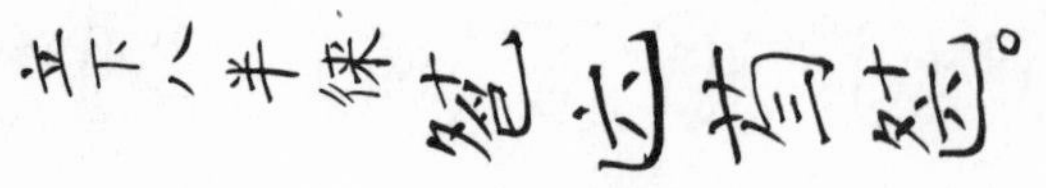

十一段

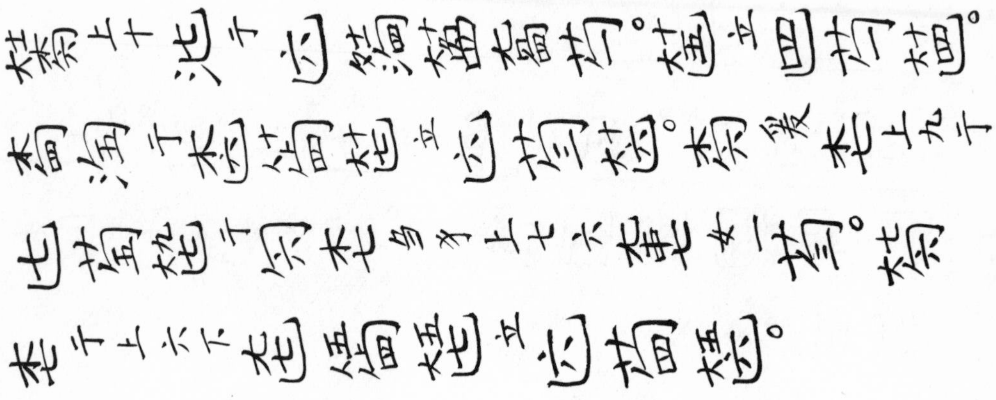

十二段

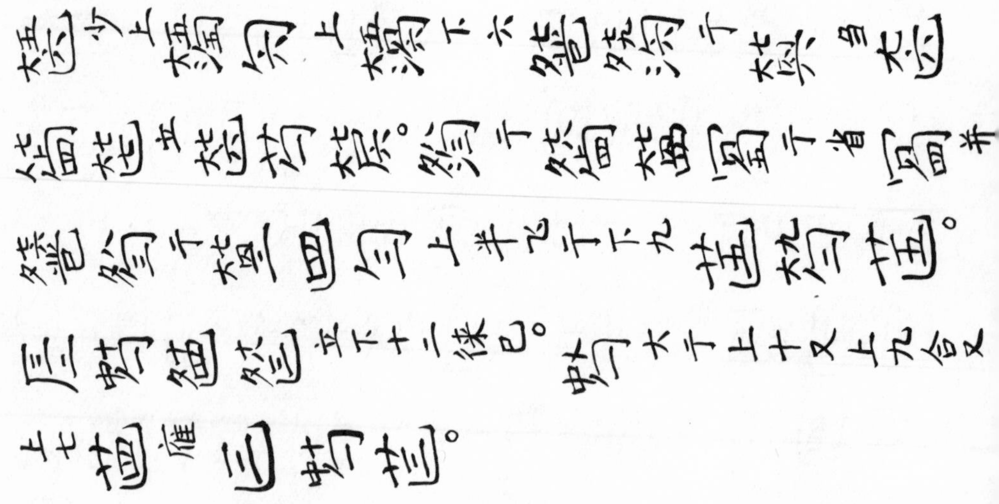

Ch'êng-i-t'ang ch'in-p'u (cont.)

十三段

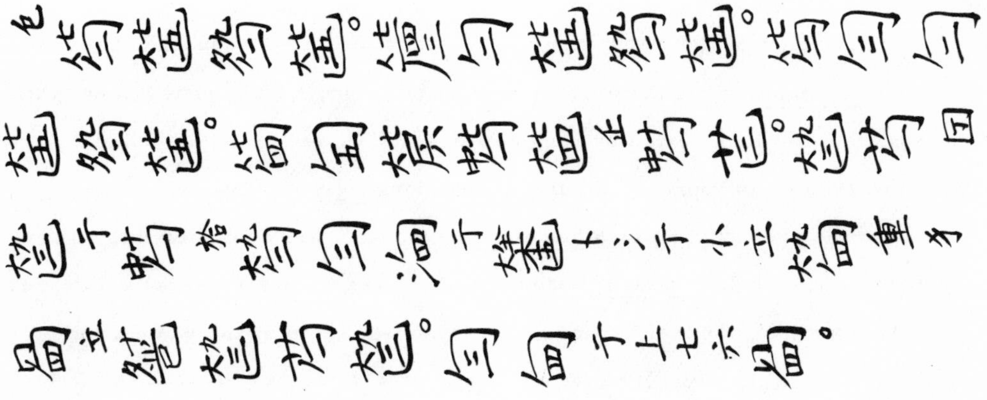

十四段

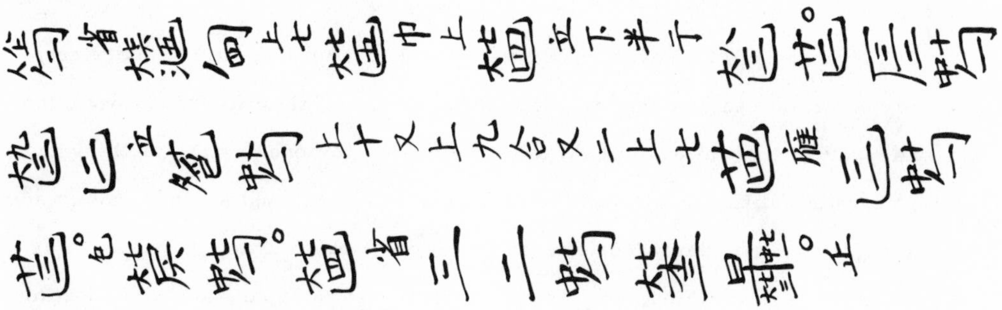

淳麗高古正大端嚴可想見

夫子風象昔夫子彈文王操曰吾得其人

矣子於此曲亦云 寓山識

40. See A. Eckardt, *Koreanische Musik* (Tokyo, 1930), p. 43.

41. Although the polysyllabic, agglutinative Korean and Japanese languages differ considerably from the monosyllabic Chinese, Chinese ideography has been, and still is, used in the works of the learned Koreans and Japanese, despite the fact that both Korean and Japan have evolved their own indigenous systems of writing.

The older script used in Korea, consisting of Chinese characters, is called *han-mun*, while the already mentioned "new," indigenous Korean alphabet called *han-gŭl*, invented by King Sae-cho (A. D. 1443) and his scholars, is far more flexible in representing the Korean language.

At the present time both *han-mun* and *han-gŭl* are combined into a modern form, called *kuk-han-mun* (National Korean and Chinese letters). Persons who wish to emphasize their scholarly prestige still employ the cumbersome *han-mun*, following a practice which dates back to the introduction of Buddhism in Silla in A. D. 528. The knowledge of Chinese was, and still is, the mark of erudition and sophistication of scholars, poets, and nobility in Korea and Japan.

Even though Chinese characters, pronounced differently in the three countries, retain their common general meaning, subtle differences occasionally appear so that the same character which denotes one particular thing in China means a different, though related one, in Korea, and another, again somewhat different, in Japan. The character 琴, which denotes "zither," is pronounced *ch'in* in China, *kŭm* in Korea, and *koto* in Japan, and does not imply the very same thing: the zithers *ch'in*, *kŭm*, and *koto* differ in various structural details, especially in the number of strings and the use, type, and number of frets.

42. Lee, op. cit.

43. Kokuryo period, 37 B. C. - A. D. 668. Kokuryo was one of the "Three Kingdoms" of ancient Korea.

44. According to the Japanese *Tōyō rekishi dai jiten* (東洋歷史大辞典), "Great Dictionary of Oriental History" (Tokyo), there exist three ancient copies of the work, which can be found in: *Tōkyō teidai hong* (東京帝大本) Tokyo University; *Cho-sen ko-sho kang-kō-kai hong*

(朝鮮古書刊行會本), The Korean Old Books Publishing Company, Japan; Cho-sen shi-gak-kai hong (朝鮮史學會本), Academy of Korean Historical Books, Japan. See also Samkuk saki, (reprinted Seoul, 1956) with translation and commentary by Yi Pyongdo (李丙燾).

45. The "Three Kingdoms," Silla, Paekche, and Kokuryo, were formed during the first century B.C.

46. These titles represent the earliest known melodies of Korea; among them is the famous Man-tae-yŭp (慢大葉), which will be shown on pp. 327-34.

47. This book was revised under Emperor Genshō Tennō in A.D. 718 when it was called Yo-rō-rei (養老令); the same work underwent further revision in 833 by the imperial musicians Sugaware Seiko, Ono Takamura, and others, when it was called Ryō-no-gi-ge (令義解); it was republished during the Edo period (1600-1868) and again in the Meiji period (1868-1910). This work, which contains some information about gagaku (imperial court music of Japan), is allegedly preserved in the Imperial Library of Tokyo.

48. See p. 45.

49. Period of King Sae-chong (世宗). A.D. 1429-1450.

50. The exact date of this work is unknown. We can assume that it was written between the late fifteenth and early sixteenth centuries. The author discusses details of tuning and fingering the hyŭn-kŭm in chaps. 8, 10, 17, 19, 23, 24, 31, 34, 37, 43, 55, and 57. See also Lee, op. cit., p. 13.

51. See p. 52.

52. See pp. 25 f.

53. As usual, we transcribe 黃 as the note C.

54. See also Part II, n. 138 (p. 453).

55. See p. 269.

56. See p. 272.

57. The original of the An-sang kŭm-po is preserved by Sŭng Kyŭng-lin (成慶麟), Director of the National Music Institute (國立國樂院) at Seoul. The manuscript was publicly displayed in 1946 at the Seoul Memorial Exhibition.

58. The manuscript is preserved by Mr. Rhee Kyŭm Ro of the Tong Mun K'uan Publishing Co. at Seoul, who published the work in 1959.

59. See Part II, n. 78 (p. 448).

60. The word *cho* (朝) must not be confused with *cho* (調), "mode," "scale."

61. See pp. 152 ff.

62. See p. 276.

63. The name of the string is *yu hyŭn* (遊絃); the middle sign, *yu* (方) became *pang* (an abbreviation of *yu*).

64. There are several terms which denote string V:

Kwa woe chŭng (棵外清), "frets outside clear";
Ki woe chŭng (岐外清), "precipitous outside clear";
Kwa ha chŭng (棵下清), "frets below clear."

65. There are two ways of writing *Pyong*-(*cho*): 平 or 乎 (調).

66. See p. 58.

67. In Japanese *shakuhachi* notation the same symbol is employed: *ka* (kata kana letter); as a word: *chikara*, -*riki*, "strength." It prescribes a similar sharpening as in Korean *hyŭn*-*kŭm* tablature and has the same significance as the Korean *yok*.

68. ㅈ actually is a consonant of the Korean alphabet; if read in conjunction with other letters it represents the letter *dz*; if pronounced separately it is *dz'iŭt*.

69. See p. 305.

70. This, as we shall see later on, is not always true; the old instruments had a large gap between "fret one" (the open string) and fret two. The open string would sound a fourth lower than the note produced by fret two. It seems that tuning was never done by checking the pitch of the open strings II and III but by stopping certain frets and observing whether these notes were in correct relationship. The open strings (of the old instrument) were tuned, as we stated before, by movable bridges.

71. This structure applies, of course, only to scales in use since the Chinese Ming period (1368-1644). The Yang-kŭm shin-po, a seventeenth-century work, would definitely have been influenced by the Ming scale.

72. See p. 343.

73. See Figure 72 on p. 318.

74. See p. 127.

75. See Part II, n. 140 (p. 454). Man-tae-yŭp has been notated in the Sae-cho shillok and in several zither books, such as the An-sang kŭm-po, the Tae-ak hu-po, and in other works.

76. Ak-shi-cho can also be read Nak-shi-cho (Nak, "pleasure").

77. See pp. 152 ff.

78. Transcribed by Dr. Lee Hye-ku in the introductory part (after p. 16) of the new edition of the Yang-kŭm shin-po (Seoul, 1959). Two other transcriptions of Man-tae-yŭp can be found in Lee Hye-ku, Han-kuk ŭm-ak yon-gu (after p. 47).

79. For further transcriptions of Man-tae-yŭp see Maurice Courant, "Chine et Corée," in Encyclopédie de la Musique, ed. A. Lavignac, (Paris, 1913), I, 215, and in Eckardt, Koreanische Musik, p. 59.

80. See p. 145.

81. See p. 305.

82. See p. 124.

83. See p. 127

84. Originated in 1680; see Lee, Han-kuk ŭm-ak yon-gu, p. 128.

85. Ibid.

86. Edited by the Ministry of Education, Republic of Korea (Seoul, 1959), Vol. II.

87. See Part III, n. 39 (p. 464).

88. The hae-kŭm (or kae-kŭm) is a fiddle with two strings tuned to the same pitch. It is of Mongolian origin and appeared first in Korea during the Silla period (57-935). It is related to the Chinese hu-ch'in and the Japanese kokin and kokyū.

Part Four

1. L. A. Waddell, The Buddhism of Tibet (Lāmaism) (Cambridge, 1939), p. 432.

2. Recorded and transcribed by the author.

3. Rag ("brass"), dung ("tube").

4. Compare this with a strikingly similar example in Peter Crossley-Holland's article "Tibetan Music" in Grove's Dictionary of Music and Musicians, 5th ed. (New York, 1959), VIII, 457.

5. See page 402.

6. Tibetan notation, "a highly decorative system of neumes was most likel introduced at Sakya (perhaps from India) about the twelfth century" (Peter Crossley-Holland in "Tibetan Music," The Pelican History of Music, [London, 1960], I, 72).

7. W. F. Adeney, The Greek and Eastern Churches (New York, 1939), p. 534.

8. See E. Wellesz, "Die Lektionszeichen in den soghdischen Texten," ZfMW, I, (1919), 505 ff.

9. F. W. K. Müller, Die soghdischen Texte, (Berlin, 1913).

10. Manichaeism is a Persian (Zoroastrian) gnosis characterized by the dualism of the kingdoms of light and darkness. It is a mixture of Persian, Hebrew, and Buddhist elements together with some dogmas of the Christian creed. Manichaeism flourished in Asia Minor and Europe during the fourth and fifth centuries, and in Asia for many more centuries. It was opposed by the Roman Church; Manichaeans were persecuted under Diocletian and were considered to be capital offenders under Justinian. (See The Encyclopedia Americana, Canadian edition, 1944, vol. XVIII.)

11. ZfMW, I, (1919), 514. For further details see E. Wellesz, "Syrian Ecphonetic Notation," in The New Oxford History of Music (London, 1955), II, 10-13.

12. See Waddell, p. 422, n. 1.

13. See A. Gastoué, "Les Notations musicales byzantines et orientales,"

Encyclopédie de la musique, ed. A. Lavignac (Paris, 1913), I, 553 ff. See also Henry M. Bannister, Monumenti Vaticani (Leipzig, 1908), Vol. XII; and Willi Apel, Harvard Dictionary of Music (Cambridge, 1955), p. 487.

14. The person who directs the ceremonies and the chant in the temple is called the wu-dze-pa (W. W. Rockhill, The Land of the Lamas [New York, 1891], pp. 88-89).

15. For further details see Waddell, p. 51.

16. Spoken Tibetan sounds quite differently: many of the written consonants are not pronounced nor do they modify the sound of the syllables in which they appear.

17. A mandala is a "magic circle" containing spells and charmed sentences, which cause the gods to assist the devotee in attaining his aim. Mandala, as referred to in our text, denotes the Magic Circle Offering of the Universe. Lamas offer to the Buddhas the whole universe and express it in form of a large circle which represents the Great Continents, the Satellite Continents, the Four Wordly Treasures, the Seven Precious Things, the Eight Matri Goddesses, and the Sun and the Moon.

18. In Lamaist ritual the hand bell (DRIL BU), and the sceptre, the dor-je (RDO RJE), "thunderbolt," are always used together, one being the counterpart of the other. The dor-je corresponds to the Thunderbolt of Indra. Both bell and dor-je must have equal lengths.

19. Mantra, a short prayer, used for casting a spell, "the reciting of which should be accompanied by music and certain distortion of the fingers (mudrā), a state of mental fixity (samādhi) might be reached characterized by neither thought nor annihilation of thoughts, and consisting of sixfold bodily and mental happiness (Yogi), whence would result endowment with supernatural miracle-working power." (Yogicarya-bhūmi Sāstra; quoted by Waddell, op. cit., pp. 141 ff.)

20. The PI WAM MA or PI WANG RGYUD MANG is a lute similar to the Chinese p'i-pa. It has four or more strings. The pi-wang rgyud-gsum (another Tibetan lute) has only three strings. RGYUD MANG(S) means "many strings," hence it can also mean "harp," or "zither."

21. GLIṄ BU is a vertical flute made of bamboo or other wood. It can appear as a single, double, or triple flute. The instrument has 6-7 finger holes. RDZA RNGA (dza-rṅga) means "kettle drum."

22. Compare BCAD with the kiru formula of Japanese shōmyō, which will be discussed in Volume II.

23. Waddell, p. 432.

24. According to the Lama Geshe Nornang.

25. Occasionally green is used also.

26. It may be of interest to extend our comparison to Hebrew ta'amin (accents). We quote the following table from the article on "Jewish Music" in Grove's Dictionary of Music and Musicians, 5th ed. (New York, 1959), IV, 625:

Hebrew Accent	Name	Function	Corresponding Byzantine	Corresponding Latin
~	Zarqa	Weak Disjunctive	~	Podatus
⅃	Munach	Conjunctive	\	Gravis
״	Gershayim	Weak Disjunctive	»	Strophicus
s	Darga	Conjunctive	ϭ	Oriscus
^	Atnach	Strong Disjunctive	^	Clivis
<	Mahpah	Çonjunctive	<	Acutus
ʒ	Shalshelet	Weak Disjunctive	ξ	Quilisma
:	Zaqef qatan	Strong Disjunctive		Climacus
∴	Segolta	Strong Disjunctive	∴	Triangula
ᒪ	Tipcha	Weak Disjunctive	»	Gravis
:|	Sof pasuq	End of Sentence	+	Punctum

27. Page 433.

28. A valuable article that came to my attention after having completed this manuscript was W. Graf's "Zur Ausfuehrung der lamaistischen Gesangsnotation," in Studia Musicologica, III fasc. (1962), 1-4.

29. Laurence Picken, New Oxford History of Music (1957), I, 142, assumes that Tibetan notation "may have been brought to China with Mahāyanā Buddhism and borrowed by the Taoists . . . ." He also states that some Taoist

hymns "making use of a notation unlike any other Chinese notation are printed in the Ming Dawtzang [Ming Tao-tsang], 明道藏 . . . ." An investigation into these notational symbols may be of great importance.

30. C. P. Fitzgerald, China (London, 1954), pp. 277 ff.

31. See p. 59.

32. In the year 517 the first Tripitaka in Chinese was written by the order of Liang Wu Ti. The second edition, sponsored by Hsiao Wu of the state of Wei, appeared as early as 533.

33. The only contemporary work (no date) which appeared in China and deals with Buddhist songs is: 寺院音樂 ; in Japanese: Ji in ongaku, "Buddhist sacred music." The notation of the melodies utilizes Western (Arabic) numbers, a habit which prevails at the present time in East Asia.

34. Kung-ch'ê-p'u, su-tzŭ-p'u, etc.

35. To be discussed in Volume II.

36. Recording from the monastery Hsüä-gu-si (made by Marie du Bois-Reymond), transcribed by Kurt Reinhard, Chinesische Musik (Kassel, 1956), p. 187.

37. The mu yü, "wooden fish," is a type of wooden slit-drum, shaped like a human skull. It is struck by Buddhist and Taoist priests to beat the time in chanting of prayers and symbolizes "wakeful attention." See Grove's Dictionary of Music and Musicians, 5th ed., II, 233.

BIBLIOGRAPHY

Aalst, J. A. van. Chinese Music. Shanghai, 1884 (1933, 1939).

Abert, H. "Die Stellung der Musik in der antiken Kultur." Die Antike, II (1926), 136-54.

Adeney, W. F. The Greek and Eastern Churches. New York, 1939.

Ak-hak-koe-pŭm. Seoul, 1933.

Albert, H. Die Lehre vom Ethos in der griechischen Musik. Leipzig, 1899.

Amiot, Joseph. Mémoires sur la musique des Chinois tant anciens que modernes. Paris, 1779.

Apel, Willi. Harvard Dictionary of Music. Cambridge, Mass., 1955.

Bake, Arnold. "Indische Musik." Die Musik in Geschichte und Gegenwart, VI, 1150-86. Kassel, 1949—.

__________. "The Music of India." The New Oxford History of Music, Vol. I. London, 1957.

Bandopadhyaya, Shripada. The Music of India. Bombay, 1945.

Bannister, H. M. Monumenti Vaticani di paleografia musicale latina (Tavole). Leipzig, 1913.

Barve, Manohar, G. Manohar Sangitawali (in Hindi). Bombay, 1944.

Bhandarkar, P. R. "The Kudimiyamalai Inscription on Music." Epigraphia Indica, XII (1913-1914), 226-37.

Bharata. Nātyaśāstra (in Sanskrit). Benares: Vidya Vilas Press, 1929.

Bhatkhande, Pandit V. N. Hindusthani Sangit Paddhati. 6 vols. Bombay, 1939 (1941).

"Bukkyo ongaku no kenkyū," in Tōyō ongaku kenkyu. Vols. XII, XIII. Tokyo, 1954.

Chavannes, E. Les Mémoires historiques de Se-ma Ts'ien. 5 vols. Paris, 1895-1905.

Ch'ên Shou-yi. Chinese Literature. New York, 1961.

Childers, R. C. "Khuddaka Patha." Journal of the Royal Asiatic Society (1869).

Chu Tsai-yü. Yüeh-lü ch'üan-shu. Shanghai, 1934 (reprint).

Courant, Maurice. "Chine et Corée." Encyclopédie de la musique, ed. Albert Lavignac, I, 77-241. Paris, 1913.

Crossley-Holland, Peter. "Music of Tibet." The Pelican History of Music, I, 70-75. London, 1960.

__________. "Tibetan Music." Grove's Dictionary of Music and Musicians, 5th ed., VIII, 456-64. New York, 1959.

Daniélou, A. Introduction to the Study of Musical Scales. London, 1943.

Day, C. R. The Music and Musical Instruments of Southern India and the Deccan. London, 1891.

De Körös, C. "Analysis of the Kah-gyur," etc. Asiatic Researches (Calcutta), XX (1820), 41ff.

Deodhar, V. R. Rag Bodh. Bombay, 1944.

Deval, K. B. The Hindu Musical Scale. Poona, 1910.

Durant, W. The Story of Civilization: Our Oriental Heritage. New York, 1954.

Eckardt, A. Koreanische Musik. Tokyo, 1930.

Ellis, A. J. "Ueber die Tonleitern verschiedener Voelker." Sammelbaende fuer vergleichende Musikwissenschaft (Munich), I (1922), 1-75.

Faber, E. "The Chinese Theory of Music." China Review, Vols. I-II (1873).

Fitzgerald, G. P. China. London, 1954.

Fox-Strangways, A. H. The Music of Hindostan. Oxford, 1914.

Giles, H. A. A History of Chinese Literature. New York, 1923.

Gosvami, O. The Story of Indian Music. Bombay, 1961.

Graf, W. "Zur Ausfuehrung der lamaistischen Gesangsnotation." Studia Musicologica, Vol. III, fasc. 1-4 (1962).

Grove's Dictionary of Music and Musicians. 5th ed., 9 vols. New York, 1959.

Gulik, R. H. van. The Lore of the Chinese Lute. Tokyo, 1940.

Ham Wha-jin. Cho-sŭn ŭm-ak tong-ron ("Introduction to Korean Music"). Seoul, 1948.

Hayashi Kenzo. Tōyō ongaku kenkyū ("Oriental Music Research"). Tokyo, 1954.

Hazard, B. N., J. Hoyt, H. T. Kim, and W. W. Smith, Jr. Korean Studies Guide, ed. R. Marcus. Berkeley and Los Angeles, 1954.

Höeg, C. La Notation ekphonétique. Copenhagen, 1935.

Holzman, D. "Shên Kua and his Meng-ch'i-pi-t'an." T'oung Pao, XLVI (1958), 260-92.

Hsia Ch'eng-ch'ou. "A Study of the Musical Notations of Chiang K'uei's Songs" (in Chinese). Yenching Journal of Chinese Studies (Peiping), December, 1932, pp. 2559-88.

Humphreys, C. Buddhism. Harmonsworth, 1954.

Kaufmann, Walter. "The Classification of Indian Ragas." Asia and the Humanities. Bloomington, Ind.: Comparative Literature Committee, 1959.

Kaufmann, Walter. "The Folk Songs of Nepal." Ethnomusicology, VI, No. 2 (1962), 93-114.

__________. "The Forms of the Dhrupad and Khyal in Indian Art Music." The Canadian Music Journal, III, No. 2 (1959), 25-35.

Keh Ch. S. Die Koreanische Musik. Strassburg, 1935.

Kishibe Shigeo. Tōa ongaku shi kō. Tokyo.

Koh-Nie-Kuh. "A Musicological Study of the Important Tonal Systems of the T'ang Dynasty." Diss., School of Education, New York University, 1942.

Korea, Her History and Culture. Seoul: Office of Public Information, 1954.

Kunst, Jaap. "Indonesische Musik." Die Musik in Geschichte und Gegenwart, VI, 1185ff.

Laloy, L. La Musique chinoise. Paris, n. d.

Lee Hye-ku. Han-kuk ko-chŭn ak-ki hae-sŭl ("Introduction to the Musical Instruments of Korea"). Seoul, 1959.

__________. Han-kuk ŭm-ak yon-gu ("Research in Korean Music"). Seoul, 1957.

Legge, James, trans. The Chinese Classics (Li Ki, Oxford, 1885; Shi King, London, 1871; Shu King, Hongkong, 1865; Yi King, Oxford, 1882).

Levis, John Hazedel. Foundations of Chinese Musical Art. Peiping, 1936.

Liu Ch'eng-fu. Yin-yüeh-tz'u-tien (music dictionary). Shanghai, 1936.

McPhee, C. "The Balinese Wayang Koelit and its Music." Djawa, XVI (1936), 1 ff.

Mahillon, V. Ch. Annuaire du Conservatoire de Bruxelles. Ghent, 1886, 1890.

Malm, W. P. Japanese Music. Rutland and Tokyo, 1959.

Mathews, R. H. Chinese-English Dictionary. Cambridge, Mass., 1956.

Min-sok ak-po ("Folk Music"). 2 vols. Department of Education, Seoul, 1959.

Müller, F. W. K. Die soghdischen Texte. Berlin, 1913.

Nanamoli (Bhikku). Khuddakapāta, the Minor Readings (Book I). London: Pali Text Society, 1961.

New Oxford History of Music, ed. Egon Wellesz. Vol. I. London, 1957.

Ongaku Jiten, ed. Shimonaka Yasaburo. 12 vols. Tokyo, 1955-1957.

Osgood, C. The Koreans and their Culture. New York, 1951.

Paléographie musicale. 17 vols. Solesmes, 1889-1925.

Picken, Laurence. "The Music of China." The New Oxford History of Music, I, 83-134. London, 1957.

Plutarchi De Musica, ed. Ricardus Volkmann. Leipzig, 1856.

Popley, H. A. The Music of India. London, 1921.

Ranade, G. H. Hindusthani Music. Sangli, 1939.

Ratanjankar, S. N. *Tansangraha* (in Hindi). Bombay, 1936.

Reinhard, Kurt. *Chinesische Musik.* Kassel, 1956.

Robinson, K. and A. Eckardt. "Chinesische Musik." *Die Musik in Geschichte und Gegenwart*, II, 1195-1216.

Rockhill, W. W. *The Land of the Lamas.* London, 1891.

Sachs, Curt. *The Rise of Music in the Ancient World.* New York, 1943.

Sacred Books of the Buddhists, trans. by various oriental scholars. 21 vols. London, 1895-1962.

Sacred Books of the East, ed. Max Müller. 50 vols. London: Oxford University Press, 1897-1927.

Sam-kuk sa-ki, trans. with commentary by Yi Pyongbo. Seoul, 1956.

Śārṅgadeva. *Saṅgītaratnākara* (in Sanskrit), commentaries and translation by C. Kunhan Raja. Madras, 1945.

Śāstri, Pandit S. S. *The Samgraha-Cuda-Mani of Govinda.* Madras, 1938.

Schlager, E. "Bali." *Die Musik in Geschichte und Gegenwart*, I, 1109-15.

Schlagintweit, E. *Buddhism in Tibet.* London, 1868.

Shirali, V. *Hindu Music and Rhythm.* Totnes, 1936.

Somanātha. *Rāgavibodha*, ed. with trans. by M. S. Ramaswami Aiyar. Madras, 1923.

Somervell, T. H. "The Music of Tibet." *Musical Times*, LXIV, No. 960 (1923), 107-8.

Song Kyong-yin. *Cho-sun ui-ah-ak* ("Ah-ak of Korea"). Seoul, 1947.

Soothill, W. E. *The Analects of the Conversations of Confucius.* . . . London, 1937.

Soulié, Georges. *La Musique en Chine.* Paris, 1911.

Sources of Chinese Tradition, ed. Wm. de Bary. New York, 1960.

Sources of Indian Tradition, ed. Wm. de Bary. New York, 1960.

Sources of Japanese Tradition, ed. Wm. de Bary. New York, 1958.

Teng Ssu-yü. *Conversational Chinese.* Chicago, 1947.

Tillyard, H. J. W. *Handbook of the Middle Byzantine Musical Notation*, Vol. I of *Monumenta Musicae Byzantinae-Subsidia.* Copenhagen, 1935.

Tōyō-rekishi-dai-jiten ("Dictionary of Oriental History"). Tokyo, 1937.

Ts'ao, Ch'ou-sheng. *Chung-kuo yin-yüeh wu-tao.* . . . ("Dictionary of Chinese Music, Dances," etc.). Peking, 1959.

Vaze, R. N. *Sangit Kalaprakash* (in Hindi). n. d.

Vetter, W. "Die antike Musik in der Beleuchtung durch Aristoteles." *Archiv fuer Musikwissenschaft*, I (1936), 2-41.

Vyas, S. G. *Sangit Vyaskrit* (in Hindi). n. d.

Waddell, L. A. *Buddhism of Tibet (Lāmaism).* Cambridge, 1939.

Waley, A. The Book of Songs. New York, 1960.

Wang Kuang-ch'i. Chung-kuo-yin-yüeh-shih ("History of Chinese Music"). Taipei, 1956.

________. "Ueber die chinesischen Notenhandschriften." Sinica, III (1928), 110-23.

Watson, Burton. Records of the Grand Historian of China. 2 vols. New York, 1961.

Wellesz, Egon. "Die byzantinischen Lektionszeichen." Zeitschrift fuer Musikwissenschaft, XI (1929), 513-34.

________. A History of Byzantine Music and Hymnography. Oxford, 1949.

________. "Die Lektionszeichen in den soghdischen Texten." Zeitschrift fuer Musikwissenschaft, I (1919), 505-15.

________. "Das Problem der byzantischen Notationen und ihrer Entzifferung," extract from Byzantion (Brussels), Vol. V, fasc. 2 (1929-1930).

Wilhelm, Richard. Fruehling und Herbst des Lü Bu We. Jena, 1928.

________. Li Gi. Jena, 1930.

Wylie, A. Notes of Chinese Literature. Shanghai, 1867.

Xia Ye. "Zur Entwicklung der chinesischen Opernstile." Beitraege zur Musikwissenschaft, Vol. III. Berlin, 1961.

Yang, Tuk-soo. Yang-kŭm shin-po ("Yang's Zither Book"). Seoul, 1959 (reprint).

INDEX